T0389691

Mozambique on the Move

Mozambique on the Move

Challenges and Reflections

Edited by

Sheila Pereira Khan
Maria Paula Meneses
Bjørn Enge Bertelsen

BRILL

LEIDEN | BOSTON

Cover illustration: Traditional female dance – Niassa Oriental 2003. Photo by Sérgio Santimano.

Library of Congress Cataloging-in-Publication Data

Names: Khan, Sheila, 1972- editor. | Meneses, Maria Paula, editor. |
   Bertelsen, Bj²rn Enge, editor.
Title: Mozambique on the move : challenges and reflections / edited by Sheila
   Pereira Khan, Maria Paula Meneses, Bjorn Enge Bertelsen.
Description: Leiden ; Boston : Koninklijke Brill NV, 2019. | Series:
   Africa-europe group for interdisciplinary studies, ISSN 1574-6925 ; VOLUME
   21 | Includes bibliographical references and index.
Identifiers: LCCN 2018049051| ISBN 9789004376885 (pbk. : alk. paper) | ISBN
   97890391100 (e-book)
Subjects: LCSH: Mozambique--Civilization. | Mozambique--History. |
   Mozambique--Politics and government.
Classification: LCC DT3320 .M69 2019 | DDC 967.905--dc23
LC record available at https://lccn.loc.gov/2018049051

Typeface for the Latin, Greek, and Cyrillic scripts: "Brill". See and download: brill.com/brill-typeface.

ISSN 1574-6925
ISBN 978-90-04-37688-5 (paperback)
ISBN 978-90-04-38110-0 (e-book)

Contents

Preface

This book takes a fresh look at Mozambique, probing and engaging the political, sociocultural and epistemic diversity the country entails in a broader dialogue with the global dimensions of economic and political powers. Indeed, although over the recent years several books have been published focusing on this country, most of them remain bound by subject-disciplinary approaches. Aiming to stimulate a broader, interdisciplinary dialogue about the complex geopolitical space that comprises contemporary Mozambique, Sheila Pereira Khan organized an international conference on Mozambique in Trondheim, Norway, in 2010. With the aim of exploring Mozambique's changes and continuities, the conference provided research challenges to scholars, students, and practitioners concerned with the country's development and future, and these were highlighted from a range of disciplines, including political science, history, macroeconomics, anthropology, literature, gender studies, art, and African Studies. As the vivid discussions that took place during the conference demonstrated, scholars were dissatisfied with how studies on Mozambique are habitually subdivided into academic topics.

While most of the contributors to this book first met at the conference, after two days of intense debate as editors we realized that our diverse interests covered much common ground, providing a panoramic view of research on Mozambique; our conviction was supported by the spirit of debate and interaction that animated the conference. Attendees commented on the multiple ways in which the papers intersected and suggested that this represented an exciting moment of convergence in academic scholarship: it was the birth of this volume. Thus, from the very beginning this volume was organized around an interdisciplinary position. It has been an absorbing process whose outcome has turned into this volume whose chapters' address Mozambique from various perspectives, intersecting the present with the past whenever needed.

Although a great number of other languages are spoken throughout the country, Mozambique's official language is Portuguese and remains the dominant language in teaching and public discourses.[1] Nevertheless, in order to reach a wide, non-Lusophone and global readership we decided to publish this book in English. By uniting scholars through their research interests in Mozambique, this choice allowed us to broaden the conditions of debate and the

---

[1] Crucially, a range of languages – with five language groups besides Mozambican Portuguese each having more than a million speakers – continue to shape everyday life and outlooks for the country's majority (Chimbutane 2015).

possibilities for reflection – including, but also going beyond, the sphere of Portuguese-speaking researchers.

Our very cordial thanks are extended to all of our colleagues who accepted to be part of this project. We really appreciate and treasure the time they dedicated to writing and reviewing their chapters. To organize a book while working in different locations and institutions was not an easy task and shaping it – as well as co-writing the introduction – became a space of academic debate. Therefore, this volume also reflects the value of academic friendships and intellectual stimulus. To write the introduction, unobtrusive help has been forthcoming from the staffs of many research libraries, including the library of Centro de Estudos Africanos of Eduardo Mondlane University, of the National Archives of Mozambique, of Centre for Social Studies from Coimbra University, among others.

Thanks for indefatigable support and interest also go most warmly to our families, many friends and colleagues for providing advice, criticisms and references along the process. All the many discussions were welcome, including especially significant exchanges with Ana Maria Gentili, Benedito Machava, Boaventura de Sousa Santos, Bruno Sena Martins, Carolina Peixoto, Elísio Macamo, João Paulo Borges Coelho, José Luis Cabaço, Margarida Calafate Ribeiro, Omar Thomaz, Teresa Cruz e Silva, among many others.

Thinking and writing-time are greatly treasured by authors. Special thanks go to several research fellowships that made possible time for research and for writing. Among these are the Portuguese Science and Technology Foundation through the fellowships PTDC/AFR/103057/2008 and PTDC / CVI-ANT / 6100 / 2014 – POCI-01-0145-FEDER-016859 (with both national funding and co-funding by FEDER through the Operational Program of Competitiveness and Innovation COMPETE 2020). In addition, the book project has received valuable support – logistical and financial – from the Department of Social Anthropology, University of Bergen and the Department of Social Anthropology, Norwegian University of Science and Technology. We would like to thank the Norwegian Research Council for their financial support allowing for copy-editing parts of this volume.

Lastly, two anonymous readers produced trenchant critiques of an early draft. This behind-the-scenes support should not go without a public expression of gratitude. They encouraged and advised upon appropriate changes to the chapters in perfect editorial style. Their suggestions helped to improve the volume as a whole, making the main arguments sharper and more insightful.

Sheila Pereira Khan
Maria Paula Meneses
Bjørn Enge Bertelsen

List of Contributors

Signe Arnfred
is a sociologist and a gender scholar. She works at Roskilde University in Denmark, where she is associate professor at the Department of Society and Globalization and part of the Centre for Gender, Power and Diversity. 2000–2006 she worked at the Nordic Africa Institute in Uppsala, Sweden, as coordinator of the research programme on Sexuality, Gender and Society in Africa. She has written a number of articles critical of development discourse on gender, such as e.g. "Women, Men and Gender Equality in Development Aid. Trajectories, Contestations" in *Kvinder, Køn og Forskning* 2011, and she is the author/editor of the following recent books and journal special issues: *Re-thinking Sexualities in Africa* (2004), "Sex and Politics, Case Africa" (special issue of NORA) 2009, *African Feminist Politics of Knowledge*, together with Akosua Adomako Ampofo (2010), and *Sexuality and Gender Politics in Mozambique. Re-thinking Gender in Africa* (James Currey, 2011).

Bjørn Enge Bertelsen
is Professor at the Department of Social Anthropology at the University of Bergen and works on issues such as state formation, egalitarianism, cosmology, violence and rural-urban connections. He has worked on Mozambique since 1998 and has authored *Violent Becomings: State Formation, Sociality and Power in Mozambique* (2016) and has recently co-edited *Navigating Colonial Orders: Norwegian Entrepreneurship in Africa and Oceania* (with K.A. Kjerland, 2015), *Violent Reverberations: Global Modalities of Trauma* (with V. Broch-Due, 2016), and *Critical Anthropological Engagements in Human Alterity and Difference* (with S. Bendixsen, 2016).

José Luís Cabaço
was born in Maputo. He participated in the struggle for the independence of Mozambique and held government positions after his country's liberation. He holds a degree in Sociology from the University of Trento, Italy, and a PhD in Anthropology from the University of São Paulo, Brazil. He was a professor at the Polytechnic University of Mozambique and Rector of the Technical University of Mozambique, where he currently is Professor Emeritus. He is the author of the book *Mozambique: Identities, Colonialism and Liberation*, ANPOCS Award 2008, edited by UNESP in Brazil, and by Marimbique Publisher in Mozambique. He has chapter in anthologies published in Mozambique, Brazil,

Italy and Portugal. He was a guest researcher at the Federal University of Rio de Janeiro in 1996 and a visiting researcher at CEBRAP in 2001. In 2016 he was a guest professor at the Anthropology Graduate Program at FFLCH (USP) and is currently a guest researcher at Unicamp. He has participated in research projects, held seminars and lectures in Mozambique, South Africa, Angola, Brazil, Portugal and Italy.

Ana Bénard da Costa

is a social anthropologist with an MA and PhD in Interdisciplinary African Studies in Social Sciences (ISCTE- Lisbon University Institute, 2003) and researcher at CEsA (Centre for African, Asian and Latin American Studies) in the Lisbon School of Economics and Management (ISEG)/Universidade de Lisboa (ULisboa) and at the Centre for International Studies (former Centre of African Studies) of the ISCTE- Lisbon University Institute in Lisbon. Currently she is carrying out research on urban development in Maputo (Mozambique) and on the links between processes of social and cultural change in Mozambican families, development and higher education. Ana Bénard da Costa is the author and co-author of several books and articles published in national and international scientific peer-reviewed periodicals and was IP and team member of nine research projects.

Linda van de Kamp

is a cultural anthropologist and assistant professor in the Department of Sociology, University of Amsterdam. Her research activities concentrate on urban regeneration, religion and ritual, transnational circulation, media, and gender and reproductive issues. Linda has done in-depth research on the emergence of Brazilian Pentecostalism in Mozambique. She is the author of *Violent Conversion: Brazilian Pentecostalism and Urban Women in Mozambique* (James Currey, 2016).

Ana Margarida Fonseca

(PhD, University of Lisbon, 2007) is adjunct professor at the Polytechnic Institute of Guarda, Portugal, and researcher of the Centre for Comparative Studies (University of Lisbon) and Institute of Comparative Literature Margarida Losa (University of Porto). She is the author of *Projectos de Encostar Mundos. Referencialidade e Representação na Literatura Angolana e Moçambicana dos Anos 80* (APE Revelation Award for Literary Essay, Difel, 2002) and of *Percursos da Identidade. Representações da Nação na Literatura Pós-Colonial de Língua Portuguesa* (Fundação Calouste Gulbenkian/FCT, 2012). Her research interests lie mainly in the area of Postcolonial Studies, Identity Studies and Contemporary Fiction in Portuguese Language (Portugal, Angola, Mozambique).

Anna Maria Gentili

is Emeritus Professor of the Alma Mater Studiorum, University of Bologna. Since 1968 she has taught African Political History and Political Development, at the Faculty of Political Science of the University of Bologna, at the University of Dar es Salaam, at the Centro de Estudos Africanos of the Eduardo Mondane University of Maputo, Mozambique. She did field research in Nigeria, Senegal, Tanzania and Mozambique. Member of the Academy of Sciences of Bologna (section social studies); Resident Member of the Alma Mater University of Bologna Institute of Advanced Studies; Chairman of the Amilcar Cabral Center, Bologna (Library, documentation and research activities on Asia, Africa, Latin America); Scientific Board of the Review Afriche e Orienti (Bologna); Member of the Academy of Sciences of Bologna (section social studies). Anna Maria Gentili's present research activities are: the crisis of the Nation state in Africa; democracy and citizenship; conflicts and conflict resolution in Africa with special reference to Southern Africa the Great Lakes and Congo/Zaire.

Randi Kaarhus

is currently Professor of Anthropology at Nord University in northern Norway, being on leave from a position as Professor of Development Studies at the Faculty of Landscape and Society at the Norwegian University of Life Sciences. Holding a PhD in social anthropology from the University of Oslo, she has carried out research both in South America and South-Eastern Africa, and has published on land rights, access to and conflicts over natural resources, livelihood strategies, food and gender. Over the last 15 years she has in particular focused on rural Mozambique, visiting all the provinces, and seeking to understand people's livelihood conditions in different parts of the country.

Sheila Khan

is a sociologist and currently a researcher at the Interdisciplinary Centre for Social Sciences (CECS.UMinho). She holds a PhD in Ethnic and Cultural Studies from the University of Warwick. Her main research topics are: post-colonial studies, with focus on the relations between Mozambique and Portugal, including the question of Mozambican immigrants in Portugal; Mozambican and Portuguese contemporary history and literature; narrative of life and identity from the global South; memory and post-memory authorities. Her most recent book is entitled *Portugal a Lápis de Cor. A Sul de uma pós-colonialidade*

(Almedina, 2015), and she has co-edited *Visitas a João Paulo Borges Coelho. Leituras, Diálogos e Futuros* (Colibri, 2017).

Maria Paula Meneses

a Mozambican scholar, is currently a Principal Researcher at Center for Social Studies of Coimbra University; previously she was a Professor at Eduardo Mondlane University, Mozambique. Her principal areas of interest include postcolonial debates in African contexts, with a focus on the debates related to the production of national history, the challenges to official historical narratives by other memory(ies) and narratives of belonging in contemporary identity struggles. Her fieldwork in Mozambique, as well as in Angola, Kenya and East Timor has contributed to broaden the study of the relationships between the modern state and traditional authorities, opening up the analysis of the multiple modernities coexisting across the Global south. In this context, she has been documenting the silenced narratives of women in frontline contexts, aiming to understand the participation of African women in local politics and in shaping the nationalist discourse. Her current research is concerned with the contemporary Mozambique archive and memory culture, with a focus on food, emotions and cultural transmissions. The goal is to magnify the forms and meaning of coexistence and dialogues across cultures generated in contact zones in the Global south, beyond the written and spoken words. Maria Paula Meneses has published articles in anthologies, edited volumes, and a range of scholarly journals. Among her most recent books is the volume coedited with Bruno Sena Martins, entitled *As Guerras de Libertação e os Sonhos Coloniais: alianças secretas, mapas imaginados* (Almedina, 2013) and *Epistemologías del Sur*, with Boaventura de Sousa Santos (Akal, 2015). She is currently completing a book manuscript on the 'collaborators' and the political use of 'treason' in the construction of independent Mozambique.

Lia Quartapelle

graduated as an economist from the University of Pavia. In 2007, she worked for a year as an economist with the Italian Development Cooperation in Mozambique, supporting the Mozambican government under Prime Minister Luísa Diogo in setting their development policies. Quartapelle was elected Deputy in the 2013 Italian national elections. In parliament, Quartapelle serves on the Committee on Foreign and European Community Affairs, the Sub-Committee on Human Rights, the Sub-Committee on Sustainable Development, and the Sub-Committee on Africa and Global Affairs. In addition to her committee assignments, Quartapelle has been a member of the Italian delegation to the

Parliamentary Assembly of the Council of Europe since 2015. She currently serves on the Committee on Political Affairs and Democracy. By 2014, Quartapelle was widely mentioned as possible replacement for Federica Mogherini as Minister of Foreign Affairs in the government of Prime Minister Matteo Renzi. In January 2016, Quartapelle was among a group of MPs who collected 118 signatures of a petition nominating the Afghan Cycling Federation women's team for the Nobel Peace Prize.

Amy Schwartzott

received her PhD from the University of Florida in 2014. An ethnographic investigation of recyclia utilized by Mozambican artists is presented in her dissertation, *Weapons and Refuse as Media: the Potent Politics of Recycling in Contemporary Mozambican Urban Arts*. This research resulted in a Centre for Conflict Studies Fellowship and two Fulbright awards. Recently authored publications in international journals and volumes include *Tydskrif vir Letterkunde/Journal for Literary Studies; Critical Interventions: Journal of African Art History and Visual Culture;* and *Representations of Reconciliation: Art and Trauma in Africa*. Ms. Schwartzott currently is an Assistant Professor of Art History at North Carolina A&T State University where she is Curator of University Galleries.

Leonor Simas-Almeida

has a BA in Romance Philology and a *licenciatura* in Portuguese literature from the University of Lisbon, Portugal, as well as a Masters and a PhD in Comparative Literature from Brown University, Providence, Rhode Island. She teaches in the Department of Portuguese and Brazilian Studies, where she also serves as Director of Graduate Studies. She has been teaching and publishing extensively in the areas of Portuguese and Lusophone African Literatures. Her more recent project, a book entitled *Literatura e Emoções: a função hermenêutica dos afetos*, is currently in press.

Anne Sletsjøe

is emeritus professor of Portuguese literature at the University of Oslo, Norway, where she taught Portuguese and Brazilian literature from most historical periods, as well as contemporary Lusophone African literature. Her scholarly work has paid special attention to Brazilian Modernism (PhD dissertation on Mário de Andrade's *Macunaíma*), to Portuguese theatre from the sixteenth century, and to Portuguese and Brazilian narrative prose from the seventeenth century (the works of Gaspar Pires de Rebelo) and the eighteenth century (Nuno

Marques Pereira's *Compêndio Narrativo do Peregrino da América*). When the literatures of the PALOP countries were included in the syllabus of Portuguese studies in Oslo in 2003, she embarked on the study of the works of Pepetela, Agualusa, Ondjaki and Mia Couto. She has, however, worked more extensively on Ungulani Ba Ka Khosa's *Ualalapi*. She was made *Oficial da Ordem do Infante Dom Henrique* in 2000.

Sandra Sousa
holds a PhD in Portuguese and Brazilian Studies from Brown University. Currently, she is Assistant Professor in the Modern Languages and Literatures Department at the University of Central Florida, where she teaches Portuguese language, Lusophone and Latin American Studies. Her research interests include colonialism and post-colonialism; Portuguese colonial literature; race relations in Mozambique; war, dictatorship and violence in contemporary Portuguese and Luso-African literature; feminine writing in Portuguese, Brazilian and African literature. She is the author of *Ficções do Outro: Império, Raça e Subjectividade no Moçambique Colonial* (Esfera do Caos, 2015) and has co-edited *Visitas a João Paulo Borges Coelho. Leituras, Diálogos e Futuros* (Colibri, 2017).

Situating Mozambican Histories, Epistemologies, and Potentialities

Maria Paula Meneses, Sheila Pereira Khan and Bjørn Enge Bertelsen

For many good reasons, interest in Mozambique has greatly expanded over recent years. Such growing interest reflects changing global configurations of economic and political powers and, particularly, shifts in ambitions for control over this part of Africa. Notable, of course, is China's complex and multi-dimensional engagement with a country such as Mozambique, partly displacing European, North American and other donor influence over national politics (e.g. Chichava and Alden 2012; Chichava, Cortês and Orre 2015; Brautigam and Ekman 2012; Wethal 2017). Moreover, given the recent upsurge in hydrocarbons (oil, gas and coal), metals (such as aluminium), wood and land – to name some key elements – the country's resources have increasingly become attractive on a global market through various so-called megaprojects, although their social, political and economic impacts have been mixed (e.g. Castel-Branco 2014; Mandlate 2015; Silva, Araújo and Souto 2015; Osório and Silva 2017). Amidst such great alterations, the Mozambican economy continues to grow and 2016 achieved an annual growth rate of 3,3 per cent (World Bank 2017).

These indicators and a range of other developments signal large-scale transformations in domains as varied as migration and labour patterns, sociocultural perceptions, political dynamics, investment possibilities, public and literary discourses about the nation-state and its ideals, or class and elite formation. In short, Mozambique is reverberating with intense processes characterized by motility and mobility – it is a country on the move in a plural, international and diverse sense.[1] The interdisciplinary character of this book, therefore, not only mirrors the diversity of studies carried out in the country, but also aims to

---

[1] For example, besides being a member of several multilateral international organizations, such as the United Nations (UN), Mozambique is a full member of the *African Union*, of *the Commonwealth*, of the *Community of the Portuguese Speaking Countries* (CPLP), of the *Organization of Islamic Cooperation*, and has a seat, as an observer, in the *Organisation Internationale de la Francophonie*. Mozambique is also member of regional, African associations, such as the *Southern Africa Development Community*.

capture and reflect the complex geopolitical space that comprises contemporary Mozambique.

1   Perceiving the Nation

On June 25, 1975, Mozambique became an independent country and, with freedom, an African and global beacon of liberation was born, inaugurating a new dawn for its inhabitants. The country celebrated having won independence from the Portuguese under the leadership of *Frente de Libertação de Moçambique* (Front for the Liberation of Mozambique) – FRELIMO – and began its journey towards nationhood and statehood. As a nationalist movement, FRELIMO was established inside and outside colonial Mozambique during the 1960s and gradually came to be the dominant nationalist organization in the struggle for independence. Retaining the name and acronym, following independence it transformed into a political party, which has remained in power during both mono- and multiparty systems and until the present day.[2]

However, as with most contemporary countries and nations, the question of what constitutes Mozambique in a more profound sense than corresponding to a formerly colonized territory, raises a number of additional issues. In particular, and over time, multiple colonial presences in the region[3] produced the geopolitical space that today is the sovereign republic of Mozambique (Pélissier 1994). Thus, the case of Mozambique crucially serves to inform various forms of postcolonial scholarship by highlighting how African territories and spaces (as well as non-African postcolonial contexts) are the products of the rise and fall of imperial forces (Meneses 2011). Unsurprisingly, the sediments of these colonial presences – including the historical configuration of boundaries, national hierarchies, and privileged identities based on notions of ethnicity, religion, race, language and civilizational inputs – were sought to be redressed with independence, primarily through politics that re-defined and re-territorialized various features and registers of the independent nation-state (Meneses and Ribeiro 2008; Bonate 2010). Specifically, the radical shift fomented by Mozambican nationalist struggles was predicated on an orientation towards a brighter future liberated from direct colonial rule – a political

---

2   Usually, the capitalized acronym FRELIMO refers to the movement until the moment of liberation, while Frelimo refers to the post-independence political party.

3   Mozambique was a Portuguese colony until independence was gained in 1975. However, as this book reveals, other colonial presences can be identified, including British chartered companies, Austrian slave traders, Indian trading companies, and numerous other entities (see also Newitt 1995 for an overview).

process where the past was discursively represented so as to serve political ends for the country's liberation movement and political party in power since independence, Frelimo (Coelho 2003, 2015; Dinerman 2006, 2009).

As in other processes of nation-building, the immediate postcolonial project was based upon a supposedly common past, in the form of a rich heritage of memories shared in the present. This 'heritage' is oriented towards a consent to live together in an indivisible way. As Ernest Renan (1996) suggested, writing about the French experience at the end of the nineteenth century, an epic past, sharing sufferings and common enemies, gives shape and direction to a cohesive core of the national community to be constituted. But, as Renan emphasizes, if common memories of the past can cement the unity of a nation, they can also contribute to creating multiple fractures. For these reasons, and as Homi Bhabha (1990, 292) points out, any national project carries the burden of constructing a collective political memory which generates multiple silences and forgets or marginalizes actors and political processes. Consequently, any view of the nation based on a politicization of the past always contains innumerable ambiguities.

We are acutely aware of the ways in which the past and its role in the present are inherent to postcolonial societies, politics, and cultures – and these aspects are approached in a number of ways in this volume. However, we also want to emphasize the movement and fluidity of the dynamic encounters generated by travelling, struggles, and shifting debates and how these aspects likewise inform Mozambican presents and pasts: Rather than exploring a dual notion of past and future, then, we underline instead the complexities of the ways in which time and space are experienced and expressed in contemporary Mozambique – specific spatio-temporal configurations that are emergent, receding, transforming or open (Cahen 1994; Bonate 2010; Meneses 2011).

Precisely due to this emergent, open and un-ended nature of Mozambique – and, arguably, also Africa more widely, as has been increasingly underlined (see, e.g., Sarr 2016; Goldstone and Obarrio 2017) – in this volume we also explore the relationships between literature, cultural expressions and academic analysis. Pursuing such intricacies, we hold, challenge us to interrogate hegemonic representations and conventional descriptions of historical and contemporary Mozambican transformations (see also Khan 2016). For the history of a country is not limited to official speeches and writings about events and facts which comprise or dictate the ontological fabric of a nation. Rather, literature and the diversity of other concrete and systematized cultural manifestations exhibit and embody a variety of other forms and strands of narrative that facilitates approaching a nation *both* as a project or a construct *and* as a movement or a form of emergence (see also Leite *et al.* 2012). Displaced voices, narratives and interpretations of that history emerge within these cultural forms, perceived as a rich and rewarding locus for bringing about new ways of challenging a hegemonic historical perspective. Taking this into account, the defiance that the texts in this volume in various ways demonstrate, is that historical representations of a country have to be approached lucidly with the certainty of multiple ways of narrating both the colonial and post-colonial Mozambican nation(s) and, therefore, past and present can no longer be fixed and fossilized terms within temporal grids. Here, the opportunity does not arise in the shape of a naïve ambition to make a singular or metrical construction of History, but rather, as Susan Sontag observes '...part of the ethical function of literature is the lesson of the value of diversity' (2011, 167, our translation; see also Coelho 2008).[4]

Reflecting such considerations, this introduction offers a way into the book both through the engaged dialogue and debate that has emerged among the authors and through the reflection on various aspects of Mozambican trajectories and dimensions. Hence, *Chapter 1* opens the book with a contextual and critical account of Mozambique's political trajectory. It looks specifically into the rural-urban divide, the recent politics of decentralization, the challenges of political mobilization in a context of dominance of a single political party and the potentially divisive influence of the donor and aid community. *Chapter 2* shifts our focus to the plight of individual refugees and the mass-mediated discourses related to the Zimbabwean migration to Mozambique, especially in the central province of Manica during the late 2000s. Based on anthropological fieldwork, the chapter contrasts analytically the kinds of local realities the Zimbabwean refugees met with how the issue was represented doubly in terms of negative stereotyping or made invisible in the Mozambican media, the latter reflecting, the author argues, a non-recognition of the Zimbabwean crisis on part of the Mozambican government. *Chapter 3* also deals with Manica Province but this chapter explores how the Mozambican past is remoulded also in terms of urban space by analysing the purported change of name of a central square in the provincial capital of Chimoio – from celebrating the Mozambican women's organization to reflecting the contested historical figure of the emperor Ngungunyane. The author interprets this shift not only at a level of national discourses of the past – where the political elite and a donor community may find it rewarding to include such figures as the emperor in an urban spatial representation –, but also by showing how the change of name evoked reactions from non-elite citizens that testify to the struggles over the nation's

---

4 The original quote reads: '... parte da função ética da literatura é a lição do valor da diversidade'.

imaginaries. The following text, *Chapter 4*, takes us to Maputo and explores its urban politics and social orders in terms of household dynamics, family strategies and spatial dimensions. Crucially, the chapter points out that processes of urban expansion as well as densification (especially of central urban areas) are accompanied by an increased migration between sections of the city as well as its surroundings which, argues the author, create important, complex and multiple bridges between urban spaces formerly identified in dichotomous terms as formal and informal, modern and traditional. *Chapter 5* shifts the focus to the analysis of the impact of mineral wealth in the country, specifically addressing the aid effects on employment. In a country still dependent on external aid, whether aid creates employment and in what sectors are fundamental questions that are analysed using, largely, a macroeconomic approach. *Chapter 6* discusses the representation of memory in the reconfiguration of Mozambican identities, by highlighting the importance of transculturation and hybridism, in order to regain the diversity inherent to the challenge of narrating the history of Mozambique through its mnemonic richness. *Chapter 7* presents an attentive and critical reading of two Mozambican novels, Mia Couto's *Jesusalém* and Ungulani Ba Ka Khosa's *Ualalapi*. Through a close reading and contextual analysis of these works, the chapter offers the reader a rigorous account of how the nation-state also writes its own narrative by challenging the official discourse and also of how from the lessons of its past human wounds it is possible to anticipate the understanding of the future. By drawing on Mia Couto's novels *Terra Sonâmbula* and *O Outro Pé da Sereia*, *Chapter 8* explores the racial, cultural, and emotional crossing paths in both colonial and post-colonial times. In the discussion of *Terra Sonâmbula* the authors unveil some of the textual strategies that reveal a clear awareness of people's suffering in a country engulfed by civil war, but also the possibility of redemption. In *O Outro Pé da Sereia* they analyse the view of the oppressed and marginalized in a colonial and slavery-based society, as well as the after-effects of colonial practices on contemporary society. *Chapter 9* brings about a painstaking examination of the intricate relationship between history, gender and cultural forms that are encompassed by so-called *capulanas* – manufactured pieces of cotton cloth that traverse the cultural landscape of Mozambique. They do this through presenting and analysing the memories and uses that *capulanas* embody, as well as by unfolding their relevance as creative and dynamic vehicles of social interaction. *Chapter 10* analyses the project *Transformação de Armas em Enxadas* (TAE) in order to discuss the potency of recycling as an artistic tool in processes of post-conflict resolution. The innovative aspect of TAE lies in the fact that recycling weapons of war into agricultural tools is not only a transformation into art or a frame towards healing and commemoration, but

also that the weapons are permanently disabled in order to prevent them being used for killing again. *Chapter 11* presents us with another notion of and
approach to culture, namely how Brazilian Pentecostal churches in Maputo
construe Mozambican culture as an entity to be overcome by its converts. Analysing Mozambican women aspiring to or already being part of the middle
class, the chapter argues that Pentecostalism, in the way that it is enacted and
lived in these contexts, gives force and shape to a particular form of agency –
one geared towards prosperity, liberation and the severance of previous kin
or familial relationships. In *Chapter 12* we are introduced to the rich and polysemic trajectory of music in Mozambique, in particular the repertoire of
revolutionary songs and their relation to the expression of politics. Seeing
these songs as comprising a discursive site, the chapter alerts us to the fact
that their articulation and performance, their singing, also constitute specific
and crucial ways of being and constituting history, as well as documenting it.
Chapter 13 brings us to the domain of epistemology, science and colonial and
postcolonial relations – interrogating the hegemony that the North has in
terms of being presented as (and presenting itself as) the origins of scientific
thought and knowledge. The chapter underlines the flaws of such a position
while, at the same time, holding up the ideal of critical thought to be influential for African and Mozambican re-assertion of knowledge, science and
epistemologies.

As can already be gleaned from this cursory introduction to the book's
chapters, the Mozambican people's struggle, the country's revolution and the
ascendance of Frelimo as a liberation movement and later vanguard political
party, profoundly shaped and continues to shape the country's multiple trajectories. However, while the fervour and celebration of national liberation in 1975
included the tearing down of colonial symbols, re-naming streets and transforming the urban landscape, the leaders of independent Mozambique mixed
national independence with political autonomy and sovereignty (Egerö 1990;
Morton 2015). That there would be challenges to Mozambique's new formal
sovereign status rapidly became painfully clear, as devastating occurrences
of violence, including a protracted civil war (1976–1992) ravaged the country.
These conflicts were supported by such foreign powers as Apartheid-era South
Africa, white-minority ruled Southern Rhodesia, and the Cold War leaders of
the USA and the USSR (see also Nordstrom 1997; Coelho 2003, 2009; Emerson
2014; Bertelsen 2016).

Nevertheless, the new national freedom and the emergent postcolonial politics remained in the hands of the movement-become-party-in-power, Frelimo,
and spurred on by the party, the political change inaugurated an era where
colonial mind-sets and its cognitive spaces were attacked. In such a context of

radical politics, alliances forged during the war of liberation (1964–1975) – for instance, of ethno-political kinds – were abandoned for a unitary political-cosmological orientation. As several chapters emphasise, including the opening and closing chapter, Mozambique's official postcolonial discourse accentuated aspects of freedom that Nandy analyses as a key to understanding postcolonial dynamics more broadly, also beyond India, namely 'freedom as an event and as an unfolding process [that] is seen as part of a longer journey towards modernity and progress' (1999, 305). In fact, this idea of journeying has framed the Mozambican imagination so broadly that a great majority of social, cultural, political, and economic experiences of the country has been, to some extent, informed by it.

While this aspect of journeying and movement is developed in several chapters, we will mention merely two instances at the political level here. First, what we can call Frelimo's 'future-orientation' has been dominant throughout the postcolonial era and has informed both radical politics of societal transformation. It has also been used explicitly in political slogans – as in Frelimo's election campaign in 1999 'Juntos por um futuro melhor' ('United for a better future') (see also Chapter 1) or, as Rønning (2015) has underlined, during the 2014 elections the term 'mudança' ('change') was equally important and, again, reflecting a futurist temporal orientation.

Second, it has also been integral to the sometimes cautious and sometimes boundless optimism of donors: these have emphasized stability of rule, increasing economic growth, and the country's wealth in natural resources, which they frequently contrast with other African countries (Moran and Pitcher 2004; Clément and Peiris 2008). However, in recent years such optimism has been strongly challenged by the emergence of elite-induced so-called secret debts, dire economic porosity and an intensification of aggressive elite-driven and predatory forms of primitive accumulation (Brooks 2017; Nogueira *et al.* 2017).

However, Frelimo's future-orientation would have remained incomplete without an epic past: characterized by shared suffering, this unitary historical narrative gave shape to a cohesive present that constituted the foundation of the imagined project of national community (Anderson 1983). Moreover, cultivating such an epic collective past immediately following independence was part of the nationalist project and was, interestingly, also reflected in a number of scholarly accounts (see, e.g., Isaacman 1978). Nevertheless, both the personal memories of those ousted from or opposed to power and the uncovering of a range of archival material gradually muddled the waters of the nationalist narrative. While this perhaps reflects a general observation that Stoler (2009, 2011, 2016) has incisively and repeatedly made about the enduring, recursive

and muddled character of imperial formations, it also emphasizes the instability of 'the past' in any political order. One example can be seen in the case of
Uria Simango: once a FRELIMO leader, marginalized in official accounts of the
liberation following his execution in 1978, he was re-centred and again debated
following a controversial biography (Ncomo 2004) which also, more generally,
introduced a broader public discussion about the history of liberation and
Frelimo.

Therefore, the dominant version of the struggle, almost enshrined in 'The'
canonical narrative of resistance against Portuguese colonialism, includes
loud silences (Meneses 2011). National celebrations of the liberation struggle
constitute a reminder of this narrative, and aim to pass on the national history
to younger generations, thus reinforcing a sense of national belonging. This involves an annual cycle of public events such as May 1 (Labour Day) and April 7
(Women's Day) – both of which are mass celebrations that inscribe significant
events and national unity onto urban landscapes (Panzer 2009; Santos 2010).
For Frelimo, the chance afforded by its position of power to narrate the history
of Mozambicans also represented a political opportunity to construct a specific
identity that countered the image of the oppressed colonial subject. Perhaps
the boldest attempt undertaken in the early post-liberation period was their
construction of 'the New Man' (*O Homem Novo*) (see also Machel 1980 [1977]).
Inspired by socialist ideas of revolutionary emancipation from colonial subjec-
tivities and societal structures, the government set out to radically transform
and re-envision what an identity beyond the oppressed colonial subject could
be. The New Man was a mainstay of much political rhetoric in the first post-
independence decade and measures were taken to implement this revolutionary vision in practice. In practical terms this meant a wide-ranging and radical
reordering of the political and social orders, including the ousting from office
and dethroning of traditional chiefs and religious leaders, large-scale attempts
at rural collectivization, and social 'cleansing' of urban areas of the 'unproduc-
tive parasites' living in the cities (Honwana 1984; Cabaço 2001; Coelho 2007;
Zawangoni 2007; Thomaz 2008; Chichava 2013; Israel 2013; Nielsen 2014; Farré
2015; Meneses 2015). Furthermore, the construction of collective state farms as
part of rural transformation was seen 'not only as rational and highly productive but as having dynamic effects on the surrounding desert of agricultural
backwardness' (Hall and Young 1997, 91; see also Mosca 2011 for a comprehensive oversight over recent Mozambican agricultural history).

Of course, debate was rife within Frelimo regarding its radical political project, the 'Mozambican revolution' and the attempted comprehensive transformation that was oriented towards transgressing inherited colonial orders and
categories. Such matters were a main topic of debate throughout Frelimo's

Congresses – the first was held in Tanzanian exile in 1962, followed by the second congress in still colonial Mozambique in 1968, until the famous 1977 Third Congress was held in liberated Mozambique (see also Pachinuapa 2009 for a memoir of these early congresses). Continuing to inform the party and to constitute an arena for ideological debate and development, the format of the congress is still crucial for Frelimo as was evidenced by its 11th held in September 2017. Reflecting changing political tides and developments both within pre- and post-independence Frelimo, these debates and dynamics are also reflected in several of the chapters in the book and, arguably, gender has continued to pose a considerable challenge to the revolution, running alongside the projects of transformation that fall under the heading of the New Man (see also Sheldon 2002; Owen 2007, 2010; Tavares 2010).

When analysing these post-independence national aspirations and radical politics, it is important to distinguish between a socially constructed category and the group that is inscribed in this category. For Mozambique, this basic distinction requires differentiating between the construction of political citizenship – such as the New Man – and other and more heterogeneous projects of what we may term cultural citizenship. Firstly, the formation of what we may call *political citizenship* following independence was accompanied by a radical levelling in terms of legal equality, independent from (and without relation to) ethnic or religious roots (Sachs and Welch 1990; Meneses 2006). This levelling movement is epitomised in a quotation sometimes used before independence by the man who would become Mozambique's first president (1975–1986), Samora Machel.[5] As leader of FRELIMO, Machel proclaimed (Machel 1974, 39):

> To unite all Mozambicans, transcending traditions and different languages, requires that the tribe must die in our consciousness so that the nation may be born.

This political motto, used during the revolutionary period of the 1970s to 1980s, reflected the party's nationalist objective, which was to encourage the

5   While the impact on Mozambique of the presidency, personality and style of Samora Moises Machel can hardly be overestimated, space limitation prevents us from going into details here. However, for works relating to biography and politics, see for instance Christie (1988), Sopa (2001) or LeFanu (2012). For literature related to his spectacular death (alongside many others) in a much-debated plane crash on South African soil in 1986, see Cabrita (2005), Robinson (2006), Milhazes (2010) or Douek (2017). For two contributions dealing with his contemporary influence on such diverse issues as contemporary rap music in Maputo and the ideological and epistemological terrain of the Mozambican political order, see Ngoenha (2009) and Rantala (2016) respectively.

emergence of a national identity absent of ethnic or religious pasts and identities (Meneses and Santos 2009).

However, and running counter to what has just been outlined, actions that constitute what we may call *cultural citizenship* set out to emphasize coexistence and dialogue among socio-cultural entities and formations, which implied the rejection of a single historical narrative (see also Chapters 3 and 10, this volume). If initially this approach was often part of a critical dialogue about the roots of contemporary representation (questioning, for instance, the geographies and semantics associated with concepts that located Mozambique far behind in the movement towards 'progress and civilization'), it later became a political tool used to construct *moçambicanidade* – a hard-to-translate term that is commonly rendered as Mozambicanness. As an artefact of hegemonic discourse, *moçambicanidade* nevertheless reflects the country's multiple struggles and construes a sense of national belonging while simultaneously being anchored in a de-historicized and de-politicized conceptualization of Mozambique (see also Bragança and Depelchin 1986; Coelho 1998; Serra 1998; Ngoenha 1999; Power 2000). The nation-building vision included the political adoption of an official version of history, which was grounded in a selective assemblage of collective memories about the colonial past, both recent and distant.

As many of the contributors to this book point out, and as argued by Penvenne (1996) elsewhere, the journey towards freedom must be seen as ongoing. Historically, one way to trace such development – or historical journey, if you will – is through analysing the origins of Mozambican nationalism in the early twentieth century where journalists, such as João Albasini, were crucial in establishing nationalist discourses.[6] However, the processes of contestation and the possibilities for pluralization have also harboured a destructive potential throughout Mozambican colonial and postcolonial history – not least during the harrowing period of warfare between 1976 and 1992, which has variously been labelled civil war, war of destabilization, post-liberation war, or war of RENAMO.[7] Beyond being devastating, extremely violent, and conditioned by a number of foreign interests that supported *Resistência Nacional de*

---

6 For a comparative study of Portuguese-speaking African countries where national independence was achieved through armed struggle, see Morier-Genoud (2012).

7 RENAMO – *Resistência Nacional de Moçambique* (Mozambican National Resistance) – was a guerrilla group that fought the Frelimo government with apartheid South African and Western support until a General Peace Agreement (GPA) was signed in 1992. Following the peace process, RENAMO transformed into a political party – now acronymized in the minor as Renamo – and, following the peace agreement, has remained the country's main opposition party. The nature of RENAMO and the dynamics of the period of warfare remain highly contested and

Moçambique (Mozambican National Resistance) – RENAMO – the war era also created new dynamics of support for non-Frelimo politics and ideologies. This became apparent in the country's first parliamentary and presidential elections following the General Peace Agreement in 1992 and the country's first parliamentary and presidential elections in 1994: The RENAMO movement then emerged as a political party – Renamo – and to many observers' surprise gained almost half of the votes. It has also done consistently well in consecutive elections (for further details on the elections, see Mazula 1995; Manning 2008 or Vines 2017).

Now, more than a quarter of a century after the war formally ended, how has Mozambique fared? While it is impossible to reply to a question of such magnitude fully here, we would nevertheless suggest that two distinct matrixes or domains for assessing the country's trajectory are visible: in one, social science and humanities insist on speaking the policy language of international organizations, development projects, and ideologies of modernization; in the other, there is an insistence on paths to be found among multiple worlds, where truth is to be found in a plurality of worldviews. The second matrix constitutes an alternative by referencing to different ways of being in the world, and to highlight the continuities, movements, and knowledges that these processes embody. An epistemological approach, we stress, comprises such matrices that convey, in various senses, alternative worlds and establishes domains where truth emerges as conversational plurality – a perspective engaged particularly in Chapter 13.

As we attempted to outline above, analyses of the past, be they undertaken in literary studies, anthropology, or political science, are never neutral and inevitably reflect the author's political, academic, and scientific position. This point is made obvious in the Mozambican case by the period of revolutionary socialism, the episodes of extreme violence associated with it, the controversies that raged until 1992 and the end of the civil war. Contemporary scholarly approaches to Mozambique – and especially those steeped in universal and universalizing neoliberal approaches to governance, aid, and development – sometimes lack a sense of direction and an appreciation for the specificity of the Mozambican journey (Ngomane 2008; Obarrio 2014). Luckily, in contemporary Mozambique, besides the scholarly, literary, and policy-making realms, musicians and artists expressly create representations of reality, combining the local with the global, the past with the present. These creative works embody a vast array of representational challenges since they articulate alternative

---

debated among scholars (see, e.g., Cahen 2002). For two opposing views, see Geffray (1991) and O'Laughlin (1992), and for a summary of debates on Renamo, see Dinerman (2006).

political, social, and cultural projects, as the songs analysed in Chapter 12 suggest, or they can ambivalently relate to national narratology, as discussed in Chapter 3. Further, as dealt with in the powerful Chapters 6 to 8, when delving into the country's rich tapestry of literary traditions – including its engagement with race, temporality and identity – it becomes evident that Mozambique is replete with diverse ways of generating new visions of the country's worlds and its possibilities; a literary and creative cosmogenetics of sorts. What these literary works analysed in these chapters testify to, is the richness of the various traditions available and their potential to challenge dominant colonial and postcolonial representations of reality (present and past) from a subaltern perspective of multiple claims (Santos and Meneses 2009; Ngoenha and Castiano 2010). This reality is also grasped by Chapters 9 and 10 which probe art – weapons and capulanas – as a means to address how Mozambicanness is addressed in on-going memorialization and identity disputes (see also Israel 2014).

From the vantage point of the postcolonial subject, the remembrance of colonial relations of power has emerged as fundamental to a range of intellectual and political agendas that make the recording, rewriting, and eliciting of colonial memories equally pertinent and charged. This tense field includes numerous biographical works on colonial officials that have been published over the last few decades, or the range of glossy photobooks on colonial Mozambique currently peddled in up-scale Maputo and Lisbon bookstores (see also Gupta 2016 [2012]). The force inherent in both biographies and photobooks – and particularly given their undertone of ruination of and nostalgia for (colonial) orders past – is often also tied to a kind of fetishization of the physical, desolate, and disintegrated places of the *l'ancien régime* (Hell and Schönle 2010). The politically charged landscape of memory charted by such colonial memorabilia, photographic reprints, and recollections reflects the ongoing difficulties inherent in the colonial situation and continually re-signifies it as a problematic and important site of inquiry.

2   Imperialism, Globalization, and Postcolonial Epistemologies

Vasco da Gama's passage across the Indian Ocean in 1498 inaugurated what has come to be known as the European renaissance: the founding moment of Western capitalist modernity which would rapidly come to dominate the world. However, other (non-European) people already inhabited this world beyond Europe – including what would later be known as Mozambique where trade circuits across the Indian Ocean had brought merchants to its western shores to trade slaves, gold, and ivory (Newitt 1995; Capela 2002; Zimba *et al.* 2006). These traders comprise longstanding communities and have a history that has also profoundly shaped the identities of coastal peoples in the region (Conceição 2006). Beyond Mozambique, and as several historical documents reveal, the Indian Ocean region may be seen as the product of migrations (voluntary and forced) that began in the first century (Abu-Lughod 1989; Jayasuriya and Pankhurst 2003; Bose 2006; Harries 2016).

These pre-Portuguese connectivities underline what is by now cliché but needs to be repeated in the face of 'born-again globalists': globalization is not a new phenomenon and in the medieval era there was already a world system based on travel and trade underpinning a global economy that was not dominated by a single country, with Europe joining these existing global economies (Dussel 2000; Wallerstein 2004). For nearly two thousand years, Africans journeyed to distant lands which were often radically different from their own politically, geographically, linguistically, and culturally. Specifically, on the western shores of the Indian Ocean, Kiswahili was the lingua franca in those regions that are usually described as part of the Swahili world, until the beginning of the twentieth century. The communities of the cosmopolitan cities that emerged in these coastal areas established broad family ties within the region; they were deeply enmeshed in transnational trading networks, initially in the historic Indian Ocean area and, more recently, through networks involving European colonialism. New positions as middlemen arose in the colonial order, such as the emergence of traders of Indian descent who were important in the Zambezia region of Mozambique in the 1800s and 1900s (Machado 2005; Teixeira 2008). This process was marked by high levels of mobility and gave rise, in Ho's characterization, to local cosmopolitanisms that 'travelled, amalgamated itself with other states, families, peoples, lands and languages' (2002, 224; see also Pinto 2010). These historical developments arguably created various open-ended, changing and rich alternative imaginations – existing, beyond the confines of imperialism and nationalism – which generated not universalism but cosmopolitanism and effected, arguably, not the erasure of the Other but the possibility for a conversational contiguity (Visvanathan 2012, 67).

The presence of specific Mozambican forms of cosmopolitanisms and of such long duration, involving a range of languages and histories outside the Eurocentric canon, raises challenging questions for a book explicitly confined to a particular nation state (see also Mignolo 1991). What are we to narrate? In which language(s)? How are we, and what are we, to translate?

If we start with language and its use, several works argue that merely a quarter of the population in post-independence Mozambique use Portuguese as its mother language (Firmino 2001; Gonçalves 2002). Thus, we must ask how we might translate native languages into Portuguese, or from (Mozambican)

Portuguese into English, without committing epistemicide[8] (Santos 1998, 103). This is particularly relevant for the case of Mozambique, where history, as well as social and political diversity, have been subsumed to a colonial past that divides lived realities into modern and traditional forms – impinging also on the present with the question of how to translate between the distinct language communities that constitute the national cultural mosaic.

Recognizing these challenges of language, cosmopolitanism and a problematic bifurcation of traditional versus modern, the editors believe that the choices an academic has to make while translating his/her research have to be seen within a broad framework that has an ethical as well as an epistemological component (Hountondji 2002; Ramose 2002). As this volume reveals, the way in which a particular culture – and Mozambique recognizes itself as a multicultural country[9] – formulates its knowledge is intricately bound up with the identity of its people, their way of making sense of the world, and the value system that holds this worldview in place. Nevertheless, and despite such diversity, as underlined by the unitary message of Samora Machel, quoted above, post-independence Mozambique is undeniably founded on a distinctly modern idea of the nation state; a polity with a strong sense of unity and collective interest. Further, and in particular following the end of the civil war (1992) and the introduction of multiparty democracy (1994), one might add that the country has made a significant investment in democracy and human rights, paralell with a government that attempts to maintain a monopoly over the legitimate means of force. On the other hand, this same state arguably fails to protect its citizens from various forms of violence and fails to deliver on the promise of rights. In such a context of contestation and paradox, and in lieu of a lack of effective collective mobilization of political opposition (but see Bertelsen 2014), non-state domains of culture become central to producing meaning against the overwhelming forces of market, state and an increasingly powerful ruling class.

However, we should not romanticize such alternatives to market, state and class power: It is crucial to recognize that when multiple means of communication are present – the oral, the gestural, the textual, the digital – to grant a special privilege to a singular script is equivalent to the erasure of such multiplicity. Paraphrasing Spivak (1988), the subaltern cannot speak when orality has been abandoned and life is ruled by the despotism of the written text. An

---

8 Boaventura de Sousa Santos defines epistemicide as the death or murder of knowledge of a subordinate culture, and hence the eradication of the social groups that possessed it (Santos 2014).

9 See article 4 of the 2004 Constitution of Mozambique.

attention to Mozambican forms of epistemicide, as the systematic destruction of other forms of knowledge, alerts us to the ways in which the conjunction of knowledge with power reduces the unbiased search for wisdom to self-serving ideology. Key here is the imperial project of a global North vis-à-vis a global South – a metaphor of exploitation and social and political exclusion – as a constitutive part of the global capitalist relationship (Santos 2006b). Inherent to this process is also a radical division between knowledges where the capacity to distinguish between true and false is attributed to modern science – a work of distinction that has generated profound contradictions and which has remained at the core of contemporary epistemological debate (Santos 2007). A crucial inroad into such work of distinction and the apparatus of the North-South divide, is provided by the work of history as a form of enactment of power: It embodies the capacity to tell not only a part of history, but also, and primordially, to expand that part into the full history. From the perspective of Europe, the 'worlding' of the world, to use Heidegger's term (1962), is a memory of colonialism and, thus, the imposition of a Eurocentric epistemology of knowledge (Meneses 2011; Khan 2015, 2017). In this sense, because most of the Eurocentric representations of the global South have yet to be decolonized, there are multiple examples showing that colonial dynamics, modes of thinking and orders did not cease to operate with Mozambican political independence in 1975. A case in point here is the concept of citizenship – normatively produced in and by institutional settings defined in the global North. All otherness, in geographic, socio-political, and historical terms, tends to become a variation of a master narrative of citizenship that still uses the semantics of this global North (see also Obarrio 2014). This implies that experiences of citizenship founded on or related to otherness are relegated to positions of subalternity.

Informed by a range of cases – historical, literary, cultural, and political – the editors and authors of this volume therefore probe whether one can still insist on a single macro-narrative of citizenship wherein subaltern positions are contained. This is also a methodological question, which results from carrying out analysis within a single analytical field. After all, the global North and the global South[10] are hyperreal terms in that they refer to imaginary figures whose geographical and epistemological referents remain indeterminate. As figures of the imaginary they are, of course, subject to contestation. Simultaneously, they are adversely positioned and reified categories speaking to and of a

---

10   The global South is commonly invoked as a metaphor of oppression and subalternity. Despite its totalizing scope, we should not forget that in the South, geographically speaking, many situations echo and replicate those of the global North.

structure of domination and subordination where the North is evoked as the centre and the South embodies the periphery (Wallerstein 2004). This being so, such a particular version of Eurocentric universalism, which continues to dominate the discourses of citizenship and belonging, may be identified in the phenomenological world of everyday relationships.

Aiming to challenge such Eurocentric universalism, several authors probe, for instance, the various notions of democracy and citizenship in operation. We would like to stress that Mozambican notions of democracy are here shown to be diverse and, crucially, that the various manifestations available suggest that the global North's notion and powerful discourse of liberal democracy is just one configuration among many possible.

Such Mozambican alternatives and challenges to the global North's dominance is a move towards undermining what Ranajit Guha (2002) has called the generalization of Western notions as the norm. Also in this book this global conundrum has presented itself as a particular problem: That developing world intellectuals feel a need to refer to Eurocentric socio-political works while Western academics do not feel any need to reciprocate (see Chapter 13). We have sought to overcome this in the chapters that follow by including several chapters and parts of these that develop the richness of epistemological positions that pose alternatives to those Western or globally Northern. As a result, various authors have generated debate and dialogue across the book. Put differently, an attempt has been made to overcome what Santos (2006b) calls 'the abyssal thought' – a phrase that alerts us to the fact that, again, also at the epistemological level, postcolonial political independence did not erase the distinctions established through the colonial division of the world.

Specifically, the diverse realities of the 'civilized world' did not incorporate the norms, knowledges, and experiences of the colonized universe. As an effect, people from the former colonies came to be represented as generally underdeveloped and lacking knowledges and experiences relevant to the old world. The persistence of this abyssal line continues to produce a profound theoretical, epistemological, and socio-political problem regarding the production of modern knowledge in the developing world. This problem – often expressed in a paradoxical manner – also goes to the very nature of social science theoretical claims, societal impacts and wider politics.

This line of probing, perhaps the very epistemology of the social sciences itself, is followed up in the anthology's final chapter. It addresses the everyday paradox for developing world's social science, namely that many developing world researchers find Western theories eminently useful in understanding their societies, in spite of their inherent ignorance of 'them'. One way to overstep this dependence is to attempt to move the centre 'to a multiplicity of locations in our languages' (Thiong'o 1993, 14), both between and within countries and continents (Comaroff and Comaroff 2012). Or, as Achille Mbembe powerfully argues, to convey analyses of history and contemporary dynamics relating to Africa and race that de-naturalize Europe as a centre altogether (Mbembe 2017 [2013]). The editors see this anthology as precisely in support of such moves that generate new encounters and embody as well as alter distinct power–knowledge nexuses that may contribute to unmoor cultural formations from the restrictive conceptual frameworks of nationalism, class, race, gender, and sexuality. Therefore, a main thrust of the chapters in this anthology emphasizes the hybridity over categorical purity, contestedness over unity, and dialogue over monologue. As Toyin Falola has observed, in his critical analysis of African Studies and the imperial dimensions to the generation of knowledge (Falola 2006, 169), national histories of Africa represent one of the powerful counters to the attempt to provincialize history. The very first task of writing and teaching national history in various African contexts is to understand the agenda of global history. Having chosen to circumscribe a territory nationally, epistemologically, and historically, we follow Falola and Mbembe in seeing the de-provincializing potential of such narratives. Indeed, this was one of the inspirations for a book dedicated to portraying a Mozambique that is agile, moving and transforming.

3   Decolonization, History, and the Past in the Mozambican Present

The dual objective of retaining the national framework, combined with the need to decentre the North–South epistemic heritage (and the inherent potential in doing so), also entails rethinking what decolonization might mean in the context of Mozambique. As noted above, African political independences did not entail the end of colonialism, broadly conceived. For one, postcolonial societies are based on development regimes the origins of which were constructed under colonial rule, creating systems of governance that inherited the colonial predisposition to excise politics from economic and administrative practice (Meneses 2006). The role of law in defining citizenship in independent Mozambique draws attention to the persistence of a Eurocentric definition of the modern state (but see Sachs and Welch 1990). The contradiction between political and cultural identities and realities, and the definition of political citizenship associated with the modern state (Macamo 2017), which is a legacy of the colonial infrastructure of representation, continued in the post-independence period. This was so despite the return or resurgence of what can be termed 'tradition' in contemporary Mozambique, mirroring, thus, other African contexts where this return is seen as both a legacy of the colonial past and a re-action to postcolonial circumstance (Perrot *et al.* 2003; Vaughan 2005; Buur and Kyed 2007; Lourenço 2010; Bertelsen 2016).

As mentioned above, in Mozambique's short post-independence history another but related political event has been significant: the civil war that, for-mally, was waged between the Mozambican state and RENAMO. In a study of the Mozambican civil war (1976–1992), Borges Coelho (2009) defines this as crucially revolving around a decision reached by part of society to rebel against the country's leadership; this section of society gives a rational basis for its actions, such as a search for material or political gain, or to exhibit some grievance. What further assumes importance in the context of understanding the Mozambican civil war is that the country's independence had repercus-sions, both internally and regionally. For one, in the 1970s, the independence movements of both Mozambique and Angola have to been seen as integral to the broader wave of colonial transitions that were taking place across the region. The rapid disappearance of the physical colonial presence left behind the atypical cases of Apartheid South Africa and Ian Smith's racist Southern Rhodesia – both countries neighbouring Mozambique.[11]

For the immediate post-independent Mozambican government, decoloni-zation implied a radical departure from the politics of the colonial past and the racialized orders of its two neighbours. This was to have consequences for the country, not least in terms of its support for nationalist guerrillas in Zimbabwe and the adoption of UN sanctions against Southern Rhodesia, with the subsequent withdrawal of diplomatic relationships between the two countries. These events caused the eruption of violent conflict with Southern Rhodesia, during which the country's secret services actively supported the creation of RENAMO (Vines 1996). However, to blame the emergence of vio-lence in Mozambique solely on Rhodesian backing – a logistical, financial and tactical support that was taken over by Apartheid South Africa around 1980 – omits a large part of the story: As Borges Coelho explains (2009), other factors, such as poverty (lack of economic opportunities and low rates of economic development), temporal distance from previous conflicts, ethnic dominance, and political instability were at the core of this conflict. In particular, the mod-ern Mozambican state's failure to recognize local social and cultural orders and practices and its antagonist politics against chiefly forms of authority, prac-tices of healing and religion etc. contributed to an armed conflict that spanned more than a decade (see also Cahen 2002; Bertelsen 2016; Morier-Genoud et al. 2018). As the civil war intensified and spread geographically engulf-ing vast tracts of the country in the mid-1980s, RENAMO began to question

---

11   Zimbabwe gained independence in 1980.

Frelimo's contention that traditional authorities were obscurantist institutions – vestiges of a feudal past that needed substitution by the party apparatus. Despite the subalternization endured by traditional institutions in colonial times, and their rejection by the state after independence in its future-oriented drive towards the realization of a modernist and socialist postcolonial society, these maintained a strong presence in the political fabric because of their beneficial proximity to the populations they administered (Geffray 1991).

Following the war, it was difficult for the traditional authorities to decide what position to take in relation to the parties involved in the conflict. By this time, however, Frelimo's attitude towards them had become more ambivalent than inimical and the so-called 'traditional authorities' (*autoridades tradicionais*) were reinstated in 2000, although formally with little power beyond the restrictive scope defined by the law (Meneses 2006; Bertelsen 2016; Obarrio 2017). This situation remains in contemporary Mozambique, with the three dominant political bodies in the country – Frelimo, Renamo, and the new political opposition party MDM (*Movimento Democrático de Moçambique* – Democratic Movement of Mozambique) – negotiating at a distance with these now re-instated traditional authorities.[12]

Analyses of Mozambique's geo-political complexity and historical trajectories are addressed by several contributions. It is important to remember, however, that in the 1990s Mozambique was frequently referred to as a case for the Red Cross, consistently gaining a low score in the United Nations Development Programme's (UNDP) Human Development Index. Over the last few years, however, Mozambique has experienced a boom, as many experts characterized the country's economic growth, and social and political progress. In 2011, it experienced 7.1 percent growth in GNP, partly due to the implementation of major infrastructure projects, and Chapter 5 is concerned with an accompanying aspect of the boom – Mozambique's expanding middle class (see also Arndt *et al.* 2012; Sumich 2018).

Nevertheless, this country that abandoned a colonial relationship less than 50 years ago, and that was subsequently riven by civil war for many long years, faces multiple challenges. For example, the country is poised to become the world's biggest coal exporter within the few next decades,[13] which will

---

12   The MDM emerged in 2009 as a breakaway from Renamo and was headed by then popular mayor of Beira, Daviz Simango. It soon became recognized as an alternative to Renamo and Frelimo and, hence, a third political force. In the national elections of 2009 and 2015, MDM won 8 and 17 (of 250) seats in the Assembly of the Republic respectively.

13   For many analysts, 2011 marked a turning point in Mozambique's economy. With the initiation of large-scale coal exports and the discovery of significant reserves of natural gas, Mozambique began exporting minerals globally. Also, the large aluminium smelter MOZAL has influenced the structure of the Mozambican economy. However, the impact

challenge the traditional roles of agriculture and transport as the core of the Mozambican economy. As several chapters touch upon, growth is not a magic bullet for reducing inequality or promoting democracy and problems regarding redistribution as well as indications of growing inequalities continue to cause concerns – a situation in no way unique to Mozambique (see Castel-Branco 2014; Mozambique News Reports & Clippings, 2016). Also, since the end of the civil war and the emergence of a multi-party democracy, Mozambique has witnessed increasing contestation concerning rights over economic redistribution, judicial authority, and the privileges of representation. Mbembe's (2000) analysis of these matters is especially relevant for the contemporary context. Taking Mbembe's challenge, one should ask whether the transition to democracy in Mozambique is in fact a struggle for the codification of new rights and privileges. Undoubtedly, these struggles, combined with worsening inequalities and corruption, have produced a ripple effect involving instances of public and private violence.[14] Further, unclear political alliances between particular civil society groups and Frelimo have produced multiple forms of privatization of state resources, funds and capacities.[15]

These contestations generate a number of questions concerning Mozambican state formation: to what extent do these challenge the state as a public good; to what extent are they an instrument for ensuring protection and safety

---

in terms of benefits for the Mozambican state, economy and society at large of these developments remain contested (see, .e.g., Castel-Branco 2010; Cunguara 2012; Kirshner and Power 2015).

14   There were street riots and protests in 2005, 2008, 2010 and a minor protest in November 2012, for example, which may be interpreted as popular expressions of resentment against the liberal policies of the state, against elite accumulation, corruption and enduring poverty, or as against state neglect in terms of, for instance, security provision (for some analyses, see Serra 2012; Bertelsen 2014; Brito *et al.* 2015; Brito 2017. More recently (August 2018) attacks by suspected Islamists groups in northern province of Cabo Delgado have been described by several analysts as stemming from economic and social grievances.

15   In 2012, there were episodes of political intimidation by Renamo party members when some of its so-called 'private troops' were arrested in the northern Nampula province. While the period since 2013 remains a period of tension and violence between Renamo and the Mozambican government, a truce agreement of sorts emerged in 2017 although the future trajectory of Renamo and, therefore, the stability of Mozambique remains uncertain with the death of long-term Renamo leader Afonso Dhlakama on May 3, 2018. Also in 2012, a more obvious blackmailing of the state occurred in Maputo when a wave of kidnappings targeted wealthier Muslim, Hindu and Ismaili communities. With the judiciary and the police unable to solve the problem, these communities threatened to vote for parties that would protect their members. There has been a rise in populist demands for cultural rights, which have been accompanied by a rise of religious movements, sometimes framed in open opposition/challenge to the state.

for individuals, in providing an arena for creating the legal conditions for the extension of political rights; and, finally, to what extent do they make possible the exercise of citizenship in its multiple forms?

One answer to these queries is that the Mozambican state – as any modern state – is constituted by the spirit of modern law and exudes, therefore, the language of legality (Obarrio 2014). As John and Jean Comaroff stress for postcolonial domains more generally (2004, 539), 'it is this spirit, this language, hegemonically retooled for the neoliberal epoch that gives postcolonial nation-states their delicate sense of unity and coherence'. The language of the law is also, we might add, what grants all states their self-proclaimed omnipotence.

Portugal's implementation of the modern colonial system in what became known as Portuguese East Africa – an area the Portuguese had sought to control since the 1500s – underwent a profound transformation during the end of the nineteenth century by radically altering the legal situation for the majority of the territory's inhabitants – particularly through the racialization of citizenship. From then on, there was a distinction (and disassociation) between the native or the indigenous person (now endowed with an ethnic identity, and therefore guaranteed only private rights, specific to a given ethnic group), and the citizen (a privilege of the civilized, guaranteed by colonial law).[16] An understanding of the impact of the racialized disassociation between native and citizen is central to understanding how colonial categories were established through a meticulous regime of rights and obligations; this was perhaps most obvious in the form of forced labour (for a case study, see Isaacman 1996). This system of forced labour, and the export of labour to South African mines (First 1983), was a crucial part of the management of rights and obligations under the Portuguese colonial regime until the last few decades before independence (Penvenne 2015).

From the middle of the 1800s, however, the Portuguese system became challenged by other colonial powers' gradual control of African territories in general and, more specifically, the politics of the Berlin conferences (1884–1885) where *de facto* territorial and sovereign control was agreed to be crucial in order to achieve international legitimacy vis-à-vis its colonies. Portugal was, put simply, required to transform itself into a modern colonial power on par with other European colonial forces – using also violent pacification to achieve this aim (Pélissier 2004). This demand heightened the Portuguese sense of superior knowledge vis-à-vis their colonial orders and subjects, which was bolstered by being endowed with legal authority. The consequent ideology, disguised in the European context as 'the civilizing mission', was quickly set in motion, and

---

16   See, for example, Mamdani (1996) and Meneses (2006).

reinforced the notion that everything should be judged and validated according to canons that emanated from continental Portugal.

These colonial power structures are not merely of regimes past, however, their remnants invade nominally postcolonial situations in ways that do not challenge the underlying colonial references. For example, post-independence Portuguese Africa was transformed into Lusophone Africa in 1992 under the organization of palops (*Países Africanos de Língua Oficial Portuguesa* – Portuguese-speaking African Countries) (Meneses 2011) – a creation that in different ways mirrors the geopolitics of yesteryear colonial Portugal. As such, the example of PALOPs reflects the limits to claims of decolonization and the problem of a single macro-narrative in this regard.

Nonetheless, for the African continent, decolonization was one of the twentieth century's foundational events (Bragança 1986). For, as Ochieng and Atieno Odhiambo (1995) have pointed out, decolonization is a much wider concept than the mere winning of independence, or the transfer of sovereign powers. It involves an exploration of dreams and an analysis of struggles, compromises, pledges and achievements. The former focuses on the nationalist, anti-colonial struggle, whereas the latter foregrounds negotiations and planning among colonial officials and colonized elites. Within Europe, decolonization meant the end of empire, and the moment when the colonial question was replaced by the immigrant question in public discourses (Sheppard 2006, 4). Such aspects of decolonization require in-depth study, in different contexts, to evaluate how a prescriptive term became a historical category – a stage in the teleological tide of history. The dominant version in historical analysis has presented decolonization as a narrative of progress, and as an extension of national self-determination, and its corollary values: liberty, equality, human rights – the reference point for which has always been France. Following the French approach, Portugal sought to avoid grappling with the question of racial or ethnic difference, or with racism. With independence, it seemed there was no longer any need to try to explain that Mozambicans were not the same as the Portuguese. Yet, the difficulty of making policies based on this difference was what prevented Portugal to allow the independence of Mozambique. For ten years, the bloody conflict – the colonial war – had forced Portugal to confront how the Portuguese state defined the boundaries of the nation. By conceiving decolonization as a tide of history, Portugal, part of the imperial West, could avoid coming to terms with what many saw in the worldwide flowering of nationalist, anti-colonial struggles – a stormy wind bringing with it other political undertakings, and other ambitious emancipatory projects. The various revolutions that unfolded across the African continent summoned the world to see the limits, paradoxes, and incoherencies of Western universalism, as well as the violence it required and thus produced, which is highlighted in Chapter 11 below. The critics of colonialism, seeking to answer Césaire's (2000, 39) question – colonization and civilization? – did not reject all the values associated with Western universalism: they also fought for a new humanism, opening up heretofore unimagined possibilities. However, according to Eduardo Mondlane (1969) – Frelimo's legendary first president and an intellectual of the anti-colonial struggle –, the colonial relationship bequeathed to Mozambique the modern state. Thus, the roots of the modern state in Mozambique are still based in many respects on features of Portuguese colonial administration.

In this sense, then, decolonization reflects dramatically the problematics produced by the colonial transition. The hybrid societies of eastern Africa found themselves in a perilous position when faced with the modern Eurocentric political projects: These were a fraught legacy of colonial rule, and spoke of black and white – a bequest of the racialization of the colonial past. Through legislation, colonial Mozambique had been inhabited by two main categories: colons (whites) and African colonized subjects – black natives. Other significant diasporic groups who originated from the Indian Ocean region were lumped together with the natives on the whole: a small group of Indians, mainly originally from Goa, 'were allowed' into the civilized group of Portuguese colons. This situation meant that both Mozambique and Angola were settler colonies[17] (Penvenne 1995).

As noted briefly above, post-independence Mozambique opted for a socialist development project, a choice that would be abandoned by the mid-1980s under pressure from the international institutions to which the country had applied for support because it was in the midst of a serious economic and political crisis (Abrahamsson and Nilsson 1996). With the drawing up of the 1991 constitution, the path of democratic capitalist development was instituted. From then on, the state[18] that had been imagined as the solution for all problems under the socialist project was represented as the main obstacle to governance, development, and prosperity. The rest of the 1990s therefore witnessed a succession of political measures aimed at privatizing state-controlled infrastructure, together with a dramatic reduction of state presence in crucial areas such as education and health. For example, during the 1990s Mozambique underwent the most wide-ranging sub-Saharan African programme for privatisation,

---

17   A settler colony was characterized by the presence of substantial numbers of migrants, mostly Europeans, who were settled relatively permanently, and who brought with them their institutions and rules. It differed from an economic colony, which had a small European presence, and different administrative relationships with metropolitan governments and their associated systems of rule.

18   Until this point, the state had been governed by a single-party system.

a process involving corrupt accumulation and rampant asset stripping as well as what Santos (2006a) has described as the deliberate production of 'a weak state'.

At a local level, the reduction of the state allowed for the stronger presence of other social and political forces that had been silenced or made invisible by the state, with which they continued to co-exist. This was the case, mentioned above, in relation to the traditional authorities – the return of which acted as a reminder of Mozambique's ethnic diversity. This coexistence, addressed by several of the present chapters, was not always collaborative and peaceful, however, especially in the field of justice (Meneses 2006; Bertelsen 2009).

As in other African contexts, in Mozambique, national identity is under perpetual construction, a topic that is addressed, from different angles, in a number of chapters, resulting in an interesting dialogue. These chapters explore the ways in which the political and cultural framework of the Mozambican nation overlaps with other imaginaries, producing new relationships, demanding new historical (re-)interpretations and contributing to reinforce a sense of national cohesion.

The end of Portuguese colonialism in South-East Africa precipitated a reorientation of local societies. The idea of the nation projected upon these former colonial territories sought actively to supplant other imaginaries, and this entailed new relationships among territory, people, and histories. While multiple social referents persisted, nationality became a primary and inescapable mode of identification. Confronted with the cosmopolitan histories of the African shores of the Indian Ocean, the national project in Mozambique – as in neighbouring countries – was challenged by ideas of identity bound to race, religion, or ethnic identity. With the transition to independence, many settler migrants – mainly white colons, but also people of Asian ancestry and mestizos – left Mozambique, each of them with a unique history (Rita-Ferreira 1998). Indeed, such departures have occurred at various times since at least the early 1960s (Pereira Leite 2001) and the migrant destinations vary widely (Khan 2009).

The social rupture produced by the transition to independence forced a fairly heterogeneous and colony-specific mixture of peoples – which often included, along with nationals of the colonizing nation, nationals of other European nations, the mixed offspring of European and indigenous unions, non-European or intermediate traders, native wives of European men, and subsets of the indigenous populations (Smith 2003, 12) – to become Mozambicans and Portuguese. Such issues and many other conceptual conundrums result from the political processes associated with decolonization.

With the political changes that took place in Portugal with the fall of the colonial-fascist regime in 1974, the decision regarding the political future of its African colonies brought about a certainty that decolonization was an inevitable stage in the progressive march of history. This stance enabled Portugal to overlook the fact that the people from these colonies had become Portuguese citizens from 1961, and to ignore many of the implications of their shared past (Meneses 2015). Through this forgetting there emerged new definitions of Portuguese identity and new Portuguese state institutions; several blind spots were in evidence in their formulation. With independence in Mozambique (as elsewhere), colonial forms of hierarchical citizenship were removed and the population became, at a legal and formal level, equal Mozambicans.

The goal of reclaiming other histories and other knowledges – alternative ways of seeing the world, if you will – has occupied a central place in nationalist and decolonization movements (Fanon 1965 [1961]), generating the call also to 'decolonize our minds' (Thiong'o 1986). This task had special challenges and assumed specific forms in Mozambique, reflecting both its colonial past and its postcolonial political choices moving through the phases of socialism and a single-party system to capitalism and multiparty democracy.

The texts that comprise this anthology reflect multiple accounts of the social, the spatial, the cultural, and the political, critically engaging differences, subalternizations, discriminations, oppressions, struggles, and resistances. However, they also expose contemporary forms of historical legacy, which are often left unwritten or disregarded, and include those of mixture and crossing-over, and form the basis of the cultural mosaic that is contemporary Mozambique. In this sense, these chapters hope to contribute to finding situations, forms, and moments of mutuality that are, in some capacity or other, generative. Across them, we can identify a shared consideration, which emphasizes the fact that the colonized did not only erect defensive walls around their notions of cultural difference. Rather, the opposite: Mozambicans have been and remain players in broad arenas of cosmopolitan thought, and, consequently, wish to contribute to the shaping of their global future (see, e.g., Ngoenha and Castiano 2010). This cosmopolitanism flows not from abstract reason but from the fertile ground of local knowledge and learning in the vernacular (Bose 2006).

4   Snapshots of Mozambique

As a country of the global South, Mozambique's geopolitical position is provided by a metaphorical cartography, that of the colonial library (Mudimbe 1988). An image prevails of Mozambique as a patchwork of distinct but self-contained, independent, internally cohesive, and structured cultures, each of which is still classified by ethnic designation. Based upon this colonial library, many think of Mozambique as the Other – the developing world – as an object of study. The dominance of this hierarchical gaze was captured by Gayatri Spivak, who argued that even when texts of developing-world authors are taught in the developed world, they are studied in ignorance of their genealogy; that is, there is little interest in the struggles that formed the historical and political contexts and times in which these texts were produced (1996, 237–266).

As editors approaching such multiple sites of marginalization and subalternity, our aim has been to retrieve the many silenced and invisible knowledges, approaches, and reflections that integrate Mozambique with the world, in a web generated by multiple relationships (including imperialism, colonialism and Eurocentric modernity). Above all, to decolonize requires challenging the colonial imaginary and its temporality. In this sense, when we speak of Mozambique and Africa, it is important to understand to what extent we are *not* referring to an intellectual product of Western colonialism. We aim to avoid the pitfall of doing 'history by analogy' (Mamdani 1996, 9), that is, the tendency to look at African historical phenomena with the core reference being European historical processes.

Thus, the contributions to this volume relate the ways in which Mozambicans negotiated the terms of their identities and belonging in colonial times, and the ways in which they are coming to terms with the present, postcolonial era. The chapters provide valuable descriptive and analytical insights of diverse kinds into the constitution of Mozambique (and into African social, cultural, and political realities). Taken in the round, this book makes the case that the experience of Mozambique has been and remains distinctive and, at the same time, it functions as a case study from which to formulate theories of citizenship, democracy, participation, and progress, from pan-African and global perspectives. This wide-ranging perspective signals the different practices that 'subalterns' are developing, sustained by signs of re-appropriation of the capacity to represent themselves, and to think reflexively about themselves, avoiding one of the most dangerous traps of modernity – the dichotomy of 'Us' and 'Others' (Ndlovu-Gatsheni 2018). These chapters, then, seek to map affinities and to broadcast very different voices. In such voices and affinities, we can recognize clear signs that the struggle to meet the challenge of decolonising the imagination continues.

Neither by losing sight of the colonial encounter and its implications, nor by suppressing the intertwining of modern colonialism with Mozambique's contemporary geo-politics and the politics of knowledge, this book aims also to evaluate the meanings of history in a situation in which the past not only is continually contested but impinges on the present in various ways. Thus, this book is concerned with beginnings, and with the intellectual ferment that is brewing in Mozambique, which is increasingly regarded as the creation and the source of its own knowledge and project of modernity. As such, it also seeks to subvert the sometimes extractive underpinning of area studies, which has a tendency to preclude dialogical encounters and confines Mozambican (and African) realities and knowledges to objecthood; in so doing, it risks reflecting historically formed and prevailing geo-political relations of exploitation, dominance and, ultimately, representation. Echoing Franco Cassamo's (1989) observation that 'decolonization means, above all, overcoming solipsism', this book, in emphasizing Mozambique as being on the move, seeks to place a bridge across the diverse knowledges available here, guided by the region's various geographies. It is our hope that our reflections will constitute a fertile soil for further research that might embark on a truly cosmopolitan journey of debates, challenges, and discoveries.

Arguably, diverse inputs into understanding the complex entity that we call Mozambique are needed now more than ever in a context where dynamics of motility, mobility and, indeed, volatility make themselves apparent through, for instance, fuelling expansive infrastructure building projects, including roads, railways, ports, electricity supply and aircraft traffic. Further, an expanding but heterogeneous middle class is also sedimenting itself in particular urban and suburban areas, tangible through both expansive house-building projects in many areas and by an increasing number of privately owned cars clogging the arteries of major cities like Maputo and Beira (Sumich 2016; Mazzolini 2016; Brooks 2017). The year 2015 also saw the celebration of forty years of independence and saw the swearing in of Filipe Nyusi from Frelimo – Mozambique's new president is scheduled to sit until 2020, a year that will mark Frelimo being in power consecutively for almost half a century.

However, the years of 2015, 2016 and 2017 also saw an increasingly politically charged situation in the country with intensified conflicts between democratic and autocratic political trajectories (Azevedo-Harman 2015; Khan 2016; Macamo 2017), assassinations of key figures in Mozambican society (Ganho 2016), as well as military confrontations between government forces and armed men affiliated with Renamo (Wiegink 2015; Darch 2016). It has also seen the slow trickle of Mozambican refugees from Tete province escaping such confrontations by fleeing into neighbouring Malawi – the existence of Mozambican refugees in 2016 bringing back memories of the almost 1 million that sought refuge there at the height of the civil war (Englund 2002). Further, increasing allegations and evidence of drug money being integral to the last decades of building booms in Maputo and other major Mozambican cities also contribute to a mixed impression of both the motors of economic growth, as well as how it is managed politically and administratively (Hofmann 2013; Hanlon 2018).

In such a context – where it is difficult to ascertain whether to concentrate on the prospects for fair weather or to look at the gathering clouds on the horizon – it strikes us as more important than ever to move beyond sensationalist headlines. If we fail to grasp *in situ* heterogeneous socio-cultural dynamics, multiple economic and political dimensions and its rich tapestry of contemporary and past trajectories of creativity, art and thought, we are unable to assess fair from cloudy weather for Mozambique. And it is precisely such insights needed for in depth assessment that this book also seeks to provide.

References

Abrahamsson, Hans, and Anders Nilsson. 1996. *'The Washington Consensus' and Moçambique*. Gothenburg: Gothenburg University.

Abu-Lughod, Janet. 1989. *Before European Hegemony: The world-system, AD 1250–1350*. New York: Oxford University Press.

Anderson, Benedict. 1983. *Imagined Communities: Reflections on the origin and spread of nationalism*. London: Verso.

Arndt, Channing, et al. 2012. Climate change, growth and infrastructure investment. The case of Mozambique. *Review of Development Economics* 16 (3): 463–475.

Azevedo-Harman, Elizabete. 2015. Patching Things Up in Mozambique. *Journal of Democracy* 26 (2): 139–150.

Bertelsen, Bjørn Enge. 2009. Multiple sovereignties and summary justice in Mozambique: A critique of some legal anthropological terms. *Social Analysis* 53 (3): 123–147.

Bertelsen, Bjørn Enge. 2014. Effervescence and ephemerality: Popular urban uprisings in Mozambique. *Ethnos*: 1–28, DOI 10.1080/00141844.2014.929596.

Bertelsen, Bjørn Enge. 2016. *Violent Becomings: State formation, sociality, and power in Mozambique*. New York: Berghahn Books.

Bhabha, Homi K. 1990. *Nation and Narration*. London: Routledge.

Bonate, Liazzat. 2010. Islam in Northern Mozambique: A Historical Overview. *History Compass*, 8/7: 573–593, DOI 10.1111/j.1478-0542.2010.00701.x.

Bose, Sugata. 2006. *A Hundred Horizons: The Indian Ocean in the age of global empire*. Cambridge, MA: Harvard University Press.

Bragança, Aquino. 1986. Independência sem Descolonização: A transferência de poder em Moçambique, 1974–1975. *Estudos Moçambicanos* 5/6: 7–28.

Bragança, Aquino, and Jacques Depelchin. 1986. From the idealization of FRELIMO to the understanding of the recent history of Mozambique. *African Journal of Political Economy* 1 (1): 162–180.

Brautigam, Deborah, and Sigrid-Marianella Stensrud Ekman. 2012. Briefing rumours and realities of Chinese agricultural engagement in Mozambique. *African Affairs* 111 (444): 483–492.

Brito, Luís de, ed. 2017. '*Agora eles têm medo de nós!' Uma colectânea de textos sobre as revoltas populares em Moçambique (2008–2012)*. Maputo: Instituto de Estudos Sociais e Económicos (IESE).

Brito, Luís de et al., 2015. *Revoltas da Fome: Protestos populares em Moçambique*. Maputo: Instituto de Estudos Sociais e Económicos (IESE).

Brooks, Andrew. 2017. Was Africa rising? Narratives of development success and failure among the Mozambican middle class. *Territory, Politics, Governance*, 1–21, DOI 10.1080/21622671.2017.1318714.

Buur, Lars, and Helene Maria Kyed, eds. 2007. *State Recognition and Democratization in sub-Saharan Africa: A new dawn for traditional authorities?* New York: Palgrave Macmillan.

Cabaço, José Luís. 2001. O homem novo (breve itinerário de um projecto). In *Samora. Homem do Povo*, ed. Antonio Sópa, 137–148. Maputo: Maguezo Editores.

Cabrita, João M. 2005. *A Morte de Samora Machel*. Maputo: Edições Novafrica.

Cahen, Michel. 1994. Mozambique, histoire géopolitique d'un pays sans nation. *Lusotopie 1994*, 213–266.

Cahen, Michel. 2002. *Les bandits. Un historien au Mozambique, 1994*. Paris: Centre Culturel Calouste Gulbenkian.

Capela, José. 2002. *O tráfico de escravos nos portos de Moçambique, 1733–1902*. Oporto: Afrontamento.

Cassamo, Suleiman. 1989. *O regresso do morto*. Maputo: AEMO.

Castel-Branco, Carlos Nuno. 2010. *Economia extractiva e desafios de industrialização em Moçambique*. Maputo: Instituto de Estudos Sociais e Económicos (IESE).

Castel-Branco, Carlos Nuno. 2014. Growth, capital accumulation and economic porosity in Mozambique: social losses, private gains. *Review of African Political Economy*, (41) S1: S26–S48, DOI 10.1080/03056244.2014.976363.

Césaire, Aimé. 2000. *Discourse on Colonialism*. New York: Monthly Review Press.

Chichava, Sérgio. 2013. 'They can kill us but we won't go to the communal villages!' Peasants and the Policy of 'Socialisation of the Countryside' in Zambezia. *Kronos: Southern African Histories* 39 (1): 112–130.

Chichava, Sérgio, and Chris Alden. 2012. *A mamba e o dragão. Relações Moçambique-China em perspectiva*. Maputo: Instituto de Estudos Sociais e Económicos (IESE).

Chichava, Sérgio, Lara Côrtes, and Aslak Orre. 2015. *A cobertura da China na imprensa moçambicana: Repercussões para o* soft power *chinês*. Maputo: Instituto de Estudos Sociais e Económicos (IESE).

Chimbutane, Feliciano. 2015. Bilingual education: enabling classroom interaction and bridging the gap between schools and rural communities in Mozambique. *International Journal of Educational Development*, 2 (1): 101–120.

Christie, Iain. 1988. *Samora Machel. A biography*. London: PANAF.

Clément, Jean A.P., and Shanaka J. Peiris. 2008. *Post-stabilization Economics in Sub-Saharan Africa. Lessons from Mozambique*. Washington, DC: International Monetary Fund.

Coelho, João Paulo Borges. 1998. Um itinerário histórico da moçambicanidade. In *Língua portuguesa. A herança comum*, ed. Fernando M.F.R. Rosas, 108–118. Lisbon: Assírio e Alvim.

Coelho, João Paulo Borges. 2003. Da Violência Colonial Ordenada à Ordem Pós-Colonial Violenta: Sobre um Legado das Guerras Coloniais nas ex-colónias portuguesa. In *Lusotopie 2003: Violence et contrôle de la violence au Brésil, en Afrique et à Goa*, ed. Camille Goirand, 175–193. Paris: Karthala.

Coelho, João Paulo Borges. 2007. *Campo de trânsito*. Lisbon: Caminho.

Coelho, João Paulo Borges. 2008. Escrita Académica, Escrita Literária. In *Moçambique. Das palavras escritas*, eds. Margarida Calafate Ribeiro, and Maria Paula Meneses, 229–236. Oporto: Afrontamento.

Coelho, João Paulo Borges. 2009. A 'Literatura Quantitativa' e a Interpretação do Conflito Armado em Moçambique, 1976–1992. Paper presented at *Pobreza e Paz nos PALOP*, Centro de Estudos Africanos ISCTE-IUL, Lisbon, November 25–26.

Coelho, João Paulo Borges. 2015. Abrir a fábula: Questões da política do passado em Moçambique. *Revista Crítica de Ciências Sociais* 106: 153–166.

Comaroff, John, and Jean Comaroff. 2004. Policing culture, cultural policing: Law and social order in postcolonial South Africa. *Law and Social Inquiry* 29 (3): 513–545.

Comaroff, Jean, and John L. Comaroff. 2012. *Theory from the South. Or, how Euro-America is evolving towards Africa*. Boulder, CO and London: Paradigm Publishers.

Conceição, António Rafael Fernandes da. 2006. *Entre o mar e a terra: Situações identitárias do Norte de Moçambique (Cabo Delgado)*. Maputo: Promédia.

Cunguara, Benedito. 2012. An exposition of development failures in Mozambique. *Review of African Political Economy* 39 (131): 161–170.

Darch, Colin. 2016. Separatist tensions and violence in the 'model post-conflict state': Mozambique since the 1990s. *Review of African Political Economy* 43 (148): 320–327.

Dinerman, Alice. 2006. *Revolution, Counter-Revolution and Revisionism in Post-colonial Africa: The case of Mozambique, 1975–1994*. New York: Routledge.

Dinerman, Alice. 2009. Débat: Regarding totalities and escape hatches in Mozambican politics and Mozambican studies. *Politique Africaine* 113: 187–210.

Douek, Daniel L. 2017. New light on the Samora Machel assassination: 'I realized that it was no accident'. *Third World Quarterly*, 38 (9): 2045–2065.

Dussel, Enrique. 2000. Europe, modernity and Eurocentrism. *Neplanta: Views from South*, 1 (3): 465–478.

Egerö, Bertil. 1990. *Mozambique. A dream undone. The political economy of democracy, 1975–84*. Uppsala: Scandinavian Institute of African Studies.

Emerson, Stephen A. 2014. *The Battle for Mozambique: The Frelimo-Renamo struggle, 1977–1992.* West Midlands and Pinetown: Helion and 30 South Publishers.

Englund, Harri. 2002. *From War to Peace on the Mozambique-Malawi borderland.* Edinburgh: Edinburgh University Press.

Falola, Toyin. 2006. Writing and teaching national history in Africa in an era of global history. In *The Study of Africa. Volume 1: Disciplinary and interdisciplinary encounters,* ed. Paul T. Zeleza, 168–186. Dakar: CODESRIA.

Fanon, Frantz. 1965 [1961]. *The Wretched of the Earth.* New York: Grove Press.

Farré, Albert. 2015. Assimilados, Régulos, Homens Novos, Moçambicanos Genuínos. A persistência da exclusão em Moçambique. *Anuário Antropológico* 40(2): 199–229.

Firmino, Gregório. 2001. *A 'questão linguística' na África pós-colonial: O caso do Português e das línguas autóctones em Moçambique.* Maputo: Promédia.

First, Ruth. 1983. *Black Gold: The Mozambican miner, proletarian and peasant.* Brighton: Harvester Press.

Ganho, Ana. 2016. The murder of Gilles Cistac: Mozambique's future at a crossroads. *Review of African Political Economy* 43(147): 142–150.

Geffray, Christian. 1991. *A causa das armas em Moçambique: antropologia de uma guerra civil.* Oporto: Afrontamento.

Goldstone, Brian, and Juan Obarrio, eds. 2017. *African Futures: Essays on crisis, emergence, and possibility.* Chicago: University of Chicago Press.

Gonçalves, Perpétua. 2002. The role of ambiguity in second language change: The case of Mozambican African Portuguese. *Second Language Research* 18: 325–347.

Guha, Ranajit. 2002. *History and the Limit of World-History.* New York: Columbia University Press.

Gupta, Pamila. 2016 [2012]. Romancing the colonial on Ilha de Mozambique. In *Emotion in Motion: Tourism, affect, and transformation,* eds. David Picard and Michael Robinson, 247–268. London and New York: Routledge.

Hall, Margaret, and Tom Young. 1997. *Confronting Leviathan: Mozambique since Independence.* London: Hurst.

Hanlon, Joseph. 2018. *The Uberization of Mozambique's Heroin Trade.* London: London School of Economics.

Harries, Patrick. 2016. Mozambique Island, Cape Town and the Organisation of the Slave Trade in the South-West Indian Ocean, c.1797–1807. *Journal of Southern African Studies* 42 (3): 409–427.

Heidegger, Martin. 1962. *Being and Time.* Oxford: Basil Blackwell.

Hell, Julia, and Andreas Schönle, eds. 2010. *Ruins of Modernity.* Durham: Duke University Press.

Ho, Engseng. 2002. Names Beyond Nations: The making of local cosmopolitans. *Études Rurales* 163/164: 215–231.

Hofmann, Katharina. 2013. Mozambique's Economic Transformation and its Implications for Human Security. In *Southern African Security Review 2013*, eds. Anthoni van Nieuwkerk, 102–118. Maputo and Johannesburg: Friedrich-Ebert-Stiftung and The Centre for Defence and Security Management, University of the Witwatersrand.

Honwana, Gita. 1984. Operação Produção. Actuação dos tribunais. Consolidação da justiça popular. *Justiça Popular* 8–9: 3–10.

Hountondji, Paulin. 2002. *Struggle for Meaning: Reflections on philosophy, culture and democracy in Africa.* Athens: Ohio University Press.

Isaacman, Allen F. 1978. *A Luta Continua: Creating a new society in Mozambique.* Binghamton, NY: State University of New York at Binghamton.

Isaacman, Allen F. 1996. *Cotton is the Mother of Poverty: Peasants, work and rural struggle in colonial Mozambique, 1938-1961.* London: James Currey.

Israel, Paolo. 2013. A Loosening Grip: The liberation script in Mozambican History. *Kronos: Southern African Histories* 39: 10–19.

Israel, Paolo. 2014. *In Step with the Times. Mapiko masquerades of Mozambique.* Athens, OH: Ohio University Press.

Jayasuriya, Shihan de Silva, and Richard Pankhurst, eds. 2003. *The African Diaspora in the Indian Ocean.* Trenton, NJ: Africa World Press.

Khan, Sheila. 2009. *Imigrantes Africanos Moçambicanos.* Lisbon: Colibri.

Khan, Sheila. 2015. *Portugal a lápis de cor. A Sul de uma pós-colonialidade.* Coimbra: Almedina.

Khan, Sheila. 2016. Moçambique 41 anos depois: 'Crónica' de uma imaturidade política. *Revista de Estudos Ibero-Americanos* 42 (3): 944–960.

Khan, Sheila. 2017. Espaços em branco, Memórias Subterrâneas da 'História' de Moçambique. Número temático, *Dinâmicas políticas, sociais e culturais em África* (org. Augusto Nascimento), *Revista TEL: Tempo, Espaço e Linguagem* 7 (3), Setembro/Dezembro.

Kirshner, Joshua, and Marcus Power. 2015. Mining and extractive urbanism: Postdevelopment in a Mozambican boomtown. *Geoforum*, 61: 67–78.

Leite, Ana Mafalda, Sheila Khan, Jessica Falconi, and Kamila Krakowska, eds. 2012. *Nação e Narrativa Pós-Colonial II – Angola e Moçambique – Entrevistas.* Lisbon: Colibri.

LeFanu, Sarah. 2012. *S is for Samora. A lexical biography of Samora Machel and the Mozambican dream.* New York: Columbia University Press.

Lourenço, Vitor Alexandre Antunes. 2010. *Moçambique. Memórias sociais de ontem, dilemas políticos de hoje.* Lisbon: Gerpress-CEA.

Macamo, Elísio. 2017. Power, conflict, and citizenship: Mozambique's contemporary struggles. *Citizenship Studies* 21 (2): 196–209.

Macamo, Elísio, and Severino Ngoenha. 2016. *Moçambique como Lugar de Interrogação à Modernidade.* Cape Town: African Minds.

Machado, Pedro. 2005. Gujarati Indian merchant networks in Mozambique, 1777–c.1830. PhD thesis. University of London.

Machel, Samora. 1974. *Mozambique: Sowing the seeds of revolution*. London: Committee for Freedom in Mozambique, Angola and Guiné.

Machel, Samora. 1980 [1977]. *Sobre os problemas, função e tarefas da juventude Moçambicana*. Maputo: Departamento do Trabalho Ideológico do Partido Frelimo.

Mamdani, Mahmood. 1996. *Citizen and Subject: Contemporary Africa and the legacy of late colonialism*. Princeton: Princeton University Press.

Mandlate, Oksana. 2015. Capacitação das empresas nacionais e conteúdo local de megaprojects em Moçambique. In *Desafios para Moçambique, 2015*, ed. Luís de Brito, et al., 247–272. Maputo: Instituto de Estudos Sociais e Económicos (IESE).

Manning, Carrie. 2008. Mozambique: RENAMO's electoral success. In *From Soldiers to Politicians: Transforming rebel movements after civil war,* ed. Jeroen De Zeeuw, 55–80. Boulder, CO: Lynne Rienner Publishers.

Mazula, Brazão, ed. 1995. *Moçambique: Eleições, democracia e desenvolvimento*. Maputo: Inter-Africa Group Press com patrocínio da Embaixada do Reino dos Países Baixos.

Mazzolini, Anna. 2016. An Urban Middle Class and the Vacillation of "Informal" Boundaries – Insights from Maputo, Mozambique. *Geography Research Forum* 36: 68–85.

Mbembe, Achille. 2000. *De la postcolonie: Essai sur l'imagination politique dans l'Afrique contemporaine*. Paris: Karthala.

Mbembe, Achille. 2017 [2013]. *Critique of Black Reason.* Durham, NC: Duke University Press.

Meneses, Maria Paula. 2006. Traditional authorities in Mozambique: Between legitimization and legitimacy. In *The Shade of New Leaves: Governance in traditional authority. A Southern African perspective*, ed. Mannfred O. Hinz, 93–119. Berlin: Lit Verlag.

Meneses, Maria Paula. 2011. Images outside the mirror? Mozambique and Portugal in world history. *Human Architecture: Journal of the Sociology of Self-knowledge* 10(1):121–137.

Meneses, Maria Paula. 2015. Xiconhoca, o inimigo: Narrativas de violência sobre a construção da nação em Moçambique. *Revista Crítica de Ciências Sociais* 106: 9–52, DOI 10.4000/rccs.5869.

Meneses, Maria Paula, and Margarida Calafate Ribeiro. 2008. Cartografias Literárias Incertas. In *Moçambique, das palavras escritas*, eds. Margarida Calafate Ribeiro and Maria Paula Meneses, 9–17. Oporto: Afrontamento.

Meneses, Maria Paula, and Boaventura de Sousa Santos. 2009. The rise of a micro dual state: The case of Angoche (Mozambique). *Africa Development* 34 (3/4): 129–166.

Mignolo, Walter. 2011. *The Darker Side of Modernity. Global futures, decolonial options*. Durham, NC: Duke University Press.

Milhazes, José. 2010. *Samora Machel. Atentado ou acidente: Páginas desconhecidas das relações Sovieto-Moçambicanas.* Lisbon: Aletheia.

Mondlane, Eduardo. 1969. *Struggle for Mozambique*. London: Harmondsworth.

Moran, Mary H., and Anne M. Pitcher. 2004. The 'basket case' and the 'poster child': Explaining the end of civil conflicts in Liberia and Mozambique. *Third World Quarterly* 25 (3): 501–519.

Morier-Genoud, Eric, ed. 2012. *Sure road? Nationalisms in Angola, Guinea-Bissau and Mozambique.* Leiden: Brill.

Morier-Genoud, Eric Michel Cahen and Domingos M. do Rosário. eds. 2018. *The War Within: New perspectives on the civil war in Mozambique 1976 – 1992* Suffolk: Boydell and Brewer.

Morton, David. 2015. Age of Concrete: Housing and the Imagination in Mozambique's Capital, c. 1950 to Recent Times. PhD thesis, University of Minnesota, USA.

Mosca, João. 2011. *Políticas agrárias de (em) Moçambique (1975–2009).* Maputo: Escolar Editora.

Mozambique News Reports & Clippings. 2016. 'Survey shows inequality doubled in six years'. Mozambique News Reports and Clippings, no. 306, 7 January 2016. Accessible at http://www.open.ac.uk/technology/mozambique/sites/www.open.ac.uk .technology.mozambique/files/files/Mozambique_306-4Jan2016_Big-Inequality-Increase_%2B_other-reserarch%20.pdf, accessed 20 January 2016.

Mudimbe, Valentin Y. 1988. *The Invention of Africa: Gnosis, philosophy, and the order of knowledge.* Bloomington: Indiana University Press.

Nandy, Ashis. 1999. The invisible holocaust and the journey as an exodus: The poisoned village and the stranger city. *Postcolonial Studies* 2 (3): 305–329.

Ncomo, Barnabé Lucas. 2004. *Uria Simango: Um homem, uma causa.* Maputo: Edições Novafrica.

Ndlovu-Gatsheni, Sabelo J. 2018. *Epistemic Freedom in Africa: Deprovincialization and decolonization.* London: Routledge.

Newitt, Malyn D.D. 1995. *A History of Mozambique.* Bloomington: Indiana University Press.

Ngomane, Nataniel. 2008. Posfácio. In *O alegre canto da perdiz*, ed. P. Chiziane, 335–336. Lisbon: Caminho.

Ngoenha, Severino. 1999. Os Missionários Suíços face ao Nacionalismo Moçambicano. Entre a Tsonganidade e a Moçambicanidade. In *Lusotopie 1999: Dynamiques religieuses en lusophonie contemporaine*, ed. Lurdes M. Silva, 425–436. Paris: Karthala.

Ngoenha, Severino. 2009. *Machel. Ícone da 1a República?* Maputo: Ndjira.

Ngoenha, Severino, and José P. Castiano. 2010. *Pensamento Engajado: Ensaios sobre filosofia Africana, educação e cultura política.* Maputo: Editora Educar.

Nielsen, Morten. 2014. The negativity of times. Collapsed futures in Maputo, Mozambique. *Social Anthropology/Anthropologie Sociale* 22 (2): 213–226.

Nogueira, Isabela et al. 2017. Mozambican economic porosity and the role of Brazilian capital: a political economy analysis. *Review of African Political Economy* 44 (151): 104–121.

Nordstrom, Carolyn. 1997. *A Different Kind of War Story*. Philadelphia, PN: University of Pennsylvania Press.

Obarrio, Juan. 2014. *The Spirit of the Laws in Mozambique*. Chicago and London: Chicago University Press.

Obarrio, Juan. 2017. Time and Again: Locality as Future Anterior in Mozambique. In *African Futures: Essays on crisis, emergence, and possibility*, eds. Brian Goldstone, and Juan Obarrio, 181–195. Chicago: University of Chicago Press.

Ochieng', William Robert, and Elisha S. Atieno Odhiambo. 1995. On Decolonization. In *Decolonization and Independence in Kenya, 1940–1993*, ed. Bethwell A. Ogot and William R. Ochieng', xi–xviii. Athens: Ohio University Press.

O'Laughlin, Bridget. 1992. A Base Social da Guerra em Moçambique: Análise de 'A causa das armas em Moçambique: antropologia de uma guerra civil', de C. Geffray. *Estudos Moçambicanos* 10: 107–142.

Osório, Conceição, and Teresa Cruz e Silva. 2017. *Corporações económicas e expropriação: raparigas, mulheres e comunidades reassentadas no distrito de Moatize*. Maputo: WLSA Moçambique.

Owen, Hilary. 2007. *Mother Africa, Father Marx: Women's writing of Mozambique, 1948–2002*. Lewisburg: Bucknell University Press.

Owen, Hilary. 2010. As Mulheres à Beira de um Império Nervoso na obra de Paulina Chiziane e Ungulani Ba ka Khosa. *Via Atlântica* 17: 43–56.

Pachinuapa, Raimundo Domingos. 2009. *II Congresso da Frente de Libertação de Moçambique (FRELIMO)*. Maputo: Elográfio.

Panzer, Michael G. 2009. The Pedagogy of Revolution: Youth, generational conflict, and education in the development of Mozambican nationalism and the state, 1962–1970. *Journal of Southern African Studies* 35 (4): 803–818.

Pélissier, René. 1994. *Historia de Moçambique. Formação e Oposição 1854–1918, vols. 1 and 2*. Lisbon: Editorial Stampa.

Pélissier, René. 2004. *Les Campagnes Coloniales du Portugal: 1844–1941*. Paris: Éditions Pygmalion.

Penvenne, Jeanne Marie. 1995. *African Workers and Colonial racism: Mozambican strategies and struggles in Lourenço Marques*. London: James Currey.

Penvenne, Jeanne Marie. 1996. João dos Santos Albasini (1876–1922): The contradictions of politics and identity in colonial Mozambique. *Journal of African History* 37 (3): 419–464.

Penvenne, Jeanne Marie. 2015. *Women, Migration and the Cashew Economy in Southern Mozambique, 1945–1975*. London: James Currey.

Pereira Leite, Joana. 2001. Indo-britanniques et indo-portugais: Présence marchande au Sud de Mozambique au moment de l'implantation du système colonial, de la fin du XIXème siècle jusqu'aux années 1930. *Outre-Mers, Revue d'Histoire* 1: 13–37.

Perrot, Claude-Hélène, and François-Xavier Fauvelle-Aymar, eds. 2003. *Le Retour des Rois: Les Autorités Traditionnelles et l'État en Afrique Contemporaine*. Paris: Karthala.

Pinto, Rochelle. 2010. A Diffused History of Race. The Portuguese Presence in the Indian Ocean. In *Eyes across the Water. Navigating the Indian Ocean*, eds. Pamila Gupta, Isabel Hofmeyr, and Michael N. Pearson, 238–257. Pretoria: Unisa Press.

Power, Marcus. 2000. Twenty-first Century Foxed: Global Media Broadcasting and the Reconfiguration of Moçambicanidade. *South African Geographical Journal* 82 (1): 47–55.

Ramose, Mogobe. 2002. *African Philosophy Through Ubuntu*. Harare: Mond Books Publishers.

Rantala, Janne. 2016. 'Hidrunisa Samora': Invocations of a Dead Political Leader in Maputo Rap. *Journal of Southern African Studies* 42 (6): 1161–1177, DOI 10.1080/03057070.2016.1253929.

Renan, Ernest. 1996. What is a Nation? In *Becoming National: A Reader,* eds. Geoff Eley and Ronald Grigor Suny, 41–55. Oxford: Oxford University Press.

Rita-Ferreira, António. 1998. Moçambique post-25 de Abril: Causas do Êxodo da População de Origem Europeia e Asiática. In *Moçambique, Cultura e História de um País*, ed. António Rita-Ferreira, 121–169. Coimbra: Universidade de Coimbra.

Robinson, David Alexander. 2006. A Case of Assassination? President Samora Machel and the Plane Crash at Mbuzini. *Postamble* 2(2): 45–64.

Rønning, Helge. 2015. Reflections on Elections in a Dominant Party State. *African Journalism Studies*, 36 (1): 149–155, DOI 10.1080/23743670.2015.1008183.

Sachs, Albie, and Gita Honwana Welch. 1990. *Liberating the Law. Creating popular justice in Mozambique*. London and New Jersey: Zed Books.

Santos, Ana Margarida. 2010. Performing the Past: Celebrating Women's Day in northern Mozambique. *Cahiers d'Études Africaines* 197: 217–234.

Santos, Boaventura de Sousa. 1998. The Fall of the Angelus Novus: Beyond the Modern Game of Roots and Options. *Current Sociology* 46 (2): 81–118.

Santos, Boaventura de Sousa. 2006a. The Heterogeneous State and Legal Pluralism in Mozambique. *Law & Society* 40 (1): 39–77.

Santos, Boaventura de Sousa. 2006b. *The Rise of the Global Left: The World Social Forum and beyond*. London: Zed Books.

Santos, Boaventura de Sousa. 2007. Beyond Abyssal Thinking: From Global Lines to Ecologies of Knowledges. *Review* 30 (1): 45–89.

Santos, Boaventura de Sousa. 2014. *Epistemologies of the South: Justice against epistemicide*. New York: Routledge.

Santos, Boaventura de Sousa, and Maria Paula Meneses, eds. 2009. *Epistemologias do Sul*. Coimbra: Almedina.

Sarr, Felwine. 2016. *Afrotopia*. Paris: Philippe Rey.

Serra, Carlos. 2012. *Chaves das Portas do Social (Notas de reflexão e pesquisa)*. Maputo: Imprensa Universitária.

Serra, Carlos, ed. 1998. *Identidade, Moçambicanidade, Moçambicanização*. Maputo: Universidade Eduardo Mondlane.

Sheldon, Kathleen. 2002. *Pounders of Grain. A history of women, work and politics in Mozambique*. Portsmouth, NH: Heinemann.

Sheppard, Todd. 2006. *The Invention of Decolonization: The Algerian War and the remaking of France*. Cornell: Cornell University Press.

Silva, Teresa Cruz, Manuel M. Mendes de Araújo and Amélia Neves Souto, eds. 2015. *Comunidades Costeiras: Perspectivas e realidades*. Maputo: Centro de Estudos Sociais Aquino de Bragança.

Smith, Andrea. 2003. Race, Class, and Kin in the negotiation of 'Internal Strangerhood' among Portuguese retornados, 1975–2000. In *Europe's Invisible Migrants*, ed. Andrea L. Smith, 9–31. Amsterdam: Amsterdam University Press.

Sontag, Susan. 2011. *Ao Mesmo Tempo*. Lisbon: Quetzal Editores.

Sopa, António. 2001. *Samora. Homem do Povo*. Maputo: Maguezo Editores.

Spivak, Gayatri Chakaravorty. 1988 [1983]. Can the Subaltern Speak? In *Colonial and Postcolonial Discourse: A reader*, eds. Patrick Williams and Laura Chrisman, 66–111. New York: Columbia University Press.

Spivak, Gayatri Chakaravorty. 1996. How to Teach a 'Culturally Different' Book. In *The Spivak reader: Selected works of Gayatri Chakravorty Spivak*, ed. Donna Landry and Gerald MacLean, 237–266. New York: Routledge.

Stoler, Ann Laura. 2009. *Along the Archival Grain: Epistemic anxieties and colonial common sense*. Princeton: Princeton University Press.

Stoler, Ann Laura. 2011. Colonial Aphasia: Race and Disabled Histories in France. *Public Culture* 23 (1): 121–156.

Stoler, Ann Laura. 2016. *Duress: Imperial durabilities in our times*. Durham, NC: Duke University Press.

Sumich, Jason. 2016. The Middle Class of Mozambique and the Politics of the Blank Slate. In *The Rise of Africa's Middle Class: Myths, realities and critical engagements*, ed. H. Melber, 159–169. London: Zed Books.

Sumich, Jason. 2018. *The Middle Class in Mozambique. The state and the politics of transformation in Southern Africa*. Cambridge: Cambridge University Press.

Tavares, Maria. 2010. Women who Give Birth to New Worlds: Three feminine Perspectives on Lusophone Postcolonial Africa. PhD Thesis, University of Manchester, UK.

Teixeira, Luisa Pinto. 2008. The Workings of the Indian Traders of Zambézia, Mozambique, 1870s–1910s. *Lusotopie* 15 (1): 39–58.

Thiong'o, Ngugi wa. 1986. *Decolonizing the Mind*. Nairobi: Heinemann Kenya.

Thiong'o, Ngugi wa. 1993. *Moving the Centre: The struggle for cultural freedoms*. Nairobi: EAEP.

Thomaz, Omar Ribeiro. 2008. Escravos sem Dono: A Experiência Social dos Campos de Trabalho em Moçambique no Período Socialista. *Revista de Antropologia* (São Paulo) 51 (1): 177–214.

Vaughan, Olufemi, ed. 2005. *Tradition and Politics: Indigenous political structures in Africa*. Trenton, NJ: Africa World Press.

Vines, Alex. 1996. *Renamo: From terrorism to democracy in Mozambique?* London: James Currey.

Vines, Alex. 2017. Warlord Democrats in Africa: Ex-Military Leaders and Electoral Politics. In *Warlord Democrats in Africa: Ex-military leaders and electoral politics*, ed. Anders Themnér, 121–155. London: Zed Books.

Visvanathan, Shiv. 2012. For a New Epistemology of the South. *Seminar* 630: 66–70.

Wallerstein, Immanuel. 2004. *World-systems Analysis: An introduction*. Durham: Duke University Press.

Wethal, Ulrikke. 2017. Workplace regimes in Sino-Mozambican construction projects: resentment and tension in a divided workplace. *Journal of Contemporary African Studies* 35 (3):383–403. DOI: 10.1080/02589001.2017.1323379.

Wiegink, Nikkie. 2015. 'It Will Be Our Time To Eat': Former Renamo Combatants and Big-Man Dynamics in Central Mozambique. *Journal of Southern African Studies* 41 (4): 869–885.

World Bank. 2017. *The World Bank in Mozambique*, available at http://www.worldbank.org/en/country/mozambique/overview, accessed January 22 2017.

Zawangoni, Salvador André. 2007. *A Frelimo e a Formação do Homem Novo (1964–1974 e 1975–1982)*. Maputo: Portos e Caminhos de Ferro de Moçambique.

Zimba, Benigna de Jesus, Edward A. Alpers, and Allen F. Isaacman, eds. 2006. *Slave Routes and Oral Tradition in Southeastern Africa*. Maputo: Filsom Entertainment.

CHAPTER 1

'No passado o futuro era melhor?': Mozambique's Democracy in Question

Anna Maria Gentili

When compared with the majority of African states, Mozambique is often described by international media and donors as a positive model of sustainable reconciliation, democratization, and successful economic growth. Since the transition agreed under the 1992 General Peace Accord,[1] multiparty presidential, parliamentary, and local elections have taken place regularly without the country reverting to war. In the African scenario of repeated, prolonged, and intractable conflicts, this has the appearance of being an outstanding success. Even though it remains one of the poorest countries in the world, growth figures since 1997 have classified Mozambique among the best performers in Africa. The ongoing debate, then, is between those looking at quantitative data showing a trend towards a steady drop of the poverty indicators and those who point out that poverty, in both rural and urban areas in its extreme forms of vulnerability and exclusion, has become more visible, essentially as a result of increasing inequality of access to basic resources and rights.

Mozambique is ruled by a government receptive to international pressures for policy reform in terms of structural adjustment and pre-set agendas of 'good governance' (Killick *et al.* 2005; Hodges and Tibana 2004; de Renzio and Hanlon 2009). It has increasingly negotiated better deals as regards international aid and investments, but has repeatedly condoned some cavalier attitudes towards human and citizen rights.

Thus, optimism about the alleged Mozambican success – which dominates international and government debate – may be curbed somewhat after reading academic and consultancy studies on the country, or specialized journalists' accounts of various aspects of governance. Such studies raise concerns regarding a democratic process that lacks transparency, a society that is tainted by rampant corruption, and a widening gulf between the privileged few with

---

* Translation: 'In the past the future was better?'

1 The General Peace Accord (GPA) between the Mozambican civil war parties, Frelimo and Renamo, that put an end to the civil war in the country was signed on October 4, 1992 in Rome, Italy.

access to resources, jointly with their clients and cronies, and the many in urban and rural areas who have little hope of making their lives more bearable. Put differently, this new era of the democratic and market 'revolution of rising expectations' following the end of the civil war, which promised freedom with prosperity, has undoubtedly opened spaces for individual accumulation, but to the advantage of a select few who have privileged access to state resources. In this way, the new democratic dispensation is perceived by the majority of 'have-nots' or 'have-less' to function as a cover to forego state responsibility for the population's well-being.

The question, then, is whether the new era of liberal democracy and market supremacy – in which 'good governance' is understood as the creation and enhancement of a good business environment through actions directed to improve infrastructure and human capital, with better access to health and education – has in fact prioritized a 'responsible politics' that seeks to expand the citizenship space for the political recognition and integration of individuals and communities. Or, are we witnessing the consolidation of technocratic governance, a sort of anti-politics machine (Ferguson 1990, 2006), in which a redeemed state defines its external and internal legitimization not in ideological terms but in the name of a renewed, centralized control that is functional in terms of the growth and accumulation priorities established by regional and international neo-liberal strategies?

1   The End of History

When Mozambique gained independence in 1975 the general state of affairs in Africa was far from encouraging: by the middle of the 1970s most sub-Saharan states were showing signs of political and economic decay, mainly because of inherited structural problems, a collapse in commodity prices, and adverse trade terms – the effects of which were multiplied by slow growth in Western industrial countries, and by governments' flawed economic policies and overspending. Furthermore, the recession caused by the Arab oil embargo following the 1973 Arab–Israeli war, and by the 1979 Iran revolution, caused a rapid increase in oil prices. At the time, this proved a decisive blow to African countries' growth and hopes of development. A similar recession among the economies of industrialized countries meant drastic cuts in aid and investment. Developing countries resorted to borrowing 'petrodollars' from commercial banks, which opened the way to disastrous debt accumulation, mostly incurred to sustain the rising costs of essentials such as oil, fertilizers, food, and manufacturing goods, but also to retain some measure of welfare services for expanding populations.

On the political front, the crisis among developing African states exposed a diminishing consensus and a collapse of legitimacy relating to increasingly authoritarian ruling elites. Most regimes lost legitimate authority and, to a large extent, the ordinary powers required to peacefully negotiate and govern internal conflicts.

However, this abrupt end to what had been the cornerstone of all national integration projects, that is, the promise of development with equity, was not merely the result of rapacious or dogmatic leaderships; rather, it was a callous decision made by powerful countries to reorder and discipline less developed countries and to leave them with no alternatives. During this era, poor countries with rapidly growing populations, the majority of whom had no access to full citizenship entitlement, were accused of living beyond their means. The World Bank, the IMF, the Reagan administration, and the governments of Margaret Thatcher and Helmut Kohl made it clear that not one cent would leave their treasuries for aid and investment if these same states did not rein in their 'irresponsible' spending. This meant drastic reforms, including less state intervention, adjustment as a promotion of free trade markets, an open-door policy to private foreign investment, privatization of assets and state enterprises, and the deregulation of domestic markets. These reforms were to be negotiated with Bretton Woods institutions as Structural Adjustment Packages, under mandatory economic and political conditionality.

The implementation of such structural adjustment measures meant the trimming of the state's responsibilities in the public domain, in which capacity building was now minimally performed for free market promotion and security issues. The state had to be reduced to assure only very basic civil rights, leaving social justice to the functioning of market forces and to charities – mainly solidarity NGOs – for the 'deserving poor'. Capital and aid partnerships with powerful local elites made state institutions more exclusive, and more accountable to external interests and donors, thus contributing to an undermining of the legitimacy of the democratization process that had been set in motion with the end of the cold war. Ideologically, the neoliberal turn was intended to 'adjust' the state to make room for market forces and democracy, promising the 'end of history',[2] and peace and prosperity for the whole world.

Since poor economic performance and faulty leadership were considered not as symptoms but as the main causes of the breakdown of legitimacy and

---

2   This expression refers to Fukuyama's position, in an article with the same title published in 1989. The author's main argument is that the rise of Western liberal democracy signals the end-point of humanity's sociocultural evolution and the final form of human government (Fukuyama 1989).

political viability of states, the focus of the new version of the developmental state became the promotion of technocratic models of 'good' governance. From decentralization to land and financial markets, from education to health system reforms, such good governance was intended to inject 'best practices' that were based on abstract, institution-building norms.

2   The Dream Undone

African states such as Mozambique, which won a late independence through liberation struggles supported by socialist countries,[3] were pushed to destruction by the proxy wars between the two blocks[4] in the final and most cruel battle for world hegemony. At the time of the liberation struggle and in the first years of independence, Frelimo conquered consensus and legitimacy for its modernizing project of nation building. This was achieved by inculcating people with the idea of progress, and the belief that it was their basic right to expect a better life, equity, justice, and full political participation. This revolutionary path faced formidable obstacles, in a region geo-strategically and economically dominated by the South African apartheid regime allied to Ian Smith's Rhodesia, which was using all possible means to safeguard the fortress of white minority rule, including direct and indirect destabilization through proxy military force.

However, Mozambique was to enjoy only a short period of enthusiasm for Frelimo's nation-building project before harsh geo-political realities set in: it was an artificially asymmetric country, lacking crucial infrastructure and skills. The impact of negative structural legacies and adverse international and regional geopolitical conditions (Saul 1985; Hanlon 1991), the option of a socialist state-centred approach to development policies, and the doctrinaire authoritarianism that antagonized customary hierarchies and modes of livelihood (Geffray 1990) – and that was too urban and southern-based – have been the subject of much discussion concerning the failure of Frelimo to keep to the promises made during the struggle for independence (Mamdani 2000; O'Laughlin 2000; Dinerman 2006, 2009; Cahen 2008).

The question of democracy, in the form of mobilization at a grass-roots level, was the object of intense political and intellectual debate in the first years of Frelimo's rule. This was natural insofar as the foundation of the new

---

3   The countries then known as belonging to the socialist block, headed by the former Soviet Union.

4   The so-called 'hot' cold wars involving countries allied either with Western nations or with the socialist block.

state revolutionary project had been based in ideals of democratization from below (Brito 1988). After independence, however, self-empowerment through mobilization was exchanged for the organization and practices of a party that chose Marxism–Leninism as the ideological expression of its modernizing nation-building project. In the early post-liberation period, the debates and differences between the mobilizing faction and the top-down Marxist–Leninist followers were intense, and often a matter of internal dispute within government. Economic and political options for development were few in a harsh situation of structural and economic backwardness, lack of resources, and foreign aggression, and resulted in the closure of all spaces for mobilization from below. This determined a deficit in Frelimo's legitimacy that opened a space for Renamo's momentous political and military offensive.

For Frelimo, imbalances in local or regional integration under the ethos of the liberation struggle, and a lack of adherence to the planned socialist economy, were dismissed either as manifestations of *obscurantismo* (backwardness), or as evil, divisive plots engineered by *inimigos* (enemies) bent on destroying the revolutionary unity of the nation. More specifically, Frelimo ideological discourse and practice blamed peasants' lack of enthusiasm or resistance to collectivization as the manifestation of a 'backward' defence of customary ways of life, as constructed by colonial subordination and as instigated by enemies of the revolution. Its anti-capitalist line made it impossible for the party to admit to what extent such resistance might be a recourse to traditional identities, or a defence of personal or community interests against top-down policies that were perceived as damaging people's livelihood strategies.

Given this situation of limited institutionalization of power, with no effective distribution of political, social, and civil rights access, the policies adopted were 'impracticable in principle and disruptive in practice' (Pitcher 2002, 89), which signalled a dramatic erosion of Frelimo's legitimacy. Together with a strategy of destabilization escalated by South African support, this situation allowed for the spread of insecurity and war.

The turn to Marxism–Leninism in 1977, and the adoption in 1980 of a Soviet-style Economic Plan and tighter military pacts with socialist countries, did not merely fail to solve enormous problems of growth and redistribution but instigated a decisive cold-war onslaught against all regional political forces aligned with what Ronald Reagan in 1980 labelled the 'evil empire'.[5] At one level, then, the aims of economic growth and the objectives of distributive justice were not met; additionally, the erosion of legitimacy was accelerated by the inability

---

5   In reference to the then Soviet Union's strategic and global military capabilities. This characterization represented the rhetorical side of the escalation of the cold war.

of the party/state to guarantee the country's regional, external, and international security.

The strategy changes that led to the 1992 Peace Accord have a long history. At the end of the 1980s, after three decades of uninterrupted war and destabilization, Mozambique was the martyr of Africa. The 16 years of war that followed the war of liberation and independence created the conditions for Mozambique to become a pawn in the final phase of the cold war in a region dominated by the South African apartheid regime. The beginning of the 1980s saw a rapid turn, from a policy of strict adherence to Soviet-inspired economic planning, and tighter economic and military relations with Eastern socialist countries, towards the realization that the Soviet Union and its allies were facing enormous political and economic difficulties of their own. They were unable to help mitigate the impact of drought, the shortage of consumer goods, increasing debt, and above all the ravaging destabilization of the war. Frelimo's realization of these aspects induced the party to appeal to the West for diplomatic and financial assistance; they obtained food aid, sanctioned by their 1982 application for membership of the World Bank and the IMF. Thereafter, it was possible to reschedule Mozambique's external debt. Arguably, the new policies decided at the 1983 Fourth National Congress of Frelimo, and the changes that came about through the signing of the Nkomati treaty in 1984,[6] began a new era of pragmatism.

The question of coming to terms with armed dissidence and its main sponsor South Africa, and the possible initiation of a fundamental economic shift towards market capitalism, had been debated intensely within the party since 1982. These political decisions were followed by concrete diplomatic steps, some of which we know about, while others, more discreet, have still to be investigated.

With regard to the military, diplomatic, and economic realities created by the drought that hit the country between 1981 and 1984, Frelimo had no choice but to appeal to an international community whose priorities were concentrated on finding a negotiated solution. Western governments wished to achieve this in collaboration with Frontline States[7] whose governments would agree to end the region's militarization and the apartheid regime in a way that would

---

6 Treaty signed in 1984 between the governments of Mozambique and (apartheid) South Africa. According to the terms of the treaty, both countries agreed not to harbour hostile forces or allow their countries to be used as launching pads for attacks on one another. Mozambique agreed to expel the African National Congress (ANC) from their country while South Africa agreed to cease its support of RENAMO, the anti-government guerrilla organization in Mozambique.

7 The Frontline States was an organization of African States established to achieve democratic majority rule in apartheid South Africa. Among the members of this organization that no longer exists were Angola, Botswana, Lesotho, Mozambique, Tanzania, Zambia and Zimbabwe.

avoid further serious trouble in South Africa and across the wider region. The decision at the end of 1982 (Ferrão 2007) to send their first accredited ambassador to the United States was another clear sign that Frelimo was aware of the winds of change following the 1979 economic recession and Reagan's presidency in the 1980s. The decision to sign the Nkomati treaty in 1984 was taken at the same time as Frelimo's first secret negotiations with Renamo.

As for the apartheid regime, the constitutional and political reforms of 1984, as well as the Nkomati treaty, were meant to save the essence of white power by showing good will towards the countries of the region brought to their knees by the increased destabilization. At the time, in South Africa and in Mozambique, the prevailing opinion among decision makers was that the confrontation could be won with only minor concessions to the 'enemy'.

However, nobody in Frelimo was under the illusion that the Nkomati agreement would put an end to South African support for Renamo or, for that matter, to Frelimo's support for the ANC. Rather, Frelimo's main objective was to gain the trust of critical Western supporters, and by this point that process had already started. British diplomats, for instance, had discovered and greatly appreciated the flexibility of President Samora Machel (1975–1986) and his staff during the difficult negotiations with the Frontline States involved in negotiations for the independence of Zimbabwe. The pragmatic attitude Frelimo displayed in coming to terms with its worst enemy provided renewed legitimacy and widespread international credibility. Thus, even if the Nkomati treaty may be argued to have failed, in that it did not bring an end to war but instead allowed its further escalation, it nevertheless exposed the dangerous militarism of the South African regime (Davies 1985). Following the treaty, Frelimo found that asking for and obtaining Western economic assistance became easier; it broadened and strengthened formal and informal support for contacts and negotiations towards a solution to the conflict.

President Machel was killed in a plane crash on South African soil in October 1986 while he was engaged in stepping up regional and international diplomatic efforts for a solution to Mozambique's security issues. The many investigations into the plane crash in Mbuzini have not yet provided a convincing explanation of South African and other actors' responsibilities. Nonetheless, only one year after the death of Machel, Joaquim Chissano's government adopted the *Programa de Reabilitação Económica* (PRE) – an economic reform plan in line with World Bank and IMF priorities – in a first step towards the demise of the state's leading role in the economy and in a move towards the adoption of wide-ranging liberalization. The first structural adjustment programs of 1987 had as their ideological corollary the formal shedding of Marxism–Leninism and of the centrally planned economy – policies thereafter decided in the 1989

5th Congress (Castel-Branco *et al.* 2001; Pitcher 2002). From this perspective, the fact that the 1992 Peace Accord defined the terms that guaranteed the adoption of democratic multiparty competition, based upon the adoption of market capitalism, may be viewed as another of the ongoing political reorientations that took place at this time.

Regionally, the first success that paved the way towards the end of the apartheid regime was the Namibia referendum (1989), which led to the country's independence through multiparty elections. The case of Namibia functioned as a negotiation workshop for the divided sides of the erstwhile cold war. Last but not least, the international community and the African Frontline States – and, as is often the case after some decisive intervention by informal but influential actors – amassed considerable funds for all the stages of the long and difficult Peace Accord negotiation and its implementation (Vines 1994).

The first transition was completed through the adoption, in 1990, of a multiparty constitution and, in 1991, of an initial set of local administration reforms. At this point, the Mozambican state had in effect to relinquish its sovereignty to supranational powers – mainly Bretton Wood institutions and United Nations organizations and programs; these powers included government and non-governmental organizations representing the community of donors.

Thus, the 1992 Peace Accord finally signed in Rome was the inevitable outcome of steps taken throughout the 1980s in specific international, internal, and regional circumstances. However, it hardly represents a model of conflict resolution (Saul 1999; Honwana 2002; Hanlon 2005). During the negotiations for peace and in the transition period Frelimo was able to accommodate its internal differences; it avoided making internal divisions public and maintained a coherent and reliable leadership, backed by nearly all African states and conditioned by considerable international experience (Sumich and Honwana 2007). Above all, Frelimo was aligned with Mugabe's Zimbabwe and with the ANC; with Mandela's liberation in 1990 and the opening of the multiparty conference. In short, these southern African countries were now emerging as a regional political force to be reckoned with.

Renamo bore the stigma of being a 'contra' organization created by Smith's regime in Rhodesia and sponsored by apartheid South Africa; it was in a position of weakness due to its frail leadership and ideology as well as because of the raw brutality it had shown on the battleground. It took a formidable array of formal and informal diplomatic machinery and a lot of international financing to make Renamo politically acceptable in the first instance;[8] thereafter, it

---

8   See, among other, Hume (1994); Morozzo della Rocca (1994); Samkange (1994); Alden (1995); Vines and Wilson (1995); Synge (1997).

was helped to reorganize from a guerrilla movement into a civil party in order to be recognized as a legitimate partner in negotiations and in the following political democratization process. Renamo's transformation from *bandidos armados* (armed bandits) to a legitimate party was thus supported by exceptional political and financial provisions during, as well as after, the transition to the second republic. Thus, the main success of the Rome peace process seemed to be not so much the 'conversion', already advanced by then, of Frelimo to multiparty democracy and to the market, but the transformation of Renamo into a legitimate political party (Vines 1994; Manning 1998; Cahen 2002).[9]

3   The Fading Trust

Knowledgeable observers of the Peace Accord negotiations, such as Brazão Mazula, have defined the negotiation and transition phase leading up to the first presidential and parliamentary elections of 1994 as a period of trust building (Mazula 1995). Crucially, such trust was made possible and successfully implemented by an extraordinary effort of formal and informal diplomacy and a well-financed UN operation, the ONUMOZ.[10]

Other arguments put forward to suggest that the Mozambican transition was successful stress the high growth rate of the Gross National Product (GNP) since 1997. Macroeconomic measures for fiscal and currency stabilization were implemented, as well as the dismantling of state enterprises and interventions in favour of privatization. Mozambican privatization has seen one of the largest sales of assets in Africa, and private actors have taken up many state responsibilities, according to the most extensive study on the subject to date (Pitcher 2002).

According to recent data, poverty seems to have declined (Ministério de Plano e Finanças 2004; da Silva Francisco and Matter 2007), but despite this progress, more than fifty percent of the population is still classified as poor,

---

9   Christine Messiant (1997) notes that those involved in the peace process were fixated on negotiating an accord between Frelimo and Renamo, and left out all other political groups; thus, the entire exercise postponed democratization to the next phase. Sumich (2007, 16), investigating the alienation and loss of Frelimo legitimacy among Maputo elites, concludes, 'democracy was introduced less to legitimize the government with the people as it was to legitimate it with the international community and to end the war'.

10   ONUMOZ – United Nations Operation in Mozambique (1992–1994) was established to support implementing the Peace Agreement of 1992. Its mandate included facilitating the implementation of the Agreement, monitoring and supporting the ceasefire, the demobilization of forces and the holding of national elections. On this topic, see also Synge (1997) and Chan and Venâncio (1998).

and mostly living in rural areas, working in agriculture, while the result of deregulation and of an increasingly precarious regional labour market has been a rise in unemployment, inflation, food prices, and basic services. In urban areas, the reduction of poverty has been slower still, suggesting that any trickle-down effect has been negligible. Educational opportunities are on the increase, but still insufficient to meet basic needs, while the expansion of private institutions implies that only those with financial resources can afford quality. Further, public services remain in short supply and are unevenly distributed, geographically and socially. While acknowledging some progress in macro data, critics of government strategies insist that accelerating progress towards diminishing poverty would require not only broad-based economic growth but also a fairer distribution of resources combined with intensified expansion of social services to the poorest in urban as well as rural areas. Crucially, the most significant expansion has taken place in the informal economy and in multiple non-state networks of survival (Cruz e Silva 2000; de Vletter 2001; Serra 2003; da Silva Francisco and Paulo 2006; Paulo *et al.* 2007).

If statistically poverty has diminished, what has increased visibly is the inequality between social classes in both urban and rural areas. All observers also note that growth is mainly a result of external intervention. Thus, regarding government strategies on where and how to intervene, and in which sectors and regions, central political and administrative powers have the upper hand in negotiating and shaping donor decision-making processes.

In this context of growth financed mainly by aid and not by internal revenue, tension occurs among political and administrative powers, 'communities', local administrations, and large segments of the population for whom multiparty democracy, the liberalization of markets, and related economic growth have led neither to a substantial reduction of poverty nor to a more equitable access to resources. General and municipal elections have been held regularly in Mozambique, since 1994 and 1998 respectively, and they have been recognized as reasonably free and fair by the international community. Since 1994 Frelimo has won all elections, maintaining its position as Mozambique's dominant, hegemonic governing party. At all elections the opposition party, Renamo, has denounced what it claims to have been fraudulent activities, and in 1998 it called for a boycott of local elections (Nuvunga 2005; Sitoe *et al.* 2005). The first multiparty elections saw high levels of participation, which was claimed as an endorsement of a revolution of rising expectations in a liberal democracy that promised prosperity for all towards a future without fear and violence.

However, subsequent elections, election results, and accusations of fraud and violence have shown that trust in the Peace Accord was fragile and, until the 1994 elections, was mainly guaranteed by the combination of the United

Nations' mission and the might of financial disbursements. Also, election after election showed that Renamo was unable to reorganize, and was burdened with an oligarchic leadership reluctant to make space for the better-educated younger generation. This was despite the fact that some of the new members recruited by Renamo among the intellectuals have revealed a potential to face up to parliamentary challenges; in many instances they were able to articulate alternative policies to those proposed by more experienced Frelimo representatives. However, at each setback Renamo tended to react by threatening to 'go back to war' – an empty threat by all accounts, since no regional or international conditions or alliances would support such a venture. On the other hand, a marginalized Renamo could still be a flag around which violent dissidence could rally – especially at the local level in areas marginalized by government policies. Last but not least, there is nothing as detrimental as repeated failure. Politically, at both central and local levels, what is clear is that rewards go to those who belong or are close to the ruling party. Investors as well as international organizations and NGOs are critical of the government (mostly in relation to corruption charges and lack of transparency), but they seem to have concluded that given the institutional fragility of the country Frelimo remains by far the more credible partner in terms of leadership capabilities. Despite the criticisms, in other words, Frelimo is still regarded as the party that will guarantee growth in the market economy, in the framework of a reformist path towards improved democratic governance.

The most salient aspect of the multiparty elections has been the decline of voter turnout in recent general elections, signalling a general increase in attitudes of apathy, discontent, and disinterest. International organizations, NGOs, and consultants have offered diverse explanations, ranging from lack of education in democracy, blurred transparency in registration and counting, disorganization – especially in remote rural areas – and a general distrust of politicians and central and local government administrators – all of whom are accused of functioning as brokers of private and patrimonial interests.

While political parties and the electoral process seem to have lost rather than gained legitimacy over time, civil society organizations continue to be weak or for the most part conditioned by whoever holds financial power, be it government institutions or foreign donors. Opting out of political engagement, taking refuge in traditional ways of guaranteeing one's survival, autonomy, and identity, or turning to various syncretic religious forms are now options for an increasing number of people who see their livelihoods increasingly threatened (Cruz e Silva 2001, 2003, 2004).

If the measure of democratic success is to be evaluated and legitimized by enlarged participation and government accountability, then competition between political parties is central. In representative democracies, parties constitute the essential link between society and public office, as they are the agencies intended to give voice to their particular constituencies; they also present electoral candidates and through competitive elections place candidates for public office. Several scholars are consistent in stressing how important the model of representative democracy is for ensuring that a mechanism is in place to encourage competition between parties, and in terms of transparency in the electoral process. Trust in the new system was initially built in Mozambique through the ethical promise that democracy would mean the adoption of a responsible mode of politics, in which parties would formulate political strategies that would respond to and discipline the demands of constituencies, negotiate with other political actors and, finally, respect the rights of the opposition and the hierarchy of institutional orders. However, the small space left to parties to devise alternative paths to development has made secondary what should have been the primary objective, that is, to represent citizens' interests and to respect the rules of fair and transparent competition for government power.

Frelimo has maintained and possibly reinforced full control of patronage resources and a monopoly of the division of state spoils, including vital aid resources. Given the country's aid dependence, and thus reflecting the externally devised politico-economic agenda, Frelimo has tended to function, and to be perceived to do so by the general public, at the service of the political class and its ability to stay in power over the long term. In other words, Frelimo is, and is perceived to be, part of the state if not constituting the whole state, drawing legitimacy from party members and electors only by monopolizing the exploitation of state resources (Pereira 2008).

4   Citizens or Subjects?

Although not included in the Peace Accord, decentralization was crucial to the donors' strategy and was seen as an essential tool for extending democratic representative governance at the local level in order to generate a full devolution of power. In 1995 the new multiparty parliament, with Frelimo as the majority party in government, chose to recognize a limited and gradual devolution of power through elections for 23 local urban bodies and ten semi-urban ones – one for each province (Ministério da Administração Estatal 2000). The right to vote in these *autarquias* was thus only granted to a (urban) minority of the population in this as well as in subsequent elections. The current administration of the 10 provinces, 154 districts, 419 administrative posts and over a thousand localities – and therefore control of their respective economic and material resources, including those coming from aid and investment – remains under the control of administrators delegated by central government.

The moves against devolution to the rural areas demonstrate the Frelimo government's victory in relation to a traditional statism, now best represented by an emerging national capitalist class. Given the still present dependence on foreign aid and finance, it remains the case to the present day that the re-capturing and consolidation of state power is crucial as a means by which to access resources and distribute them and thus as an instrument with which to build alliances with selected provincial and local interests, whether via private entrepreneurs or community and traditional authorities.

Contrary to past occurrences, government authorities now pay homage to customs and recognize difference – as can be seen in the proliferation of eth-nic identity discourse and in the instrumental measures that recognize some functions as belonging to traditional authorities (Buur and Kyed 2005; Gon-çalves 2006; Kyed and Buur 2006; Florêncio 2008). However, continuity with first republic policies is striking: all the reforms seem to be based on the per-sistence of a dual vision of national society and of citizenship rights, which are represented by a decentralization governance model that separates urban and rural communities. This policy concedes to the former some limited political rights, and leaves the latter under centralized state rule. The majority of the rural population is left 'homeless' in political terms, with only secondary rights in relation to how they want to be governed and by whom.

It can therefore be argued that the decentralization chosen in 1997 contin-ues to negate equal citizenship rights for the majority of the rural population, insofar as second-class citizens are bound by legally recognized 'communities', and by local political and administrative structures that nevertheless remain centralized and hold the power to decide how benefits will be distributed. The peasant populations, collapsing the memory of the racial hierarchical dual-ism[11] of colonial times with today's reality of dual citizenship, are encouraged to move away from voting, and to take refuge in ethnicity or religious affilia-tions that provide them with a sense of belonging and justice.

It is for these reasons that we need more nationwide comparative research on the ways in which decentralization has been appropriated at the local level. In many instances conflicts have increased, giving way to fragmentation and an informalization of instances of power and authority, thus leaving space for

11 Euclides Gonçalves's ethnographic survey in Inharrime (2006) concludes that the whole process resembles a colonial style indirect rule system of native administration as com-munity leaders are expected to act as government representatives.

multiple forms of ethnicization and xenophobia against those who 'do not belong'. And thus one sees the paradox of the party in power: it defends central-
ization in name of the reconstruction of the nation state; on the other side,
it is impossible to consolidate the nation exactly because of the policies of
'decentralization' being proposed.

Frelimo has shown a remarkable ability to adapt to new international imperatives in order to maintain control of the state apparatus. Today, the party
is not so much criticized because it has so rapidly abandoned socialist ideology – the bedrock of Mozambican patriotism – to passionately embrace
neo-liberalism, but because it is holding democracy hostage, on the whole to
reinforce its monopoly over all positions of privilege derived from control of
foreign aid and investment.

Elections and decentralization both show how citizenship remains unequal; this has become ever clearer as the growth deriving from the effects of
structural adjustment are seen to benefit a minority at the expense of the vast
majority. Inequality has become more visible, considering that the demand for
the expansion of social services such as education and health has escalated,
while privatization has made access prohibitively expensive for most.

While social movements are emerging, mainly in urban areas, they continue
to be led and mainly constituted of elite, educated, middle-class social groups
that are heavily dependent on aid money; they are critical of power, but lack
the support and the strength to call to task an unaccountable executive and a
malfunctioning legislature, or to counter the power and impunity of corrupt
interest groups. Nevertheless, in rural areas and in the most marginal urban
areas there is a growing informal dynamic of protest. The fact that the vote in
the new democratic dispensation is increasingly void of any political influence
is aiding in such an informalization of politics and protest – over which the
government holds little or no control.

There is a real tension here, created by the possibility of a centralizing party
state, whose policies are guided by the imperative to control the division of
aid and investment spoils, collapsing under the grievances of the majority of
the rural and urban population, who consider that democracy and citizenship
entitlements are only intended for the privileged few who can afford them.
This tension risks leading to less governability, which is already visible in an
increase of uncontrolled criminality. In this scenario the danger is a further
drifting apart of the polity, with a minority of mostly modern urban citizens
who, through donor-promoted governance, will enjoy spaces of freedom, freedom of information, capitalist development accumulation, and opportunities,
while the majority of the 'poor', conceived and treated as a world apart, will
continue to be regarded and treated as subjects.

References

Alden, Chris. 1995. The UN and the resolution of conflict in Mozambique. *Journal of Modern African Studies* 33 (1): 103–128.

Brito, Luis de. 1988. Une relecture nécessaire: La genèse du parti-État Frelimo. *Politique Africaine* 29: 15–27.

Buur, Lars, and Helene M. Kyed. 2005. *State Recognition of Traditional Authority in Mozambique: The nexus of community representation and state assistance*. Discussion Paper 28, Nordiska Afrikainstitutet, Uppsala, Sweden.

Cahen, Michel. 2002. *Les Bandits. Un historien au Mozambique*. Paris: Centre Culturel Calouste Gulbenkian.

Cahen, Michel. 2008. A la recherché de la défaite: Notes sur une certaine historiographie de la 'Révolution' et de la 'Contre-Révolution' au Mozambique et sans doute ailleurs. *Politique Africaine* 122: 161–178.

Castel-Branco, Carlos Nuno. 2008. *Aid and Development: A question of ownership*. Working Paper 1, Instituto de Estudos Sociais e Económicos, Maputo, Mozambique.

Castel-Branco, Carlos Nuno, Christopher Cramer, and Degol Hailu. 2001. *Privatisation and Economic Strategy in Mozambique*. Discussion Paper 64, United Nations University / World Institute for Development Economic Research, Helsinki, Finland.

Chan, Stephen, and Moises Venâncio, eds. 1998. *War and Peace in Mozambique*. New York: St. Martin's Press.

Cruz e Silva, Teresa. 2000. Identidades étnicas como fenómenos agregadores num espaço social urbano: Os casos de Mafalala e Chinhambanine. In *Racismo, Etnicidade e Poder: Um estudo em cinco cidades de Mocambique*, ed. Carlos Serra, 195–208. Maputo: Livraria Universitária, Universidade Eduardo Mondlane.

Cruz e Silva, Teresa. 2001. Entre a exclusão social e o exercício da cidadania: Igrejas 'Zione' do Bairro Luís Cabral na cidade de Maputo. *Estudos Moçambicanos* 19:61–68.

Cruz e Silva, Teresa. 2003. A Igreja Universal do Reino de Deus em Mocambique. In *Igreja Universal do Reino de Deus: Os novos conquistadores da fé*, ed. Ari Pedro Oro, André Corten, and Jean-Pierre Dozon, 123–136. São Paulo: Paulinas.

Cruz e Silva, Teresa. 2004. Continuidades e rupturas na definição da 'normalidade' religiosa em Moçambique e consequentes processos de exclusão social: O caso do movimento Zione na Cidade de Maputo (1980–1990). In *Persistência da história: Passado e contemporaneidade em África*, ed. Clara Carvalho and João de Pina-Cabral, 293–306. Lisbon: Imprensa de Ciências Sociais.

da Silva Francisco, Antonio A., and Konrad Matter. 2007. *Poverty Observatory in Mozambique*. Basel: Gerster Consulting.

da Silva Francisco, Antonio A., and Margarida Paulo. 2006. *Impacto da Economia Informal na Protecção Social, Pobreza, Exclusão: A dimensão oculta da informalidade em Moçambique*. Maputo: Cruzeiro do Sul.

Davies, Robert. 1985. *South African Strategy towards Mozambique in the post-Nkomati Period: A critical analysis of effects and implications.* Research Report 73. Uppsala: Scandinavian Institute of African Studies.

de Renzio, Paolo, and Joseph Hanlon. 2009. Mozambique's contested sovereignty? The dilemma of aid dependence. In *The politics of Aid: African strategies for dealing with donors*, ed. Lindsay Whitfield, 246–270. Oxford: Oxford University Press.

de Vletter, Fion. 2001. *Mozambique's Urban Informal Sector: A neglected majority.* Maputo: Ministério do Trabalho.

Dinerman, Alice. 2006. *Revolution, Counter-revolution and revisionism in post-colonial Africa: The case of Mozambique, 1975–1994.* London: Routledge.

Dinerman, Alice. 2009. Regarding totalities and escaping hatches in Mozambican politics and Mozambican studies. *Politique Africaine* 113: 187–210.

Ferguson, James. 1990. *The Anti-politics Machine: 'Development', depoliticization, and bureaucratic power in Lesotho.* Cambridge: Cambridge University Press.

Ferguson, James. 2006. *Global Shadows: Africa in the neo-liberal world order.* Durham, NC: Duke University Press.

Ferrão, Valeriano. 2007. *Embaixador nos USA.* Maputo: Ndjira.

Florêncio, Fernando. 2008. Autoridades tradicionais vaNdau de Moçambique: O regresso do indirect rule ou uma espécie de neo-indirect rule? *Análise Social* 2: 369–391.

Fukuyama, Francis. 1989. The End of History? *The National Interest*, 16 (Summer 1989): 8–16.

Geffray, Christian A. 1990. *La Cause des Armes au Mozambique: Anthropologie d'une guerre civile.* Paris: Karthala.

Gonçalves, Euclides. 2006. Local Democracy and the Politics of Recognition: Implications for land management in Inharrime, Mozambique. Paper presented at 11th conference of the International Association for the Study of Common Property, Bali, Indonesia, June 19–23.

Hanlon, Joseph. 1991. *Mozambique: Who calls the shots?* Bloomington, IN: Indiana University Press.

Hanlon, Joseph. 2005. Bringing it all together: A case study of Mozambique. In *Postconflict Development*, ed. Gerd Junne and Willemijn Verkoren, 273–288. Boulder, CO: Lynne Reiner.

Hodges, Tony, and Roberto Tibana. 2004. *Political Economy of the Budget in Mozambique.* Maputo: DfID.

Honwana, João. 2002. Mozambique. What nexus among peacemaking, peacekeeping, and development? In *The Causes of War and the Consequences of Peacekeeping in Africa*, ed. Ricardo R. Laremont, 195–221. Portsmouth, NH: Heinemann.

Hume, Cameron. 1994. *Ending Mozambique's War: The role of mediation and good offices.* Washington, DC: United States Institute of Peace Press.

Killick, Tony, Carlos N. Castel-Branco, and Richard Gerster. 2005. *Perfect Partners? The performance of programme aid partners in Mozambique 2004.* Maputo: Programme Aid Partners.

Kyed, Helene M., and Lars Buur. 2006. New sites of Citizenship: Recognition of traditional authority and group-based citizenship in Mozambique. *Journal of Southern African Studies* 32 (3): 563–581.

Mamdani, Mahmood. 2000. Indirect rule and the struggle for democracy: A response to Bridget O'Laughlin. *African Affairs* 99 (394): 43–46.

Manning, Carrie. 1998. Constructing opposition in Mozambique: Renamo as political party. *Journal of Southern African Studies* 24 (1): 161-189.

Mazula, Brazão. 1995. As Eleições Moçambicanas: Uma Trajectória da Paz e da Democracia. In *Eleições, Democracia e Desenvolvimento*, ed. Brazão Mazula, 26–77. Maputo: Inter-Africa Group Press com patrocínio da Embaixada do Reino dos Países Baixos .

Messiant, Christine. 1997. La paix au Mozambique: Un Succès de l'ONU. In *Les chemins de la guerre et de la paix*, ed. Roland Marchal and Christine Messiant, 49–105. Paris: Karthala.

Ministério da Administração Estatal, Governo de Moçambique. 2000. *Estratégia e Política de Desenvolvimento Autárquico em Moçambique*. Maputo: Direcção Nacional de Desenvolvimento Autárquico.

Ministério do Plano e Finanças, Governo de Moçambique. 2004. *Pobreza e Bem-estar em Moçambique: Segunda avaliação nacional*. Maputo: Direcção Nacional do Plano e Orçamento.

Morozzo Della Rocca, Roberto. 1994. *Mozambico, una Pace per l'Africa*. San Paolo: Cinisello Balsamo.

Nuvunga Adriano, ed. 2005. *Multiparty Democracy in Mozambique: Strength, weaknesses and challenges*. Johannesburg and Maputo: EISA.

O'Laughlin, Bridget. 2000. Class and the customary: The ambiguous legacy of the *Indigenato* in Mozambique. *African Affairs* 99 (394): 5–42.

Paulo, Margarida, Carmeliza Rosário, and Inge Tvedten. 2007. *'Xiculungo': Social relations of urban poverty in Maputo, Mozambique*. Report no. 13. Bergen: Chr Michelsen Institute.

Pereira, João C.G. 2008. Antes o 'diabo conhecido' do que um 'anjo desconhecido': As limitações do voto económico na reeleição do Partido Frelimo. *Análise Social* 2: 419–442.

Pitcher, Anne. 2002. *Transforming Mozambique: The politics of privatisation, 1975–2000*. Cambridge: Cambridge University Press.

Samkange, Stanlake. 1994. L'ONU et le processus de la paix au Mozambique. *Le Trimestre du Monde* 25: 147–176.

Saul, John. 1985. *A Difficult Road: The transition to socialism in Mozambique*. New York: Monthly Review Press.

Saul, John. 1999. Inside from the outside? The roots and resolution of Mozambique's un/civil war. In *Civil wars in Africa: Roots and resolution*, ed. Taisier M. Ali and Robert O. Mathews, 123–168. Montreal and Kingston: McGill-Queen's University Press.

Serra, Carlos. 2003. *Em Cima de Uma Lâmina: Um estudo sobre precaridade social em três cidades de Moçambique.* Maputo: Imprensa Universitária.

Sitoe, Eduardo J., Zefanias Matsimbe, and Amílcar Pereira. 2005. *Political Parties and Political Development in Mozambique.* Johannesburg: The Electoral Institute for Sustainable Democracy in Africa.

Sumich, Jason. 2007. *The Illegitimacy of Democracy, Democratisation and Alienation in Maputo, Mozambique.* Working Paper series 2, London School of Economics, London.

Sumich, Jason, and João Honwana. 2007. *Strong Party, Weak State: Frelimo and state survival through the Mozambican civil war. An analytical narrative on state making.* Working Paper 23, London School of Economics, London.

Synge, Richard. 1997. *Mozambique: UN peacekeeping in action, 1992–1994.* Washington, DC: United States Institute of Peace Press.

Vines, Alex. 1994. *No Democracy Without Money: The road to peace in Mozambique, 1982–1992.* London: Catholic Institute for International Relations.

Vines, Alex, and Ken Wilson. 1995. The Christian churches and the peace process in Mozambique. In *The Christian Churches and Africa's Democratisation*, ed. Paul Gifford, 130–147. Leiden: Brill.

CHAPTER 2

Mirrors and Contrasts: Zimbabwe and Zimbabweans in Manica, Mozambique

Randi Kaarhus

During 2008, waves of people crossed the border from Zimbabwe into Mozambique. In neighbouring Zimbabwe, the 2008 elections had presented a serious political challenge to the party in power since independence. The response of the ruling ZANU-PF,[1] its officials and supporters had been mounting violence and persecution directed towards – real and suspected – opponents, making tens of thousands seek refuge across the borders. The major part of these migrants headed for South Africa (UNHCR 2010). But thousands also crossed into Mozambique and the border province of Manica in particular. By June 23, 2008, the UN Refugee Agency (UNHCR) had made large-scale plans for the reception of Zimbabwean refugees, including two potential refugee camps sites in Manica Province (UNHCR 2008). These plans were, however, never effectuated. In fact, the flow of Zimbabweans into Mozambique in 2008 was only the peak in a steady flow of people seeking livelihood opportunities and shelter from the economic crisis which followed the 'Fast Track' land reform launched by President Mugabe in 2000. This influx of Zimbabweans was basically treated as a non-topic by Mozambican authorities, and while seeking to address the responses of Mozambican authorities to the Zimbabwean crisis, this chapter will also provide insights into the experiences of the Zimbabweans: Why did they come? What did they meet when crossing the border? How did they experience the changing realities of present-day Mozambique?

The material and analyses presented here draw upon field research in Manica Province, carried out under a research project funded by the Norwegian Research Council.[2] Field research in Manica Province took place during four periods between October 2007 and October 2009, totalling 4 months. The author conducted 36 in-depth interviews with Zimbabweans living in Manica Province, in addition to a large number of informal conversations with

---

1 The Zimbabwe African National Union – Patriotic Front. It has been the ruling party in Zimbabwe since independence in 1980, led by Robert Mugabe until 2017.
2 The project 'In the Shadow of a Conflict' was funded through the Norwegian Research Council programme 'Poverty and Peace' from 2007 to 2009.

© KONINKLIJKE BRILL NV, LEIDEN, 2019 | DOI:10.1163/9789004381100_004

Mozambicans and Zimbabweans in Manica as well as some on the Zimbabwean side of the border. The identities of the Zimbabweans are kept strictly anonymous in order to protect their privacy, since most of them could not avoid getting involved in some form of extra-legal practices when trying to make a living in Mozambique. The overall analyses presented here, situating the immigrants within the shifting realities of contemporary Mozambique, are, furthermore, based on the author spending altogether three years in the country between 1999 and 2011.

1 Brief Background – With No Statistics on the Mozambican Side

The year 2000 was for many in Mozambique the year of the great floods. In Zimbabwe, also, the year came to mark a political watershed of sorts as a majority of Zimbabweans did not support President Mugabe's party ZANU-PF in a constitutional referendum. What started out as a process to revise the constitution developed into a contest between the governing ZANU-PF and the gathering forces of the opposition, turned into a referendum on ZANU-PF's rule since independence in 1980. At the time it was broadly seen as the first serious challenge to the party-in-power since Zimbabwean independence (Alexander 2006, 184; Raftopoulos 2009, 211). Soon after the referendum, fairly well-organized War Veterans initiated a series of land invasions on commercial ('white') farms. Supported by the President and officially legitimized through a new and radical Fast Track Land Reform programme, the land occupations resulted in an increasing number of evictions of both (white) farm owners and (black) farm workers. By February 2003, the Commercial Farmers Union estimated that 2.300 of their members were no longer 'farming' in Zimbabwe (IDMC 2008, 31). A small group had, however, with the acceptance of the Mozambican president Chissano, left Zimbabwe to establish themselves as commercial farmers in the Manica Province. Since then the Zimbabwean farmers in Manica have been the target of both studies, publications, and a lot of debate (Manica 2006; Hanlon and Smart 2008, 71–88; Hammar 2010).

But the 'Zimbabwean farmers' in Manica constitute only a fraction of the actual number of Zimbabweans who have crossed the border into Mozambique. Real numbers are, however, unknown as none are classified as 'refugees' by Mozambican authorities nor are they reported as refugees by the UNHCR. While it has been reported that Zimbabweans in Mozambique are mainly found in the provinces of Manica and Tete, and to some extent in Gaza, in addition to the major cities, Maputo and Beira (Kiwanuka and Monson 2009, 31), numbers and official statistics are lacking. When asked to give an estimate for

Manica Province, well-informed interviewees would provide the author numbers that ranged from 4.000 to 30.000 or 40.000, or more – estimates reflecting
the lack of official numbers. I will argue that the lack of any official statistics
also contributes to make the Zimbabweans in Mozambique paradoxically invisible in public debate, while – as everybody knows – they are 'everywhere'.

2   Who Are the Zimbabweans in Mozambique?

Let me introduce a few of the Zimbabweans I interviewed in Manica Province in the period 2007–2009, starting with a young man, *Nelson*.[3] Nelson had
grown up in one of the suburbs of Harare, and lived there with his family until
2005. Then the suburb was destroyed, during what he – and most Zimbabweans in Manica – referred to as 'Tsunami time'.[4] *Tsunami time* was when large-
scale evictions and demolitions of informal housing and business structures
destroyed numerous low-income *urban* areas in Zimbabwe. This was, however,
a man-made tsunami, carried out by Zimbabwean authorities in 2005 under
the official name of Operation *Murambatsvina*.[5] It started in Harare, and was
officially presented as an initiative to clean up and restore order in urban slums
(Sachikonye 2006). At the time it was noted that among the residents in the
targeted low-income suburbs there were many Mozambican migrants and
their descendants – mainly people who had sought refuge in Zimbabwe during the Mozambican civil war (1977–1992) and had not thereafter returned to
Mozambique. One of the reasons for staying was that Mozambique came out
of the post-independence war as one of the poorest countries in sub-Saharan
Africa, while Zimbabwe in a regional perspective was still a relatively prosperous country. Some of these 'Mozambican Zimbabweans' also lived in Nelson's
neighbourhood in Harare.

After the 2005 'Tsunami' destroyed their house, Nelson's family split up. His
mother left for Botswana in search of a new livelihood, while his sister got involved in prostitution seeking to raise money to go to South Africa. He felt the
Tsunami left him with 'a broken family'. But a friend of his, who had already

---

3   All informants and interviewees referred to are anonymised. Italics are used when introduc-
ing new 'names'. The quoted interviews were conducted between March and October 2009.
4   Referring to the (natural) tsunami that swept the coasts of the Indian Ocean during Christ-
mas 2004.
5   The Shona term *murambatsvina* has been translated as 'Clear the filth' or 'Clean out the trash',
while the official translation used by the UN was 'Restore Order' (ICG 2005:1). The same UN
report indicated that this Operation resulted in an estimated 700.000 men, women and children 'losing their homes, their source of livelihood or both' (ICG 2005, 2).

decided to leave the country for good, helped him with some start capital based on a small shop in Harare and some goods. Nelson took up cross-border trading, and first travelled to Botswana to buy cosmetics to sell back in Harare. With increasing demand for foodstuffs in Zimbabwe, and informal reports about Mozambique as 'cheap', he turned to Manica for groceries. His base was the small shop he had taken over from his friend, and in this way he was able to make a living. But, in 2007 he found that trade was becoming more difficult. In Zimbabwe it was made illegal to 'walk with *forex* [foreign currency]'. Young people like Nelson were also under surveillance by police who wanted to make sure the youth supported ZANU-PF: 'They came to my place and asked: "What was the last rally that you attended?" Then the police took all the groceries in the shop and said: "Our children are also starving...."' The police also took his passport, saying: "You have travelled a lot; you are the ones who are spreading the wrong message about our country".

In 2008, Nelson had once more crossed over to Manica to buy groceries. On his return he was arrested and beaten up by the police. Late in the evening they let him go. But the next morning he got a telephone call, and learnt that a fellow traveller had been killed by the police: 'I thought, I am the next one!' In shock, he left at once, travelling back to Manica, only carrying the clothes he wore and his cell phone – 'to avoid suspicion'. At the border crossing at Machipanda,[6] he said he had left something behind during his last visit, and just came to pick it up. But this time he came to Manica to stay: 'It was escaping death, it was the only way'. Nelson himself had no family in Mozambique, but he had a Mozambican friend who had come to Zimbabwe during the civil war. His friend's brother had spent the years of war in Malawi, but had since returned to Manica. Here this brother made a living as a *curandeiro* (traditional healer). In his very modest shelter, the *curandeiro* also made a space for Nelson letting him sleep on the ground, 'sharing a blanket among five people'. Though he really appreciated the hospitality of his friend's brother, the *curandeiro,* Nelson soon fell into a deep depression.

Another 'Tsunami' victim among my Manica informants was a woman of Mozambican descent, *Laura.* She was born in Manica, but while still an infant her mother and father brought her along to Harare in 1981 during the height of the civil war. Laura grew up and went to school in Harare. She learnt to speak Shona[7] and English – no Portuguese – and married a Zimbabwean, who

---

6 Machipanda is the major point of formal border crossing between Zimbabwe and Mozambique. It is situated in Manica Province on the main road (the 'Beira Corridor') from Harare to the port of Beira on the Indian Ocean.

7 Shona is an official language in Zimbabwe. More on the language situation below.

worked as a teacher. He died already in 2000, leaving her widowed at the age of 19, with two small children. After that 'life became hard', she said. She started selling tomatoes in the streets, and managed to save some money that she used for cross-border trading. For Laura, the fact that part of her family still lived in Manica made her venture into cross-border trading in Mozambique, bringing rice and cooking oil, later sandals and shoes, to sell back in Harare, where she had a market stall in a flea-market area. However, in May 2005 when returning to Harare her stall had been destroyed and all the goods taken. Then, on short notice, the house where she lived with her two children was also destroyed. The 'Tsunami' struck her twice; 'and they said it was a clean-up!' It left her not knowing what to do. When her Mozambican family learnt about what had happened, they put together and sent enough money for her to travel with her children to Manica by bus, once again through the border crossing at Machipanda. She 'came with nothing', since the 'Tsunami' had destroyed all her capital, and started to look for work. But to find a more or less permanent job to make a living turned out to involve a series of new challenges.

The majority of the Zimbabweans who have left the country since 2000 have headed for South Africa. Many have also gone to Botswana, the UK, and the USA (Raftopoulos 2009, 222). What characterises many of the Zimbabweans who have ended up in Mozambique is in this context that they actually 'came with nothing'. Some, because they – like Laura – left Zimbabwe in a situation of loss and desperation; others because their economic resources were already exhausted, and they knew they had to pay for a passport, in addition to transport, and maybe bribes, not only to go overseas, but also to cross into South Africa. Not only for people in the border provinces but also in major cities like Harare, Mozambique increasingly appeared as an option when they found the situation in Zimbabwe unbearable.

3   Some Economic Aspects of Border Crossing

Both Nelson and Laura were involved in cross-border trade as a source of livelihood *in* Zimbabwe before eventually seeking refuge and a new life in Mozambique. They only came when the foundations of their lives had been seriously shattered. The fact that they eventually decided to leave Zimbabwe for Mozambique, should, however, also be understood against the backdrop of shifts in the economic development in the two countries. According to the World Bank (2010), GDP per capita in Zimbabwe was in the year 2000 calculated to USD 594, while it was USD 234 per capita in Mozambique. Annual growth rates, then, show different trajectories: For Mozambique, in 2001 the annual growth rate per capita was 9 per cent and 3 per cent in 2003, while for Zimbabwe it was *minus* 3 per cent (2001) and *minus* 10 per cent (2003). By 2005, the calculated GDP per capita in Zimbabwe had fallen to USD 274 while it had increased to USD 320 in Mozambique, and thus surpassed the GDP of Zimbabwe (World Bank 2010). Between 2000 and 2005 formal employment in Zimbabwe was further estimated to have shrunk by 20 per cent (Sachikonye 2006, 13). The flip side of the coin was the marked expansion in the informal economy – ranging from flea-markets and individual travellers providing basic food from neighbouring countries, to black-market foreign currency transactions and illegal mineral extraction, including gold panning in the border areas in Manica Province.

From 2005 onwards, a steadily aggravating political and economic crisis in Zimbabwe resulted in a continuous flux of people crossing the border back and forth. Many only came to buy basic commodities to bring back to Zimbabwe, where the shelves in the grocery shops were usually empty. Some, like Nelson and Laura, would enter Mozambique at the formal border crossing point at Machipanda. In this period of economic and political crisis in Zimbabwe, the formal visa requirements for passing the border were relaxed, with the introduction of one-day border passes for citizens without passports (Kiwanuka and Monson 2009). Large numbers of Zimbabweans depended either on food aid, on relatives travelling to neighbouring countries as informal traders, or on remittances from migrant family members. According to Raftopoulos (2009, 222): 'In 2005/6 it was estimated that half of the families in the two major cities of Zimbabwe were in receipt of remittances from workers in the diaspora'.

Since the defeat in the 2000 constitutional referendum, ZANU-PF had increasingly used 'race and the unequal division of land' in a political mobilisation taking the shape of a 'redefined nationalism' (Alexander 2006, 11). The party and its leader, President Mugabe, furthermore represented its stance as 'part of a longer history or pan-Africanist and anti-imperialist struggles' (Raftopoulos 2009, 202). At the same time, the opposition mobilised around the Movement for Democratic Change (MDC), formed as 'a multi-class, cross-racial alliance', which focused on labour issues and human rights, and confronted the state with 'a language of democratisation' (ibid., 211).

The Zimbabwean elections in 2008 were followed with intense interest – and growing concern – by international media. Taking place in March, and including both parliamentary and presidential elections, the results were released in April, after a month's delay. They showed that after 28 years in government, ZANU-PF had lost its majority position in parliament, while none of the presidential candidates had received an absolute majority of votes. A presidential run-off was called, followed by an up-scaling of violence that, according to Raftopoulos (2009, 229), was 'inflicted by the ruling party on the electorate, as punishment for its loss in the March election and as a warning against the repeat of such a vote'. During this period, the number of people crossing the border into Mozambique peaked, and the presence of Zimbabweans in the border areas became highly visible. In the border town of Vila de Manica the streets were lined with young men equipped with portable stalls trying to sell soap, sugar, cigarettes or sweets; but ready to fold up their stalls and run when the Mozambican police appeared. The whole town was, somehow, involved in a desperate struggle for survival on the one hand, and control of an escalating influx of people, on the other.

In the Manica area, people living on both sides of the border would still cross the border 'informally', on foot, following the narrow paths like they had 'always' done, through the forests, hills or mountain passes of the Chimanimani mountains. There is a long history of cross-border interactions and trade in the Manica area, as well as of violent conflict and expansionist politics. In the late 1880s, Cecil Rhodes formed the British South Africa Company to promote British colonisation of the area, while the *Companhia de Moçambique* (Mozambique Company) was established to expand Portuguese control between the Zambezi River in the north and the Sabi River in the south (Newitt 1995, 369). The present-day border was established through a 1891 treaty between Portugal and the British, settling the 'mini-scramble for Manyika' (Bhila 1982, 232). Different dynamics and histories of cross-border relations in the Manica area have been extensively described (e.g. Alexander 1997; Hughes 1999; Tornimbeni 2007) and in this literature a shift can be identified when comparing accounts from the 1990s and after 2000: While Hughes (1999, 544) reports that Zimbabweans in the border community of Vhimba in Chimanimani 'could hardly imagine fleeing to a land they identified as backward, violent and poor', Tornimbeni (2007, 498) refers to a recent flow of Zimbabweans, though 'their number is unknown' in his analysis of the politics of land and human mobility in TseTserra on the Mozambican side.

In October 2008, I crossed the border in the opposite direction of most people these days, from Mozambique into Zimbabwe, using one of the footpaths in the Chimanimani. At this time, a cholera epidemic had broken out, adding to Zimbabwe's economic and political crisis – cholera deaths also being reported in the border communities on the Mozambican side. In interviews on the Zimbabwean side, I learnt that they had to walk over to Mozambique to get basic commodities, such as sugar, cooking oil, and soap. They would usually cross over to Mozambique on foot once a week, or once every two weeks. Sitting at the edge of a family field ready for planting, with harvest time only the coming year, we all looked at the path leading back to Mozambique, which from this perspective seemed like a haven of plenty and safety. Back in Manica

Province in the late afternoon, heading towards Chimoio on the dusty roads of Sussundenga District, we saw lines of minibuses – *chapas* – overloaded with people and large bundles and bags of commodities heading in the opposite direction, towards the sunset and the Zimbabwean border.

In the account presented here, the local cross-border interactions and movements constitute a more long-term backdrop to the sudden large-scale influx of Zimbabweans crossing the border in search of food, income, or refuge in Mozambique. It was the total influx of people, the local and longer-distance cross-border movements combined, which surged during the first decade of the 2000s, reaching a peak in the year 2008.

4   Perspectives in the Mozambican Media

How was the situation in the border areas with Zimbabwe in this period perceived and represented in Maputo – by the Government, in the media, or in public debate? In Nyamnjoh's work (2005, 4), he holds that 'in Africa the so-called old media are yet to take over from the indigenous forms of communication'. Rønning (2009, 254f), focusing more specifically on the influence of the media in Mozambique, sustains that being still an elite medium, newspapers voice different views and conflicts 'between different subgroups and factions of the politico-economic elite'. When playing such a role, the press is, according to Rønning, buttressed by a Press Law (*Lei no 18/91*) which is considered one of the most liberal in Africa (2009, 249).

Analysing newspapers from 2007 to 2009, I found that the Mozambican press did neither give any broad coverage to the situation *within* Zimbabwe, nor to the political challenges presented to the Mozambican government as a result of Zimbabwe's economic and political crisis. The exception was the period of Zimbabwean elections of 2008, when, suddenly, the media's attention was directed, not only towards the political contest itself, but also to the responses of the regional political forums of the SADC.[8] A number of newspapers closely followed the post-election process in Zimbabwe, providing their audience with somewhat diverse interpretations of the situation as it developed.[9] In April 2008, an extraordinary summit of SADC was called in Lusaka to

---

8 Southern African Development Community.

9 This section is based on a systematic reading of the following Mozambican newspapers: *Notícias, O País, Zambeze, Diário de Moçambique* and *SAVANA*. While *Notícias* is the official newspaper and is still government controlled, *O País, Zambeze, Diário de Moçambique* and *SAVANA* are independent newspapers owned by private media groups or cooperatives.

discuss the situation in Zimbabwe after the first round of elections. After this summit, the Maputo-based weekly paper *SAVANA* reproached the participants for not taking a clear stance and leaving the summit with 'their hands full of nothing' [*as mãos cheias de nada*].[10] The editorial of the newspaper *Zambeze* directed its criticism more directly towards President Mugabe, with a warning about 'what is happening here next door in our neighbouring Zimbabwe'.[11] *Zambeze,* alleged that this was not only 'a flagrant case of abuse of power and an undisguised violation of justice and the fundamental democratic rights of the people of that country, but also a signal of warning that something very serious is happening in our region...'.[12] *Zambeze* also took a step further, drawing a comparison with the Mozambican elections in 1999 and alleging parallel cases of rigging of election results in the two countries:

> If in this Zimbabwean electoral process of 2008, the manoeuvre used has been the recounting of votes, some nine years earlier, in Mozambique, the counting of votes was interrupted in order to make possible a cooking of results that it was convenient to announce...[13]

The following week, on 23 April, President Mugabe's main opponent in the elections, Morgan Tsvangirai, landed at Maputo Airport in a tour of regional capitals. He was still waiting for the release of the results of the presidential elections on 29 March. Reporting from the visit, *Zambeze* draws another parallel, between the role of Renamo's leader Afonso Dhlakama in Mozambique, and that of Morgan Tsvangirai as the leader of MDC in Zimbabwe. As the candidate who had most likely won the first round of elections, Tsvangirai is solemnly received by the leader of the Mozambican opposition 'in his office'.[14] After meeting with Dhlakama, Tsvangirai also met with Joaquim Chissano – in his capacity as leader of the Forum of former presidents in Africa. Chissano, however, was very cautious in giving any explicit interpretation of the situation

---

10   'Flashes da Cimeira de Lusaka', *SAVANA* 18.04.2008. All translations from Portuguese by the author of this chapter.

11   'Democratização sempre adiada: África Austral precisa urgentemente de novas mentalidades', Editorial, *Zambeze* 17.04.2008.

12   *Zambeze*, ibid.

13   *Zambeze,* ibid. The official results of the elections in Mozambique in 1999 was that the governing Frelimo got 48,55 per cent of the votes in the Parliamentary elections, while the opposition's RENAMO-UE got 38,7. In the presidential elections, Frelimo's candidate Joaquim Chissano got 52,3 per cent of the valid votes, while Renamo's Afonso Dhlakama got 47,7. As much as 9,37 per cent of the votes were categorized as invalid (nule).

14   'Eleições no Zimbabwe continuam a mexer: Morgan Tsvangirai não aceitará nenhuma 2ª volta nas presidenciais', *Zambeze* 24.04.2008.

in Zimbabwe. After meeting Tsvangirai, he said to *SAVANA*: 'We will follow the situation and will be in contact when possible, but for the time being we can do nothing more'.[15] Finally, Tsvangirai had a brief meeting with the Mozambican President Guebuza, whose office had apparently been very reluctant to organize such a meeting, and where Tsvangirai was received 'through the back door'.[16]

During the same week, a public meeting in Maputo to discuss the situation in Zimbabwe is also reported in the media. Several panellists thought that the line of silent diplomacy followed by SADC should continue until 'all peaceful means have been exhausted'.[17] Others held that in this process, SADC had been badly discredited. A common concern was, however, the need to avoid an escalation of violence, with the post-election violence in Kenya in January 2008 looming as a worst-case scenario. At the meeting, '... all agreed that it is necessary to avoid a war in Zimbabwe'. More generally, it was observed that:

> ... Africa is at the moment going through a 'phase of transition in leadership' in the sense that those who have governed since independence are or at least should now be 'giving room for leaders from the new generation'...[18]

On 26 April, the Beira-based newspaper *Diário de Moçambique* also gave a summary of different positions voiced at the Maputo meeting concerning Zimbabwe. *Diário* points out that the fact that Morgan Tsvangirai was eventually received by President Guebuza means that 'Mozambique recognises the existence of a *real crisis* in this African country'.[19]

The newspapers concur in referring to the existence of particularly close links between Mozambique and Zimbabwe, their personification being the relationship between the leaders of the struggle for independence, Samora Machel and Robert Mugabe. As key historical figures they are, in a sense, placed in a sphere beyond mundane criticism. In Mozambique, Machel is already an icon and serves as a symbol, not only of the achievements of Independence, but for many also as a symbol of the earlier – true and uncorrupted – Frelimo party. In the case of Mugabe, the situation was different. He was still an active politician, and an increasingly controversial president struggling to stay in power.

---

15   'Guebuza recebe Tsangirai pela porta dos fundos: Gaffe diplomática', *SAVANA* 25.04.2008.
16   *SAVANA,* ibid.
17   'SADC é cúmplice?', *O País* 25.04.2008.
18   *O País,* ibid.
19   Emphasis in original. 'Maputo reconhece "crise real" no Zimbabwe', *Diário de Moçambique* 26.04.2008.

What we can observe when analysing Mozambican media reports on Zimbabwe during April and May 2008, is that political contradictions, parallels, and dilemmas literally flood the printed pages. But the historical relationship between the freedom fighters makes it difficult to relate in any un-biased way to a neighbouring country in severe crisis. In *SAVANA,* on 2 May 2008, the outspoken columnist Machado da Graça questions the 'silence'. Under the heading '*Are we going to continue being silent?*' [*Continuamos em silêncio?*] he directs his criticism towards Mozambican civil society regarding Zimbabwe:

> ...it remains regrettable, this lack of response on the part of our Civil Society when confronted with what is happening. As far as I know, it is only the Mozambican Human Rights League [*Liga Moçambicana dos Direitos Humanos*] that has spoken out loudly. It is time that more voices join in [...] to say publicly that what is happening in Zimbabwe is completely unacceptable and should stop immediately.[20]

During my fieldwork in Manica, in an interview with a representative for one of the locally based NGOs, I understood that they actually tried to target humanitarian migrants from Zimbabwe. But they were 'closely monitored' by the Mozambican Government, and had to keep their activities targeting Zimbabweans 'within certain limits' to be able to continue working. Turning the *SAVANA* columnist's question back to the press: How did they report on the situation of Zimbabweans who are *in* Mozambique as a result of the 'completely unacceptable' situation? In 2007, *SAVANA* gave the following information on the – then – economic situation in Zimbabwe:

> The economy of Zimbabwe is at present among the most devastated in the world, as represented in the highest inflation rate on the planet (7000 per cent) [...] Since 2000 there is a deep crisis, in addition to the hyper-inflation, a high unemployment rate, poverty, and a chronic lack of fuel, food and foreign currency.[21]

This information was, however, given under the heading: 'Zimbabwean prostitutes assaulting Manica and Sofala' [*Prostitutas zimbabweanas assaltam Manica e Sofala*], and the story of the article was an – alleged – open quarrel between a Zimbabwean and a Mozambican woman, both involved in sex work in Beira:

---

20   Machado da Graça: 'Continuamos em silêncio?' *SAVANA* 02.05.2008.
21   'Crise económica na terra de Mugabe: Prostitutas zimbabweanas assaltam Manica e Sofala', *SAVANA* 02.11.2007.

Angry and shouting, the Mozambican woman accused the Zimbabwean of taking her client and charging too low rates. 'It is a disloyal competition. These Zimbabweans are destroying our business', she claimed.[22]

In addition to the gendered bias of this particular representation of the 'Zimbabwean issue', it is worth noticing the virtual absence of the issue in the official daily newspaper in Mozambique, *Notícias*. While this absence may reflect the Mozambican Government's support for SADC's 'silent diplomacy' approach to Zimbabwe, one could still argue that such support does not have to be silent. Why, then, this absence of official voices on the 'Zimbabwe issue' in the Mozambican media? In 2008, the independent press in Mozambique actually initiated a debate, but the official media, including *Notícias*, did not respond. Maybe the Zimbabwean crisis presented a mirror reflecting political challenges that Frelimo itself also fears, and for that reason kept silent?

5   Shelter from a Crisis

On May 2, 2008, the Electoral Commission in Zimbabwe announced that Mugabe and Tsvangirai had received respectively 43.2 and 47.9 per cent of the votes in the presidential elections. With these results, a second round of presidential elections was announced to take place on June 27, 2008 (ICG 2008:5). ZANU-PF's response to Mugabe losing the first round of elections was to launch a systematic campaign of violence, seeking to dismantle opposition structures and intimidate opposition activists and voters (ICG 2008:6). One of my key Mozambican informants in Manica District, which I will call *A*, had meanwhile, with growing concern, observed the influx of Zimbabweans into Mozambique:

> A lot of people came over the border, from March onwards. They came fleeing – beaten, burnt... But then we believed the problem would be solved with the second round of elections... There were whole families who came crossing over. Early in the morning, we could see people walking in the forest, Zimbabweans, carrying something to sell to get food. They may not have been allowed to cross the border. But the forest has many paths... After the second election day ... there were thousands coming, thousands! Desperate. Many, most of them, to get food.

---

22   *SAVANA*, ibid, 02.11.2007.

A also mentions another, contrasting cross-border phenomenon: Buses of Mugabe-supporters, with people wearing t-shirts saying *I am with Mugabe* crossing at Machipanda during the period of elections. These were people 'with money in hand' [*com dinheiro na mão*], heading for the Shoprite supermarket in the provincial capital of Chimoio. 'Shoprite is huge, but they emptied the place...', *A* observed.

By April 2009, most of the young men lining the streets of Vila de Manica in 2008 had either returned to Zimbabwe or travelled further into Mozambique. But some of the women had stayed behind in Manica. Around 80 – some of them with children – were living in the former waiting hall of the old railway station. They were sleeping on pieces of cardboard on the cement floor, each occupying a few square meters with a bundle of clothes or a couple of plastic bags. They told me they were trying to make some money by cooking snacks, *sadza*,[23] to sell (for MZN 10) at the local market.[24] Many had come 'through the bush' instead of through a formal border crossing, and had neither passports nor identity papers.

Joyce was among these and had come to Manica in late 2007. Growing up in a small town on the road between Harare and Bulawayo, she had been to college, where she studied interior decoration. But in the middle of an economic crisis, it was impossible to find a job in interior decoration. With no income, 'there was no food'. And in 2007, even with the salary of a normal job you could not buy anything, she said. Joyce started travelling to Botswana to buy and sell commodities. When she first came to Mozambique, it was because some people said it was 'easy to cross the border' and 'it is very cheap in Mozambique'. While she stayed in Manica, the situation in Zimbabwe deteriorated. In Mozambique she earned at least some money, but it was a mixed experience:

> You know, the Mozambicans ... most of them are so friendly. Just the police, they come at night and say they want money ... If you walk at night, they will take your money; they ask you *50 mil*.[25] Only if you have got a passport, they won't. You keep on working [selling *sadza* at *10 mil*]... They ask you *50 mil* every time. They are too rough, the policemen; and especially those *guarda fronteiras* [border guards], you know them? I think they harass us because we have got poverty in Zimbabwe. That is why they harass us. If South Africans come here to stay, they don't do that.

---

23   Cooked as a sort of dumplings.

24   MZN 10 at the time equalled USD 0,30.

25   That is, MZN 50. The amount known to be charged by Zimbabwean sex workers was approximately MZN 30–50.

> Because South Africans, they have got everything... I'm struggling. Mozambique is too tough.

The women at the Manica railway station describe a situation of desperation, and serious contradictions. In their report, Kiwanuka and Monson say that it is a 'widespread belief that the majority of women migrants are sex workers', and therefore they are 'often targeted for police harassment, arrest and deportation' (2009, 44). Another of my key informants in a local civil society organisation working with health and HIV prevention, let me call her *B*, says that among the women sex workers, the majority actually have children and family in Zimbabwe, who depend on the remittances they are able to send or bring with them back home. Their families in Zimbabwe are often unaware of what 'trade' they are involved in across the border. However, according to B, only a limited number of Zimbabwean migrants were actually involved in sex work. Her estimates were about thirty women in Chimoio and twenty in Vila de Manica. Still, all the Zimbabwean women I interviewed in Manica had, in some way or other, to deal with the reputation of Zimbabwean women being involved in prostitution.

The 'gendered' actions of the Mozambican police, aimed at targeting – assumed or real – Zimbabwean sex workers, reflect the broader political context: In Mozambican media, the migration of livelihood-seeking Zimbabweans into Mozambique has been represented as an influx of women engaged in prostitution – which is an illegal activity. This particular focus becomes an element in a more general misrepresentation of the Zimbabwean issue. Another of my informants among civil society workers in Manica, let me call him *C*, illustrates this point with an example: 'One day, 20 Zimbabweans may be captured as "illegal migrants" at the border; or the police may arrest 40 for deportation or repatriation'. These actions may be met with acclaim by their superiors in the police hierarchy. At the same time, these police actions contribute to misrepresent the real scale and complexity of the problem, according to *C*. The fact that the Zimbabwean crisis has driven large numbers across the border '... is not an issue in the Government's official discourse'. The Government 'is not interested in recognising that there *are* refugees ... in spite of seeing the problem. For political reasons, they don't want to recognize it'. And *C* concluded: 'It takes a lot of courage to contradict the official discourse'.

6   Mozambique is Too Tough?

Can we talk about a clearly defined *domestic policy* towards the Zimbabweans who crossed into Mozambique? My informant *C* claimed: 'The Government holds that local society, local communities, can absorb this population'.[26] When insisting that these people would 'naturally' merge into the local population, it also referred to the historical connections and cross-border relationships between (present-day) Mozambique and Zimbabwe. These relationships have, in turn, been facilitated by the use of the same, or mutually comprehensible, local languages. In Zimbabwe, in addition to English, *Shona* is a national language, together with *Ndebele*. Most Zimbabweans speak or at least understand 'modern Shona', which represents a standard in relation to a continuum of closely related varieties or 'dialects', including Ndau and Manyika. In Manica Province in Mozambique, a majority of the population speaks what from a Zimbabwean perspective can be classified as Shona dialects, such as *Ndau/Cindau* (29%), *Manyika/Cimanyika* (15%) and *Tewe/Citewe* (21%) – in total 65% of the population (Mwitu 1999, 14).[27] One of my Zimbabwean informants in Chimoio, *Eduardo,* said: 'It is easier in Manica Province, one speaks Shona, one speaks in Cimanyika, and they can understand each other easily'. In informal settings, at the market, making contacts and communicating with local people, Zimbabweans easily get along with Shona. But, Eduardo continued, in Mozambique, 'when you go into somebody's office, you have to speak in Portuguese... the paperwork here, it is all in Portuguese'. None of the Zimbabweans I met knew any Portuguese before they came. Most shared the experience of acute helplessness, not being able to understand or communicate in the official language in critical situations. Or having to pay; as several Zimbabweans told me: 'The police stops to greet you *"Bom dia,"* and when you reply, they know you are not from here'.

For most of the Zimbabweans I met, going to Mozambique to seek a livelihood would have been inconceivable 10–15 years earlier. Even the children of Mozambican migrants in Zimbabwe would not learn Portuguese at home. They told me: 'Our parents did not expect us to come here', or: 'Everybody looked down on Mozambique then'. *Farah,* whose parents migrated from Mozambique to Zimbabwe in the 1960s, said that Portuguese was taught as a third language in secondary schools in Zimbabwe, but 'nobody would choose Portuguese'. After arriving in Mozambique, not knowing how to communicate in the official language was, however, only one element in the unexpected 'culture shock' experienced by the great majority of the Zimbabweans interviewed in Manica. Let me turn back to Nelson. He had regularly been travelling to Mozambique, but only seen part of Mozambican realities before he came to stay:

---

26 Both scholars and policy-makers have since the early 1990s lent support to a notion of 'emigrants as flexible opportunists', which may also be questioned (Hughes 1999, 535).

27 Figures based on the 1997 General Census in Mozambique.

I didn't even know what to expect... But I was shocked... When I came
here, it was a nightmare. I had never been to the residential areas, only
Shoprite and the highway. When I came, the place I went to stay... to sleep
on the floor, sharing one blanket... I sold my phone to contribute, for the
lodging. With a small job, I got enough to buy soap to have my clothes
washed... But we have to adapt, there is no choice!

7   The Political Construction of Invisibility

From the 1980s onwards, post-independence political leaders in many African
states – including Mozambique and Zimbabwe – struggled under the pressure
of neoliberal economic and political principles imposed from the outside (Alexander 2006; Hanlon and Smart 2008). After the implementation of the so-
called 'rolling back of the state', according to Dorman, Hammett, and Nugent
(2007, 20), one way for political leaders to deal with the political challenges
confronting the 'unstable and fragmented' states that were the outcome of
these processes, was to claim control over the definition of citizenship and
nationhood. An effective way of maintaining such control is to 'cast a negative other against which to rally their nation' (ibid.). Under the pressure of
multi-party elections, political leaders have 'sought to manipulate citizenship
and redefine nationhood; making nations by creating strangers' (ibid., 8). This
perspective may explain aspects of the political processes that over the last
decade have shaped the complex crisis Zimbabwe. Beginning in the 1990s, the
category of strangers in Zimbabwe increasingly seems to have merged with
that of internal enemies. Also in local communities, especially where the pressure on land is high, it was reported that membership was increasingly been
defined in exclusive, and at times violent, terms (Alexander 2006, 183).

Why does the internal political development in Mozambique during the last
decades seem to have taken another path? On the one hand, the country has
struggled to recover from the disastrous civil war. When the established political leadership look across the border to Zimbabwe, what they (want to) see is
a mirror of themselves as historic and heroic freedomfighters in the position
of political power. At the same time, the devastating outcomes of the struggle
of the Zimbabwean political leadership to *stay* in power has presented the Mozambican political leadership with some real challenges; including how to deal
with the increasing flow of immigrants across the border. My argument here
has been that the response of the Mozambican political elite has to a very limited extent been to cast the Zimbabwean migrants as 'negative others'. Rather,

we have seen the construction of *invisibility* to deal with the fact that large numbers of people have fled the neighbouring state led by the elder freedom fighter. The Mozambican central authorities' non-recognition of the Zimbabwean crisis through rendering Zimbabwean migrants officially *invisible* also has its local – and more concrete – parallels. Almost all the Zimbabweans I interviewed in Manica had acquired Mozambican identity papers – most of them illegally through paying local officials to get identity papers documenting that *X* was born in Mozambique by Mozambican parents, or stating that *X* is a Mozambican citizen. For Zimbabweans with means, this has been considered a necessity in order to sustain a livelihood. Those who have been unable to acquire such papers, like the women at the old train station in Manica, become extremely vulnerable, facing dire problems of survival in Mozambique.

The practices of the local 'corrupt officials' can in fact be seen as local responses in line with the national policy towards Zimbabwean migrants. Making Mozambican identity papers easily available at a reasonable price, some local officials contribute in their own way to make the Zimbabweans invisible *as Zimbabwean citizens* in Mozambique. With Mozambican identity papers the immigrants have – voluntarily or not – officially merged into the local population. They cannot any longer be registered as Zimbabweans, even if Mozambican authorities at some point should wish to do so, and make the 'invisible' Zimbabwean issue into more visible statistics.

This chapter has described some of the social and political dynamics associated with the large-scale influx of Zimbabweans into the Mozambican border province of Manica during the first decade of this century. The analysis of individuals' narratives and national press stories point to a regional political situation, in which Manica Province is part of a much larger 'political field' (Bertelsen 2016). The chapter has also underlined that Zimbabwe became enmeshed in escalating economic and political processes of 'exclusion', associated with violent – but nevertheless government-supported – 'counter movements' (Hall, Hirsch and Li 2011, 9) to the established commoditization of land. In a comparative perspective, it may be necessary to look beyond the 'creation of strangers' in the struggle over nationhood and power in Zimbabwe, and look at the processes of exclusion regarding landownership in both countries. In Mozambique, the exclusionary dynamics that usually accompany contemporary processes of large-scale conversion of land into some form of private property is still in an incipient phase. However, with the powers of commoditization and exclusion increasingly structuring access to land in Mozambique, the 'inclusive' use and manipulation of citizenship described here may also soon become a feature of the past.

References

Alexander, Jocelyn. 1997. The local state in post-war Mozambique. *Africa* 67 (2): 1–26.

Alexander, Jocelyn. 2006. *The Unsettled Land.* Oxford: James Currey.

Bertelsen, Bjørn Enge. 2016. *Violent Becomings:* State Formation, Sociality, and Power in Mozambique. New York: Berghahn Books.

Bhila, Hoyni H.K. 1982. *Trade and Politics in a Shona Kingdom.* Harlow: Longman.

Dorman, Sara, Daniel Hammett, and Paul Nugent. 2007. Introduction: Citizenship and its Casualties in Africa, in *Making Nations, Creating Strangers: States and citizenship in Africa,* ed. Sara Dorman, Daniel Hammett and Paul Nugent, 3–26. Leiden: Brill.

Hall, Derek, Philip Hirsch, and M. Li. Tania 2011. *Powers of Exclusion.* Singapore: NUS Press.

Hammar, Amanda 2010. Ambivalent Mobilities: Zimbabwean Commercial Farmers in Mozambique. *Journal of Southern African Studies* 36 (2): 395–416.

Hanlon, Joseph, and Teresa Smart. 2008. *Há Mais Bicicletas – Mas Há Desenvolvimento?* Maputo: Missanga/CIEDIMA.

Hughes, David McDermott. 1999. Refugees and Squatters. *Journal of Southern African Studies* 25 (4): 533–552.

ICG. 2005. Zimbabwe's Operation Murambatsvina. *Africa Report* No 97, 17 August 2005. https://www.africaportal.org/publications/zimbabwes-operation-murambatsvina -the-tipping-point, accessed 10 August 2018.

ICG. 2008. *Negotiating Zimbabwe's Transition.* International Crisis Group Policy Brief- ing, 21 May 2008. https://www.files.ethz.ch/isn/55937/b51_negotiating_zimbabwes _transition.pdf, accessed 10 August 2018.

IDMC. 2008. *The Many Faces of Displacement: IDPs in Zimbabwe.* Internal Displace- ment Monitoring Centre, Geneva. http://www.internal-displacement.org, accessed 5 February 2010.

Kiwanuka, Monica, and Tamlyn Monson. 2009. *Zimbabwean Migration into Southern Africa.* Report, Forced Migration Studies Programme, WITS University, Johannes- burg, November 2009.

Manica. 2006. Manica: miracle or mirage? *Mozambiquefile – AIM* No. 360, July 2006.

Mwitu, Juliana C. 1999. *Situação Linguística de Moçambique.* Maputo: KEPA.

Newitt, Malyn. 1995. *A History of Mozambique.* London: Hurst & Company.

Nyamnjoh, Francis B. 2005. *Africa's Media, Democracy and the Politics of Belonging.* London: Zed Books.

Raftopoulos, Brian. 2009. The Crisis in Zimbabwe, 1998–2008. In *Becoming Zimbabwe,* ed. Brian Raftopoulos and Alois Mlambo, 201–232. Harare and Johannesburg: Weav- er Press and Jacana.

Rønning, Helge. 2009. The Influence of the Media. In *The Power of Communication: changes and challenges in African media,* ed. Kristin S. Orgeret and Helge Rønning, 1–22. Oslo: Unipub.

Sachikonye, Lloyd M. 2006. *The Impact of Operation Murambatsvina/Clean Up on the Working People in Zimbabwe*. Report, March 2006. http://archive.niza.nl/docs/200608281522024680.pdf, accessed August 10 2018.

Tornimbeni, Corrado. 2007. 'Isto foi sempre assim': The Politics of Land and Human Mobility in Chimanimani, Central Mozambique. *Journal of Southern African Studies* 33 (3): 485–500.

UNHCR. 2008. *Map of Zimbabwe situation*. Detailed map, 23 June. http://www.unhcr.org/publications/maps/487f12012/zimbabwe-situation-map-detailed, accessed 7 August 2018.

UNHCR. 2010. *Mozambique: 2010 Regional Operations Profile – Southern Africa*. http://www.unhcr.org, accessed 29 January 2010.

World Bank. 2010. *WDI Online – World Development Indicators*. http://documents.worldbank.org, accessed 8 August 2018.

CHAPTER 3

From Celebrating Female Emancipation to Emplacing Emperor Ngungunyane: Remoulding the Past in Mozambican National Narratology

Bjørn Enge Bertelsen

Reflecting a general pattern, Mozambique has been the subject of intense nation-building processes throughout the entire postcolonial era. Following the country's 1975 liberation from Portuguese colonial domination, FRELIMO (*Frente de Libertação de Moçambique*, Front for the Liberation of Mozambique) embarked on a politically informed full-scale transformation of the former colony (Newitt 1995). As in other contexts of rapid and dramatic political transformation, violence, and regime shifts, the Mozambican postcolonial era involved varied attempts to re-cast the nation's past, present, and future. Such a process of continued re-molding is integral to what can be called a 'national narratology' of Mozambique – a process fomented primarily by Frelimo, both in its initial guise as a political movement and thereafter as it re-constituted itself as a revolutionary political party from 1977 onwards.

However, the narration of a Mozambican past fit for the revolutionary present following independence was also significantly shaped by the country's defiance in the face of military and political aggression from the racist, white minority regimes of Rhodesia, South Africa, and other countries in the region and beyond.[1] Radical postcolonial politics in Mozambique in the face of external (and, with time, internal) aggression, its colonial legacy and, of course, the civil war (1976–1992) with RENAMO (*Resistência Nacional Moçambicana*, Mozambican National Resistance) have jointly produced complex, multiple, and intense processes of narration at different societal levels and in various domains. These trajectories have meant, for instance, that the politics of memory is part and parcel of political debate, as experienced during national election campaigns when historically informed accusations are frequently exchanged between Renamo and Frelimo candidates. At the local level – as

---

1 Political regimes that historically supported aggression against independent Mozambique included, for instance, Malawi and Kenya (Hedges 1989; Dinerman 1994). As observed by Austin (1994), several rightwing and Christian organizations in the United States and Europe also supported RENAMO during different periods.

I found in a study of Manica Province, a rural community close to Chimoio[2] (Bertelsen 2002, 2016) – conflicting versions of historical events and allegiances have translated into tense and multiple processes of narration and silence.

This chapter, however, analyses narration neither in terms of a Renamo–Frelimo dichotomy (Cahen 2002), nor in strict literary terms (see, for instance, Laban 1998; Saúte 1998; Rosário 2008, or numerous chapters in this volume); nor does it analyse narration in the sense of popular accounts of past violence (see Gersony 1988; Magaia 1988). Instead, it approaches narration from two directions: firstly, in terms of the changing semiotics of urban state space and, secondly, as a collective and heterogeneous social practice beyond state narratology. Empirically and specifically, it explores the case of a recent change to the name of a public square in Chimoio (and associated reactions to the change), from Praça da OMM[3] to Praça Gungunhana. It does so in order to elucidate crucial processes of transformation in Mozambican state narratology. It will be argued here that such changes demonstrate that *narration* of the past must be seen as linked both to state formation in general and to processes of territorialisation of state power more specifically. As Feldman has pointed-ed out (2004, 164–165), powerful state-dominated processes – as that of the postcolonial Mozambican period – is characterized by 'politicized anamnesis [which] constantly requires the re-auditing of "residual" marginal, repressed, denied, and unreconciled historical fragments that can call the present into question, and to political accountability'. It is important that we recognize the challenges imposed on such state-driven processes by subversive and alternative memories.

1   The Epic: State Formation, Narratology and Territorialisation

My anthropological work has shown that not only is memory of the past present – sometimes painfully so (Broch-Due and Bertelsen 2016) – but also that its force assumes multiple forms.[4] For instance, civil war violence has been transmogrified into various forms following peace in 1992, and aspects of the past continuously impinge on the present in this regard: from popular

---

2   Manica Province is located in Mozambique's eastern and central part bordering Zimbabwe.

3   OMM is an acronym for *Organização da Mulher Moçambicana* (Mozambique Woman's Organization), Frelimo's feminine organisation.

4   From 1998 I have undertaken numerous periods of urban and rural fieldwork in and around the provincial capital of Chimoio, Manica Province, with the most recent fieldwork there carried out in January 2016. In addition, multiple fieldworks have been carried out in Maputo between 2012 and 2017.

accounts that have been told in efforts to regain, re-enact, and re-generate the dynamics of the social (Bertelsen 2002) to the ways in which the past has been present – and kept alive – in bellicose rhetoric during election campaigns (Bertelsen 2004a, 2004b). However, such preoccupation with the past is not only concerned with civil war violence or the colonial era (see, for example, Zimba *et al.* 2006). As has been shown in other studies, it also addresses processes of state formation and the social dynamics of the traditional field (Igreja 2014; Bertelsen 2016). Such processes are crucial for understanding recurring spates of lynchings (Serra 2008; Bertelsen 2009a), imaginaries and experiences of punishment (Bertelsen 2011), incidents of police violence (Bertelsen 2009b) or in the dynamics of public unrest, demonstrations or urban uprisings (Bertelsen 2014, 2018).

The relevance of a memorialized past transcends such domains, however, and this chapter addresses a facet that I found striking when arriving for the first time in Mozambique in 1998: the past was not only a powerful domain of collective and individual memory but also a realm with which the Mozambican state was energetically and visibly concerned. Such engagement was perhaps most apparent in the urban spaces where numerous murals depicted both key past events and aspirations for future developments. As Sahlström (1990) has asserted, in analysing the graphic expressions of revolutionary posters in Ethiopia and Mozambique – and as Deleuze and Guattari (1980) have argued more generally – recent and emerging regimes are oriented towards re-inscribing their spaces through territorialisation. In the case of newly independent Mozambique, this involved aspirations towards the de-territorialisation of the semiotics of the Portuguese colonial regime, including urban relics, spaces and murals.

Indeed, murals are a key expression for and format of such an ambition of de-territorializing the colonial visual expression and replacing this with inscribing a sequenced national past in its place. Commonly, these post-independent murals are awarded key spots in the urban landscape in almost all parts of Mozambique, usually in the *Praça dos heróis* (Heroes' Square) that are found across the country. Taking the mural in Chimoio as an example, national Mozambican history is represented and sequenced here in squared paintings, moving from left to right, as follows: an image of colonial repression (Africans behind bars, whips being swung, barbed wire) with a nascent resistance movement hinted at on the right-hand side; a depiction of the formation of a national liberation movement under a national flag and the leadership of Frelimo's first president Eduardo Mondlane (1920–1969), with the first guerrillas from liberation movement retreating into the forest on the painting's right-hand side; a description of full-fledged war against the Portuguese colonizers – a struggle encompassing women and men, peasants and guerrillas; a mural depicting a mature liberation movement, with guerrillas sporting uniforms and attacking in formation, under the leadership of legendary Frelimo leader and Mozambican first president Samora Machel (1933–1986); a depiction of Portuguese colonial troops in retreat from the onslaught of the liberation movement, led by much-despised General Kaúlza de Oliveira de Arriaga (1915–2004), who commanded the military campaign in Mozambique between 1969 and 1974; and a final mural depicting the apotheosis of liberation, centring on a triumphant Samora Machel hailed by his troops to his left and the Mozambican people to his right, with elements of what came to be the Mozambican flag in the background, including the emblematic crossed Kalashnikov and hoe.

The sequenced murals (such as the one in Chimoio) in Heroes' Squares across Mozambique encapsulate the violence of colonial repression, the heroic and collective struggle for independence, the valiant leaders of the Mozambican revolution, and the aspirations for a bright socialist future following Frelimo becoming a party in 1982. Such narration of the past, present, and future must also be understood as integral to the spatial and semiotic effects – as these were inscribed onto the urban landscape – brought about by radical change to what might be called a national cosmology in the post-independence era. Arguably, a central aim of such narration was to merge the historical liberation struggle and the ongoing battles for a socialist Mozambique with the Frelimo party and state. Or, to put it differently, it was a means by which to link and seamlessly integrate party, people (*o povo*), and nation in a tale of the country's formation, present, and future (see also Coelho 2013; Pitcher 2006).

At the level of state formation, such a merging of the past, present, and future consolidates the post-independence party in power as the wielder of the nation's master narrative. Such a narrative produces what Bakhtin (1986) termed the epic – the tale in which the past is a story of heroism, leading up to present-day rule. In Chimoio, as elsewhere in Mozambique, the postcolonial state minutely re-inscribed its urban landscapes at a range of levels in such epic narratives (Bakhtin 1986) – not confining itself to the key location of Heroes' Square. For instance, the post-independence celebration of the epic nature of the liberation struggle encompassed the re-naming of large urban territorial entities: the capital Lourenço Marques became Maputo, and Vila Pery became Chimoio. Furthermore, new names for the *bairros* typically memorialized significant dates from the heroic struggle, as in *Bairro 25 de Junho* (June 25, Independence Day), or dates selected from a more encompassing transnational socialist cosmology, as in *Bairro 1 de Maio* (May 1, International Worker's Day). Additionally, it was integral to Frelimo's vanguard politics to visually imbue public buildings – such as the interior walls of classrooms – with murals depicting familiar slogans and Frelimo logos. Such murals replaced colonial era classroom images of the president of the council and crucifixes. In schools in Chimoio, a recent display included a series of three murals in which, from left to right, there was a painting of a maize cob encircled by a mechanical gear, with the text 'Production'; the centrepiece was a version of the Frelimo logo with the text 'Frelimo' underneath an open book, with the crossed hoe and Kalashnikov; on the right was the Tanzanian logo with the text *Ujamaa* – a word meaning 'extended family' in Kiswahili but which was used to describe Tanzania's post-independent radical politics – underneath the crossed hoe and sledgehammer, as well as a burning fire underneath a red star.

These concrete inscriptions of the past – as well as the futurity of ideological aspirations, one might say – onto urban space exemplify on a semantic and iconic level Frelimo's cultivation and dissemination of the party as eternally safe-guarding the past, present, and future of the nation (see also Dinerman 2006). As Coelho (2010, 1) has argued, 'The memory of the liberation struggle in particular, has represented a powerful means both of implementing the national project and of legitimising political power, resulting in a less than flexible narrative often in tension with subaltern memories' constituting, as he has argued elsewhere, a 'liberation script' (Coelho 2013). Furthermore, this cultivation of the past is in keeping with Frelimo's appropriation and reformation of socialist state centrism, as also found in Angola and Tanzania.[5] The post-liberation re-configuration of territorial semiotics and the transformation of the urban landscape itself – sometimes conjuring novel cosmologies of epic proportions onto such spaces – are significant aspects of state formation as well as regime signifiers.[6] The vast array of semiotic-spatial techniques of inscription reveals a crucial dynamic of *capture* and *erasure/re-inscription*, which work to dis-embed meanings and memories and replace them with state insignia (Deleuze and Guattari 1980). Territorial and spatial aspects of post-independence state formation, such as those exemplified above, underline a complexity that *transcends* the cadastral demarcation of borders or technologies of urban planning.[7] Instead, these instances of deliberate change to physical as well as

---

5   The political aesthetics of socialist Mozambique are clearly shaped by historical trajectories of colonialism, indigenous art forms, and international politics, as demonstrated in Sahlström's (1990) comparison of Mozambican political posters with those from Ethiopia. See also Schwartzott, Arnfred and Meneses, and Meneses in this volume.

6   Elsewhere (Bertelsen 2002, 2016) and informed by Bakhtin (1981, 1986), I have developed the argument of 'epicness' as central to ongoing Frelimo efforts to construe itself as the collective, moral, and encompassing force that gave birth to the nation, while continuing to safeguard its existence against internal and external forces.

7   As analysed, for instance, by Sidaway and Power (1995).

semiotic space by local agents of the state can be analysed as points of entry into how the territorializing dynamics of state formation are central to narrating the Mozambican nation.

2   A Novel *Praça*

Given the above argument about the post-liberation national inscription of the past, present, and future onto urban space, it is perhaps unsurprising that a striking feature in the urban landscape in central Chimoio has been the continued up-keep of the murals in the *Praça dos heróis*. During my many fieldwork trips to the city, there has been a continuous re-painting of the murals and slogans on the school walls, and of other insignia of the epic struggle – all reflecting what one might call the Frelimo cosmology of the past. It was therefore with considerable surprise that I, and some of my interlocutors, received news about an important (but as yet incomplete) change that had been announced in Chimoio in January 2007. While no one from the Conselho Municipal in Chimoio could neither provide documents about the change of name of the place nor confirm whether this was a decision that came from Maputo or *O Partido* (the Party, a colloquial term for Frelimo), they all confirmed that the change had taken place in 2007. Moreover, at that time, many of my interlocutors increasingly made reference to *Praça Gungunhana* (Gungunhana Square), named after the Nguni ruler of Ngungunyane.[8]

Ngungunyane was the last ruler of the Gaza Empire (Wheeler 1968; Bertelsen 2012), governing vast territories in what later became Manica province and beyond. The immediate context for his rule was the Gaza state, established in 1821 in Tembe, south of today's Maputo, following political leader Soshangane's defeat of the polity of Ndandwe de Zwide. While in part antagonistic to the Portuguese colonial rule and sometimes opposing it actively, Ngungunyane is known for having sent three envoys to Lisbon in 1885, eventually negotiating a treaty between the Portuguese crown and the Gaza state – an arrangement that also secured the Gaza emperor's fiscal and trading privileges (Wheeler 1968). However, the polity under Ngungunyane's rule was unstable and ridden by civil war (1859–1862), not least in Zambézia, which contributed to the leader moving the location of the imperial capital on several occasions. The capital assumed immense importance at this time, as it was around these territorial cores that subjects were recruited to the army, and riches (often

---

8   In various texts, the name of the emperor is spelt Goungounyane, Gungunyana, Gungunhana, Gungunhama, Gungunyane, Ngungunhane, or Ngungunyana. In keeping with Gerhard Liesegang's seminal work and research (1996), I use the spelling Ngungunyane.

cattle) were amassed by the state's elite. Areas peripheral to the capital were deemed tributary and were ruled by Gaza overlords, who collected taxes in annual, often violent, sweeps. Eventually, however, the stability negotiated with Lisbon deteriorated: following a series of military battles with the Portuguese and Ngungunyane's subesequent arrest in 1895, he was subsequently taken to Lisbon and eventually exiled to the Azores, where he died in 1906 (Liesegang 1996; Bertelsen 2012).

3   (Re-)asserting Southern Dominance

Rather surprisingly, when querying interlocutors about Chimoio's novel *praça* these historical features of Ngungunyane's ascension, rule, and demise were not prominent in their responses. Rather, people were concerned that it was the *Praça da OMM* (OMM Square) – that was now, apparently, being renamed.[9] Among my interlocutors, this re-naming and re-valorisation of a prominent urban square remained a hot topic for quite some time. Many who were critical of the Frelimo government clearly interpreted it in terms of the historical dominance of the Nguni era and, more broadly, as southern Gaza power having found yet another contemporary expression. In the words of Afonso, an elderly Renamo veteran:[10]

> A: Frelimo would like to put the Shangaan [the dominant
>   ethnic group in southern Mozambique and the current Gaza
>   province] everywhere! This is not something new.
> B: But Ngungunyane – is he not from here [Chimoio]?
> A: Ah! They say that. But he is much more from the south than
>   from the centre. Samora [Machel] asked for the bones from
>   Portugal because he died in São Tomé and Principe. The
>   bones are there in Maputo.

For Afonso, the renaming in Chimoio was an insidious way of re-asserting southern primacy of the Shangaan group over the centre. This Shangaan

---

9   Although OMM's relationship to Frelimo is essential to understanding the gendered dimension of Mozambican politics and the changing role of women from the liberation struggle to the present day, it falls outside the scope of this chapter (see Katto 2014 and West 2000 for two excellent ethnographically based analyses). See also studies of the politics of gender inside and outside OMM and their ambivalent relation to Frelimo by Silva and Andrade (2000), Arthur (2004), Osório (2004), Santos (2010), Arnfred (2011) and Miedema (2016).

10   All translations from interviews are my own. Interlocutors' names have been changed because of the sometimes sensitive issues broached during fieldwork.

dominance is popularly thought to be integral to the Frelimo political dynamic, and to be historically continuous with the Gaza orientation of Nguni polities. In recalling and celebrating the brutal rule of an invading king from the south, who also enslaved many maTewe, maSena, and maNdau – ethnic groups that also constituted important parts of the Renamo movement (see MacGonagle 2002) – the dominance of the south, for many interlocutors, had found yet another symbolic manifestation. The interpretations by Afonso (and others) also conform to MacGonagle's (2002, 2008) analyses of oral history among chiNdau-speakers in central Mozambique. MacGonagle documents that the memory of Ngungunyane is prominent and that, contrary to endeavours of memorialization that are integral to national narratology, the ruler is popularly remembered as a violent tyrant and an impostor.[11]

One could argue that such a vision of Frelimo and southern dominance is flawed due to some re-allocation of national symbolically important figures within the national urban geography and that such redistribution and emplacement also takes place with the opposite direction (i.e. not from the South to the Centre or the North). For instance, a central but very short street in Maputo, straddled between Rua Agostinho Neto and Rua Kwame Nkrumah, is named Rua Kamba Simango. Hailing from an area in Central Mozambique generally seen as Ndau, Kamba Columbus Simango (c. 1890–1967) was a mission-educated ethnomusicologist with degrees from Hampton Institute and Columbia University in the US and had worked academically and politically with figures such as anthropologist Franz Boas and W.E.B. Du Bois. However, while he is considered as central for some intellectuals and politicians in Central and Northern parts of the country, the naming of an insignificant street for him as late as 2009 and the downplaying of him as the first Mozambican intellectual (in relation to anthropologist and Frelimo founder Eduardo Mondlane), remains a problematic aspect of the country's postcolonial historiography (Chichava 2013).

Furthermore, while the naming of a short street in Maputo took place in 2009 (and, thus, after the events of 2007 analysed here), such renaming in the capital would not generate as many historically informed political reactions and interpretations as the renaming of the central square in Chimoio. In order to understand why this is so, we need to probe connections between Ngungunyane's rule and the subsequent form of Portuguese colonial rule.

---

11   The memory of Ngungunyane has also been popularized in literature. A famous instance is Mozambican writer Ungulani Ba Ka Khosa's work *Ualalapi* (1987), which charts the complexities and ambivalences surrounding the historical figure of Ngungunyane (see also Banks 2003 and Sletsjøe in this volume).

4   **Company Rule, Emperor Ngungunyane, and Memories of a Violent Colonialism**

As noted above, for Afonso and others, the emplacement of Ngungunyane evoke memories of a brutal past that was (directly and indirectly) associated with his rule. Specifically, memories were evoked of the era of the *Companhia de Moçambique* – a corporate state regime (Kapferer and Bertelsen 2009) that the Portuguese administration imposed in the region of Manica. It dominated large areas of central Mozambique (including Manica) until its dissolution in 1941 (Allina 2012; Neil-Tomlinson 1987). For instance, Maria, an elderly woman from a locality I will call 'Honde', outside Chimoio, recalled the following during an interview in 2008:

> M: Ah! This new place in town [*Praça Gungunhana*]. I do not like it!
> B: Why? It is just a place, isn't it, on the road to Vila Manica and Machipanda [the nearest Mozambique–Zimbabwe border crossing]?
> M: Ngungunyane! It is not good. This place used to belong to Mozambican women – all women. But now to give it to such a man – it is no good. Do you know what he [Ngungunyane] did?
> B: Yes...
> M: [Interrupting...] He came from the south to dominate [*para dominar*] us – killing our men, taking the women and children, forcing people to work. He did not like our rituals – he was afraid of them! But he had lots of men and took all we had.
> B: But did he not also fight the Portuguese?
> M: Ah, they say that. But it is a lie; he worked with the Portuguese all the time. And after they [the Portuguese] killed him, look what happened: his soldiers became Portuguese soldiers. It all started with him and the Portuguese continued it. Afterwards, more and more whites [*muzungus*] came and took our land or forced us to work. I do not like it.

In order to understand such a memory, it may be helpful to frame it within the specific trajectory of Portuguese colonial administration – a process in Mozambique that was gradual, contested and, in some places, rather ephemeral in terms of attaining measurable sovereign control. More generally, despite its gradual refinement in practices of domination, the colonial state administration regularly employed violence against populations to quell resistance and to subordinate people to colonial machinations. René Pélissier (2004), for example, has chronicled the Portuguese colonial campaigns from 1844 to 1941 and quotes the governor of Beira who, in a letter in 1917, gave instructions to his military commander to use the Nguni mercenary fighters at his disposal (there were about 15,000), and to embark on a punishing expedition after the Barué Rebellion of 1917 (Barué being located close to Chimoio). As is well-documented, this was one of the last major rebellions against the Portuguese colonial rule, fifty years before Frelimo initiated its military struggle in the 1960s (Artur 1996).

Such military campaigns went hand in hand with the emergence of a new sovereign power in the region: the *Companhia de Moçambique* (hereafter 'the Companhia'). As noted by Fernando Sacaduro, a long-term employee of the Companhia, its emergence was crucially linked to the downfall of Ngungunyane (Sacaduro 1928, 59):

> With the defeat of Gungunhana [Ngungunyane] and with our effective and real possession of the lands, the rebellions ceased and today the peoples are perfectly pacific and obedient to the authorities to whom they present their problems to be resolved and to whom they pay the tribute of vassalhood, through the hut tax or the poll tax [*mussoco*].[12]

However, although the Companhia itself – as well as employees like Sacaduro – emphasizes the break with Ngungunyane (and there are clear merits to this argument), the situation needs to be further explained. As Newitt (1995, 261) points out, the Nguni tributary state – an often violent form of extraction remembered by Maria, above – gradually developed into what was to become the Companhia from the late 1800s. Further, the Companhia's violent techniques of capture, taxation, and forced labour exhibit statist dynamics similar to the Nguni state. Such resemblance and continuation can be clearly seen in the fact that the Companhia directly employed vast numbers of Nguni mercenaries as a company police force employed in campaigns of pacification, as Sacaduro's 1928 remark also underlines.

In Manica province, the practical results of such a long-term process of violent capture and spatial reconfiguration, which were by no means confined

---

12   The original text reads '[c]om a batida do Gungunhana, e com a nossa posse effectiva [*sic*] e real das terras, cessaram todas as rebeliões e hoje os povos encontram-se perfeitamente pacíficos e obedecendo às auctoridades, a quem apresentam os seus milandos para serem resolvidos e a quem pagam o tributo de vassalagem, por meio do imposto de palhota ou de mussoco'.

to the era of the Companhia, resulted in the transfer of control of land to Portuguese and other European farmers, as well as the subordination of African populations to their control and production schemes. Neves (1998) details the ways in which the forced labour regimes in the post-Second World War period reinforced a long-term trend of evasion from repressive forces through migration: from former Nguni raids to the Companhia's wild sweeps to recruit labour, African communities met these events with flight – frequently effecting permanent or temporary relocation. In the same post-War period, the huge demand for child labour on white settler farms and sugar plantations in Manica, Chimoio, and Buzi (and, later, from cotton producers and the textile industry, such as the once-important TextAfrica in Chimoio) severely affected African communities.[13]

What is remembered by Maria and others are precisely these long-term connections between the violence of capture by Nguni forces – Ngungunyane's original cadres – and the gradual transformation from his imperial formation to Companhia rule, maturation of colonial rule, and its accompanying violence. Thus, experiences of historical violence, colonial domination, and its external rule are integral to these collective memories of hardship and suffering. Crucially, the dynamics of collective memorialization frequently oppose state-centric narratologies, which Heroe's Square and Praça do Gungunhana exemplify (see also Ribeiro 2005; Basto 2013).

5   Subverting National Narratology: Appropriation, Memory and De-territorialisation

Both Afonso's and Maria's non-conformist interpretations exemplify ways in which the state semiotics of narration – as in the renaming from OMM to Ngungunyane – is frequently counteracted by alternative memories. For Afonso, the renaming reflected a long-standing political legacy of Frelimo as dominated by southern Mozambican interests in general and by the Shangaan group in particular (see also Serra 2000). Thus, the renaming of a particular site in Chimoio's urban landscape was interpreted as an expression of such historically conditioned dominance. Maria, on the other hand, interpreted the shift in terms of a longer historical trajectory wherein Ngungunyane and (remnants of) his polity were indistinguishable from the violence and the long-term hardships associated with memories of many different polities.

---

13   As asserted, for instance, by Isaacman and Peterson (2003), the rise of Nguni domination also related to how they invaded, transformed, and took over the so-called *prazo* system in operation in the Zambézia region.

Frelimo held a majority in Chimoio city council in 2007, as they did for the whole post-independence period, reflecting the party's dominance in much of Mozambique in general. Their shift away from spatially celebrating OMM is perhaps understandable, as the OMM organization seems to be considerably weakened at a local level (Disney 2008). Furthermore, the move to include a former Nguni ruler in a national pantheon of heroes is not entirely new. For instance, Ribeiro (2005, 267–268) explores this in tracing early Mozambican nationalist attitudes towards Ngungunyane. As Ribeiro points out, already at the beginning of the twentieth century, leading nationalist João Albasini, expressing himself in the journals *O Africano* and *O Brado Africano*, was already regarding Ngungunyane as responsible for unifying southern Mozambique. Nevertheless, the renaming of the site in Chimoio arguably signifies a more recent shift in Frelimo-dominated national narratology, in which Ngungunyane is increasingly re-codified as having fought an anti-colonial struggle. In other words, in Frelimo elite circles Ngungunyane is in the process of entering the pantheon of national liberation guarded and erected by Frelimo.

This shift can also be seen in literary form in a series published by Plural Editores in Maputo, entitled Colecção Personalidades Moçambicanas (Mozambican Personalities Collection). As of late 2016, the series titles listed as available include, perhaps unsurprisingly, *Ngungunhane, Eduardo Mondlane, Josina Machel, Samora Machel* and *Maria de Lurdes Mutola*. The text on Ngungunyane (Almada 2010) presents his rule, family, feasts, and battles against the colonizers, before ending the work with his death. Crucially, on the final page (2010, 30), Almada divulges that Samora Machel demanded the return of Ngungunyane's bones in 1983; following their return, Ngungunyane's remains were interred in Fortaleza de Maputo (Maputo Fort) in 1985. Around this time Machel also proclaimed Ngungunyane as an anti-colonial hero (Basto 2013; see also Bertelsen 2012). In this fashion, the book mirrors the re-naming of urban places to enshrine Ngungunyane in the nation's mythical past; it attempts to weave together threads from both the liberation struggle and Ngungunyane's era. Indeed, the format, narrative, and sequence of Almada's work concur with Bakhtin's notion of epicness, outlined earlier; these elements characterize Mozambican postcolonial aspirations to sequence and order a past that serves the present.[14]

Tellingly, there are yet further examples of re-naming taking place in Mozambique: as widely broadcast during June, July, and August 2011, statues of former Mozambican President Samora Machel were to be erected in all provincial capitals. While I was carrying out fieldwork in July and August 2011, the

---

14   See also Afolabi (2005) for the relevance of such production to liberation in Lusophone Africa.

reason for placing such a statue in Chimoio's central square was the subject of much discussion. Popular views ranged from whether the base and its statue would fall down, as there were rumours that both were produced in China (while it was actually produced in North Korea), to some concern that the spirit of Samora would return to haunt Chimoio's inhabitants.[15] Political jokes may be interpreted in many ways and they need to be seen in relation to Mozambique's commonplace employment of subversive oral forms in the shape of, for instance, songs ridiculing the colonial powers (Vail and White 1983). However, in the case of the mirth surrounding the Samora statue, the joking may be seen as a subversive critique of Frelimo's political instrumentalization of the Samora legacy – pointing to a general trend in postcolonial countries in which the containment of memory is increasingly difficult (see Werbner 1998).

As argued elsewhere (Bertelsen 2014), the very notion of 'popular power' (*poder popular*) introduced under Samora's presidency (1975–1986) has officially been discarded from Frelimo's rhetorical arsenal in the era of neoliberal democracy that has dominated politics since the 1992 peace agreement and the first presidential and multiparty parliamentary elections in 1994. While retaining fragments of socialist rhetoric, the central notion of popular power has, nonetheless, been re-animated and re-interpreted in the popular rhetoric surrounding the spate of lynchings and summary justice in the first decade after 2000 (Bertelsen 2009a). However, this notion has also resurfaced in political music, such as Azagaia's rap song *Povo no poder* (People in power) (Azagaia 2008). The song, issued just two weeks after the 2008 urban riots, was a play on the notion of *poder popular* – and as a song criticizing the government it was seen as accompanying these urban protests, where varieties of this conceptualization of collective power, politics, and justice also emerged (Groes-Green 2010; Bertelsen 2014).

What do such disparate instances as Maria's memories of past violence, Afonso's accusations of continued southern dominance, jokes about the Samora Machel statue, and the 'de-regulated' use of memories and legacies of *poder popular* have in common? For one thing, in a broad sense they all demonstrate the subversive and oppositional potentiality inherent in processes of state signification and narratology. Put differently, the force of the narrative rhetorical thread, or the force of historical figures inscribed onto state domains and public places, is non-total and non-finite: power, then, is always in excess of what can be controlled. Thus, its expressions, institutions, and forms may

---

15   Following the inauguration in Maputo of the Samora Machel statue on the 25th anniversary of his death, October 19, 2011, ceremonies to unveil further such statues took place in Mozambican provincial capitals in October and November 2011.

always be challenged, undermined, resisted, de-territorialized, transmogrified, or appropriated (see also Mbembe 2001). More generally, as Vološinov (1973) claimed, all signs ideologically produced – as in the productions in public places with specific narrative content – may be subverted, as such signs are semiotically non-finite.

For this reason, it remains important for those working on Mozambique – and others working in, on, and for postcolonial countries – to grapple with the many ways in which changes in national narratology are engaged at a popular level. Popular engagement provides potential for the forging of new perceptions of politics – be this via processes of inscription, changes to a national pantheon of historical figures, or the redefinition – as in Chimoio – of an urban square. In the latter, where once the emancipatory achievements of Mozambican women were celebrated, now an emperor is hailed about whom many are ambivalent, at best. Such changed perceptions of, as well as the perceptions of change to, the rhetoric and narratology of Mozambique's main party may well shift voters' attention to other possibilities or alternative readings of Frelimo politics. More broadly, the as-yet-unfinished transition from Praça OMM to Praça Gungunhana is a poignant instance of how any polity may seek to impose a narratology onto the (urban) spaces it commands; in doing so, states aim to limit, cordon off, or diminish subversive accounts that potentially undermine their collective, unifying narrative.

6   Conclusion

The political narratology of state formation is always integral to processes of territorialisation and de-territorialisation. In Mozambique, state-dominated narratives of a past struggle that was violent yet heroic have been integral to postcolonial politics. Such is the pervasiveness of this violent past, appropriated and inserted into almost all urban spaces, that it has been almost universally tangible in most domains of the social and political landscape. Crucially, it has also been visible in the urban physical landscape, as we have seen in the case of the re-naming of the town squares. The shift in naming discussed in this chapter, from Praça da OMM to Praça Gungunhana, however minor it may seem, represents a shift in the narratology of the Mozambican nation from celebrating (aspirations towards) female emancipation to emplacing an emperor within the pantheon of the nation. For all those studying Mozambique, beyond its gendered implications – a dimension not analysed in this chapter but no less essential – such a shift is important for at least two additional reasons: firstly, it may herald transformations in how the Mozambican state politics of memory is subject to both national and international recon-figurations of the past. This may concern the last decade's international aid providers and donors, who emphasize decentralization, democratization, and the recognition of non-formal authorities, groups, and cultures. From this per-spective, the inclusion of Ngungunyane can be interpreted as an expression of a novel political economy of statehood (see also Orre 2010). Secondly, such transformations open up new avenues for social recall that do not necessarily emanate from the state (Israel 2013, 2014; see also Feldman 2004). By dethron-ing OMM and substituting a place of memory for the figure of Ngungunyane, the Mozambican state is broadening the space of political recall to include fig-ures from the pre-Frelimo period. While such a shift may be seen as inclusive, it is also subject to specific and situated readings of the past. In the present context of Chimoio and nearby rural areas, the move to include and re-empha-size Ngungunyane was, thus, interpreted within an oppositional context, and evoked memories of a violent past.

These two points – that a Mozambican politics of memory is subject to in-ternational and national reconfigurations of state power, and the opening up of new avenues of social recall – underline the importance of monitoring and analysing processes of narration at various levels. It is also important to note that such readings as this chapter has offered should go beyond the capital of Maputo spatially, and beyond elite circles politically. Further, such processes of narration are varied and offer rich material for understanding both the politics of elite formation and ongoing social dynamics that are external to the elite and its world. Arguably, monitoring official narratology, its material effects (in the form of places and statues, for instance), and its popular reception presents us with a concrete context from which to better understand the contested na-ture of the imaginaries of the Mozambican nation.

References

Afolabi, Niyi. 2005. Empowering paradigms: Prophecy, mythology, and ancestrality in the liberation of lusophone Africa. In *Tradition and Politics: Indigenous political structures in Africa*, ed. Olufemi Vaughan, 143–156. Trenton, NJ: Africa World Press.

Allina, Eric. 2012. *Slavery by any Other Name. African life under company rule in colonial Mozambique*. Charlottesville: University of Virginia Press.

Almada, João Vaz de. 2010. *Ngungunhane*. Maputo: Plural Editores.

Arnfred, Signe. 2011. *Sexuality and Gender Politics in Mozambique: Rethinking gender in Africa*. London: James Currey.

Arthur, Maria José. 2004. Fantasmas que assombram os sindicatos: Mulheres sindicalistas e as lutas pela afirmação dos seus direitos. In *Moçambique e a Reinvenção da Emancipação Social*, ed. Boaventura de Sousa Santos and Teresa Cruz e Silva, 173–206. Maputo: Centro de Formação Jurídica e Judiciária.

Artur, Domingos do Rosário. 1996. *Makombe: Subsídios à reconstituicão da sua personalidade*. Maputo: Arquivo do Património Cultural (ARPAC).

Austin, Kathi. 1994. *Invisible Crimes: US private intervention in the war in Mozambique*. Washington, DC: Africa Policy Information Center.

Azagaia. 2008. *Povo no Poder*. Maputo: Cotoneterecords.

Bakhtin, M.M. 1981. *The Dialogic Imagination*. Austin: University of Texas Press.

Bakhtin, M.M. 1986. *Speech Genres and Other Essays*. Austin: University of Texas Press.

Banks, Jared. 2003. Violence and the (re)writing of history: A reading of *Ualalapi*. In *Seasons of Harvest: Essays on the literatures of lusophone Africa*, ed. Niyi Afolabi and Donald Burness, 135–162. Trenton, NJ: Africa World Press.

Basto, Maria-Benedita. 2013. The Writings of the National Anthem in Independent Mozambique: Fictions of the Subject-People. *Kronos: Southern African Histories* 39 (1): 185–203.

Bertelsen, Bjørn Enge. 2002. 'Till the soil – but do not touch the bones'. Histories and memories of war and violence in Mozambican re-constructive practices. Cand. Polit. Diss., University of Bergen, Norway.

Bertelsen, Bjørn Enge. 2004a. 'It will rain until we are in power'. Floods, elections and memory in Mozambique. In *Rights and the Politics of Recognition in Africa*, ed. Harri Englund and Francis B. Nyamnjoh, 169–191. London: Zed Books.

Bertelsen, Bjørn Enge. 2004b. 'The traditional lion is dead'. The ambivalent presence of tradition and the relation between politics and violence in Mozambique. In *Lusotopie 2003: Violence et politique dans les espaces lusophones*, ed. Camille Goirand, 263–281. Paris: Éditions Karthala and Centre d'Étude d'Afrique Noire (CEAN).

Bertelsen, Bjørn Enge. 2009a. Multiple sovereignties and summary justice in Mozambique. A critique of some legal anthropological terms. *Social Analysis*, 53 (3): 123–147.

Bertelsen, Bjørn Enge. 2009b. Sorcery and death squads. Transformations of state, sovereignty, and violence in postcolonial Mozambique. In *Crisis of the State. War and social upheaval*, ed. Bruce Kapferer and Bjørn Enge Bertelsen, 210–240. New York: Berghahn Books.

Bertelsen, Bjørn Enge. 2011. 'Entering the red sands'. The corporality of punishment and imprisonment in Chimoio, Mozambique. *Journal of Southern African Studies*, 37 (3): 611–626.

Bertelsen, Bjørn Enge. 2012. Ngungunyane, in *Dictionary of African Biography. Vol. 4*, eds Henry Louis Gates, Jr. and Emmanuel Akyeampong, 465–466. New York: Oxford University Press.

Bertelsen, Bjørn Enge. 2014. Effervescence and ephemerality: Popular urban uprisings in Mozambique. *Ethnos: Journal of Anthropology*, DOI: 10.1080/00141844.2014.929596.

Bertelsen, Bjørn Enge. 2016. *Violent Becomings: State Formation, Sociality, and Power in Mozambique*. New York: Berghahn Books.

Bertelsen, Bjørn Enge. 2018. Composing texts and the composition of uprisings: Notes on writing the postcolonial political, in *The Composition of Anthropology: How Anthropological Texts Are Written*, eds Morten Nielsen and Nigel Rapport, 56–72. London: Routledge.

Broch-Due, Vigdis, and Bjørn Enge Bertelsen, eds. 2016. *Violent Reverberations: Global modalities of trauma*. New York: Palgrave Macmillan.

Cahen, Michel. 2002. *Les bandits. Un historien au Mozambique, 1994*. Paris: Centre Culturel Calouste Gulbenkian.

Chichava, Sérgio Inácio. 2013. Unlike the other whites? The Swiss in Mozambique under colonialism. In *Imperial Migrations: Colonial communities and diaspora in the Portuguese world*, ed. Eric Morier-Genoud and Michel Cahen, 149–167. Houndmills: Palgrave Macmillan.

Coelho, João Paulo Borges. 2010. Memory, History, Fiction. A Note on the Politics of the Past in Mozambique. Paper presented at École des Hautes Etudes en Sciences Sociales, Paris, 21 to 22 October 2010. Available at http://www.ces.uc.pt/estilhacos _do_imperio/comprometidos/media/jp%20borges%20coelho%20text.pdf, accessed 22 November 2014.

Coelho, João Paulo Borges. 2013. Politics and contemporary history in Mozambique: A set of epistemological notes. *Kronos: Southern African Histories* 39 (1): 10–19.

Deleuze, Gilles and Félix Guattari. 1980. *A Thousand Plateaus: Capitalism and schizophrenia*. London: Continuum.

Dinerman, Alice. 1994. In search of Mozambique: The imaginings of Christian Geffray in *La Cause des Armes au Mozambique: Anthropologie d'une guerre civile*. Book review. *Journal of Southern African Studies* 20 (4): 569–586.

Dinerman, Alice. 2006. *Revolution, Counter-revolution and Revisionism in Post-colonial Africa: The case of Mozambique, 1975–1994*. New York: Routledge.

Disney, Jennifer Leigh. 2008. *Women's Activism and Feminist Agency in Mozambique and Nicaragua*. Philadelphia: Temple University Press.

Feldman, Allen F. 2004. Memory theatres, virtual witnessing, and the trauma-aesthetic. *Biography* 27 (1): 163–202.

Gersony, Robert. 1988. *Summary of Mozambican Refugee Accounts of Principally Conflict-related Experiences in Mozambique*. Washington, DC: Bureau for Refugee Programs.

Groes-Green, Christian. 2010. Orgies of the moment: Bataille's anthropology of transgression and the defiance of danger in post-socialist Mozambique. *Anthropological Theory* 10 (4): 385–407.

Hedges, David. 1989. Notes on Malawi–Mozambique relations, 1961–1987. *Journal of Southern African Studies* 15 (4): 617–644.

Isaacman, Allen F., and Derek Peterson. 2003. Making the Chikunda: Military slavery and ethnicity in Southern Africa, 1750–1900. *International Journal of African Historical Studies* 36 (2): 257–281.

Israel, Paolo. 2013. A loosening grip? The liberation script in Mozambican history. *Kronos: Southern African Histories* 39 (1): 10–19.

Israel, Paolo. 2014. *In Step with the Times: Mapiko Masquerades of Mozambique*. Athens, OH: Ohio University Press.

Kapferer, Bruce, and Bjørn Enge Bertelsen. 2009. The crisis of power and reformations of the state in globalizing realities. In *Crisis of the State: War and social upheaval*, ed. Bruce Kapferer and Bjørn Enge Bertelsen, 1–26. New York: Berghahn Books.

Katto, Jonna. 2014. Landscapes of Belonging: Female Ex-Combatants Remembering the Liberation Struggle in Urban Maputo. *Journal of Southern African Studies* 40 (3): 539–557.

Khosa, Ungulani Ba Ka. 1987. *Ualalapi*. Lisbon: Caminho.

Laban, Michel, ed. 1998. *Moçambique: Encontro com escritores*. 3 vols. Oporto: Fundação Eng. António de Almeida.

Liesegang, Gerhard. 1996. *Ngungunyane: A figura de Ngungunyane Nqumayo, Rei de Gaza, 1884–1895 e o desaparecimento do seu Estado*. Chimoio: Arquivo do Património Cultural.

MacGonagle, Elizabeth. 2002. A mixed pot: History and identity in the Ndau region of Mozambique and Zimbabwe, 1500–1900. PhD diss., Michigan State University.

MacGonagle, Elizabeth. 2008. Living with a tyrant: Ndau memories and identities in the shadow of Ngungunyana. *International Journal of African Historical Studies* 41 (1): 29–53.

Magaia, Lina 1988. *Dumba Nengue: Run for your life. Peasant tales of tragedy in Mozambique*. Trenton, NJ: Africa World Press.

Mbembe, Achille. 2001. *On the Postcolony*. Berkeley, CA: University of California Press.

Miedema, Esther. 2016. 'Let's Move, Let's Not Remain Stagnant': Nationalism, Masculinism, and School-Based Education in Mozambique. In *Childhood and Nation: Interdisciplinary engagements*, ed. Zsuzsann Millei and Robert Imre, 183–206. New York: Palgrave Macmillan.

Neil-Tomlinson, Barry. 1987. The Mozambique Chartered Company, 1892–1910. PhD diss., SOAS, University of London.

Neves, Joel Maurício das. 1998. Economy, Society and Labour Migration in Central Mozambique, 1930–c. 1965: A case study of Manica Province. PhD diss., University College London.

Newitt, Malyn. 1995. *A History of Mozambique*. London: Hurst.

Orre, Aslak. 2010. Entrenching the Party-state in the Multiparty era: Opposition parties, traditional authorities and new councils of local representatives in Angola and Mozambique. PhD diss., University of Bergen, Norway.

Osório, Conceição. 2004. Poder político e protagonismo feminino. In *Moçambique e a Reinvenção da Emancipação Social*, ed. Boaventura de Sousa Santos and Teresa Cruz e Silva, 145–171. Maputo: Centro de Formação Jurídica e Judiciária.

Pélissier, René. 2004. *Les Campagnes Coloniales du Portugal, 1844–1941*. Paris: Éditions Pygmalion.

Pitcher, Anne. 2006. Forgetting from above and memory from below: Strategies of legitimation and struggle in postsocialist Mozambique. *Africa* 76 (1): 88–112.

Ribeiro, Fernando Bessa. 2005. A invenção dos heróis: Nação, história e discursos de identidade em Moçambique. *Etnográfica* 9 (2): 257–275.

Rosário, Lourenço do. 2008. *A Narrativa Africana de Expressão Oral*. Maputo: Texto Editores.

Sacaduro, Fernando. 1928. Usos e costumes de Quiteve, Território de Manica e Sofala (1). *Boletim de Sociedade de Geographia de Lisboa* 46 (3/4): 53–74.

Sahlström, Berit. 1990. Political Posters in Ethiopia and Mozambique: Visual imagery in a revolutionary context. PhD diss., University of Uppsala, Sweden.

Santos, Ana Margarida. 2010. Performing the Past: Celebrating Women's Day in northern Mozambique. *Cahiers d'Études Africaines* 197: 217–234.

Saúte, Nelson, ed. 1998. *Os Habitantes da Memória: Entrevistas com escritores moçambicanos*. Maputo: Embaixada de Portugal, Centro Cultural Português.

Serra, Carlos, ed. 2000. *Racismo, Etnicidade e Poder: Um estudo em cinco cidades de Moçambique*. Maputo: Livraria Universitária.

Serra, Carlos, ed. 2008. *Linchamentos em Moçambique I (uma desordem que apela à ordem)*. Maputo: Centro de Estudos Africanos, Unidade de Diagnóstico Social, Universidade Eduardo Mondlane.

Sidaway, James D., and Marcus Power. 1995. Sociospatial transformations in the 'postsocialist' periphery: The case of Maputo, Mozambique. *Environment and Planning A* 27: 1463–1491.

Silva, Terezinha da, and Ximena Andrade. 2000. *Woman in Mozambique / Mulher em Moçambique*. Maputo: Centro de Estudos Africanos, Universidade Eduardo Mondlane.

Vail, Leroy, and Landeg White. 1983. Forms of resistance: Songs and perceptions of power in colonial Mozambique. *American Historical Review* 88 (4): 883–919.

Vološinov, V.N. 1973. *Marxism and the Philosophy of Language*. Cambridge, MA: Harvard University Press.

Werbner, Richard B. 1998. Smoke from the barrel of a gun: Postwars of the dead, memory and reinscription in Zimbabwe. In *Memory and the Postcolony: African anthropology and the critique of power*, ed. Richard B. Werbner, 71–102. London: Zed Books.

West, Harry. 2000. Girls with guns. Narrating the experience of war of Frelimo's 'Female Detachment'. *Anthropological Quarterly* 73(4): 180–194.

Wheeler, Douglas. 1968. Gungunyane the negotiator: A study in African diplomacy. *Journal of African History* 9 (4): 585–602.

Zimba, Benigna de Jesus, Edward A. Alpers, and Allen F. Isaacman, eds. 2006. *Slave Routes and Oral Tradition in Southeastern Africa*. Maputo: Filsom Entertainment, Lda.

CHAPTER 4

Urban Transformation, Family Strategies and Home Space Creation in the City of Maputo

Ana Bénard da Costa

The spatial and demographic configuration of today's Maputo (see figure 4.1) with around one *million* people living in the city and about 1.8 *million* in the metropolitan area[1] is more than the creation of those who inhabit the city than of those supposedly in charge of it. Attempts at imposing zoning regulations are invariably thwarted by private interests' business, commerce, and the families who put their savings and earnings into building homes in the various areas of the existing and emerging city. A result of complex, often obscure, processes of monetary accumulation, or merely the fulfilment of the 'put a little by every day' method of saving, these homes range in size and standard from modern apartment blocks and luxury villas to the thousands of more modest (and often unfinished) dwellings that spread for miles across the city. Inherent in this dynamic process of 'independent' building is a mesh of conflicts of interest. Such conflicts arise in a context in which there co-exist different, and contradictory, legal interpretations of the possession, appropriation, and use of land and property.

This chapter follows one of the overall aims of this volume in exploring the diverse ways in which the Mozambican nation is perceived and depicted. It does so by questioning the relevance of certain dichotomy-based theoretical models (the idea of a dual city comprising tradition and modernity, for example) for the analysis of this exceptionally dynamic and constantly changing urban context. Such analysis is undertaken by contrasting various studies into the lives of Maputo families with an argument relating to emerging forms of 'urbanism as a way of life' in Maputo. In particular, this chapter investigates the nature and impact of the creation of 'home space'. This concept was developed by the research team of the program Home Space in African Cities[2] and refers

---

1 Between 1997 and 2007 the population of the city of Maputo increased 13.2 percent. In 2007 the city had 1,094,315 inhabitants; the total population of the Maputo metropolitan area (which includes the city of Matola) was 1,766,823 inhabitants (Instituto Nacional de Estatística 2012).

2 'Home Space in African Cities' was funded by the Danish Research Council for Innovation, 2009–2011, under the management of Jørgen Eskemose Andersen of the School of

FIGURE 4.1 Maputo

to the spaces within which the majority of African urban residents dwell – dwelling being both a place and a process. Creating *home spaces* thus involves spatial and social practices, but conceptually, *home* is above all else a culturally defined concept (Andersen 2012; Jenkins 2012).

The study of social and cultural change processes in families has been the author's research focus in Maputo since 1992 (author publications); in 2009 I entered into a research project on emerging forms of 'urbanism as a way of life' in Maputo, investigating the nature and impact of the creation of home space. A group of architects and urban planners, together with three anthropologists (myself included), and Mozambican university students conducted fieldwork mainly between December 2009 and February 2010. This chapter analyses the data collected in December 2009 on built environment dwellings and on household socioeconomics. The survey covered a sample of 100 sites located from north of the university campus to near Marracuene town, 35 kilometres

Architecture, Copenhagen. The programme was based on a conception and research design created by Paul Jenkins of the School of the Built Environment, Heriot-Watt University / Edinburgh School of Architecture and Landscape Architecture. The fieldwork was undertaken with participation by students of architecture and anthropology from Universidade Eduardo Mondlane, and had key involvement from architect Silje Erøy Sollien and academic Judite Chipenembe. Generous support from the Mozambican institutions, and time donated by the Edinburgh and Lisbon institutions in terms of their academics' input, have been a key aspect of the programme's success.

from Maputo centre. This fieldwork comprised one of three components of the Home Space project and took place in a representative section of the large peri-urban areas of Maputo city.[3]

All these neighbourhoods belong to the part of town that used to be known as *Bairros de caniço* (reed neighbourhoods), although most houses now are not made of reed and these parts of the city are called simply *bairros*. But the *bairros* – as explained below – are interlinked with the *Cidade de cimento*[4] (cement city) and cannot be understood by employing dual categories that classify these parts of the same city as opposite realities, labelling one as *formal* and *modern* and the other as *informal* and *traditional*. Instead, both *bairros* and *cidade de cimento* must be seen as *informal* and *traditional* as well as *formal* and *modern*. All these aspects – formal and informal, traditional and modern – are interlinked in complex and dynamic ways. Since the articulations exist, either we define the terms in a classic, dichotomic, and monolithic way,[5] or we adopt (as in this analysis) a perspective in which culture is seen as dynamic, intra- and inter-relational.[6]

In the social context analysed in this chapter and, indeed, in every society, there is a permanent and complex interaction between modernity and tradition. Modernity refers to elements that directly relate to the innovative aspects of a society, but the perceptions held by social actors about what is new (modern) are always shaped by the ideological frameworks available to them, and result from lived or transmitted experiences. Neither is tradition something static and intangible, but rather the outcome of dynamic negotiations that allow the permanence of ideological frameworks over time (Amselle 1990; Geschiere et al. 2008). In other words, the persistence of tradition in the present means the updating and re-creating of the ideological frameworks that

---

3   The sample draws partly on previous surveys (1990 and 2000) and partly on the trends of more recent urban expansion.

4   In Maputo, as in many African cities, the architectural fabric is a dual structure inherited from colonialism. We can distinguish between two clusters: 'Cement city', once the domain of 'white people', with its masonry buildings, metal, roads, plumbing, electricity, and a significant concentration of social infrastructure and services; and the 'reed neighbourhoods' in which, in the colonial era, the 'indigenous' population resided.

5   To oversimplify: modern refers to the historical dynamic that started with the Enlightenment, and tradition to all that is opposed to the former (see Eisenstadt 1991); formal designates all that the state regulates, informal refers to all that it does not. On formal/informal economy see Roberts 1994; Maldonaldo 1995; Hugon 1999; Navalha 2000; Chen 2003; AlSayaad and Roy 2004; Hansen and Vaa 2004; Yusuff 2011.

6   On this perspective see, for instance, Gluckman 1956; Balandier 1963, 1969, 1971; Turner 1969; Geertz 1973; Rosaldo 1980; Ortner 1984; Olivier de Sardan 1985, 1988, 1998; Turner and Bruner 1986; Bierschenk 1988; Geschiere 2008.

legitimize the present through past times that are constantly evoked and reinvented. Values and identities are anchored in these past times, whatever our perspective or level of analysis: individual, household, national, regional, or transnational. It is in the evoking of past times that identities and values are re-created, and it is from this interpretative re-creating that change and innovation (modernity) are born. However, viewing the social facts of the present through traditions and customs, as noted by Jean-Loup Amselle (1990, 62), is not enough to make intelligible the traditional facts that also result from present existing conditions. Likewise, any examination of innovative and modern elements that does not take into account the traditional ideological frameworks that shape the perceptions of social actors does not allow us to understand the social present

This perspective has led to the hypothesis presented here that the modern model of *home spaces* (quite different from the traditional model, as explained below) coexists and is interlinked with traditional forms of home space use, and that these are related to the way families organize relationships among and between family members and the outside world. The anthropologists involved in the socioeconomic survey allowed us to create an overall view of home spaces in order to choose a limited number of cases (19) for the ethnographic study, which took place in May/June 2010. As analyses of the data collected in the ethnographic study are not complete at the moment this chapter was written, this analyses compares the author's previous findings (author publication) regarding the way Maputo families lived and created their city, with some ideas that arose from the data collected in the socioeconomic survey (December 2009) of 50 home spaces (half of the sample) from Urban District number three[7] (Bairro Polana Caniço A e B) and Urban District number four (Bairros 3 de Fevereiro, Mahotas, and Laulane).[8]

1 Maputo: Demographic Evolution and Urban Mobility (1975–2013)

In demographic terms from 1975 to the early 80's, the city of Maputo has experienced a moderate population growth at an average annual rate of 3.6%, a result of the influx of population migrating to the capital city as a consequence

---

7 Those districts and district number 5 contained 74 percent of the population of Maputo: District 3: 222,756, or 20.4 percent; District 4: 293,461, or 26.8 percent; District 5: 26.6 percent, or 290,696 inhabitants (Instituto Nacional de Estatística 2012).

8 These cover areas in the above-mention previous surveys and thus constitute an important (and fairly unique) longitudinal study opportunity embedded within the Home Space project (Jenkins 1991, 2001).

of the country's independence (linked to the opening up of new work and training opportunities). Since the census in 1980 until the following census in 1997, the population of Maputo doubled from approximately 540,000 inhabitants to almost one million. The population growth was more pronounced until the end of the war, (1992), with an average annual rate of 4.5%, decreasing from 1991 to 1997 to an average annual rate of 1.7%. In the following decade (1997–2007), the growth rate of the population of Maputo was 13.2%.

The Maputo population growth from the beginning of independence was followed by an urban mobility process between the different areas of the city. During a first stage, when most of the city's real estate that was rented or had been abandoned by settlers was nationalized, and the barriers that in colonial times prevented the settling of Africans in the 'white city' vanished many inhabitants from the periphery 'occupied' the cement city. This situation did not last very long and soon many Africans who had 'less suited' behaviour but had moved to flats on the modern Maputo buildings (the cement city) were relocated (in the best of cases) in the periphery of the city or their original homeland. Similarly, land was nationalized ('from the Rovuma [River] to Maputo') including the whole peripheral area of Maputo.[9]

This complex population movement and the fact that there was no census in 1990 create difficulties to the analysis of the demographic evolution of Maputo between 1980 and 1997 and explain disparities between the different estimates that were made during the last years of war and the post-war period. These differences express uncertainties regarding the number of war-displaced people that have flowed into Maputo and uncertainties as to the number of those who returned to their homelands after the reestablishment of peace (Vivet 2012).

In Maputo the coincidence of the time of economic liberalization (Structural Adjustment Programme) with demographic growth resulting essentially from the rural exodus caused by the war, dramatically aggravated life conditions for the great majority of the city population. Particularly affected were the populations that inhabited the peripheral neighbourhoods of the city since it was mainly these areas that the war displaced people settled. It's important to stress, however, that the '*cidade de cimento*' and its inhabitants were not immune to the effects of war: the displaced also settled in 'abandoned' buildings in the '*cidade de cimento*' and many inhabitants in this area accommodated relatives from the countryside who escaped the war.

---

9 The process of acquiring plots or cultivations areas in the periphery of Maputo went through different stages from colonial times to the turn of the century. On this subject, see Mendes 1989; Lachartre 2000.

The population increase in the periphery areas has evolved in two ways: through geographic expansion of the periphery and through an increased density of housing in the various neighbourhoods. The relative distance from the municipal districts to the city centre determines population density, which is lower in the districts that are further away from the centre, even though these were precisely the ones that experienced higher density growth during the 1990s and in the following decade (1997–2007) when the northern areas of the city experienced the most significant population increase (on this subject see Instituto Nacional de Estatística 2012; Jenkins 2012). At the same time, in these areas, there are also some expensive weekend houses with well-tended gardens and *machambas*.

In the *cidade de cimento* there has also been an increase in construction. Land that was not built on during the colonial era now has expensive private houses on it, or huge commercial buildings (hotels, shopping centres, multinational offices), or it is in the process of being developed. Some *bairros de caniço* are being replaced by expensive condominiums; new and modern buildings have emerged. Such urban prosperity, however, is only for the few, and most of the population still live in the *bairros*. Most of these *bairros* have only had running water and electricity installed in recent years and some areas are still without such basic facilities. Furthermore, apart from some interesting new initiatives regarding garbage collection, basic sanitation continues to be practically non-existent.

In order to understand the way Maputo inhabitants cope with these social, economic and demographic changes the author conduct several studies during these last decades that share the same analytical option: the focus on families.

2   Why Families?

The reason this research and previous studies concentrates on families and not on households is that studying households by themselves does not allow us to understand the survival and reproduction strategies deployed at household level. In order to understand these strategies, it is necessary to consider all those family members who live in a home space unit and all those who live in other home-spaces but have existing relationships of interdependence that are significant to the household. These relationships can be identified through observation and informants' description of their relationships with other family members residing in the same house, the same neighbourhood, or elsewhere.[10] The real size of the family is therefore 'limited in practical terms by the obligations of reciprocity that a person develops and maintains in the selection of his/her relatives' (Cohen 1981, 64–65).

In the present research project, where home space is the main analytical unit, the data have so far confirmed that family analysis is relevant in explaining the way residents create their home space and define family boundaries. For instance, the circulation of family members and goods among different home spaces belonging to related family members is constant and frequent. Further, this includes relatives who live elsewhere, but who may have ownership rights to houses and land just because 'they are family', as it was expressed by interviewees.

Many interviewees expressed in various ways the importance of other family members, besides those living with them, in the creation of their *home-space*. For example, some of those family members that live apart help with money and work in terms of building the house; sometimes the house, or the land on which it is sited, was inherited from family members; in some cases, it was through family members that they knew there was land available on which they could build their houses:

> The bricklayer who built the house is my stepfather; he came to build this part; he has been a bricklayer for many years. To my stepfather I only gave some money but he didn't charge me; I only gave him ... A bricklayer I don't know I would have to pay more. (Man, 38 years old, interview, December 19, 2009) (see figure 4.2)

> This land was inherited by my mother. All this was ours; we divided it and gave it to the family members and the others they sold it. (Man, 42 years old, interview, December 12, 2009)

> The house belongs to my late father, but it is my responsibility. We didn't buy; we built it a long time ago. I do not remember the year; I know it was before the independence; we came to the neighbourhood when it was bush and did not have any houses. (Woman, 45 years old, interview, December 10, 2009)

---

10   For example, the a priori assumption that legal minors belong to the family of their parents, even when they actually live with other relatives, is questionable. These families belong to different ethnic groups and came from different geographical areas; they live in the same urban environment in a context of social change. These families are 'traditionally' included in kinship systems that are not only different from Western systems but also differ widely in this context. And, as Geffray (2000, 23; my translation) notes, there is 'error' and 'ambiguity' in the 'use of Western kinship labels to describe the kinship of others, as though our words – unlike the words of all other societies – were endowed with a universal value'.

So, in this sense, the notion of family resembles a circular argument. It exists because relationships among members enable survival and social reproduction strategies to be put into action – and residential strategies are one of the most significant of these. Such strategies, once put into action, preserve, develop, and create the different ties (and spaces) on which the family is founded.

However, it is not always possible to determine all types of relationship – their frequency and importance, and the power relations involved – that exist between family members. This is especially so when the family is divided into two or more geographical areas and *home space* members change all the time. Basic questions then arise. To whom does the house belong? Who inherits? Who provides resources to build the house? Who decides what to do, how, and when? As confirmed in this survey from December 2009, there are no easy answers to such questions. And even when there are, they can change over time, or according to the person that answers them.

It was also considered important to the research to understand the meaning that notions such as *ownership* and *belonging* have for different family members. We needed to establish whether in the social and cultural context in which this research was carried out, there are sometimes fundamental relationships of reciprocity between and among relatives that live far away from each other. These relationships of reciprocity are based on common symbols

FIGURE 4.2 A Maputo family

and identity factors (name, land of origin, common ancestors), and they cannot be understood without taking into consideration the long chain of ancestors in the daily life of the family (author publication).

In Maputo, family types, structures and relationships, and *home space* creation and organization are inter-related issues. Different family types and changes in family structures and relations, result from, and simultaneously create, different *home space* construction possibilities (or ideals). These processes are dynamic, constrained by social, cultural, political, and economic micro and macro contexts, and also by social reproduction strategies that relate individuals to specific, but not necessarily unique, social unities. Above all, in this social and economic context, family types and *home space* creation are ongoing processes of change that are paradoxically anchored in ideals of permanence and durability.

3   Maputo Families: Origins, Types, and Networks

All the families in the study live in Maputo, the political, administrative, and economic capital of a vast country; but most were (and still are) natives of the rural provinces of southern Mozambique, or descendants of families from that region. It is interesting to note that in the cases analysed, about 63 heads of family were born outside the Maputo metropolitan area. My previous research (author publication) concluded that all families had more or less regular links with the homeland, but this situation seems to have changed. For instance, only 23 percent of families claim to have a *machamba*[11] in their homeland, and only 29.7 percent said they consider their place of birth (or the place of birth of their husbands) to be their homeland.

Apart from this, differences in family types[12] – of those who have lived for longer or shorter periods in the city – are still not significant: most were and still are *extended families*[13] with an extremely heterogeneous composition

---

11   A large or small agricultural plot.

12   This analysis largely complies with the typology employed in the 1997 census for different kinds of household: monoparental families consist of father plus children, or mother plus children; nuclear families consist of father, mother, and children, or a childless couple; the extended family denotes a family whose composition differs from all those listed above. Most extended families comprise members from the mother's and the father's side, and are not necessarily organized around the oldest members. Flexibility is the common denominator, and the extended family can take many different forms.

13   This information coincides (insofar as is possible, as different units of analysis are used) with the findings of the 1997 census, which indicated that most households in Maputo are composed of extended families (Instituto Nacional de Estatística, 1998).

involving relatives (at least one) from both descendent lines and different generations. Some of those interviewed have sons or daughters living with close relatives somewhere in Maputo or in the countryside, or they have nephews and nieces living with them. On this subject, one woman said: 'I gave my son to my sister; she couldn't have children' (aged 39, interview, December 2, 2009). Another woman said: 'My niece [19 years old] has lived with me since she was seven years old; my sister didn't know how to take care of her' (aged 47, interview, December 3, 2009).

This type of family, different from both traditional southern Mozambican extended families and the modern nuclear family, may have emerged for a number of reasons: from a need to create and maintain the ties of solidarity that enable mutual assistance, from an inability to survive on a single source of income, and from an awareness that the greater its isolation and the fewer its members, the higher the risk that the family will fail to survive and reproduce. But this type of family is also the product of a specific context in which space is a scarce and precious resource, and house building a huge and expensive project that few can begin (let alone complete) alone (see also Nielsen 2010).

Another important issue concerns family relations among kinship members that live in different houses and/or neighbourhoods in Maputo. In a previous study (author publication) it was noticed that the same family has different nuclei in dissimilar economic and social neighbourhoods in the city, and/or they had moved from neighbourhood to neighbourhood during the last 30 years. As one young man commented: 'I would like to go back to town, to Alto-Maé, where I lived until I was 11 years old; could be to a flat' (19 years old, interview, December 12, 2009).

The importance of family networks still seems to explain and allow for this mobility, and families continue to move to and within the city. In the December 2009 survey only 17 percent of those interviewed lived in their present house before independence, while others had arrived during the last three decades (almost in equal number for each decade). The majority of interviewees (59 percent) had lived in other Maputo neighbourhoods before they moved to their present house; the remaining interviewees had either arrived directly from the countryside (10.6 percent) or were born in that *bairro* (17 percent). The importance of family networks is also visible in the relatively high number of interviewees (21.2 percent) to whom the plot on which they now live was given (*cedido*) to them by relatives. Finally, it was also possible to see the importance of family networks in the even higher number of interviewees (72 percent) who said that when they needed help they asked their relatives (from both descendent lines).

4   Mobility Processes in Maputo

The mobility process outlined above, which effectively connects different parts of the city, is dependent on complex family strategies. The reasons for families' mobility and spatial urban distribution are related to factors such as economic changes affecting family budgets, changes in the work activities of family members, and in their work location, and increases in rental fees for houses and plots of land associated with administrative laws and with the formal and informal market that regulates (not always in the same direction) urban transactions and major urban projects. These movements are also connected to other urban transformations: for instance, the localization of markets and streets with more or less circulation; improved or deteriorating communications between the different areas; the emergence of both wealthy and poor neighbourhoods built in relation to or as a result of auto-construction and spontaneous land occupation.

For all these reasons, families move through the city; many go to places far from the centre. The most fortunate fulfil their dreams of big houses with nice sea views or big gardens where they can have their rich *machambas*. The others, the vast majority of the urban population, attempt to make the best possible choice between different priorities. These priorities include: distance from places where various income activities take place (markets, *machambas*, urban centres, and distant neighbourhoods); land and rental prices; the profits that can be acquired when selling well-situated houses (and sometimes a good spot *is* an economic resource; for instance, for a restaurant, a shop, a hairdressing salon); space needed for all the family members that live with them (essential contributors to the domestic budget); or the money they can make renting rooms or houses to strangers. The renting process is relatively rare amongst the cases studied (2 percent) but there were some, who either have other houses or are in the process of building them, who said they would like to move and to rent out the house in which they were currently living:

> I want to rent this house, most of the time my mother and stepfather are in Nampula and I'm building my house in Albasine. That house is mine and I will keep it for my grandsons. (Woman, 39 years old, interview, December 2, 2009)

In some cases, we observed that families had built a second house in the backyard, renting it to other families; some had built extra rooms with their own door for independent access for renting. For all these reasons, houses are important in family strategies and most people, rich or poor, save to have one, or to improve the one they already have. Day by day, week by week, month by month, year by year, depending on their finances, they save for one more concrete block, to build one more room, to fix the roof, to paint a wall, to adapt to fashionable architectural styles. But they will also sell or rent the house if a good opportunity to earn money comes along. Sometimes these transactions end badly, and one woman told us one such story: she owned a big plot with trees, a *machamb*a, and when her husband died she had to sell parcels of the land to have money to live on, and also to be able to buy concrete blocks to change their *caniço* house into a house made of cement.

These dilemmas between house investments and land or house selling can also be analysed in relation to social actors' representations regarding the future of their houses. Many interviewees did not answer when asked about what would happen to their houses if they moved way (25 percent): a few said they would like to rent, and others that they would like to keep the house for their children and grandchildren. This contradicts other information regarding the number of houses owned by families in Maputo. Almost half the interviewees said they have another house and/or plot, or are in the process of building/acquiring one. Most of these new houses are in distant neighbourhoods from the city centre, such as Marracuene district. One of the explanations for this mobility was that in Marracuene it was easier to obtain a *Direito de Uso e Aproveitamento da Terra* (DUAT).[14] The difficult choices between saving and selling are related to other major issues that are interrelated and occur at all levels of family life; indeed, they are explicit in the various strategies developed.

The first major contradiction closely connected with the aforementioned urban movement occurs between the family's need to preserve unity (which is dependent on the combination of revenue and products brought in by family members working in different economic sectors and activities) and the economic and spatial dispersion that both threatens and supports this social unity. Another important contradiction is shown in the excerpts below, in the need people have to be included in social networks of solidarity – the family being one of the most important:

---

14   A document provided by the Conselho Municipal of each city, as proof that someone has the right of use of a specific plot of land. In Maputo (city centre and neighbourhoods) it is difficult to obtain a DUAT and few people have them. Most of those interviewed said they did not have one and some explained all the legal and bureaucratic processes they had been involved in, in order to try to get this sorted out.

> Family is very important. I have six brothers and one of them helps me in my business because my parents are dead. I have another brother who sells cars and he also helps me. (Woman, 31 years old, interview, December 9, 2009)

The experienced impossibility of improving their lives if they did not develop 'selfish' practices that allowed the satisfaction of individual material needs was also evident in interviews:

> Another advantage [of the house where she lives] is that it is away from the family. When I was in Hulene I was always at odds with my uncle. My family wanted to see me poor. (Woman, 45 years old, interview, December 14, 2009)

> Mozambican families are not all alike; there are brothers who can be well, have the chance to get work for their brothers and they don't do it ... They see their brother suffering and they are laughing ... and they say: 'When I went to school you played'. People of Maputo, you had to see it, even family members, help each other? No! ... In my family there are some rich ones [older brother] but he doesn't want to help anyone. I never asked him for work; I know he will never help me. (Man, 42 years old, interview, December 18, 2009)

This kind of contradiction involves a complex juxtaposition of values (trust, truth, and solidarity, alongside calculation, mistrust, and material self-interest), which social actors try to resolve in the best way they can (Geschiere 1994; Casal 2001; author publication). When this is impossible, it can initiate the breaking apart of some of the social commitments on which the previously mentioned networks were based (families, for example); this can lead to a breakdown in alliances that would otherwise have tended to perpetuate the social unit. However, this process is not necessarily irreversible: there is always the possibility of 'circulation' among solidarity networks. It is possible for individuals and families to establish new alliances with other social units (new matrimonial alliances, for instance) and for them to develop dynamic and versatile processes of social reproduction.

More generally and as we have seen in the excerpts, social actors' attitudes explain why the different nuclei of the same family in Maputo are both *together and apart*, and why family strategies can join different city neighbourhoods in a complex network that is built upon flexible economic and social relations among different houses belonging to the same family (see figure 4.4). These

FIGURES 4.3 & 4.4 Houses in Maputo Bairros (1999, 2009)

relationships involve different kinds and levels of change that are not necessarily reciprocal in time or in kind, or regular, but all of them contribute to the preservation and reinforcement of all aspects (economic, emotional, and symbolic) of family ties.

5   Home Space Changes

That family relations are changing is visible in the architectural styles people choose in the ongoing process of building their houses. Some years ago (1998–1999), many houses were built with *caniço*, usually with independent constructions spread across the yard, interspersed with trees and little *machambas*. With few exceptions, the houses are now made of concrete blocks and in many instances the buildings occupy the whole plot, leaving no space for trees and shade. Families live together under the same roof and only a few have more than 10 members (4.2 percent; 57.2 percent have between 5 and 10 members).

These new construction models, which tend towards an increasing concentration of various rooms under the same roof, are visible everywhere: from new and apparently expensive houses to new, inexpensive, unfinished ones – the latter leaving *projected houses* as a figment (see figure 4.3) of the owner's imagination. In these modern house models when some outside space exists, the tendency (or the desire) is to cover it with cement because 'sand is dirty'. From the data available it is difficult to analyse to what extent this modern construction model reflects a change in the family structure and existing relationships, and/or causes the changes taking place at a family level.[15] To what extent this model reflects a trend of smaller families, or the nuclearization of families, is difficult to know at this stage of the research, as mentioned above. But there is no doubt that this modern model and its material objects (furniture, for instance) represent what these families consider to be a modern house, and what they consider that a modern house must contain.

The existing house for a few, and the dream house for all, has all its rooms under a single roof, including bathroom, toilet, and kitchen, as well as a living room with sofas, a dining room, ornaments, and so on. It would be interesting to explore how families use their modern houses, furniture, and objects. How will they occupy the different rooms, and to do what?

---

15   I observed in my previous research that this modern urban model of spatial concentration makes polygamy more problematic even than in other urban contexts – in Maputo and in other cities in sub-Saharan Africa; polygamy does not always imply the co-habitation of the various wives (see Loforte 1996; Hasseling and Lauras-Locoh 1997).

In previous research I ascertained that in some cases the only person that eats at the dining table is the head of the family. Additionally, even when families have a bathroom inside the house, they have another one outside and that is the one they use, because they say the bathroom inside the house consumes more water (with a flush toilet and taps with running water). In the December survey, the research team found that family members spent most of the time in the outside space, sitting on mats or chairs, preparing food or just being there. With few exceptions, interviews took place outside.

Together, these aspects led to the hypothesis presented above that these modern house models coexist and interlink with traditional forms of *home space* use and are related to the way families organize relationships among family members and the outside world. These changes are expressed by family members when they argue that they rely on help from their relatives, but that they do not necessarily get the required help, which is evident in the following interview extract:

> Help is complicated. I was in the hospital and I sent an SMS to my older brother, asking him to buy me some medicine. When he read the word 'buy' he never showed up. Who helped me then was my younger brother but then I had to pay him back. (Woman, 47 years old, interview, December 3, 2009)

It seems reasonable to conclude that families are changing, then. Moreover, the city is growing and people are moving, or wish to move, as far away as the neighbourhoods of Jafar and Guava in Marracuene district (35 kilometres from the city centre), or further away still, in some instances. However, they still have relatives living in more central neighbourhoods, and if life conditions change (divorces, and deaths of parents, husbands, wives) they also have the opportunity to move to their house or plot:

> My brother-in-law is renting his house and now is coming to live with us. He is building a house in our backyard. (Man, 27 years old, interview, December 10, 2009)

6   Conclusion

On the city and in municipal districts, mobility continues. The changes that have taken place since independence have been accompanied by political, social, and economic processes, particularly in Maputo, using different economic and social reproduction strategies. Spatial mobility (urban–urban, rural–urban, and urban–rural) is an integral part of those strategies. Maputo families move from place to place because they choose or are forced to. In this process they earn money, lose money, earn social prestige or lose social prestige, destroy and create, build and rebuild social networks. The houses they can afford to build, the houses they own, or the houses they are forced to sell, or are unable to maintain, mirror or map their social mobility. This is a social mobility that the rich hide and simultaneously show with the high walls they build around their plots, and that the poor have to show because they cannot afford to build concrete walls around their houses to replace the 'ugly *espinhosa* [thorny hedge] that doesn't keep the burglars away' (Man, 43 years old, interview, December 7, 2009).

It would appear that this mobility has taken place over the last 30 years in most Maputo families' lives, regardless of the side of the city our research focused on. Land is a resource, and especially urban land and houses; it is part of a complex series of business transactions and trade undertaken by rich and poor alike. With these business and trade transactions they try to make a profit or protect themselves from legislation that during this time has regulated transactions, constructions, property, and rental markets in urban and peripheral areas of Maputo.

As explained in this chapter Maputo's population growth during these last decades has not been uniformly distributed between the *cidade de cimento* and the *bairros de caniço*. It is mainly the latter that is growing in terms of inhabited area and population density. However, this growth is not supported by urban planning in terms of maintenance or infrastructure investment, except in a few cases (Jenkins 2004, 2012; Kamete and Lindell 2010).

But apart from these obvious differences separating these two parts of the city (*cimento* and *bairros*), and the fact that both prosperity and poverty tend to move the urban *bairros* further away, it is important to bear in mind, as we have seen here, that these same factors of prosperity and poverty create complex bridges between neighbourhoods, and that such links need to be studied if we are to understand the people that live in and shape this dynamic African city.

References

AlSayaad, Nezar, and Ananya Roy, eds. 2004.*Urban informality: Transnational perspectives from the Middle East, Latin America and South Asia*. Lanham: Lexington Books.

Andersen, Jørgen Eskemose. 2012. *Understanding 'Home Space' in the African city: Socio-economic study report.* Copenhagen: Royal Danish Academy of Fine Arts.

Amselle, Jean-Loup. 1990. *Logiques métisses, anthropologie de l'identité en Afrique et ailleurs.* Paris: Payot.

Balandier, Georges. 1963. *Sociologie Actuelle de l'Afrique Noire: Dynamique sociale en Afrique centrale.* Paris: Presses Universitaires de France.

Balandier, Georges. 1969. *Anthropologie Politique.* Paris: Presses Universitaires de France.

Balandier, Georges. 1971. *Sens et Puissance.* Paris: Presses Universitaires de France.

Bierschenk, Thomas. 1988. Development projects as arenas of negotiation for strategic groups: A case study from Bénin. *Sociologia Ruralis* 28 (2/3): 146–160.

Casal, Adolfo Yáñez. 2001. Valor dos homens e das coisas. *Cadernos de Estudos Africanos* 1: 99–124.

Chen, Martha. 2003. Rethinking the informal economy: In an era of global integration and labour market flexibility. *New Delhi Seminar* 531.

Cohen, Abner. 1981. *The Politics of Elite Culture: Explorations in the dramaturgy of power in a modern African society.* Berkeley, CA: University of California Press.

Eisenstadt, Shmuel Noah. 1991. *A Dinâmica das Civilizações: Tradição e modernidade.* Lisbon: Cosmos.

Geertz, Clifford. 1973. *The Interpretation of Cultures.* London: Fontana Press.

Geffray, Christian. 2000. *Nem Pai nem Mãe. Crítica do Parentesco: O caso Macua.* Lisbon: Caminho.

Geschiere, Peter. 1994. Parenté et argent dans une société lignagère. In *La Reinvention du Capitalisme,* ed. Jean-François Bayart, 87–116. Paris: Karthala.

Geschiere, Peter, Birgit Meyer, and Peter Pels. 2008. Introduction to *Readings in Modernity in Africa,* ed. Peter Geschiere, Birgit Meyer and Peter Pels, 1–7. Oxford: James Currey.

Gluckman, Max. 1956. *Custom and Conflict in Africa.* London: Blackwell.

Hansen, Karen Tranberg, and Mariken Vaa, eds. 2004. *Reconsidering Informality: Perspectives from urban Africa.* Uppsala: Nordiska Afrikainstitutet.

Hesseling, Gerti, and Thérèse Lauras-Locoh. 1997. Femmes, pouvoir, sociétés. *Politique Africaine* 65: 3–20.

Hugon, Philippe. 1999. *Economia de África.* Lisbon: Vulgata.

Instituto Nacional de Estatística. 2012. *Recenseamento Geral da População e Habitação 2007. Indicadores socio-demográficos distritais. Maputo Cidade.* Maputo: Instituto Nacional de Estatística.

Jenkins, Paul. 1991. *Housing and Living Conditions in Two Peri-urban bairros of Maputo city.* Maputo: UNDP-UNCHS.

Jenkins, Paul. 2001. *Emerging Land Markets for Housing in Mozambique: The impact on the poor and alternatives to improve land access and urban development*; An action research project in peri-urban Maputo. Edinburgh: Edinburgh College of Art/ Heriot-Watt University, School of Planning & Housing.

Jenkins, Paul. 2004. Beyond the formal/informal dichotomy: Access to land in Maputo, Mozambique. In *Reconsidering Informality: Perspectives from urban Africa*, ed. Karen Tranberg Hansen and Mariken Vaa, 210–226. Uppsala: Nordiska Afrikainstitutet.

Jenkins, Paul. 2012. *Understanding 'Home Space' in the African city: Context report*. Copenhagen: Royal Danish Academy of Fine Arts.

Kamete, Amin Y., and Ilda Lindell. 2010. The politics of 'non-planning' interventions in African cities: Unravelling the international and local dimensions in Harare and Maputo. *Journal of Southern African Studies* 36 (4): 889–912.

Lachartre, Brigitte. 2000. *Enjeux Urbains au Mozambique: de Lourenço Marques a Maputo*. Paris: Karthala.

Loforte, Ana Maria. 1996. Género e Poder entre os Tsonga de Moçambique. PhD diss., Instituto Superior de Ciências do Trabalho e da Empresa, Portugal.

Maldonaldo, Carlos. 1995. The informal sector: Legalization or laissez-faire? *International Labour Review* 134 (6): 705–728.

Mendes, Maria Clara. 1989. Slum and Squatter Settlements in Maputo, Mozambique: structure and perspectives. In *Slum and Squatter Settlements in Sub-Saharan Africa: Toward a planning strategy*, eds Robert A. Obudho, and Constance C. Mhlanga, 219–230. New York: Praeger Publishers.

Navalha, Felisberto Dinis. 2000. Captação de Poupanças dentro do Sector Informal em Moçambique: O caso do sector informal financeiro em Maputo. Diploma diss., Universidade Eduardo Mondlane, Mozambique.

Nielsen, Morten. 2010. Contrapuntal Cosmopolitanism: Distantiation as social relatedness among house-builders in Maputo, Mozambique. *Social Anthropology* 18 (4): 396–402.

Olivier de Sardan, Jean-Pierre. 1985. Sciences sociales, africanistes et faits de développement. In *Paysans, Experts et Chercheurs en Afrique Noire: sciences sociales et développement rural*, ed. Pierre Boiral, 27–43. Paris: Karthala.

Olivier de Sardan, Jean-Pierre. 1988. Peasant logics and development project logics. *Sociologia Ruralis* 28(2/3): 216–226.

Olivier de Sardan, Jean-Pierre. 1998. *Anthropologie et Développement*. Paris: Karthala.

Ortner, Sherry B. 1984. Theory in Anthropology Since the Sixties. *Comparative Studies in Society and History* 26(1): 126–166.

Roberts, Bryan. 1994. Informal Economy and Family Strategies. *Journal of Urban and Regional Research* 18 (1): 6–23.

Rosaldo, Renato. 1980. *Ilongot Headhunting, 1883–1974*. Stanford: Stanford University Press.

Turner, Victor. 1969. *The Ritual Process: Structure and anti-structure*. Harmondsworth: Penguin Books.

Turner, Victor, and Edward M. Bruner, eds. 1986. *The Anthropology of Experience*. Urbana, IL: University of Illinois Press.

Vivet, Jeanne. 2012. Déplacés de Guerre dans la Ville. La citadinisation des deslocados à Maputo (Mozambique). Paris: Karthala.

CHAPTER 5

A Possible Triangle: Employment, Aid, and Mineral Wealth

Lia Quartapelle

Over the last decades, aid has been a subject in any discussion on economic development in Mozambique. However, both the literature and the policy-making have paid scant attention to the effects of aid on the structure of the Mozambican economy. In particular, aid effects on employment are only now beginning to be considered quantitatively in the literature, despite its potentially important policy implications. For Mozambique, this investigation is of particular interest, since the country is so dependent on aid. In this context, some observers have been critical of its effects on the economy (see, e.g., Hanlon and Smart 2009), while others suggest that aid might have an impact on the quality of institutions and on the citizen–government relationship (Hodges and Tibana 2004; de Renzio and Hanlon 2008). Whether aid creates employment and in what sectors are related issues that also need to be addressed, given the policy relevance of the topic, as well as debates about the effects of aid on the economy.

Moreover, according to de Brito (2009), amongst others, since 2005 Mozambique has entered a new stage in terms of its economic history: the country's economic development is now based on recent mineral discoveries, which are changing the structures of external dependence, wealth distribution, growth, and patterns of employment creation. This change is leaving unscathed the characteristics of Mozambique as a 'rent economy' since it is moving from aid to mineral resources as main drivers of economic activity (Auty 2007).

Given these circumstances, an assessment of the role played by aid in an area of economic development such as employment creation is all the more important. It may help our understanding of what has happened beneath the surface of the Mozambican miracle of economic growth and it could also help predict the evolution of the 'rent economy' scheme experienced by Mozambique.

1 The Donors' Darling

What is known as international aid bureaucracy works in cycles. It selects one or a few countries in which it is considered important – almost fashionable – to intervene. It inundates these countries, the donors' darlings, with aid flows for a period of time – often around ten years. During and after this period, the aid bureaucracy strives to demonstrate that aid works in that specific situation. Finally, it leaves, having achieved little when measured against the amounts of money spent.

In Africa this general pattern can be identified in a number of cases: Ghana in the 1980s, and Uganda and Ethiopia in the 1990s (Dowden 2009). Arguably, Mozambique constituted the donors' darling of the first decade of the twenty-first century. If trends in aid disbursements to Mozambique since the 1980s are examined, it is clear that the country has changed its stance towards international aid. While in the first years following independence Mozambique was an outcast from the circuits of international aid, the mid 1980s saw a shift towards increasing aid dependence: aid flows registered a rising trend. In 2008 they again reached the unprecedented levels of 1992 – the year of the peace agreement, and the beginning of the costly demobilization of troops.

If we look at relative aid trends, that is, at the relationship between aid and gross national income (GNI) (table 5.1), aid represents over 20 percent of GNI between 2000 and 2010.

This means that per capita over the period 2000–2007 every Mozambican has received on average US$67 per year. Comparatively, over the same period, Uganda and Tanzania, which have the same per capita GDP as Mozambique, have received on average, respectively, US$39 and US$40 per person per year. Not only does this show that international aid represents an important part of national income, it also suggests that aid performs a vital economic role. As table 5.2 shows, 'foreign aid has been the predominant source of investment funds' until the gas boom (Jones 2009, 15), and it can thus be considered a key ingredient in what has been termed the 'Mozambican miracle'.[1] According to Jones (2009), overseas development aid (ODA) in Mozambique has provided

TABLE 5.1   Aid as a share of Mozambique GNI, 2000–2012

Year	2000	2001	2002	2003	2004	2005	2006	2007	2008	2009	2010	2011	2012
AID/GNI	2.5	5.5	5.1	3.5	3.2	1.2	5	4.4	1.8	1.3	1.2	6.9	4.6

SOURCE: WORLD BANK DEVELOPMENT INDICATORS, 2014. AUTHOR'S ELABORATION

---

1   For usage of this term, see for instance Reibel 2010. However, the real nature of the Mozambican miracle has been widely questioned (for example, Hanlon and Smart 2009; Hanlon 2010). Recent World Bank data seem to confirm some of this scepticism: Mozambique is one of the few countries in sub-Saharan Africa where poverty between 2003 and 2008 increased, albeit marginally.

the majority of investment funding since independence. In 2000, for example, aid accounted for over 70 percent of the currency needed to finance so-called non-mega projects. Additionally, ODA contributed to most publicly financed investments until the commodity boom and especially discoveries in gas fields resulted in a stellar increase in FDIs, as can be seen from table 5.2, below.

For these reasons, and as stated in many other works (for example, IDD and associates 2006; Jones 2009), aid in Mozambique represents a crucial part of the government budget: revenues, despite efforts by the government resulting in a steep increase, cover roughly half of government expenditure and thus need to be augmented with additional – mainly foreign – resources (see table 5.3). Even rents deriving from the mineral resources in the country have not yet changed this trend.

Aid dependence is just one of the stages of the evolution of the Mozambican economy (although it is not the final stage), which, passing through stages of Portuguese rule, independence, and economic recovery following the civil war, has nonetheless maintained its colonial structure (de Brito 2009). In particular, aid has played a vital part in strengthening the role of the public sector, as well as in determining the patterns of investment and the phases of change in the country's productive structure. In this way, ODA determines general

TABLE 5.2   Investments and domestic savings in Mozambique as share of GDP, 2004–2012

	2004	2005	2006	2007	2008	2009	2010	2011	2012
Domestic savings/GDP	6.7	0.5	8.4	4.4	4.7	2.7	9.6	14.7	8.2
Investments/GDP	18.3	17.7	17	15.3	17.6	14.9	21.3	39.1	53.8
FDI/GDP	4.3	1.9	2.6	5.2	5.7	9.3	13.6	22.7	36.4

SOURCE: IMF DATA MAPPER 2014. AUTHOR'S ELABORATION

TABLE 5.3   Expenditure and revenue as a share of GDP in Mozambique, 2004–2012

	2004	2005	2006	2007	2008	2009	2010	2011	2012
Government Expenditure/GDP	24.8	22.9	27	28.1	27.8	32.6	32.9	33.7	32.6
Revenue, Excluding Grants/GDP	13.1	14.1	15	15.9	15.9	17.6	19.6	20.8	23.3

SOURCE: WORLD BANK DEVELOPMENT INDICATORS 2009. AUTHOR'S ELABORATION

trends in public spending. On average, for example, between 2000 and 2007, aid accounted for half (50.9%) of the state budget, which means that public spending depends heavily on aid availability. Therefore, financial stability is ensured by aid flows, and increases in the state budget depend heavily on aid inflows, as shown in figure 5.1 below.

To an extent, the state can now be viewed as the single most important donor agency in the country. In Mozambique, donor agencies decided to gradually reduce the number of projects that they manage directly, and they have moved to new modalities of aid, such as budget and sectoral support, which leave the government in charge of the implementation of actions using aid

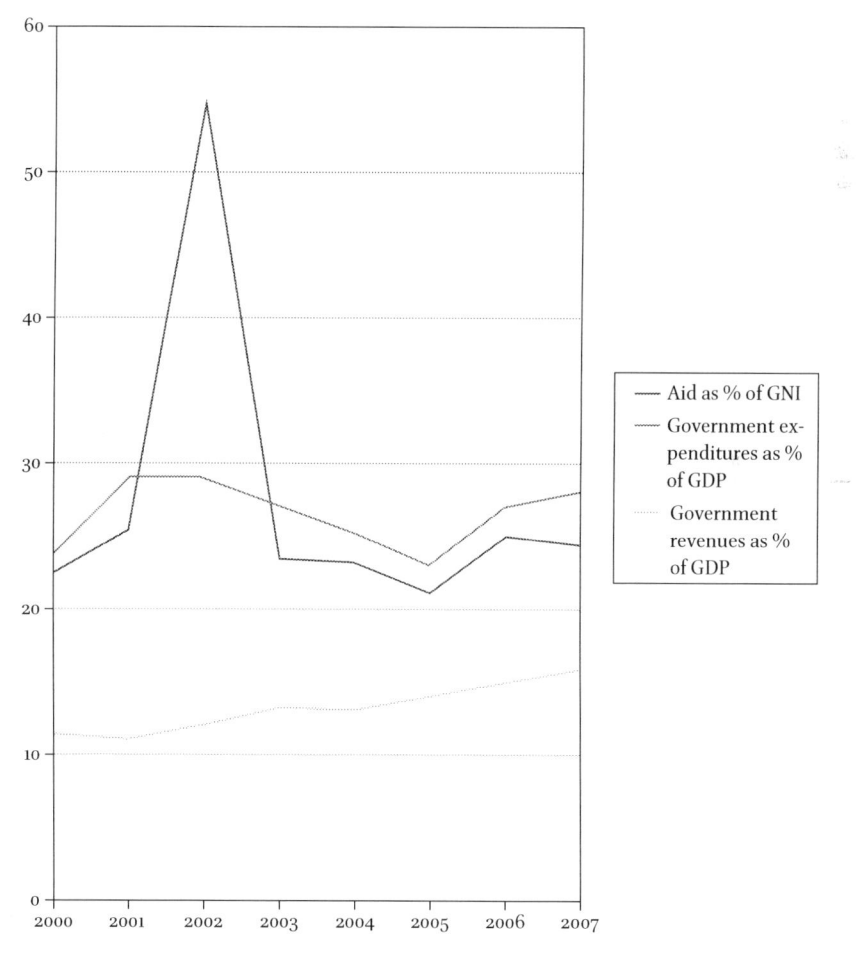

FIGURE 5.1   Overall fiscal balance, including and excluding grants as a share of GDP
SOURCE: IMF DATA MAPPER 2014. AUTHOR'S ELABORATION

monies. If we look at how aid money is spent in the country, using OECD data referring to the years 2004 to 2008, on average more than 20 percent of aid spent here is disbursed via budget support, while according to other estimates, in 2008 almost 75 percent of aid was spent via the public sector. This happens because most donor agencies extensively employ budget support and sectoral programs: both instruments channel resources via the state, making the state the de facto single most important implementing agency in the country. In-country estimates suggest that sectoral support almost equals budget support. Thus, it can be hypothesized that as much as 40 percent of ODA in the country is disbursed via sector and budget support (see Table 5.4).

The adoption of aid modalities such as sectoral and budget support, which have a higher content of policy when compared to projects, poses a challenge to the policy space open to the Mozambican government. For instance, the government has limited capacity to decide on national budget priorities because it is bound by an agreement with donors over the share of public expenditure that it has to allocate to education, health, and other priority sectors. While budget support is a form of aid used only in those countries where the government is committed to poverty reduction, fiscal and macro-economy stability, and good governance, nevertheless, it is difficult not to wonder whether there is any potential for the emergence of a set of alternative political priorities, given the weight of donor contributions for the survival of the Mozambican state service-delivery machine, and thus for the legitimization of the political elite. Perhaps indicative of how entrenched the current state of affairs is, no opposition party has yet put forward a proposal of radical reorientation of public expenditure.

Debates about the breadth and scope of autonomous prioritizing by Mozambican polities remain open. There is no conclusive evidence. Some researchers argue that the government manages to follow its own agenda (Castel-Branco 2011), others air concerns that external accountability has a priority over internal accountability (Ilal 2008), others still suggest that donors act as a catalyst in certain policy processes (Manning and Malbrough 2010). However, all the published work agrees that there is debate over national policies not

TABLE 5.4   Share of ODA spent via the state, 2004–2008

Year	2004	2005	2006	2007	2008
Via public channels	5.8	4.9	0.5	0.1	74.6
Budget support	7.0	8.1	7.8	6.5	28.8

SOURCE: OECD-DAC DATABASE. AUTHOR'S ELABORATION

only in national political circles, but also among the donor community; over time, it is likely that both sides shape decisions, one way or another.

Since the changes of the mid 1980s, new donors have come to play a part in Mozambique, and their importance has increased alongside the discovery of the region's mineral resources. For example, on the day of then President Guebuza's inauguration into his second term in office (October 28, 2009), he met with Chinese Minister of Commerce Chen Deming. Later, Minister Deming and Mozambique Finance Minister Manuel Chang agreed on a loan of US$14.7 million to Mozambique. Chinese interests in the region are closely matched by Brazilian and Indian interests,[2] although it is difficult to monitor the scale of resources coming from non-OECD donors, including both emerging countries and so-called vertical funds. Despite the advances of the OECD tracking system to include also non-DAC donors and despite the efforts in Mozambique which resulted in the ODAMoz database, there is no official tracking system for these resources, but they are undoubtedly increasing following more recent investments in the country.[3]

The impact of aid on the real economy and on its structure has yet to be ascertained. Mozambique is an agricultural-based economy and presents similar characteristics to those of most sub-Saharan African countries: 80 percent of its population works in this field of activity. However, only 32.6 percent of its GDP comes from this sector (Almeida Matos *et al.* 2014, 5) , which means that agricultural production is often carried out at subsistence level and is often labour rather than capital intensive (Arndt *et al.* 2000, 3). For these reasons, in order to stimulate a structural transformation of the economy, the 2011–2014 Action plan to reduce poverty put forward by the Mozambican government aimed at increasing agricultural productivity (Governo de Moçambique 2011).

At the beginning of the 2000 decade, the contribution to GDP made by private sector business was much the same it had been just before independence, which means that post-war efforts have gone mainly towards restructuring

---

2 China remains Africa's most significant economic partner amongst the BRICS nations, although Brazil has stepped up its economic ties in the region. In Mozambique, Brazilian companies Vale and Odebrecht have made an investment currently worth $1.3 billion, in order to exploit one of the largest reserves of coal in the world in Moatize. Other Brazilian and Indian enterprises are involved in substantive investment projects in railways and coal extraction in Tete province.

3 One reason for the difficulty in accounting for emerging donors' aid is that new donors often provide funds that are a mix of profit and grant elements. It is widely documented in the literature on emerging donors that an upsurge in commercial interests increases aid-like funds (DIE 2008; Kragelund 2008).

existing capacity rather than stimulating new forms of production. The so-called mega-projects (large inflows of FDIs for large-scale investments), have contributed to adding productive capacity in the industrial sector, despite their limited impact on local businesses and economic diversification and broad-base growth (UNCTAD 2012). Services retain a 47.4 percent share of GDP (Almeida Santos *et al.* 2014, 5), which is a little above their share of the economy prior to independence. High public expenditure (used to provide basic services to a large proportion of the population) pays for the majority of the service sector. In this sense, aid spending risks creating an economy that is service- rather than production-oriented.

Mega-projects have come under close scrutiny from observers both inside and outside the country for their effects on the structure of the Mozambican economy and their impact on national capacity for revenue mobilization. According to Castel-Branco and Ossemane (2010), even the World Bank and the IMF have come to recognize that megaprojects contribute little to poverty reduction and sustainable growth, while the fiscal incentives present a high ratio of costs and benefits in terms of social welfare. Megaprojects have contributed to sporadic investment growth but there are few signs of widespread welfare attributable to foreign capital (UNCTAD 2012).

Compared to other sub-Saharan countries Mozambique has a fairly outward-looking economy. Arguably, this basic structure of the economy is derived from decisions taken during colonialism and, also, Mozambique's geographical position. Historically and contemporarily, Mozambique has also provided manpower to the extractive industries of South Africa, which in turn have provided valuable remittances, especially to the southern provinces.

Most observers agree that Mozambique's growth potential – especially in the private sector – is still underdeveloped, mainly due to the state of the infrastructure, the poor quality of human capital, and the business environment. Aid disbursements are not proactively helping in these areas, being too much influenced still by the conclusion of the so-called Washington Consensus: that aid should only create the required preconditions for market forces to unleash their potential (Hanlon 2006).

Besides this, it is widely questioned whether aid is bringing new employment to the country, especially in the face of a lack of structural transformation of the Mozambican economy since independence (Jones and Tarp 2013, 5). According to a study (Tvedten *et al.* 2009, 16), poor people in Mozambique emphasize their lack of employment as the main reason for their poverty. According to Jones and Tarp (2012, 36) the lack of jobs is perceived as a particularly acute problem among the urban youth. At the same time, education, the universal provision of which has been a main aim of aid disbursement across the country, is not identified as an opportunity to be lifted out of poverty. On one hand, families do not believe that education guarantees access to the country's limited employment opportunities; on the other, unemployment seems to be higher amongst educated youngsters (World Bank 2009). The perception of available resources – heightened by the aid bonanza – coupled with rising inequality and a lack of formal employment is creating situations of increasing violence and the potential for instability (Hanlon 2010).

2　　Aid and Poverty in Mozambique

In February 2008 and again in September 2010, Maputo and other cities experienced 'bread riots' that ended in a number of fatalities. On both occasions the riots broke out following an increase in the price of food and other subsidized goods (chiefly, petrol and thus public transport) (see Bertelsen 2016 for an analysis). Although unpleasant per se, these episodes of violence were also read as worrying cracks in the Mozambican miracle. To most internal and international observers, these were the visible signs of a credible risk for a country heretofore portrayed as an African success story: Mozambique appeared to be on the verge of becoming yet another dysfunctional African state. Democracy did not seem to be working very well. The economic miracle also seemed volatile when consumers felt so oppressed by price increases that they took to the streets and committed violent acts.

There is heated debate inside and outside Mozambique policy and academic circles over whether poverty is being reduced, and in what ways aid is contributing to this. Measuring poverty is not an easy task in itself, and the debate is certainly caught up in this difficulty. While there is no conclusive evidence, discussion so far suggests that 'poverty [in Mozambique] is not being reduced, at least not as quickly as previously thought' (Cunguara and Hanlon 2010, 21). The sluggish agricultural sector seems to account for much of the slow progress (Arndt *et al.* 2011), especially after 2000, that is, after the initial recovery following the end of the civil war.

Of course, this situation is not only a problem of objective measurement: the dynamics of inequality and perceptions of poverty and inequality are also important factors. Politics has already adapted to the new reality: in the country's political discourse, a rhetoric of fighting against poverty has replaced a rhetoric of fighting against colonialism and postcolonial influence (de Brito 2007). However, policy measures aimed at reducing poverty and inequality seem not to work effectively. Thus, an investigation into the dynamics linking aid flows and employment creation would be both useful and timely and it would add to the existing literature trying to explain why, so far, the Mozambican miracle has been to an extent jobless (Jones and Tarp 2013).

3   Mineral Resources: Beyond Aid?

The discovery of the Mamba gas field, off the coast of Quirimbas Island, has definitively altered Mozambique economic prospects: from a poor, re-sourcesless and aid-dependent country, Mozambique turned to be a resource-abundant country, with the potential to foster development diminishing its dependence from donors. It also increases the challenges the country has to face in the coming years with reference to its development path (Castel-Branco 2010). The gas discoveries are not fully accounted yet (Crook 2012, 31), have not yet unleashed their full effect on the Mozambican economy but have positioned Mozambique as the third African gas producer.[4] In addition, Mozambique's mineral bonanza pre-dates this discovery of gas: mineral findings since 2007 (iron, coal, heavy sands, tantalum) mean that 'mining output … [has] expanded by 27% during the first half of 2011', according to government data published by the Economist Intelligence Unit in the November 2011 Country Report.

Such findings challenge the importance of aid as a source of financing (Osman 2010). Data on aid, which started decreasing from 2012, as well as tensions between donors and the Mozambican government in March 2014[5] suggest that with the decline in aid dependency comes a more dialectic relationship between donors and the beneficiary. It could also be the beginning of the diversification of sources of revenue, given the mineral discoveries and the start of many megaprojects in the region. According to the World Bank (2014, 5), 'taxes paid by oil, gas and mining companies have increased manifold from US$39.5 million in 2008 to US$112.7 million in 2011'. However, it is difficult to ascertain the impact of revenues as most of the mineral resources, starting with gas (and the prospected discoveries of oil), has yet to materialize (Almeida Santos *et al.*, 2014 forecast that a sizeable effect on public finance will be felt as of 2020). In order to appreciate the possible impact of energy resources on growth, investments, and exports, it is necessary to refer to earlier work on the impact of mineral wealth in Mozambique.

---

4   *Mozambique country analysis note*, in the US Energy Administration Information, August 20, 2014, http://www.eia.gov/countries/country-data.cfm?fips=mz.

5   *Donor relations are under strain*, in Economist Intelligence Unit, March 15, 2014, http://www.eiu.com/public/subscriber_only.aspx.

According to estimates made by Aurélio Bucuane and Peter Mulder in 2007 – that is, when natural gas and oil exploration had not yet made any notable discoveries – it was expected that non-natural resource exports would grow by an annual 10 percent, pushing the value of non-natural resource exports from US$365 million in 2000 to almost US$6,500 million in 2020. It should be noted that according to the OECD Development Directorate (OECD-DAC), international donors disbursed US$987 million in 2000. If Bucuane and Mulder's predictions hold – albeit recent hydrocarbon discoveries suggest they have provided gross underestimates – non-natural exports over the next decade will overtake and possibly replace aid as a source of foreign exchange.

Data now available on oil reserves were not available at the time of their study, and Bucuane and Mulder (2007) also made some hypotheses about the contribution of the hydrocarbon sector – and especially oil – to the Mozambican trade balance. They hypothesized that full exploitation of oil would start in 2015; they proposed three possible scenarios, on the basis of Mozambique's hydrocarbon reserves being very small (as in Tunisia), medium (as in Brazil or Libya) or large (as in Norway). Exports by 2020 would increase by an additional US$3.5 billion in the first scenario, and by US$30 to US$60 billion in the other two cases. Estimates need to be adjusted given that up to this point in time Mozambique is known to have only gas, not oil, reserves.

Even if the presence of non-natural resources could provide Mozambique with a source of income that, according to these authors, would amount to almost $1,000 per capita over a period of 20 years, this would not happen without an associated cost. Growth based on abundant primary commodities is known to be haphazard: the risk of what is referred to as the 'resource curse' is high.[6] On the political side, mineral riches tend to encourage conflict over the control of resources, and they tend to sustain authoritarian regimes. In terms of macro-economic and commercial matters, mineral-rich economies that do not diversify their exports tend to depend heavily on market conditions – that is, on price levels as well as on the availability of willing buyers – for their subsistence. The volatility of prices of primary products, and the declining terms of trade, constitute important factors explaining the persistent underdevelopment and external dependence of African oil-exporting countries such as Angola and Nigeria. The discovery of mineral riches in this respect will not free

---

6 'Resource curse' means that resource-rich countries grow at a lower rate than resource-poor countries (Auty 2001). Although some countries have managed to escape the curse (such as Botswana, Chile, and Australia), and although recent research has questioned the validity of the resource curse paradigm, preferring other articulations of it (Wright and Czelusta 2004), the record of African countries falling prey to it is high.

Mozambique from external dependence. It has to consider that the majority of energy extracted in Mozambique today (mainly from hydropower) is exported (Mulder 2007).

Moreover, foreign investments in Mozambique have already increased and will rocket in the near future: Italian-owned ENI alone has announced that it will invest about €50 billion in the country over the next few years. By comparison, net foreign direct investments (FDIS) in Mozambique in 2009 amounted to US\$78 billion. Castel-Branco estimates the contribution of hydrocarbon exploration to the share of investments to Mozambique. In 2007, for example, coinciding with the first non-natural resource explorations, FDIS increased to over US\$5.5 billion, from less than US\$100 million the year before. A disaggregated analysis shows that Mozambique is highly dependent on foreign sources of capital, especially for the investment necessary for non-natural resource exploitation. Therefore, while mineral wealth seems to reduce dependence on foreign donors, it increases dependence on foreign buyers and foreign investors. Mozambique growth prospects in this respect remain particularly vulnerable to commodity prices: the recent 30% decrease in metal prices is matter of concern (World Bank 2014, 5).

The discovery of mineral riches also matters in terms of employment. There are many concerns about the sustainability of growth based on mineral wealth in terms of poverty reduction and inequality consequences. If the benefits of growth from aid for the Mozambican population living in poverty are widely questioned, growth that comes from the exploitation of mineral resources is even more widely criticized. In this regard, the first studies concerned with the impact of mining on local communities are eye-opening: Kabemba and Nhancale (2012), for example, find that two coal mining companies in Mozambique, Vale and Rio Tinto, are undermining local entrepreneurship through mechanisms of procurement and through extensive use of imported materials. In this context a study of aid employment dynamics is crucial in terms of helping to influence the practices of the international companies that are exploiting Mozambique's mineral resources.

4   Is Aid Better at Job Creation?

One of the most recent assessment of the employment situation in Mozambique was carried out by Inquerito à Força de Trabalho (IFTRAB), which undertook a cross-sectional survey between 2004 and 2005, involving 17,800 individuals (17,151 respondents). This survey is representative at national and provincial levels. While a detailed description of IFTRAB's data can be found in the Mozambican national statistics (Instituto Nacional de Estatística 2006), some insights into the relationship between employment levels and variables are significant in the present context. The definition of employment refers to the ILO definition, adapted to the Mozambican reality (INE 2006, 11–2), in which a person is employed if s/he is at least 15 years old and either

(a)   worked at least one hour in the seven days before the survey, either in waged employment or in household production; or

(b)   did not work in the seven days prior to the survey but has employment. That is, s/he was on leave, on sick leave, on strike, etc.

The adaptation to Mozambique is achieved by including in the unemployed population the following categories:

(a)   casual workers;

(b)   self-employed workers without employees and without regular occupation;

(c)   self-employed workers without employees and with a regular occupation, who did not work in the period of the survey due to economic reasons;

(d)   household workers without a wage and without a regular occupation;

(e)   household workers without a wage who did not work in the period of the survey.

Table 5.5 shows the proportion of employed and unemployed people according to individual characteristics (sex, age, education, sector of activity, and mode of employment). The majority of the surveyed population is male. The age groups between 20 and 40 years constitute almost 50 percent of the total population surveyed. The education level is low: more than two-thirds of those surveyed have five years of schooling or less, while agriculture is the main sector of activity. More than 75 percent of the population is self-employed. Thus, it may be said that most of the people who work in agriculture are self-employed.

It seems from the data that more females than males are unemployed; more older individuals are unemployed than younger ones; people that are employed have lower mean years of education; employed individuals tend to comprise the majority in urban areas; amongst unemployed people there are less people that are self-employed; employed people have slightly smaller families than unemployed ones; singles and widows are over-represented amongst unemployed people; finally, unemployed people own on average a higher number of goods.

Given these changes and the challenges facing the Mozambican economy, it would be interesting to investigate the job-creation effects of aid spending at the provincial level in Mozambique.[7]

---

7   The findings in this section are based on author's (author publication) empirical work, which in turn is based on IFTRAB data and provincial budget allocations; see McCoy and Cunamizana (2008).

TABLE 5.5   Characteristics of employed and unemployed population 2004

		Employed	Unemployed	Total
Sex	Male	70.4	67.7	68.2
	Female	29.6	32.3	31.8
Age	10–19 years	1.7	3.3	1.97
	20–24 years	8.7	9.2	8.8
	25–29 years	13.4	13.5	13.4
	30–34 years	14.0	11.2	13.5
	35–39 years	12.7	11.1	12.4
	40–44 years	12.0	10.3	11.7
	45–49 years	10.0	9.2	9.9
	50–54 years	7.7	7.0	7.6
	55–59 years	6.1	6.1	6.1
	60–64 years	5.2	5.8	5.3
	65 years or more	8.5	13.3	9.5
	No information	0	0.2	0
Education	No schooling	26.1	22.3	25.4
	EP1 (5 years)	45.8	44.1	45.5
	EP2 (7 years)	14.31	17.3	14.9
	Higher education (12 years or more)	13.8	16.4	14.3
Sector of activity	Agriculture	62.1	71.9	62.7
	Non-agricultural sectors	37.9	28.1	37.3
Self-employment	Waged employment	25.1	9.6	24.2
	Self-employment	74.2	87.0	75.0
	Domestic workers	0.6	3.4	0.8

SOURCE: IFTRAB 2004/05. AUTHOR'S ELABORATION

In the meantime, two questions concerning aid spending effect on employment creation are addressed here: whether aid creates employment, and whether aid acts as an instrument of structural transformation of the Mozambican economy, increasing employment in one sector while reducing it in another.

In terms of the overall effect of aid on employment, the empirical findings suggest that when controlling for individual characteristics (which the literature and previous analysis of the dataset have shown as making a differ-ence in terms of employment creation[8]), aid has no significant effect on the level of employment at the provincial level in Mozambique.

Instead, the analysis of sectoral employment suggests that aid is an impor-tant factor in terms of structural transformation of the economy. As observed in Ravallion (1987), aid seems to reduce employment in the agricultural sector while it increases employment in manufacturing. The effect of aid on employ-ment in the service sector is insignificant. This could be due to the fact that the service sector includes a wide array of activities, from public employees to street vendors. It could be hypothesized that the effect of an increase in aid could have different effects on various categories.

Finally, the effects of aid spending on self-employment and on the formal sector are examined. Aid increases the likelihood of being self-employed, ei-ther as the sector includes all individuals who have declared themselves to be self-employed (74.2% of the overall employed population), or only those that are self-employed, but not in the agricultural sector. This distinction has been made because agricultural self-employment is by far the main type of employ-ment in the agricultural sector (over 96% of the population employed in agri-culture is self-employed).

Individuals who respond that they receive salaries, or who are employed in the public sector, or in a registered company in the private sector, belong to the formal sector. Aid seems to decrease the level of employment in the formal sector.

Using, in particular, the 2005 IFTRAB data collected by INE, and data on aid spending analysed in McCoy and Cunamizana (2008), the hypothesis that aid reduces unemployment has been tested. The hitherto unreported findings suggest, perhaps surprisingly, that aid does not significantly reduce unemploy-ment. The data suggest instead that aid has an effect on sectoral employment. For instance, while aid decreases employment within the agricultural sector it increases employment in manufacturing, while it has no effect on employ-ment in services. Moreover, aid increases self-employment, while reducing employment in the formal sector of the economy. Admittedly, these findings are limited by the availability of data referring to aid disaggregated at the pro-vincial level, which would allow the analysis to be expanded to aid activities not connected to the state's capacity to deliver them. The new IFTRAB data,

---

8   These are: sex, age, individual's education level, health status, goods owned by the individual, rural area of residence, two dummies for marital status, a variable referring to the size of the family, and some dummies controlling for the province of residence and the region of residence.

which should become available in 2012, could help us to further understand the dynamics of employment over time, and could be matched with more precise disaggregated data that have been collected over the years via the system of official development assistance to Mozambique. Despite these limitations, some preliminary conclusions may be drawn.

5   Conclusion

This chapter has investigated the issue of aid effectiveness on the employment level in Mozambique; the study is situated within an overall socio-economic context of different forms of aid impact on Mozambique's history and patterns of governance. It relates these issues to the emerging and recent challenges of mineral exploitation.

The first conclusion concerns aid as an instrument of modernization of the economy. In fact, if we assume the perspective of classic development economics (found mainly in Arthur Lewis's 1954 work), economic development occurs in the context of a structural change in the economy. More specifically, a country starts developing when the importance of the agricultural sector declines and the manufacturing and service sectors acquire importance, in terms of both share of GDP and employment. In Mozambique, as suggested by the empirical analysis, aid increases the share of people employed in the manufacturing sector and reduces those employed in agriculture; thus, it can be said that aid has some influence on the pattern of modernization of the economy. Mozambique, in fact, is considered an aid success story, insofar as targeted aid has sustained economic and political stabilization in the country, which in turn has attracted direct foreign investment (Auty 2007, 13).

The possible consequences of this process of structural transformation in terms of inequality and a push towards urbanization must be further investigated, however, with caution and concern. Recent events, chiefly the 2008 and 2010 riots over the increase in the price of primary goods, suggest that perceptions of inequality and of absent benefits from aid spending are acutely felt also by an increasing number of the urban population. The transformational effects of aid need to be weighed against these worrying signs, as well as against the concern that aid does not increase overall employment: it only shifts employed people from one sector to another.

Secondly, the results suggest that aid can have an effect on the formalization of the economy. If aid reduces formal activities, it can be said that aid is pushing Mozambique towards an informalization of its economy. This is an important part of the process of structural transformation of the economy outlined above. However, the consequences in terms of the resilience of the economic system must be taken into account, given the buffer role that the informal sector plays in times of crisis.

Finally, and as has been shown, the link between aid and employment might be significant for the upcoming dynamics of development and employment creation that the exploitation of mineral wealth might bring about. On the one hand, aid provided the first source of rent that the Mozambican economy has enjoyed. A careful study of the dynamics that have governed the links between aid flows and employment creation in the country could set the stage for a more effective and balanced use of rents deriving from mineral wealth as regards employment and development. On the other hand, there is much (national and international) concern over the distributive consequences of the rents deriving from the exploitation of natural resources. A virtuous interplay among government's legitimate process of prioritization, citizens' needs and aspirations, private sector interests, and donors' external scrutiny could help address some of these concerns from an early stage.

References

Almeida Santos, Andre, Luca Monge Roffarello, and Manuel Filipe. 2013. *Mozambique Profile for the African Economic Outlook*. Paris: OECD.

Arndt, Channing et al. 2011. *Explaining Poverty Evolution: The case of Mozambique*. Working Paper 17, United Nations University / World Institute for Development Economic Research, Helsinki.

Arndt, Channing, Henning Tarp Jensen, and Finn Tarp. 2000. Structural characteristics of the economy of Mozambique: A SAM-based analysis. *Review of Development Economics* 4 (3): 292–306.

Auty, Richard M. 2001. The political economy of resource-driven growth. *European Economic Review* 45:839–946.

Auty, Richard M. 2007. *Aid and Rent-driven Growth: Mauritania, Kenya and Mozambique compared*. Research paper 35, United Nations University / World Institute for Development Economic Research, Helsinki.

Bertelsen, Bjørn Enge. 2016. Effervescence and Ephemerality: Popular Urban Uprisings in Mozambique. *Ethnos* 81(1):25–52.

Bucuane, Aurélio, and Peter Mulder. 2007. Exploring natural resources in Mozambique: Will it be a blessing or a curse? Paper presented at the Instituto de Estudos Sociais e Económicos conference, Maputo, 19 September 2007.

Castel-Branco, Carlos N. 2010. Economia extractive e desafios de industrialização em Moçambique. In *Desafios para Moçambique,* ed. Luis de Brito et al., 19–109. Maputo: Instituto de Estudos Sociais e Económicos (IESE).

Castel-Branco, Carlos N. 2011. *Dependência de ajuda externa, acumulação e ownership: Contribuição para um debate de economia política.* Maputo: Instituto de Estudos Sociais e Económicos (IESE).

Crook, Leonard. 2012. *The future of natural gas in Mozambique: towards a gas master plan – executive summary.* World Bank working paper 80683. Washington, DC: World Bank.

Cunguara, Benedito, and Joseph Hanlon. 2010. *Poverty is Not Being Reduced in Mozambique.* Crisis States Working Paper series 2, Crisis States Research Centre, London.

de Brito, Luis. 2007. Discurso político e pobreza em Moçambique: Análise de três discursos presidenciais. Paper presented at Instituto de Estudos Sociais e Económico's inaugural conference, Maputo, 19 September 2007.

de Brito, Luis. 2009. *Moçambique: De uma economia de serviços a uma economía de renda.* Boletim n° 13. IDeIAS. Maputo: Instituto de Estudos Sociais e Económicos.

de Renzio, Paolo, and Jospeh Hanlon. 2008. Mozambique: contested sovereignty? The dilemmas of aid dependence. In *The Politics of Aid: African strategies for dealing with donors,* ed. Lindsay Whitfield, 246–270. Oxford: Oxford University Press.

DIE. 2008. *Financing for Development Series: Southern non-DAC actors in development cooperation.* Briefing Paper 13, German Institute for Development, Bonn.

Dowden, Richard. 2009. *Africa: Altered states, ordinary miracles.* London: Public Affairs.

Economist Intelligence Unit. 2011. *Mozambique Country Profile.* London: EIU. Available at http://country.eiu.com/Mozambique, accessed 02 November 2012.

Governo de Moçambique. 2011. Plano de acção para redução da pobreza 2011–2014. Maputo. Available at http://www.mpd.gov.mz/index.php?option=com_docman&task=doc_download&gid=189&Itemid=50&lang=en, accessed 02 November 2012.

Hanlon, Joseph. 2006. Government and donors should promote the economy. Unpublished discussion paper available at http://www.open.ac.uk/technology/mozambique/pics/d60674.doc, accessed 02 November 2012.

Hanlon, Joseph. 2010. Mozambique: 'The war ended 17 years ago, but we are still poor'. *Conflict, Security and Development* 10 (1): 77–102.

Hanlon, Joseph, and Teresa Smart. 2009. *Há mais Bicicletas mas Há Desenvolvimento em Moçambique?* Maputo: Universidade Eduardo Mondlane.

Hodges, Tony, and Roberto Tibana. 2004. *Political Economy of the Budget in Mozambique.* Maputo: DfID.

IDD and Assoc. 2006. *Evaluation of General Budget Support*: Synthesis report. Glasgow: DfID.

Ilal Abdul. 2008. *Aid Effectiveness: The case of Mozambique*. Maputo: Trocaire CAFOD Eurodad.

Instituto Nacional de Estatística. 2006. *Inquérito Integrado à Força de Trabalho*. Maputo: Instituto Nacional de Estatística.

Jones, Sam. 2009. *Whither Aid? Financing development in Mozambique*. DIIS Report 2009: 08. Copenhagen: Danish Institute for International Studies.

Jones, Sam, and Finn Tarp. 2013. Jobs and welfare in Mozambique. WIDER Working Paper n. 2013/045. Helsinki: UNU/WIDER.

Jones, Sam, and Finn Tarp. 2012. *Jobs and welfare in Mozambique*. Country case study for the 2013 World Development Report. Washington, DC: World Bank.

Kabemba, Claude, and Camilo   Nhacale. 2012. Coal versus Communities: Exposing poor practices by Vale and Rio Tinto in Mozambique. Open Policy Paper, Southern Africa Resource Watch Johannesburg.

Kragelund, Peter. 2008. The return of non-DAC donors to Africa: New prospects for African development? *Development Policy Review* 26 (5): 555–584.

Lewis, Arthur. 1954. Economic development with unlimited supplies of labour. *The Manchester School* 22 (2): 139–191.

Manning, Carrie, and Monica Malbrough. 2010. Bilateral donors and aid conditionality in post-conflict peacebuilding: The case of Mozambique. *Journal of Modern African Studies* 48 (1): 143–169.

McCoy, Simon and Imarciana, Cunamizana. 2008. *Provincial budget allocations in the health, education and water sectors: an analysis 2003–2006, DNEAP Working paper 58E*, Maputo.

Mulder, Peter. 2007. *Perspectivas da Energia em Moçambique*. Discussion paper 53, Direcção Nacional de Estudos e Análise de Políticas, Ministério de Planificação e Desenvolvimento, Maputo.

Osman, Abdul Magid. 2010. Financiar o desenvolvimento. In *Desafios para Moçambique 2010*, ed. Luis de Brito et al., 229–239. Maputo: Instituto de Estudos Sociais e Económicos (IESE).

Ravallion, Martin. 1987. *Market Responses to Anti-Hunger Policies: Effects on wages, prices and employment*. Working paper 28, United Nations University / World Institute for Development Economic Research, Helsinki.

Reibel, Aaron J. 2010. An African Success Story: Civil Society and the 'Mozambican Miracle'. *Africana* 4 (2): 78–102.

Tvedten, Inge, Margarida Paulo, and Carmeliza Rosário. 2009. *Monitoring and Evaluating Mozambique's Poverty Reduction Strategy PARPA, 2006–2008: A synopsis of three qualitative studies on rural and urban poverty*. CMI Report 5. Bergen: Chr. Michelsen Institute.

UNCTAD. 2012. *Investment policy review*. Mozambique. Geneva: UNCTAD.

World Bank. 2009. *Africa Development Indicators: Youth and employment in Africa*. Washington, DC: World Bank.

World Bank. 2014. Mozambique economic update. Paper 89921. Washington, DC: World Bank.

Wright, Gavin, and Jesse Czelusta. 2004. Why economies slow: The myth of the resource curse. *Challenge* 47 (2): 6–38.

CHAPTER 6

(Re)configurations of Identity: Memory and Creation in the Narrative of Mia Couto

Ana Margarida Fonseca

The relationship between identity and memory has been a constant concern in the literary production of Mozambican writer Mia Couto, from *Vozes Anoi-tecidas* (Voices made Night) (1987),[1] his first collection of short stories, to his latest novel *As Areias do Imperador* (2017). Author of more than two dozen works, including short stories, novels, and some poetry, Mia Couto's work distinguishes him from others in his representation of hybrid identities, made from the mixing of distinct traditions and voices, based on his own experience as the son of Portuguese, on one hand, and, on the other, as a biologist working in rural areas in close contact with traditional habits and beliefs. While his professional life enabled him to maintain direct contact with remote populations throughout the country, his childhood in Beira[2] constituted the first immersion in the cultural diversity of Mozambique. Couto affirms that he grew up in a city where the borders between colonizers and the colonized, whites and blacks, rural and urban people were never static, which allowed him to cross over the margins that would condition his future position both in aesthetic and ethical terms.[3]

It is in this way that, in harmony with his life experience of cultural diversity, yet contrary to the perspectives of colonial and neo-colonial powers, Couto

---

1   I wish to thank María del Carmen Arau Ribeiro for her invaluable help with the translation of this text. *Voices Made Night*, trans. David Brookshaw, African Writers Series, Portsmouth, Heinemann, 1990.

2   Beira is the second largest city and busiest port in Mozambique. It lies in the central region of the country in Sofala Province, where the Pungue River meets the Indian Ocean. The city prospered as a cosmopolitan port with different ethnic communities (Portuguese, Indian, Chinese, indigenous Africans) employed in administration, commerce, and industry.

3   'Beira always had difficulty in organizing its space in the colonial fashion. (...) The colonists really wanted to push the Africans far away. But the blacks always stayed there, on the other side of the street. My city was condemned to be a border place – between the sea and the continent, between Europe and Africa, between Catholicism and the religion of the forefathers. Deep down I shared an equal condition with the city: both of us were creatures of the border, between the sea and land, between the rural and the urban, between Europe and Africa. (...) The city is an umbilical cord that we create after we are born' (Couto 2005, 150).

has defended a notion that the Mozambican nation grows stronger specifically as a result of the denial of essentialisms and dichotomies. This rootedness in the Mozambican reality does not mean, however, an insistence on the regional or the local, for what emerges in his works is a desire for universality that refuses gratuitous exoticism, affirming Mozambique and its/his literature as part of a wider context that extends beyond the borders of region, country, and continent.

This chapter will explore the novels *Venenos de Deus Remédios do Diabo* (Venoms from God Remedies from the Devil) (2008) and *O Último Voo do Flamingo* (2000).[4] The objective is to find a comparative vision, bearing in mind the changes and transformations seen in Couto's narratives over the years, albeit aware of the noteworthy ethical and thematic coherence of this Mozambican writer. The representation of memory and the role of creation in the reconfiguration of national and literary Mozambican identities constitute the main issues that will be considered on this voyage through Mia Couto's writing and, more generally, as regards the relationship between literature and his writing of the nation. As for his own path as a writer, and with specific reference to *Venenos de Deus Remédios do Diabo*, Couto (2008c) observes:

> I wrote 23 books; all of them deal with diverse topics. There is, yes, a central concern in all of my writing: the negation of a pure and unique identity, the investment in the search for interior diversities and the affirmation of plural and mestizo identities.[5]

The idea of *mestiçagem* constitutes, in fact, the guiding force of his vast body of fiction, presented as an innovative and creative confluence of traditions, trends and diverse influences. Although a theoretical discussion of the concept lies beyond the scope of the present chapter,[6] *mestiçagem* is here understood as one of cultural acceptance, in alliance with the concepts of transculturation, and hybridism. All of these concepts translate the idea of transgression of borders and, notwithstanding the history of each, some common points can be detected to better describe a model of understanding of cultural interactions in colonial and postcolonial situations.

---

4 *The Last Flight of the Flamingo*, trans. David Brookshaw, London, Serpent's Tail, 2004.
5 For the sake of non-Lusophone readers, citations from essays written in Portuguese are translated. In the case of excerpts from the literary work of Mia Couto, the original is provided in footnotes.
6 See Gruzinsky (1999), Mignolo (2000), and Peres-Torres (2006).

Recognized as a term of Hispanic origin,[7] most of the theory comes from South America, where the affirmation of *mestizaje* is integrated into the official discourse of national identity. Walter D. Mignolo connects the mestizaje concept to racial or ethnic hybridism, while the more recent term *transculturation*, adopted by postcolonial criticism, is used to describe mixed ways of life and cultural patterns. Given its connotations of social and cultural transformation, Mignolo (2000, 167–169) believes that transculturation as a concept is more appropriate for understanding processes of identification that involve continuous interactions and negotiations among culturally distinct people. If this can be understood in the Latin American context, since the rhetoric of mestizaje (understood as the miscegenation among Europeans, blacks, and Indians) has been used in nationalist speeches as a way to mitigate racial tension, the distinction loses relevance in the African context, particularly in relation to Lusophone literatures and cultures. Mia Couto and others, such as José Eduardo Agualusa, for example, take mestizaje to relate first to culture and only secondarily to race.

Thus, *mestiçagem* represents a negation of dichotomies, of authoritarian discourse, and of the imposition of a sole point of view, be it European or African, colonial, neo-colonial, or even postcolonial. Without paternalism, the Mozambican writer denounces the mystification of a given idea of African-ness (and, by extension, of Mozambican-ness) that sustains its essence, resulting in a reproduction of the colonial model of separation of cultures and the reactivation of a given notion of 'exoticism'. *Mestiçagem* thus understood translates into a productive restless attitude, situating literary writing at the confluence of diverse cultures, all of which are important to the aesthetic and ethical positioning of the African writer. The border situation of the writer makes him a privileged spokesman in a changing world, in which the lines of separation asserted by unilogical discourse are continually crossed.

In referring here to a confluence of cultures, there is no assumption of the existence of a primitive state of 'purity', in which traditions, people, and cultures meet, separated by clear lines. In fact, all cultures throughout time have been characterized by a mix of peoples, races, languages, and traditions, such that neither totally impermeable borders nor peoples who are not tainted by contact with that which is diverse can be located throughout history. Thus, contrary to the absolute separation of colonial ideology, and of much anti-colonial

---

7   On the controversial origins of the term, see Laplantine and Nouss (1997), who place it in the Renaissance; it was used as a means by which to designate racial mixing among the discoverers and the indigenous people. See also Gruzinski (1999, 38), who places the term's origins in medieval Spain, to designate Christians who were allied with Muslims.

thought, postcolonialism defends a notion that the colonial relationship necessarily activates mechanisms of cultural interaction, thus exposing its eminently dialogical nature. Stuart Hall (1996, 247) points out the importance of
this contribution, which rattles belief in the possibility of returning to an original purity in spaces that have been subject to colonization:

> the long-term historical and cultural effects of the 'transculturation'
> which characterised the colonising experience proved (...) to be irrevers-
> ible. The differences, of course, between colonising and colonised cul-
> tures remain profound. But they have never operated in a purely binary
> way and they certainly do so no longer. (...) [The transition to the postco-
> lonial] obliges us to re-read the binaries as forms of transculturation, of
> cultural translation, destined to trouble the here/there for ever.

Affirming the border condition of the author does not mean perpetuating
the separation between the 'I' and the 'other' (a liminal space, which would
then have to be filled), but rather to recognize that the locus of the African
intellectual – and probably of any intellectual – implies crossing and transgressing limits of geographic, cultural, and temporal territories. Contrary
to cultural monolithism, the writer is challenged, in one sole gesture, to de-
nounce asymmetries and look for syntheses, in a vision that is decentred and
tries above all to find intercommunication and encounters.

For Mae Henderson, the definition of border intellectual underlines precisely the potential for crossing paths as a privileged place for reflection and cultural production as follows: 'an authorial subject position that occupies the inter-
stitial space of the crossroads as a site of potential transgression – interrogation
and production – in a contested living and working domain' (1995, 3). When
Couto (2000) describes himself as a 'smuggler between two worlds' – Africa
and the West – he seems to accentuate the skill of transgression enabled by the
placement of the writer or intellectual at the interstices of cultures, through
the questioning of himself and the plural world in which he is located.

In this context, the proximity of the concept of *mestiçagem*, as understood
and defined by Mia Couto, to the prevailing concept of hybridization, cannot
be ignored. Of the varying uses of *mestiçagem*, the most applicable here is
that cultural encounters do not result simply in superimposing the dominant
culture, nor in overlooking the oppressed, but result instead in a new form
that unites distinct cultural traces neither of which can then be separately
identified. This apparent paradox between sameness and difference is thus described by Robert Young (1995, 26).

> Hybridity thus makes difference into sameness, and sameness into difference, but in a way that makes the same no longer the same, the different no longer simply different. In that sense, it operates according to the form of logic that Derrida isolates in the term 'brisure', a breaking and a joining at the same time, in the same place: difference and sameness in an apparent impossible simultaneity.

In the border space that opens up to these productive cultural encounters – the Third Space, to employ Homi Bhabha's concept – the identification processes reject any permanence and remain open to the change that the presence of the other provides. Bhabha proposes that the production of meaning requires passage through a Third Space between the 'I' and the 'you', the split space of enunciation, which represents both the general conditions of language and the specific implications of the enunciated in an involuntary performative and institutional strategy (Bhabha 1994, 36). Ambivalence in the act of interpretation is thus introduced and the mirror of representation is destroyed, which translates the impossibility of 'pure' or 'original' cultures, even before dealing with the specific historical circumstances on which hybridism is founded. The discursive conditions of the enunciation guarantee that there are no fixed or immutable meanings and that any cultural symbol can be translated, re-historicized, and reread (Bhabha 1994, 37).

In an interview, Mia Couto (2008b) stated,

> there is always the danger of thinking that it [*mestiçagem*] came about because there are two pure lines which then are mixed. But those pure lines are already mixed. *Mestiçagem* is our very condition.

This idea that an anteriority made of untouched cultures does not exist seems to be crucial, in the sense that it reinforces an understanding of hybridization or *mestiçagem* as an affirmation of the border condition of cultures, as outlined above. Thus, not only the essentialisms inherent to colonial discourse and most anti-colonial discourse but also the eventual omission of the asymmetries that result from the power exercised on the part of hegemonic cultures are denied. In fact, hybridism may not represent, as could be thought, the dissolution of borders but rather the affirmation of their permeability and instability, retaining its dialectical structure which highlights the cultural crossings that take place in the contact zones. Thus, the conscience of the conditions of inequality in colonial and postcolonial spaces cannot be erased, avoiding what many have considered to be a significant celebration of cultural fusion.

Instead, the concept of hybridism, as proposed by Bhabha and others, has the potential for resistance; it is this sense upstaged in many of its uses in postcolonial contexts,[8] which moves it decisively closer to Couto's notion of mestiçagem. In effect, in his narratives, and without exception, a consciously and voluntarily undertaken project of *mestiçagem* pervades, representing an expression of mobile frontiers, continually crossed, which not only open spaces for resistance but also incite the inversion of an historic and social state marked by inequality, poverty, and abuse of power arbitrarily exercised. The confluences and syntheses that Mia Couto exposes are not mere literary artifice; they emerge from a life that, concretely, brings together the people who live on the social and geographic margins of Mozambique and gives them a voice – a subaltern voice that, as Spivak observes, remains almost always silenced. As a result, the unilogical discourses – political, cultural, historical – are threatened by the ambivalence sown through literary texts that repeatedly cross the borders of rationalities, values, beliefs, and cultural bias.

In *Venenos de Deus Remédios do Diabo* these concerns are clearly established and are part of the continuity that is established in Couto's narrative. The story takes place in Vila Cacimba (Town of Fog), a remote land in Mozambique, to which Portuguese doctor Sidónio Rosa goes in search of the mulata Deolinda, whom he had met at a conference in Lisbon, and with whom he had fallen in love. When he arrives at the town, the doctor discovers that his beloved has gone away on an internship, whence begins his long wait, divided between his work at the local health centre and his daily visits to Deolinda's parents – Munda and Bartolomeu Sozinho. Doubts as to the young woman's return grow as an intricate web of assumptions, hints, and contradictory versions emerge, fed by comments from Munda, Bartolomeu, and Alfredo Suacelência – the administrator/mayor of Vila Cacimba. In the end, there is just one certainty – Deolinda's death. The doctor departs the land of fog; his last vision is of a messenger in a grey dress scattering the white flowers of forgetting.

A narrative about loneliness and loss, *Venenos de Deus Remédios do Diabo* is also a story about identity and its confusion. In part, this concerns personal identity, since the characters become involved in a complex game of lies and truths, deceiving themselves and those around them. However, it is also about collective identities, inviting an exploration of the concepts of race and nation that follows a number of Couto's previously developed topics. The title itself

---

8   In addition to the work by Bhabha and Young referred to here, other important work problematizes the concept of hybridization; for example, Parry (1986), Aijaz Ahmad (1997), Loomba (1998), and Dirlik (1994). In the Portuguese context, see Miguel Vale Almeida (2000, 2006),
    Boaventura Sousa Santos (2001, 2002), and Paulo de Medeiros (2006).

points to the frequently raised concepts of good and evil, leaving glimpses that, in this novel, what appears to be the solution becomes a problem and vice versa. The subtitle – *As incuráveis vidas de Vila Cacimba* (The Incurable Lives of Vila Cacimba) – also suggests a dysphoric ambience; the town and, by extension, its inhabitants, suffer from an incurable pain which no medicine, neither Western nor African, can cure. As will be revealed, this is not a discourse of defeat, but rather a consciousness that, much like the *cacimba* (fog) in which the village is constantly ensconced, these times no longer hold immutable truths, clear borders, or definitive beliefs.

Just as in *O Último Voo do Flamingo*, the story begins with the arrival of a European to a remote location in Mozambique to complete a mission on African soil. Nevertheless, the motivation in each story differs: while the Italian, Massimo Risi goes to Tizangara as a UN investigator to solve the strange case of the 'blue berets' (UN soldiers) that have exploded; Sidónio Rosa's motive for the medical mission in Vila Cacimba is all about trying to meet his beloved again. However, the sense of nostalgia and cultural shock are similar across the two books. Both protagonists feel overtaken by the reality of the 'other', whom they do not understand and about whom they know nothing. Immersion in this reality changes them, modifies their perception of the world, and rattles the certainties of Western rationalism that had been heretofore unquestioned. In both books, the dislocation of the postcolonial subject runs in the opposite direction to what is usually observed: the (ex-)colonized are not those who migrate to the (post-)Imperial space; instead, the (ex-)colonizers are the ones who move to the space of the other and there discover the fallacies of Western cultural hegemony.

This sense of uprootedness is not limited to characters of European origin; Mozambican characters also feel helpless, expressing a sense of perplexity in relation to the profound cultural and material transformations that have occurred in their surroundings. In *Venenos de Deus Remédios do Diabo*, the omnipresence of loneliness dominates the lives of the protagonists, leaving them isolated even within their own families, neighbours, and the people they have known all their lives. Deolinda's mother, the mulata Munda, recognizes that, in Vila Cacimba, the 'assimilated mulatos and blacks'[9] are scarce:

> Few and helpless, sharing secret complicities and suffering from the same sense of being an orphan. The culture they were raised in is long gone, in another time, another universe. The lie is the only remedy left to them

---

9 'mulatos e pretos assimilados'.

against that solitary distance. As Munda says: just one mortal sin can cure the illness of living.[10]

COUTO 2008A, 147

The fragmentation of identity that is glimpsed in these words suggests a sense of exile within their own land and their own country, brought about primarily by the profound changes that have taken place in Mozambican society and culture. In this as in other works, Couto draws attention to realities often ignored by elites within and outside Mozambique: the abandonment to which populations far from major urban centres are fated; the arbitrariness of local power holders out to get rich; cultural desegregation; the inability to rebuild traditional structures of social support after decades of war and isolation. In the microcosm of Vila Cacimba, the figure of the administrator, Alfredo Suacelência,[11] represents the corruption inherent in the workings of the political powers in the postcolonial nation:

> Suacelência orders that the health center be closed to the public whenever he uses its services. And the doctor accepts, complacently. Just as he does not report the proof that Suacelência takes food, medicine, gas, sheets and mattresses from the warehouse. The Portuguese accepts that he is too complacent. But he does not know how to react before a universe made of businessmen without businesses and public workers who only perform private tasks.[12]
>
> COUTO 2008A, 45

The passivity of the doctor before the abuses of power that he witnesses in the small Mozambican locality can be understood as a metonym for the complacency of the West towards corrupt leaders in the African space (and not just in Mozambique); they are perpetuators of a neo-colonial state that leaves the

---

10   'Poucos e desamparados, partilhando secretas cumplicidades e sofrendo de um mesmo sentimento de orfandade. A cultura que os criou está longe, noutro tempo, noutro universo. A mentira é o único remédio que lhes resta contra essa solitária lonjura. Como diz Munda: apenas um mortal pecado pode curar a doença de viver'.

11   *Suacelência* is a play on *Sua Excelência*, in Portuguese: a title of great deference equivalent to 'Your Excellency'.

12   '(...) Suacelência ordena que o posto de saúde seja encerrado ao público sempre que ele faz uso dos seus serviços. E o médico aceita, complacente. Como se cala perante as evidências que Suacelência desvia do armazém comida, medicamentos, combustível, lençóis, colchões. O português aceita que é demasiado complacente. Mas ele não sabe como reagir perante um universo feito de empresários sem empresa e de funcionários públicos que apenas desempenham funções privadas'.

people entirely vulnerable to disease, hunger, and violence. Alfredo Suacelência is, thus, just one more in a long line of characters through whom Couto exposes the corruption of powers, as is also the case with Estêvão Jonas, the administrator of Matimati in *The Last Flight of the Flamingo*. However, while this narrative highlights Estêvão's implacable ambition, and his decisions that threaten the very survival of the community, in Alfredo's case, the representation of vices mixes with a certain Bakhtinian grotesque. Thus, the abundant sweat, alcoholism, and haughty lines make him laughable, deconstructing fear and tyranny, which is reinforced by the fact that, by the end of the novel, he is sacked from his job and is the target of an attempted poisoning.

The borders of identity are fluid and blurred: one of the more evident signs of this permeability is found in the act of naming. When the inhabitants of Vila Cacimba give Sidónio a new name – Sidonho – they amalgamate the Western name Sidónio with the word *sonho* (dream), foreshadowing an identity alteration which, otherwise, is well-accepted by the Portuguese: 'The doctor even liked this rebaptism that makes him more amenable to being other'[13] (Couto 2008a, 13). On the other hand, Bartolomeu, on another doctor's visit, unexpectedly accuses him of not calling him by his full name and thus of stealing 'his finest identity, his given name'[14] (Couto 2008a, 94), just as the Portuguese had stolen the names of slaves in times past. Later, however, Sidónio discovers that the Western name by which Bartolomeu Augusto Sozinho would like to be addressed is not, after all, his original name. The old black man 'had colonized himself'[15] (Couto 2008a, 110), refusing to take on his African name – Bartolomeu Tsotsi[16] – and instead taking on the identity branding that the colonizer had imposed on him.

Such con-*fusion* of names – Western and African – illustrates the impossibility of secure lines to separate the oppressor from the oppressed, name chosen and name imposed. Lies and truth are constantly confronted, making it difficult to understand which is the true name when the mask is confused with the face. In the incurably mestizo world in which characters move, any pretension to authenticity becomes a fruitless mission since there no longer exists any essence to be recovered: there are only provisional representations of identities in permanent (re)construction.

---

13   'O médico até gostou desse rebaptismo que o torna mais à disposição de ser outro'.
14   'a sua identidade maior, o seu nome de raiz'.
15   'se colonizara sozinho'.
16   Tsotsi means, in some African languages, bandit or gang member, which motivated Bartolomeu to change his name, when he considered becoming a mechanic.

Returning, then, to the idea of exile as a means by which to accentuate the relations of belonging that are questioned in this novel in an ongoing interlacing of individual and collective dimensions, it is clear that not a single character seems to feel s/he belongs to just one land and just one country. For different reasons, Bartolomeu and Sidónio are on a voyage that goes far beyond the physical trips they have made. 'We go abroad when our land has left us',[17] Couto notes (2008a, 108), and thus expresses the problem of identity for someone who feels distanced from a national, ethnic, or local group. In fact, even the Portuguese doctor confesses that upon his departure for Mozambique he did not go solely to find Deolinda; he left, just as his father had, on a kind of inner exile, which was a result of a sense of loneliness that was not confined to historical circumstances. His father had escaped 'the void that lies beyond political regimes'[18] (Couto 2008a, 109), and the son, forty years later, follows his example.

Reflecting upon the issue of place in postcolonialism, Bill Ashcroft notes that all constructions and disruptions of place lead to the question, 'Where do I belong?' which is not necessarily asked in relation to a physical space, as in the case of diasporas. Creative representations of place can even consist of ways of resisting its confines since, as the author points out, it is much more than a physical space that is being depicted:

Place is never simply location, nor is it static, a cultural memory which colonization buries. For, like culture itself, place is in a continual and dynamic state of formation, a process intimately bound up with the culture and identity of its inhabitants. Above all place is a *result* of habitation, a consequence of the ways in which people inhabit space, particularly that conception of space as universal and incontestable that is constructed for them by imperial discourse. (Ashcroft 2001, 156)

On the part of both characters – ex-colonizer and ex-colonized – a disquiet is thus revealed in the dislocations they have experienced, within and beyond the African continent. This movement across what was once the territory of the Empire rewrites colonial history itself, unveiling the impossibility of accepting a single culture, identity, or race. It is thus, within the context of uprootedness found in the colonial references, that Couto underscores the experience of dislocation which results from the relation between the colony and the metropolis.[19]

---

17   'Saímos para o estrangeiro quando a nossa terra já saiu de nós'.
18   'do vazio que está para além dos regimes políticos'.
19   In an interview for the novel's launch, Couto says: 'I believe that not only in literature, but in the imaginary of Mozambican people, the colonial past was well resolved. You have to

In fact, for Bartolomeu Sozinho, colonialism offers an opportunity to have the greatest experience in his life – his work as a mechanic on the ship *Infante D. Henrique*, in the service of the Companhia Colonial de Navegação (Colonial Navigation Company). Having satisfied his need to get away, and seen as a hero by his countrymen, each return represents a reinforcement of the vanity of being the only black man among the crew. Rancorously, Alfredo calls him 'a decorative black',[20] and minimizes the importance of what he has done, saying that he has been 'a crew member merely as an instrument of a lie: that there was no racism in the Portuguese empire'[21] (Couto 2008a, 26). Indeed, Bartolomeu understands only too well the existence of racism, for he felt it every time he disembarked in Portugal, but that was not the whole truth. Over the years, he has hidden the existence of a mulato daughter, Isadora, fruit of a chance relationship, and that is why the news of the *Revolução dos Cravos* (Revolution of the Carnations) in April 1974 had been an occasion of mourning and sadness for him rather than a cause for joy. With the end of his trips to Lisbon, Bartolomeu knew that he would never again see his daughter; consequently, a historic moment of collective celebration (in Portugal, it meant the end of the dictatorship while, in the colonies, it meant the inevitable end of the colonial regime) is transformed into an insurmountable personal defeat for Bartolomeu.

Thus, in the work of Mia Couto and particularly in this narrative, the idea that different truths coexist at the same time and place is quite present even within a single character, whose truth is not dependent on coherence. Only by recognizing this can we understand old Bartolomeu's gesture when he resolves to burn the flag of the Companhia Colonial de Navegação, which he had kept for decades as testimony to happier times. By accusing Sidónio Rosa of treating him in the fashion of early slave owners, and by suggesting that in his dreams he had seen Sidónio with a gun in his hand ready to kill, Bartolomeu follows another truth that coexists within himself – that of the black man embittered by race and disrespected by racism, vengeful after the oppression he has suffered. Nevertheless, when the old man violently insults the collective values that he supposedly ought to esteem, to which of these truths is he referring?

---

think that the independence of Mozambique took place as a result of an armed struggle that create disruption of well-ingrained culture' (Couto 2008c).

20   'preto decorativo'.

21   'tripulante apenas como instrumento de uma mentira: de que não havia racismo no império lusitano'.

The hoarse, crazed old man cries, 'The liberty crap is over! The cursed nation is over!' (...) No one knew exactly to which nation or to which freedom old Bartolomeu was referring. Perhaps the offended nation was a small room in which he had closed himself. And cursed freedom was the possibility of visiting the past and travelling again in fallen colonial ships.[22]

COUTO 2008A, 95

Nation, empire, and liberty arise as problematic concepts here, reinforcing the idea that no static borders exist between the self and the other. The narrative does not seem to be about a manifestation of imperial nostalgia but rather about a difficulty of identification with the postcolonial nation, explained in large part by the distance from centres of power, suggested earlier.

Yet another dimension of alterity must be added to these concepts, as it has relevance to the African context: race. Reference was made earlier to colour prejudices that existed in the colonial period and persisted after its end; it is now clear that, even among Africans race, creates hierarchy and segregation. The marriage of Bartolomeu to Munda is unacceptable to both families; Munda believes that the connection to a black 'retards the race', while Bartolomeu sees the son's choice of a mulata as a betrayal. Faced with these reservations, the couple takes advantage of the subjectivity implicit in the definition of race. If, for his in-laws, Bartolomeu defines himself as 'extremely mulato',[23] he describes his fiancée to his parents as 'almost black'[24] (Couto 2008a, 31). Thus, the colour stereotype is subverted and the permeability of borders is once again evident. Sidónio himself tires of 'having' race when he realizes that his skin colour marks him with an identity (Portuguese and a doctor) that he sometimes would like to omit, either because it exposes him to others too much or because it relegates all the other dimensions of his personality to the background. Finally, Munda is best able to synthesize the lesson to be learned: 'You have no colour, Doctor. People do not have colours. Or they have colours that have no name' (Couto 2008a, 66).

Home, homeland, nation, race – in each case, the places of collective belonging seem to be uninhabitable, or at least difficult to access. Against the

---

22   'O velho, rouco, enlouquecido, grita: — Acabou-se a merda da liberdade! Acabou-se a puta da nação! (...) Ninguém sabia exactamente a que nação e a que liberdade o velho Bartolomeu se referia. Talvez a ofendida nação fosse o pequeno quarto onde ele se havia enclausurado. E a amaldiçoada liberdade fosse a possibilidade de visitar o passado e voltar a viajar em falecidos navios coloniais'.

23   'extremamente mulato'.

24   'quase negra'.

evils of solitude, from exile to uprootedness, there seem to be two paths to choose between: dreams, or the passage of time. Yet, both are ambivalent – halfway between remedy and venom, the divine and the diabolical. Although Bartolomeu considers dreams to be evil, they end up being a way to avoid the dysphoria in which there is no hope or redemption: 'Dreaming is a way of lying to life; a revenge against destiny that is always too little too late'[25] (Couto 2008a, 155). As for time, 'the handkerchief for all tears',[26] in the words of Munda (Couto 2008a, 154), its role becomes superlativised throughout the narrative. This occurs through sentences and sayings that show the determining influence of temporality on all dimensions of human existence, providing glimpses of the fact that, in the end, time itself will be the great protagonist of this novel.

Note that, in this context, time, or rather, the awareness of its passing, is essential for the definition of identity. Memory work is indispensable for the constitution of not only personal but also collective identities, considering memory as a practice that recreates and transforms elements of the past according to changes that have occurred in the meantime. As such, the past is dynamic and contentious; as explained by Antze and Lambek (1996, xxix), it is a dialectic between remembering and forgetting:

> The past is a treacherous burden, which would crush us if we did not continuously divest ourselves of its weight. Forgetting here is as much an active process as remembering: both require effort and energy. Identity of any kind requires steering a course between holding on and letting go. Identity is not composed of a fixed set of memories but lies in the dialectical, ceaseless activity of remembering and forgetting, assimilating and discarding.

In *Venenos de Deus Remédios do Diabo* we observe the difficult relations Mozambicans have with their collective memory as a people and as a nation, through characters who have little ability to deal with the passage of time. In truth, Bartolomeu is not the only one who lives ambivalently with his memories of colonial times and his voyages aboard the *Infant Dom Henrique*. Munda, the administrator, and even Sidónio, find themselves hesitating between a lost world and a world that is unknown to them, since the personal and community references they had seemed to fall apart around them. In a

---

25   'Sonhar é um modo de mentir à vida, uma vingança contra um destino que é sempre tardio e pouco'.
26   'lenço de toda a lágrima'.

way, everything is suspended, supporting the maxim inscribed in the narrative, 'living is a verb without a past'[27] (Couto 2008a, 56).

The presentation of suspended time culminates in the appearance, near the German cemetery, of an ambiguous figure, on the border between dreams and reality – a pregnant, squalid woman who holds an armful of *beijos-de-mulata*, the white flowers of forgetting. Magical realism emerges here as a way to draw attention to a non-rationalist world model that blends with the Western world-view. Actually, it is Sidónio Rosa, the European schooled in the laws of science, who sees the ghost-like spectre, provoking the same perplexity in him as that felt by Massimo Risi, the Italian investigator in *The Last Flight of Flamingo*. In both cases, a mestizaje of world models is sought: instead of erasing cultural specificities, they are made visible, dignifying African cultural inheritance. Couto thus exposes a problematic and chaotic reality that does not conform to the single voice of conventional realism, as Brenda Copper (1998, 32) notes here:

> Hybridity, the celebration of 'mongrelism' as opposed to ethnic certainties, has been shown to be a fundamental aspect of magical realist writing. A syncretism between paradoxical dimensions of life and death, historical reality and magic, science and religion, characterizes the plots, themes and narrative structures of magical realist novels. In other words, urban and rural, Western and indigenous, black, white and Mestizo – this cultural, economic and political cacophony is the amphitheatre in which magical realist fictions are performed. The plots of these novels deal with issues of borders, change, mixing and syncretizing. And they do so, and this point is critical, in order to expose what they see as a deeper and true reality than conventional realist techniques would bring to view.

As elsewhere in his writings, Couto denounces the loss of social ties, the corruption of leaders (such as the administrator), generalized poverty, and the vestiges of insanity left by the civil war (the 'tresandarilho' soldiers[28]). Forgetting seems to be the response to a deep-seated pessimism, nearly annihilation, which can actually be understood through acceptance of the possibility of collective reinvention, outlined above. Thus, if the identity work presupposes the

---

27   'viver é um verbo sem passado'.
28   'Tresandarilho' is a neologism created by the author from the term 'andarilho', which means someone who walks very quickly and frequently. In the narrative, the soldiers suffer from a strange disease – meningitis or a spell, depending on the reading of the reality – that makes them wander incessantly through the village, like crazed men.

ability to remember and to forget, in this case venom can be the remedy, which is condensed in the contradictory and ambivalent title of the novel.

The ending of *Venenos de Deus Remédios do Diabo* otherwise resembles the *O Último Voo do Flamingo,* given that both narratives end with the town, which is a metaphor for the state of suspension of the country, in a state of suspension itself:

> The Portuguese follows the pit-ridden road as if floating along the current of a river. (...) The doctor peeks out the back window but the town is no longer visible. A heavy fog has forbidden glimpses and memories of the town. There is the taste of time suspended in that dust. As if Sidónio's trip had neither departure nor arrival. Perhaps that is why, instead of acacias and baobabs, he is met by a winding line of homes from his own Lisbon. Sidónio Rosa, after all, really only now is leaving his homeland.[29]
>
> COUTO 2008A, 187

As this is also an allegory of the difficulty of 'belonging' among the Mozambicans, and of the many challenges of a shared identity, this work seems to unmask a more intimate – even a more human – dimension than Couto's previous novels. The identity quests of Bartolomeu, Munda, Sidónio, or of any other of the characters – including the absent but not forgotten Deolinda – form a universal drive, overcoming the limits of the nation or even the continent. David Brookshaw (2008, 139) similarly affirms that Couto evokes not just the cultural pluralism of his country but also calls out 'to our global souls, to our own plural identities'.

This perspective does not clash with the deep rootedness of the contradictions and difficulties felt in the contemporary Mozambican nation because, in Couto's writing, the individual and the collective are interlaced to construct identity images which question, simultaneously, the existing communities, the memories in permanent redefinition, and the utopias of an improved future. As Paulo de Medeiros (2010, 204) rightly notes,

> literature has the possibility of imagining models for society that allow for a reflection on modalities for change. Literature might even be said

---

29 'O português segue pela estrada esburacada como se flutuasse sobre as ondas de um rio. (...) O médico espreita pelo vidro de trás, mas a Vila deixou de ser visível. Uma espessa neblina a tornou interdita a olhares e lembranças. Há nessa poeira o sabor de um tempo suspenso. Como se a viagem de Sidónio não tivesse partida nem chegada. Talvez por isso, em lugar de acácias e imbondeiros, ele assista ao vagaroso desfilar do casario da sua Lisboa. Afinal, Sidónio Rosa apenas agora está saindo da sua terra natal'.

to be a privileged medium to shape cultural memory, to problematize the ways in which societies come to construct themselves, that is, how they both remember and forget what they believe to be their defining characteristics.

At the end of *Venenos de Deus Remédios do Diabo*, there are questions to which there are no clear answers: to whom does Deolinda's love belong after all? Is Bartolomeu guilty of incest? Did she die of AIDS, or of an abortion? Was she Munda's daughter, or sister? And was Munda Alfredo's lover? For these questions there are only versions, lies, and indistinguishable truths, all of which, in the end, posit the impossibility of defining a singular identity.

As observed by Phillip Rothwell (2004, 33), in relation to another Couto novel,

> If truth re-lies on tradition, the loss of a truth presupposes the questioning of the tradition that has enabled the truth. A process of rigorous deracination unsettles the text at the level of the thematic, syntactic, and semantic, but it is a process that is always marked by being grounded on the tradition that it relativizes.

In effect, Couto follows the lesson of the great Mozambican poet José Craveirinha: 'I am not divided; I am dispersed'.[30] Averse to essentialisms and speeches on authenticity, Couto defends the idea of a 'supranational nation' (Couto 2005, 93) in which there are neither exclusions nor divisions and, above all, where no one is owner of the truth.

Permeable, uncertain and disquieting, the borders continue to be the privileged space for the presentation of mestizo identities that, for Mia Couto and all those who, like him, are disturbed, are working identities, in a constant state of reinvention.

References

Ahamd, Aijaz. 1997. The politics of literary postcoloniality. In *Contemporary Postcolonial Theory*, ed. Padmini Mongia, 276–293. London: Arnold.

Almeida, Miguel Vale de. 2000. *Um Mar da Cor da Terra: Raça, cultura e política da identidade.* Oeiras: Celta Editora.

---

30   'não estou dividido, estou repartido' (Laban 1998, 54).

Almeida, Miguel Vale de. 2006. Comentário. In *Portugal Não É um País Pequeno: Contar o Império na pós-colonialidade*, ed. Manuela Ribeiro Sanches, 360–367. Lisbon: Cotovia.

Antze, Paul, and Michael Lambek. 1996. Introduction. In *Tense Past: Cultural essays in trauma and memory*, ed. Paul Antze and Michael Lambek, vii–xxxviii. New York: Routledge.

Ashcroft, Bill. 2001. *Post-colonial Transformation*. London: Routledge.

Bhabha, Homi. 1994. *The Location of Culture*. London: Routledge.

Brookshaw, David. 2008. Indianos e o Índico: O pós-colonialismo transoceânico e internacional em *O Outro Pé da Sereia*, de Mia Couto. In *Moçambique: Das palavras escritas*, ed. Margarida Calafate Ribeiro and Maria Paula Meneses, 129–140. Oporto: Afrontamento.

Cooper, Brenda. 1998. *Magical Realism in West African Fiction: Seeing with a third eye*. London: Routledge.

Couto, Mia. 2005. *Pensatempos*. Lisbon: Caminho.

Couto, Mia. 2008a. *Venenos de Deus, Remédios do Diabo*. Lisbon: Caminho.

Couto, Mia. 2008b. Mia Couto: A mestiçagem é a nossa própria condição. *Jornal de Letras, Artes e Ideias*, June 18.

Couto, Mia. 2008c. As negas malucas de Mia Couto. *Jornal do Brasil* June 14. Available at http://ardotempo.blogs.sapo.pt/87482.html.

Couto, Mia, and Luísa Jeremias. 2000. Sou um contrabandista entre dois mundos. Interview conducted by Luísa Jeremias. *A Capital* May 25.

Dirlik, Arif. 1994. The postcolonial aura: Third World criticism in the age of global capitalism. In *Contemporary Postcolonial Theory*, ed. Padmini Mongia, 276–293. London: Arnold.

Gruzinski, Serge. 1999. *La Pensée Métisse*. Paris: Fayard.

Hall, Stuart. 1996. When was 'the post-colonial'? Thinking at the limit. In *The Post-colonial Question: Common skies, divided horizons*, ed. Ian Chambers and Lidia Curti, 242–260. London: Routledge.

Henderson, Mae. 1995. Introduction. In *Borders, Boundaries and Frames: Essays in cultural criticism and cultural studies*, ed. Mae G. Henderson, 1–30. London: Routledge.

Laban, Michel. 1998. Encontro com José Craveirinha. In *Moçambique. Encontro com Escritores*. Vol. iii. Oporto: Fundação António Engenheiro de Almeida.

Laplantine, François, and Alexis Nouss. 1997. *Le Métissage*. Paris: Flammarion.

Loomba, Ania. 1998. *Colonialism/Postcolonialism*. London: Routledge.

Medeiros, Paulo. 2006. Apontamentos para conceptualizar uma Europa pós-colonial. In *Portugal Não É um País Pequeno. Contar o Império na pós-colonialidade*, ed. Manuela Ribeiro Sanches, 339–358. Lisbon: Cotovia.

Medeiros, Paulo. 2010. Ghosts and hosts: Memory, inheritance and the postcolonial condition. *Diacrítica* 24 (3): 201–214.

Mignolo, Walter D. 2000. On gnosis and the imaginary of the modern/colonial world system. In *Coloniality, Subaltern Knowledges, and Border Thinking: Local histories/ global designs*, ed. Walter D. Mignolo, 3–43. Princeton, NJ: Princeton University Press.

Parry, Benita. 1986. Problems in current theories of postcolonial discourse. *Oxford Literary Review* 9 (1/2): 27–58.

Peres-Torres, Rafael. 2006. *Mestizaje: Critical uses of race in Chicano culture*. Minneapolis: University of Minnesota Press.

Rothwell, Phillip. 2004. *A Postmodern Nationalist: Truth, orality and gender in the work of Mia Couto*. Cranbury, PA: Bucknell University Press.

Santos, Boaventura de Sousa. 2001. Entre Próspero e Caliban: Colonialismo, pós-colonialismo e inter-identidades. In *Entre Ser e Estar: Raízes, percursos e discursos da identidade*, ed. Maria Irene Ramalho and António Sousa Ribeiro, 23–85. Oporto: Afrontamento.

Santos, Boaventura de Sousa. 2002. Para uma sociologia das ausências e uma sociologia das emergências. *Revista Crítica de Ciências Sociais* 63: 237–280.

Spivak, Gayatri Chakravorty. 1994. Can the subaltern speak? In *Colonial Discourse and Post-colonial Theory: A reader*, ed. Patrick Williams and Laura Chrisman, 66–111. Harlow, UK: Longman.

Young, Robert J.C. 1995. *Colonial Desire: Hybridity in theory, culture and race*. London: Routledge.

CHAPTER 7

Dialogues with the Past – and with the Future: *Ualalapi* and *Jesusalém*

Anne Sletsjøe

Emperor Ngungunhane of Gaza was defeated by the Portuguese in 1895 and taken as a prisoner to Ilha Terceira. In Ungulani Ba Ka Khosa's historical novel *Ualalapi,*[1] at the hour of his departure the emperor delivers a prophecy, predicting the disasters to come. The book roughly covers this period of the nation's history until the end of the war against colonial rule. As Patrick Chabal notes, *Ualalapi* is 'the first work of fiction to deal explicitly with [Mozambique's] pre-colonial past' (1996, 85). In Khosa's text, having left behind a wasteland of death and destruction, the fallen emperor brings his predictions to a close on a more personal note:

> Our history and our habits will be slandered in the schools under the vigilant eyes of the men dressed like women, who will oblige the children to talk about my death and to call me a criminal and a cannibal.[2]

Although focused on the battle between the native ruler and the colonial forces, and on the emperor's personal historic reputation, Khosa's dialogue with the past in *Ualalapi* – in accordance with the nature of all prophecy – also extends to the times that are to come: that is, in relation to the author's own recent past as well as in relation to the time at which he is writing.[3]

---

1   Published in Mozambique in 1987. First Portuguese edition by Caminho in 1990. The edition referred to here is the second edition by Caminho from 1998.

2   'A nossa história e os nossos hábitos serão vituperados nas escolas sob o olhar atento dos homens com vestes de mulher que obrigarão as crianças a falar da minha morte e a chamarem-me criminoso e canibal' (*Ualalapi*, 121). All translations from the Portuguese are my own.

3   As stated by Jared Banks (2003, 137–139), *Ualalapi* problematizes not only the modern colonial history of Mozambique, but also, ultimately, the political leadership of the independent nation. When interviewed by Michel Laban in 1992, Khosa confirmed this: 'Fundamentalmente, tinha duas intenções: por um lado, tirar o mito do Ngungunhane, porque, na altura, já se falava na transladação das ossadas do homem para cá. Então queria tirar o mito porque o Samora Machel, na fase final, já estava a ter aqueles gestos, aquela pose quase napoleónica – inclusive ele foi a Chaimite, que foi a primeira capital do Império de Gaza ... Foi esse sentido

© KONINKLIJKE BRILL NV, LEIDEN, 2019 | DOI:10.1163/9789004381100_009

In Mia Couto's 2009 novel, *Jesusalém*, after several years of self-inflicted isolation Silvestre Vitalício, a subject of post-independent Mozambique, is leaving behind another wasteland. In a former military camp in the middle of nowhere, he has founded his Jesusalém, living there with his two young sons and his 'mistress', the donkey Jezibela. He is assisted by his blindly loyal 'second in command' – a war- traumatized former soldier who, like his forefathers, has fought on the wrong side. His grandfather fought against Ngungunhane, his father with the colonial police, while he himself fought with the Portuguese against the forces of liberation. From time to time, the people of the small community are visited by a relative, who is their only link to the outside world, and the character who finally organizes their re-introduction to it. As his self-constructed 'world outside the world' collapses, Silvestre Vitalício is brought back to the city he once came from, although he is now a physical and psychological wreck. There, in the familiar urban environment, he will spend his last days in the patient care of his youngest son, Mwanito, 'the tuner of silences',[4] who is also the narrator of the story. Compared with *Ualalapi*, the span of historical time with which *Jesusalém* enters into dialogue is limited; we are dealing with a historical perspective of about two decades. The group leaves the camp sometime in the late 1980s and the story ends in an urban environment five years later. This means that Couto is also dealing with the years following national independence, and he takes his story to the end of the civil war.

The reader may well ask if Couto in his dialogue with the past in *Jesusalém* is to some extent picking up the thread left by Khosa in *Ualalapi*. Are we to understand that the essence of Ngungunhane's prediction of disasters to come remains a valid description of post-war Mozambique in the year 2009? By taking a comparative look at the complex narrative and thematic structures at work in *Ualalapi* and *Jesusalém*, the present chapter will answer this question by exploring the ways in which the authors of these two novels have made use of the nation's traumatic and violent past in their literary projects. Rather than closely comparing the fictional 'facts' with those of history, I will discuss how the two novels, as narrative strategies, explore important moments in the nation's history, and thereby challenge even extra-fictional reality – the contemporary society in which they were written.

---

que eu quis dar à história. Tinha em vista o lado ditatorial–ainda que se chamasse 'ditadura do proletariado'–do próprio regime vigente' (Laban 1998, 1069–1070). See also Afolabi (ed.) 2010.

4   'o afinador de silêncios' (*Jesusalém*, 13).

1 Didactic Simplicity and Narrative Complexity

African novels and short stories written in Portuguese and published after independence have, on a whole, not succumbed to the ideological and aestheticized strategies of the embedded 'revolutionary romanticism' so popular with both European and Latin-American socialist realist writers of the twentieth century.[5] Even the, aesthetically speaking, somewhat inadequate novel *Kikia Matcho – O desalento do combatente* (Kikia Matcho – The dejection of the combatant) – published in 1999 by Filinto de Barros – presents the reader with a clear-eyed description of the social and political disasters of post-independence Guinea-Bissau, and the justified disillusionment felt by the majority of its people. This feeling of disillusionment is strongly expressed in much fiction recently published in Mozambique and Angola. With specific reference to Mozambique, Ana Mafalda Leite describes this as 'a period of reflection displaying a positive critical distance to the actual present and the historical past'.[6] With the publication of *Jesusalém*, this 'positive critical distance', in itself a description close to euphemism, has been replaced by a much harsher attitude. Up to a point, this attitude parallels that of the most shattering contemporary novels written in Angola, and above all those by José Eduardo Agualusa. In his novel *Barroco Tropical* (Tropical Barroque), also published in 2009, Agualusa updates the disturbing scenarios depicted in his 1996 novel *Estação das Chuvas* (Rainy Season), transporting his description of daily life in Luanda to the year 2020. This work not only presents a bleak perspective, but also a frightening picture. Couto and Agualusa seem to be inspired by a mutually felt need to state that the last two decades have provided little – if any – cause for optimism.

Although Couto's approach is psychologically more interiorized than this might suggest, it is even more apparent in *Jesusalém* than it was in earlier novels that dealt more directly with the reality of war and human suffering, such

5 When asked by Michel Laban to describe his own development as a writer, Khosa points, first of all, to the North-Americans Hemingway, Steinbeck and Faulkner. After that he read Garcia Márques, Cortázar and Borges and discovered magical realism. 'E entro no mundo do realismo mágico e começo a encontrar alguma ponte em relação a toda a realidade minha, africana–que também é um mundo mágico. E começo a ver que talvez haja maior semelhança neste tipo de literatura' (Laban, 1055). 'Do Brasil, estamos um pouco distantes' (1079). As to Portuguese literature, the main source of influence has come from poetry. And although he finds both Saramago and Lobo Antunes interesting, neither has influenced him aesthetically.

6 'um período de reflexão sobre o presente actual e o passado histórico, que manifesta um distanciamento crítico positivo' (Leite 2010, 219).

as *Terra Sonâmbula* (Sleepwalking Land), published in 1992.[7] Both *Ualalapi* and *Jesusalém* contribute to ongoing debates about cultural identity from a historical perspective that embraces even that of the future. Epic in their narrative approach – although *Ualalapi* is more consistently so than *Jesusalém* – both texts point to the extraordinariness of the worlds they describe.

In *Ualalapi*'s account of the rise and fall of Emperor Ngungunhane, the historical significance is easily understood;[8] here, the epic style is further enhanced by a number of supernatural events. Despite its brevity, from a narratological point of view *Ualalapi* is a rather complex text, being divided not into chapters but into six *Fragmentos do fim* (End fragments). In their description of the reign of Ngungunhane – which is chronologically structured but not in a linear form – the fragments highlight specific figures and events. Each fragment is introduced by extra-literary passages quoted from administrative documents of the period, or by reflections made by the narrative voice. In each case, the introductory text is followed by the author's personal dedication – to fellow writers and friends – of the dramatic episode to be told. In three of the fragments, there is also a quotation from the Bible: the second fragment is preceded by a quotation from the book of Job (39:42), the third by a quotation from the book of Revelations (Chapter 18), while the final fragment, *O último discurso de Ngungunhane* (Ngungunhane's last speech), opens with a quotation from Matthew (Chapter 24). The structuring through fragments – formally separated from each other by introductory quotations from a variety of literary sources, including historical documents that conflict in their presentation of historical 'truth' – functions like a series of warnings to the reader, who is about to enter Khosa's fictional arrangement of his historical material.[9]

---

7   When interviewed by Laban in 1992, Couto states that he, both as a poet and writer of prose, has been greatly influenced by Portuguese poetry. Unlike Luandino Vieira, he does not incorporate a high level of African words in his fictional language: 'Mesmo usando estes processos que são exteriores à norma, eu estou trabalhando dentro da língua portuguesa e poucas vezes eu vou pegar num vocábulo de outras línguas moçambicanas'. He does, however, point to the Brazilian Guimarães Rosa as a source of inspiration: 'Guimarães Rosa deve ser referido de facto como um grande mestre nesta experimentação da língua portuguesa' (Laban, 1019–1020). After publishing his first work of prose in 1987, Couto was criticized for using 'a language that nobody speaks', and for being a white man writing about traditional themes. Khosa, who himself was struggling with literary censorship (his *Ualalapi* was considered 'aggressive'), defended him. At the heart of the problem, as Khosa assessed it, was the period of literary transition and consolidation that the nation was going through.

8   See also 'Self and Other in *Ualalapi*' (Sletsjøe 2010).

9   Although the author's dedication to each fragment is not, strictly speaking, consistent with a Western generic classification of the text, as a single integral fictional text, I cannot agree entirely with Ana Mafalda Leite (2005, 155–156) when she describes Khosa's organization of the work as six short stories functioning as independent unities that are, at the

In order to emphasize this underlying didactic aspect of the work, a *Nota do autor* (Author's Note) precedes the fictional text. This note has two objectives: on the one hand, to position Ngungunhane within the context of colonial history and, on the other, to distinguish between what, historically speaking, is 'unquestionably the truth' and incidents that *might* be 'true'. Another quotation – preceded by four epigraphs quoting two historical figures, both describing the impression Ngungunhane made on them – is from Agustina Bessa Luís: 'History is a controlled fiction',[10] which seems to comment directly upon what is, in fact, Khosa's main objective in *Ualalapi* – the transformation of factual history into fiction: this emphasizes the link between two different kinds of storytelling, or two different strategies for the distribution of historical material. Bessa Luís's quotation raises an important point, then – the extra-literary potential of the literary text, which is also to be found in Khosa's own Author's Note.

With regard to narrative structure, Couto's *Jesusalém* shares some of the formal characteristics of Khosa's novel, divided as it is into three books and a large number of introductory texts. The first, *Livro Um – A Humanidade* (Book Number One – Mankind) deals with everyday life in Jesusalém before an intruder, Marta, a white Portuguese woman, makes her entrance. *Livro Dois – A Visita* (Book Number Two – The Visit) describes the problematic and violent co-existence between this woman and the male inhabitants of the camp in the following weeks and months. Each of the first two books has six chapters, or sub-chapters, while *Livro Três – Revelações e Regressos* (Book Number Three – Revelations and Returns) has four sub-chapters. Here the reader learns what happened after the abandonment of Jesusalém and the disclosure of all the secrets of the past.

The three books are preceded by a pertinent quotation from Hermann Hesse's *Die Morgenlandfahrt* translated into Portuguese: 'The history of the world is nothing / but a picture-book reflecting / the most violent and blindest / of all human desires: the wish to forget'.[11] Thus highlighting what may be seen as a main objective of Couto's entire fictional work to date – the imperative to remember – Hesse's words go to the heart of the concept of *Jesusalém* and the main character's strategy of regression: life without memory. Book Number

---

same time, dependent on each other, and the introductory quotations as 'declarations of paratextual intentions'.

10   'A História é uma ficção controlada' (*Ualalapi*, 15). Agustina Bessa Luís is a well-known Portuguese novelist – author of several historical novels.

11   'Toda a história do mundo não é mais / que um livro de imagens reflectindo / o mais violento e mais cego / dos desejos humanos: o desejo de esquecer. Hermann Hesse, *Viagem pelo Oriente*' (*Jesusalém*, 7).

Two is introduced by an unidentified quotation from Jean Baudrillard reflecting on being born and on living – always accompanied by death. Khosa was asked to review the novel on the day of its publication; his online review, 'Escrever com alma: A viagem interior de Mia Couto' (Writing with the soul: The interior voyage of Mia Couto), discusses Silvestre's strategy of regression, which is also a denial of the right to dream; that is, of the right to a future. Khosa's point of departure is a scene in which the protagonist tells his two sons, 'you can neither dream nor remember. Because I myself do not dream, nor remember'.[12] This amounts to the creation of a new world, in which 'There is the need to inaugurate a new order, a new grammar, a syntax outside the chaotic, disturbed world where they lived before'.[13]

Khosa's review also discusses the author's division of the work into books. Drawing on the protagonist's self-righteous obsession with God, an aspect of the novel that I will discuss shortly, Khosa points to the biblical associations inherent in this familiar structure. When it comes to the poems used by Couto as introductory texts not only to every book but also to every sub-chapter, however, Khosa's naming of these as Psalms, and of the poets who wrote them, as psalmists, seems less appropriate or convincing. Nevertheless, although presenting man's obsessive and abjuring fight with the expulsed Christian God at the heart of this dramatic story, Couto has chosen texts written by four contemporary women poets – Brazilians Adélia Prado and Hilda Hilst, Argentinian Alejandra Pizarnick, and Portuguese Sophia de Mello Breyner Andresen – to accompany his own fictional text, thus emphasizing perspectives that support, oppose, and, finally, transcend it. In contrast, as we have seen, Khosa included three biblical quotations amongst his texts in Ualalapi, serving as introductory perspectives on a novel whose religious context is that of animism and idolatry, and where the Christian faith is regarded by the protagonist in terms of political and racial suppression.

In both cases – although more so in Khosa's novel than in Couto's – the reader's access to the text will be challenged to some extent by the complex narrative structure that departs from the more overtly didactic ambitions of some other African novels written in Portuguese over the last decades, such as

---

12 'vocês não podem nem sonhar nem lembrar. Porque eu próprio não sonho, nem lembro' (Jesusalém, 20).

13 'Quer-se inaugurar uma nova ordem, uma nova gramática, uma sintaxe fora do mundo caótico, desordenado, onde outrora viveram' (Khosa 2009, 2). Ironically, the secluded Jesusalém may also, in a bizarre way, be compared to the labour camps established by the regime. There 'persons in need of correction' could be held prisoners for years, even until death. Khosa himself came to the camp in the city of Lichinga in February 1978. 'era uma espécie de Sibéria cá do sítio para onde iam os reeducandos todos' (Laban, 1051).

Kikia Matcho, and some of the earlier works of Angolan writer Pepetela.[14] Taking their implicit social, political, and historical criticisms a step further, Couto and Khosa, through extensive use of intertextuality, acknowledge the aesthetic competence of their reading public by replacing more traditionally monologic messages with ambiguity. Given the implicit dialogic quality of these two texts, and although both writers' historical assessment is pessimistic, the message is in neither case one of total disillusionment. This applies to Couto's novel especially, with its near-contemporaneous perspective.

In order to discuss in more detail whether some elements of hope for the future and of constructive healing in the present can be inferred from these novelistic communications with the past, it will be helpful to take a closer look at how these two novels deal with some of the recurrent themes of Mozambican literature over the last few decades.

2   Four Recurrent Themes

The first theme concerns the attitude adopted by an individual towards the collective social body. Within their different historical and psychological contexts, both *Jesusalém* and *Ualalapi* discuss the making of a man and the transformation of a nation. The cultural context of *Ualalapi* presents the reader with a violent and ruthless man – a royal pretender blinded by ambition. In this strictly hierarchic cultural and social structure, Ngungunhane is not initially destined to be the next *hosi*, or chief: his brother Mafemane is. However, Ngunhunhane tells his warrior Ualalapi to kill Mafemane. Ngungunhane then assumes power, becoming a *hosi* who is renowned for his cruelty. The final defeat that occurs eleven years later is as much the ruin of himself as a man as it is the downfall of a society and its traditional way of life, culture, and territory – all of which he, like his father and grandfather before him, has defended. Depicted as being neither within the Nguni community nor outside it, the fictional Ngungunhane is a moral exemplar. From holding real power of command over thousands of warriors and a vast territory, he is eventually reduced, like the Nguni people itself, to insignificance.

---

14   When questioned about contemporary writers from Guinea-Bissau and Cape Verde Islands, Khosa admits, in 1992, that he does not know them very well. As to Angolan literature, he expresses himself in favour of Pepetela and of Agualusa, but does not find Luandino's work very interesting. 'Admiro obviamente as obras do Pepetela. Do Luandino, algumas coisas ... Isto não retira que ele é um grande escritor ... Estou a gostar muito do Agualusa: por um lado, introduz a própria realidade e, por outro, tem alguma preocupação estética–o que dá à obra o seu valor universal' (Laban, 1077).

The battle is fought here against an external enemy – the same enemy that generations later fights Silvestre Vitalício and his comrades in *Jesusalém*, only to be replaced soon after by the brutal conflicts of civil war. Silvestre Vitalício's ambition seems to be the opposite of that of Ngungunhane, who is fighting to stay in history: Silvestre fights to disappear from it. When the war against the Portuguese is over, Silvestre finds himself unable to adjust to civilian life; he regresses into an imaginary world of war, where he turns into a tyrant, violently suppressing everyone around him. By taking a small community of madness and despotism as his point of departure from which to discuss loyalty, patriotism, truth, and moral integrity, Couto seems in *Jesusalém* to suggest that the process of healing is now the responsibility of every human being, victim and aggressor alike. If so, is the author providing a strategy by way of which a demand for national maturity and reconciliation may be met? I believe he might be.

The second theme, gender, addresses the relationship between men and women in Mozambican culture and contemporary society. This has been presented as a problematic issue in most African fiction in Portuguese over the last few decades. According to Couto and Khosa, male attitudes towards women are depreciatory and violent, and lack compassion. Within the all-male community of Jesusalém even remembering women is banned. From a wider perspective, however, the author's choice of the four female poets who provide complementary authorial voices is a significant one. It was Silvestre's need to forget the tragic death of Dordalma – literally, Soul-pain – his beautiful wife and mother of the two boys, that initially disrupted his mental balance. Most of all, he needs to obliterate from his memory the fact that he let her down in a moment of extreme need after a gang rape. The fact that he could not, or would not, help and comfort the woman he loved, resulted in her committing suicide during the night. Her fate marked and brutalized him for the rest of his life. His reaction has been to ban every memory of her and to take his family with him into the wilderness, so that the world could cease to exist, and he could stop hurting. Nevertheless, Dordalma's presence is felt everywhere – through his frantic rejection of her memory and through the two boys' constant efforts to keep her memory alive.

Into this violent male society of non-communication comes Marta, uninvited and unwelcome. She is a young white Portuguese woman in search of her missing husband and also, eventually, in search of herself. Silvestre wants to have her shot, an order the older boy disobeys. She opposes Silvestre and becomes a vital instrument in the destruction of Jesusalém, as her resistance worsens his mental stability and makes him physically ill. Later, she also takes it upon herself to inform the youngest boy of what really happened to Dordalma. In a long letter to the boy towards the end of the story, Marta describes

Silvestre's attitude towards his wife as: 'Wasn't he the legitimate owner of her life?'[15] This attitude resembles the way women are treated by the socially more resourceful and physically more powerful males in *Ualalapi*, and especially by Ngungunhane himself. Notably, there is a single exception to this objectifying and oppressive treatment of women: Damboia, a member of the court, is a ruthless, evil woman who has a bad influence on the emperor, thereby causing extensive damage to the community.

In *Jesusalém* Marta is a kind of fixer, uninhibited by the material and cultural conditions defining and limiting womanhood in the society she has come to visit; she is a resourceful woman who sorts everything out, brings people together, and enables them to set their lives in motion once more. Her research into the history of her own family as well as that of the two boys plays a vital part in relation to the third theme to be discussed: writing. First, there is her diary, which is read by the youngest boy. Against his father's orders he has been taught to read and write, in secret, by his elder brother. The finding of an abandoned diary, which proves to be a vital source of information, is a well-established narrative device and has been used by Couto before, notably in *Sleepwalking Land*, where the young protagonist/narrator finds the diary of a dead man. In part, the anonymous diary provides the boy with the motivation to continue his own struggle to live; in the end, it also provides him with a link to his enigmatic past. There are several points of similarity between this nameless boy and Mwanito, the young narrator in *Jesusalém*. To both, reading is forbidden or strictly discouraged, and in both cases it qualifies them to live their own lives, giving them the necessary courage to look towards their futures. For Mwanito, the boy with no remembered past, writing represents – as Shirley de Souza Gomes Carreira (2010, 93) terms it – a fundamental step in the construction of a memory, in the same way as narrating provides a passage into the world of experience.

This activity, or rather, the intended beneficial effects of reading and writing, also affects one of the characters in *Ualalapi*. Ngungunhane has a son, Manua, who betrays his father and the Nguni tradition by associating himself with the white man and his culture. Although a complete failure, and seemingly ignorant of the fact that he is despised by his father and the whites alike, he embraces the Portuguese as part of a strategy of senseless personal ambition; mostly, however, he acts from a deeply felt conviction that his father's way of life has neither future nor value. Unlike the diary found beside the corpse of the unknown man in *Sleepwalking Land*, and equally unlike the written

---

15   'Não era ele o legítimo proprietário da vida dela?' (*Jesusalém*, 261).

material found by Mwanito in *Jesusalém*, Manua's legacy to the world has no effect whatsoever on the people who find it; it remains as futile as his own wasted life.

In *Jesusalém* the written legacy that Marta leaves for Mwanito consists of more than just her diary. Later, she writes letters to the boy, who is now nearly sixteen years old, after their return to the world outside Jesusalém. In these letters, all the enigmas of the past are explained. By stressing the importance of the written word to such a dramatic extent, and by tracing the writings explicitly and solely to the European stranger, Couto also engages in a discussion of traditional orality as opposed to the imported culture of writing. This is a theme dealt with in academic terms by several researchers of African literature and culture. As outlined above (with respect to both novels), this is connected with issues of formal narrative structure and informs the ways in which such writers seek methods by which traditional oral narrative patterns may be transplanted into and continued within the narrative context of writing. Furthermore, by attributing both the solving of the enigma of the family history and the authorship of the written testimonies instrumental in this process of discovery to the white Portuguese female intruder, Couto seems to consider cooperation between the new independent nation and its old, reformed, colonial ruler as a decisive factor for any future development. In this process, even the women of the fictional universe will play an important part. That more than half of the poems that open each chapter were written by Portuguese Sophia de Mello Breyner Andresen substantiates this reading of Couto's proposal.

In *Ualalapi*, as indicated here, the status of the written word is more precarious, due to the fact that the only written document in the story is Manua's half-burned diary, found after his death in the debris of the imperial capital Mandlakazi. Writing about *Ualalapi*, Ana Mafalda Leite states,

> The imposing of writing on a society dedicated to the oral tradition represents an element of destabilization. Here writing is not a result of a normal historical evolution, but rather reflects a necessity imposed by exterior forces.[16]

In the diary, and albeit with trembling hands, Manua proudly states that, as emperor, 'I shall be among the first, in these African lands, to accept and take

---

16   'A imposição da escrita numa sociedade de tradição oral é um elemento de desiquilíbrio.
      A escrita aqui não é um produto da evolução histórica normal e responde a uma neces-
      sidade imposta pelo exterior' (Leite 1998, 90).

over the noble habits of the whites'.[17] The issue of writing – represented as the first step taken by Manua in this process of evolution – cannot be disconnected from Ngungunhane's prediction of future Portuguese supremacy. In *Jesusalém*, on the other hand, the effect is not one of disruption but of a deeply felt psychological and physical healing. Mwanito experiences an unlimited expansion of his mind with this knowledge: 'I cease to be blind only when I write'.[18] In his review of Couto's book, Khosa comments upon this statement specifically: 'Writing has made itself organic, has transformed itself into yet another of the bodily senses. Without it, the blindness is boundless'.[19] What we observe here is a concept of writing taken beyond that 'normal historical evolution' claimed by Leite, quoted above, and beyond the cultural limits that have traditionally defined the opposition between orality and writing in an African literary context.[20]

Finally, there is the theme of religious faith and its symbolic references. In *Ualalapi* the spiritual setting is one of animism, ancestral cult and magical rites: if the established religious or cultural codes are violated, disaster strikes. Khosa's story provides several examples of this.[21] In the first place, the eponymous warrior Ualalapi has done as he was told and killed the rightful inheritor of the Nguni throne. He is struck by a nameless fear and utters a desperate 'no!' before disappearing into the dark forest, never to be seen again. The offensive deed is reflected in nature as well as in the fate of the poor man's family, who will perish without his protection; it is also seen as a bad omen for the years to come. The new emperor needs his ancestors' consent, as he needs the

---

17 'Serei dos primeiros, nestas terras africanas, a aceitar e assumir os costumes nobres dos brancos' (*Ualalapi*, 100).

18 '– *Deixo de ser cego apenas quando escrevo*' (*Jesusalém*, 292).

19 'A escrita tornou-se orgânica, transformou-se em mais um dos sentidos do corpo. Sem ela a cegueira é incontornável' (Khosa 2009, 3).

20 Later, Ana Mafalda Leite (2005, 149–156) considers what she calls Khosa's choice of the short story as *Ualalapi*'s narrative unity to be closely connected to the opposition between African oral tradition and the imposition of a written culture. She sees the short stories in question as belonging to a universe in which the temporal dimension is mythical and undefined – typical of the traditional oral universe and its didactic and moralizing functions. Of the two basic narrative models in this tradition, the ascending and the descending, Khosa's work belongs to the latter, describing a transformation of the protagonist as degradation. Leite also discusses Mohamadou Kane who, in *Roman Africain et Tradition* (1983), establishes six criteria for the survival of oral literature. Kane's fifth and sixth criteria are dialogic structure and generic imbrications, imbrication meaning the absence of rigid boundaries separating literary genres. As already noted, I find that both these criteria apply to *Ualalapi*.

21 See also 'Dead and alive. The reviving dead protagonist in contemporary Luso-African fiction' (Sletsjøe 2011).

supernatural power that comes with it. Manua's diary reads: 'When I become emperor, I shall eliminate all these ways that are contrary to our Lord, father of heavens and Earth'.[22]

The situation in which he finds himself while writing this – vomiting his guts out aboard a Portuguese ship – may be seen as the gods' and the ancestors' revenge on him for deserting them and not paying them the respect they require. Here, as in previous examples concerning outstanding female members of the Nguni community, the extraordinary happenings provoke an enduring physical reaction. The nameless wife of the warrior Ualalapi cries herself to death as soon as she feels that the deed she has foreseen and dreaded has been done:

> She entered the hut and did not come out again until she herself and her son were dead, drowned as they were by the tears that for eleven days and eleven nights kept flowing from her protruding eyes.[23]

Damboia, the cruel younger sister of the late king Muzila, dies from incessant menstrual bleeding. During her prolonged agony the emperor neglects his ritual duties,[24] and consequently, the most incredible and frightening things happen, both within Nguni society and in the surrounding natural environment. Following Damboia's death, it begins to rain, 'and on the surface of the water the still-born babies of the women that had always dreamt of having children, appeared'.[25] Her death causes further disasters as it provokes the emperor's brutal revenge on groups considered to hold a negative opinion of her. Although linked to female fertility and the sexual gratification of the more powerful male, the disastrous deaths of these women point predominantly, and ominously, to Emperor Ngungunhane himself, and to a sombre future for the Nguni people. In the case of Manua, the vomiting of gargantuan and disemboweling proportions continues for hours, filling the ship and the sea

---

22   'Quando eu for imperador eliminarei estas práticas adversas ao Senhor, pai dos céus e da Terra' (*Ualalapi*, 100).

23   'Entrou na cubata e não mais saiu até à morte do filho e dela, afogados pelas lágrimas que não pararam de sair dos olhos desorbitados durante onze dias e onze noites' (*Ualalapi*, 35).

24   'He unilaterally suspends the important annual traditional ritual, *nkuia*, a sort of ritual atonement which has the objective of renewing, restoring, regenerating and improving the physical and spiritual well-being of the people living in the community. According to tradition, the ritual could only be postponed as a result of the death of the king' (Bamisile 2010, 321).

25   'Na manhã seguinte começou a chover e à superfície das águas apareceram nados-mortos das mulheres que sempre sonharam ter filhos' (*Ualalapi*, 71–72).

around her, to the horror and disgust of the white passengers. However, this incident is far from the only one in which the whites in their encounters with the African enemy find themselves, terrified and incredulous, confronting powers and events beyond their previous experience. Within Khosa's narrative, these strange, supernatural incidents have no logical explanation.

When examining the religious aspects of Couto's novel it is important to consider the Portuguese title itself: *Jesusalém*. In Brazil the novel was published as *Antes de nascer o mundo* (Before the world was born) – in itself a reminder of the book of Genesis. In being so obviously a reference to Jerusalem (*Jerusalém* in Portuguese), the author's play on words throughout the novel keeps referring in an ambiguous way to this golden city of hope and peace, while at the same time comparing this with the hopelessness and stillness of the worldly society he describes. Indeed, the father's conversation with his children communicates this fact: '– *The world is no more, my children. There's only Jesusalém left. ... – And is there no one else in the world? ... – We are the last ones'.*[26] In addition, before entering into this barren land every member of the small community has to be re-baptized or, rather, de-baptized, and the ambiguous nature of the text is intensified by their double identities.

The name Jesus-além has further theological implications. The second part, *além*, means 'at the other side', 'of the other side'; in this particular context, the name means something like Jesus 'beyond', as in 'out of reach'. This obsession with the absence of Christ suggests the distorted messianic nature of the narrative. As explained by the young narrator on the first page, 'That was the land where Jesus would have to come to de-crucify himself'.[27] Thus, Christ is not awaited by Silvestre Vitalício as the redeemer of man – that is, of Silvestre Vitalício himself – but is seen as the guilty party in need of redemption. At the entrance to the camp there is a mast, used during the colonial war as a flagstaff. According to the youngest son, his father used this to erect a huge crucifix: 'Over Christ's head he put a board where one could read: "Welcome, Lord God." And this was his creed: – *One day God will come to beg our forgiveness'.*[28] Although keeping within the context of the Christian faith, there is still to be found in *Jesusalém*, and specifically in Silvestre Vitalício's dealings with the divine, a great deal of the bargaining attitude more typical of traditional animistic practice. Part of the psychological nature of *Jesusalém*, and an essential

---

26   ' –*O mundo acabou, meus filhos. Apenas resta Jesusalém. ... – E não há mais ninguém no mundo? ... – Somos os últimos' (Jesusalém,* 23).

27   'Aquela era a terra onde Jesus haveria de se descrucificar' (*Jesusalém,* 13).

28   'Por cima da cabeça de Cristo ele fixou uma tabuleta onde se podia ler: "Seja bem-vindo, Senhor Deus." Esta era a sua crença: – *Um dia, Deus nos virá pedir desculpa' (Jesusalém,* 23).

part of *Ualalapi*'s epic and anthropological framework, the 'supernatural' and these human interactions with religious dimensions have a symbolic quality in the work of Couto and Khosa, and their linking together of past and present concerns.

3   Dialogues with the Future

By way of a preliminary conclusion, it seems pertinent to rephrase the question asked initially: is *Jesusalém* just another bleak, true-to-life description of traumas, misery, and disillusionment in the aftermath of the colonial and civil wars – or is there some cause for optimism in this rather depressing story? As already indicated, I think there is a measure of optimism discernible here. Couto's novel may certainly be read as yet another realist description of the past and present situation in Mozambique. Although the epic solemnity of the language is never lost, the sense of other-worldliness that characterizes the opening part of the text gradually recedes into the background, allowing the dramatic scenes of the daily life of a disturbed man and his family to unfold. Even so, the mentally and morally crippling society of Jesusalém *does* end, and it is possible to see Silvestre Vitalício and his sons as symbolic figures. Silvestre is the patriarch, with his shortcomings and his violence, and his inability to put things right and take responsibility for his own actions: he is a symbol of the nation's past, at death's door. Like him, the nation refuses to grieve for its past, and instead of remembering the sufferings, it opts for oblivion; indeed, fighting this collective amnesia even today may be seen as an ongoing leitmotif in Couto's novels. Consequently, the secluded Jesusalém may be understood as Mozambique itself. By remembering the violent past of which they were the victims, the two young sons – representing the future of the nation – will hopefully come to terms with it, and in a constructive and mature way turn themselves into subjects of their own lives.

A final observation: in both the novels discussed, the epigraphs – in the form of extracts from historical documents, biblical quotations, poetic fragments, or integral lyrical texts – provide the reader with an extra-textual framework that explicitly opens a dialogue with other texts. Both novels also contain intertextual references of a kind familiar to the contemporary reader; that is, references that are not identified by the author and thus depend upon the reader's resourcefulness and knowledge. In his review of *Jesusalém*, Khosa not only discusses in some detail the poems' function as epigraphs, but also expands on what he identifies as the intertextual link between *Jesusalém* and Cervantes' *Don Quixote*. His point of departure is the novelty of the old Spanish text: its ambiguity. The fact that there is no single truth, but several truths, holds good in the world taken on by Don Quixote, in the world *not* taken on by Silvestre Vitalício, and in the world that was conquered and later lost by Emperor Ngungunhane. With regard to the world of Ngungunhane, as discussed above, the concept of ambiguity has additional meanings or consequences, as a result of the extensive presence of the supernatural at work in the narrative.

In Khosa's comparative reading of the texts by Cervantes and Couto, the two protagonists' opposing ways of confronting the outer world is essential to our understanding of them:

> In Cervantes, D. Quixote goes into the world, undoing injustice and protecting ladies ... In *Jesusalém* the characters go out of the world searching through the labyrinths of their interior life, forgetting about injustices made and eradicating ladies from their memory ... In both cases, the journey. In one, the journey from the imaginary to reality, in the other, from raw, bloody reality to inner imaginary.[29]

Khosa might have added that in both cases the protagonist is, in the end, forced to return from his deluded perception of the world to be reintroduced to what is, by majority vote, called real life – an experience he does not survive. If Khosa had considered his own novel in these terms, he might have added a description of its protagonist as a man who goes out to conquer the world, traverses the labyrinths of power, imposes what he sees as justice, and eradicates every man and woman from his memory until he is forced to enter a reality so different that it must have seemed imaginary.

Whatever literary resonance each reader finds here, the complexity of the extratextual and intertextual dialogues at work in *Jesusalém* and in *Ualalapi* enables Couto and Khosa to conduct another kind of dialogue with the past. This dialogue is intellectual, and transcends both the historical ruins of the Nguni people and the confines of Jesusalém – the sanctuary that was turned into a prison. It also transcends the limits of the Mozambican nation and its cultural history, and in so doing, these texts implicitly communicate not only with their Lusophone literary heritage but with the intellectual legacies of the world.

---

29   'Em Cervantes, D. Quixote sai para o mundo, desfazendo injustiças e protegendo damas ... Em Jesusalém os personagens saem do mundo e pervagam pelos labirintos da vida interior, esquecendo injustiças e riscando damas da memória ... Nos dois a viagem. Num, do imaginário à realidade, noutro, da realidade crua, sangrenta, ao imaginário interior' (Khosa 2009, 1).

References

Afolabi, Niyi, ed. 2010. *Emerging Perspectives on Ungulani Ba Ka Khosa. Prophet, Trickster, and Provocateur*. Trenton, NJ & Asmara, Eritrea: Africa World Press.

Agualusa, José Eduardo. 1996. *Estação das Chuvas*. Lisbon: Dom Quixote.

Agualusa, José Eduardo. 2009. *Barroco Tropical*. Lisbon: Dom Quixote.

Bamisile, Sunday. 2010. Womanhood in *Ualalapi* and *Orgia dos Loucos*. In *Emerging Perspectives on Ungulani Ba Ka Khosa*, ed. Niyi Afolabi, 307–328.

Banks, Jared. 2003. Violence and the (Re)Writing of History: A Reading of *Ualalapi*. In *Seasons of Harvest. Essays on the Literatures of Lusophone Africa*, ed. Niyi Afolabi and Donald Burness, 135–162. Trenton, NJ & Asmara, Eritrea: Africa World Press.

Barros, Filinto de. 1999. *Kikia Matcho – O desalento do combatente*. Lisboa: Caminho.

Carreira, Shirley de Souza Gomes. 2010. Memória, esquecimento e identidade: a configuração dos narradores em *Antes de nascer o mundo*, de Mia Couto. *Mulemba* 1 (3): 87–97.

Chabal, Patrick, ed. 1996. *The Postcolonial Literature of Lusophone Africa*. London: Hurst & Company.

Couto, Mia. 1992. *Terra Sonâmbula*. Lisbon: Caminho.

Couto, Mia. 2009. *Jesusalém*. Lisbon: Caminho.

Khosa, Ungulani Ba Ka. 1990. *Ualalapi*. Lisbon: Caminho (2nd edition 1998).

Khosa, Ungulani Ba Ka. 2009. Escrever com alma. A viagem interior de Mia Couto. http://escrever-com-alma.blogspot.com/2009/08/ungulani-ba-ka-khosa-escritor_31.html, accessed 22 September 2011.

Laban, Michel. 1998. *Moçambique—Encontro com Escritores*, vol. III. Oporto: Fundação Eng. António de Almeida.

Leite, Ana Mafalda. 1998. *Oralidades & Escritas nas Literaturas Africanas*. Lisbon: Colibri.

Leite, Ana Mafalda. 2005. Modelos críticos e representações da oralidade africana. *Via Atlântica* 8: 147–162.

Leite, Ana Mafalda. 2010. A Dimensão Anti-Épica da Moderna Ficção Moçambicana: *Ualalapi* de U.B.K. Khosa. In *Emerging Perspectives* on Ungulani Ba Ka Khosa, ed. Niyi Afolabi, 219–230.

Sletsjøe, Anne. 2010. Self and Other in *Ualalapi*. In *Emerging Perspectives on Ungulani Ba Ka Khosa*, ed. Niyi Afolabi, 203–219.

Sletsjøe, Anne. 2011. Dead and alive. The reviving dead protagonist in contemporary Luso-African fiction. In *Pluralité des Langues, Pluralité des Cultures: regards sur l'Afrique et au-delà*, ed. Kristin Vold Lexander, Chantal Lyche, and Anne Moseng Knutsen, 129–138. Oslo: Novus.

CHAPTER 8

Racial, Cultural and Emotional Crossing Paths: Mia Couto's Hopeful Pessimism in *Terra Sonâmbula* and *O Outro Pé da Sereia*

Leonor Simas-Almeida and Sandra Sousa

> One of the things that I find more tragic in this whole
> process of consecutive wars
> is that we stopped being friends with the future.
> We don't trust it. I am a pessimist with hope.
>
> MIA COUTO

⁙

> Alas, Portugal, Portugal
> What are you waiting for?
> You have one foot on a boat
> And another on the bottom of the sea
> Alas, Portugal, Portugal
> While you keep waiting
> Nobody can help you.
>
> JORGE PALMA

⁙

1 A Nexus between Two Novels?

Terra Sonâmbula (1992)[1] and *O Outro Pé da Sereia* (2006)[2] explore the violence and the arrogance of power in both colonial and postcolonial times. In the discussion of *Terra Sonâmbula* we aim to unveil some of the textual strategies that reveal a clear awareness of people's suffering in a country engulfed by civil war, but also the possibility of redemption. We look at a different historical

---

1 Published in an English translation as *Sleepwalking Land* in 2006.
2 Translation: *The Mermaid's Other Foot*. This novel has not yet been translated into English. Therefore, all translations are our own.

context in *O Outro Pé da Sereia* in order to emphasize the view of the oppressed and marginalized in a colonial and slavery-based community, as well as the after-effects of colonial practices on contemporary society, especially in matters of race relations. It seems that in displaying these societal problems the author is calling for change and believing in its feasibility. Although accused of offering an almost defeatist view of the Mozambican historical process (Venâncio 1992, 50), Mia Couto's fictional texts are imbued with hope – as can be seen in the two novels explored over the course of this chapter. Although separated by more than a decade, and despite vast differences in terms of themes and plotlines, the presence of a strong positive subtext brings them together, which, in the end, constitutes our main argument.

2   Doom and Redemption in *Terra Sonâmbula*

As its title signifies, *Terra Sonâmbula* portrays a land so devastated by the horrors of a long war that it has become a place where vigilance and slumber, mirroring the extreme poles of life and death, are too intertwined to be viewed as opposites. It follows two parallel, though always implicitly – and sometimes explicitly – crisscrossing storylines, which unfold during the catastrophic war between Renamo and Frelimo that ravaged the country for many years. Both macro-stories are epic in their own distinct ways: one consists of Kindzu's adventures traveling through a scorched land; the other shows Muidinga's equally perilous journey to escape war. Perhaps the most curious of the ties that bind them is that Muidinga's peregrination is narrated in chapters that alternate with his reading of Kindzu's notebooks (found next to his dead body), which report his own trials and tribulations. It all comes together in the end in a mostly surrealistic, symbolic fashion.

   Terra Sonâmbula was first published in 1992, the same year in which rival organizations Renamo and Frelimo finally accepted that they had to put an end to the armed conflict that had torn Mozambique apart for seventeen years since independence.[3] It is Couto's first novel, and it is also his bleakest work. Yet its subtext points to the regeneration of collective hope, and this has been noticed by several critics.[4] Our intention here is to take this notion a little

---

3   For an account of the conflict between Renamo and the Frelimo government see, for example, Malyn Newitt, *A History of Mozambique* (1995, especially Chapter 20, 'After Independence', 541–578) and *Confronting Leviathan. Mozambique since Independence*, by Margaret Hall and Tom Young (1997).

4   Niyi Afolabi, for example, believes that '[t]hrough the subversion of anguish and misery, the characters, even when they die or lose their loved ones or possessions, usually convey a message of regeneration' (2001, 118). In another example, Philipp Rothwell also claims that

further by means of a close reading of specific narratorial devices that generate a sense of redemption in the midst of utter misery.

Terra Sonâmbula is composed of interwoven stories that intersect, multiply, and nourish each other. The protagonists are both storytellers of and 'listeners' (Couto 2006b, 92) to various narratives, which fit neither an organized linear structure nor any simple nexus of causality. Words spoken, or read aloud, as in the case of Kindzu's notebooks, are from the beginning invested with a magical power to alter the quotidian, imbuing it with fantasy and newness. An imaginative and visionary dimension is highlighted by the frequent intrusion of dreams that assume a primordial relevance in the text. Visions and hallucinations cross through every chapter of this novel, the ending of which takes the form of a prophetic dream. Furthermore, alongside this oneiric component are various narratives of events, some more realistic than others, that transform the universe inhabited by the characters.[5]

Terra Sonâmbula readily evokes the cultural context that informs it, by means of its themes, its narrative structure (which mimics the African tradition of storytellers[6]), and also by the creolization of its language, whose flexibility seems apt for expressing a particular worldview. We will examine below some of the strategies used in this text, the polysemy of which betrays its author's 'hopeful pessimism'. More specifically, the aim here is to track Couto's attempt to recreate a microcosmos in which an ancestral tradition of appropriating the real through the mythic is threatened by, among other factors, a 'process of consecutive wars', with their corollaries of corruption and unspeakable suffering. In a present characterized by apocalyptic decomposition, the narrative is infused with some hope for the future, subtly woven into every textual strand. The omnipresence of intertwined stories in itself represents the reinvention of a reality that would be lethal if devoid of imagined alternatives. According to the poet in 'Burnt Norton', 'human kind cannot bear very much reality' (T.S. Eliot 1960, 14). Surely, this must be the reason why humans have been endowed with language and its poetic function, granting them every sort of fiction capable of minimizing and, at times, redeeming the tragedy of life.

When Kindzu asks the Indian Surendra why he wants him to believe in what he has not seen, the answer is simple: 'because I don't want you to suffer' (Couto 2006b, 20). Later, as an adult, Kindzu understands the saving power of

---

during the 'country's darkest hour in the 1980s and early 1990s', Couto was attempting 'to persuade fellow Mozambicans to dream of an order not based on binary distinctions such as ... good and bad'; he was calling on them 'to dream a dichotomy-transcended reality into existence' (2004, 90).

5 Carmen Tindó Secco (2006, 261–286) insists upon the oneiric and magic dimensions of Couto's fiction.

6 On this tradition, see for example Lourenço do Rosário (2008).

fantasy: 'Farida at least had an island with an improbable lighthouse, and a ship that would come from the land of the fairies' (Couto 2006b, 105). On the other hand, when war approaches ever closer to Kindzu's village, he gradually becomes aware of having lost the power of fabulation, as well as the power of seeing beyond fear and pain: 'at night we no longer dreamed. Dreams are the eyes of life and *we were blind*' (Couto 2006b, 9; our italics). The use of the plural here means that dreaming is not restricted to the individual but gains collective resonance. It must be articulated, that is, it must be verbalized and shared with others in order to be able to rename the world and to establish ties of communal solidarity. The written word viewed by Kindzu's relatives as 'the knowledge and witchcraft of the white men' is, nonetheless, accepted and desired. Thus, Taímo's son, with the help of Pastor Afonso, his teacher and friend, 'gained this passion for letters and became a scribbler of papers, as if through them [he] could awaken the magic' (Couto 2006b, 18). Following the same line, we witness Muidinga's belief in the magic power of language, revealed in his implicit association of Kindzu's notebooks with the imagination necessary for human survival.

Above all, what is most notable here is the text's plurality of voices, rendered in its multiple narrators and numerous tales. Absent any pretense of neutrality and naturalistic omniscience, the reader is confronted with the subjectivity of the various characters who tell their stories. Although the chapters alternating with Kindzu's notebooks are narrated in the third person, the subject of the narrative never adopts an objective posture, nor is s/he invested with unquestioned authority. Furthermore, there are several instances when a third-person narrator refrains from interpreting the actions or the emotions of the characters. Indeed, throughout the book, a narrator's gloss is avoided.

As already noted, the reader is not in presence of a single plot, subordinated to the logic of chronological and diegetic progression, but rather confronted with a paratactic structure: episodes add up in a sequence that could extend infinitely, suggesting accumulation instead of a hierarchy of themes and meanings. Yet, while organized in a sequence of correlated stories, the novel nonetheless attains a degree of unity that must be perceived if the reader is to appreciate the text's complex significance in its entirety.

The stories of *Terra Sonâmbula* are constructed as a variety of narrative types: from the *fable* of the bull, lovesick for a heron, to visionary dreams, among which is a *parable* of palm trees filled with forbidden fruits, along with an *allegory* of a country devastated by hunger, unchecked greed, and cruelty – embodied in a whale that is stabbed while still alive – or portrayed in the very *symbol* of a land that sleepwalks, between night and day, or life and death. Rather than try to define these narrative forms rigorously, describing the distinctions that would better define them, it seems more useful – considering our purpose of understanding the textual fabric as a whole – to identify the fundamental relationship between the diverse components of this fabric, following the signs that point to their common denominator, which is a dominant rhetorical mode, that of allegory, in the broad sense of figurative and polysemic discourse. Under the generic designation of 'allegorical mode' we are therefore incorporating a body of narrative forms that are identifiable by specific (although unstable) *differentiae*, given that all of them have in common aspects that are important to the present approach.

According to a secular tradition begun in the Middle Ages and firmly established in the Renaissance, when interpreting allegory, the literal sense is ignored as mere appearance, that is, as a pretense; it is the second, figurative meaning that must be taken as the only pertinent one.[7] It seems, however, that *Terra Sonâmbula* illustrates well the redefinition of allegory provided by more recent rhetoricians who believe that if a text says one thing and means another, it both says and means two things. Therefore, *Terra Sonâmbula* constitutes a perfect paradigm of crisscrossed, simultaneous, not vertically hierarchical, *signifieds*. For example, at the linguistic level, the creation of neologisms is accomplished through the association and juxtaposition of new meanings (or extra meanings), by way of a contiguous process that in no way implies the elimination or subtraction of what the original words signify. A random example among innumerable others: '*Andam bambolentos*' (they walk with swaying gait) (Couto 2006b, 1) – where the notion of vacillatory movement contained in the word *bamboleante* (swaying) is associated with that of the slowness signified by *lentos* (slow).

Still another form of interconnected verbal structures may be observed in the paragraph that opens the novel, where a landscape (which can be read as a synecdoche of the country) is described thus: 'They were dirty colours ... no longer daring to rise into the blue on the wing' (Couto 2006b, 1). Later, in the chapter titled 'The letters of the dream', Muidinga observes, 'The colour blue has the right name. For it has the same sound and letters as the word "TRUE," as if it were almost its twin sister' (Couto 2006b, 31). *Azul* (blue), he discovers, is

---

7 Angus Fletcher (among modern theorists, he is one of the most dedicated rehabilitators of allegory as a literary genre) echoes what for centuries it was common to say about this particular rhetorical figure: 'allegory does not mean what it says it means, but instead turns the open and direct statement into something other' (Fletcher 1964, 2). This notion of 'something other' can be explained etymologically (derived from *allos* + *agoreuin* – respectively meaning inversion or *alieniloquium* and the words proclaimed in the *agora*, that is, the public space), thus confirming the traditionally accepted assertion that allegory 'destroys the normal expectations we have ...that our words mean what they say' (Fletcher 1964, 2).

a palindrome of *luz* (light),[8] and the relationship between the two concepts is thus made obvious. Accordingly, the connection between the two quoted passages is also made explicit: the absence of light in the landscape is compared to the weight of darkness and/or the impossibility of gaining any access to light, or to any elevation above the earth, if only at the level of dreams, fantasy, and creative power. The absence of blue/*azul* is equated to the absence of the '*as letras do sonho*' (the letters of the dream) – the same ones that Muidinga writes on the sand when for the first time he perceives that he knows how to write and use his own imagination to find hidden similarities between concrete and abstract entities, or between the words that refer to them.

Just as the literal and figurative meanings of language align horizontally, so too, at the level of diegesis, do History and Fiction peacefully coexist or intersect. A poetic universe, built in accordance with the laws of probability and necessity established by its narrators, interferes with the mimesis of historic reality. In other words, facts and fantasy constantly interact and, at times, are reciprocally allegorized. Thus, throughout the novel there run a series of public circumstances concerning colonialism, postcolonialism, war, corruption, hunger, sickness, refugee camps – all interspersed with fantastic stories, apparitions, and various wonders. Neither dimension overshadows the other; rather, they are mutually nourished, each being reflected in the other.

As for the characters, they are each as much fantastic or magical creatures as they are representations of people or groups from Mozambican history. One of the figures who best exhibits this double status is the Portuguese colonial Romão Pinto. Romão has died and become a ghost when the reader first makes his acquaintance,[9] yet he incarnates a specific colonial stereotype from pre-independent Mozambique: the rude and ignorant settler, an incurable racist and sexist, capable of destroying with his own hands his entire property when the decolonization process forces him to share it with others, or abandon it altogether. Moreover, he personifies the unscrupulous ex-colonizer who after independence is willing to ally himself to corrupt local powers, thus prospering from the misery of others.[10]

---

8   Obviously, the translator (Brookshaw) found a way of circumventing the problem of translating this play on words – '*luz/azul*' – by substituting 'blue/true'.

9   Much more recently (in 2006), João Paulo Borges Coelho has created a dialogue between colonial ghost characters and post-independent Mozambicans in his novel *Crónica da Rua 513.2*.

10 Corrupt government officials in a post-independence Mozambique are a strong presence in *Terra Sonâmbula*, representing their negative influence in the building of a country better than Mozambique had been while still a colony. Alongside Romão Pinto, the '*administrador*' Estevão, Shetani, Assane, Antoninho and the '*milicianos*' (the militia men)

The characters all fold upon themselves and/or multiply. Junhito, however, deserves special consideration, given that he represents the character whom rhetoricians would consider the most pure form of allegory: the personification of an abstract concept. Even before his birth, Taímo had decided to call him 'Twenty-fifth of June', which was 'too much of a name' (Couto 2006b, 9). He is Kindzu's youngest brother, who had been ordered by his father to change 'body and soul, into the appearance of a hen' (Couto 2006b, 11). He then began living in the chicken coop to escape a dire prediction of one day perishing at the murderous hands of passing marauders. Following his metamorphosis, the rooster Junhito (he assumed the appearance of a male) later disappears, and it is only at the end of the novel that he is recovered in a prophetic dream in which he regains human form. It seems obvious that the homonym for the date of the proclamation of Mozambican independence symbolizes the joy that many associate with this historical event, but also, and most especially, the perils the new nation was forced to confront. This symbolism notwithstanding, Junhito is as capable of having feelings as the other characters. After all, in *Terra Sonâmbula*, the novel's self-referentiality never dismisses the ability to represent an outside reality, and always projects at both levels the regenerative force of the poetic word.

Moreover, the epic dimension of the text is also a fundamental part of how language's redemptive power is represented in this novel. As far as Kindzu's journey is concerned, it closely conforms to the model of a quest – a personal journey of initiation undergone by an epic hero. This type of underlying heroic structure has been defined in the following generic terms:

> [There are] three foundational moments: the calling, the journey itself, and the return. After having recognized the call to adventure (and refusing it would mean to start an inverse process of self-destruction) the hero separates himself from the familiar world of the community to which he belongs, and departs into the unknown world. There he encounters fantastic powers, some of which help him while others oppose him ... From the point of view of his community, the return of the hero constitutes the purpose and the only justification for his long absence.
>
> MACEDO 1980, 33–34; our translation

---

appear together at the end of *Terra Sonâmbula*, portraying the enemies of Mozambican independence, and being finally defeated by the strong spirit of the nation incarnated in Kindzu, who has turned into a '*Naparama*', that is, a neotraditionalist militia fighting for justice.

The moment of 'calling' is readily identifiable in Kindzu's narrative, implying his quest for the *naparamas*, and later, for Farida's child, Gaspar. As for the journey itself, alternatively helped or hindered by the fantastic powers and obstacles that emerge, it is narrated in detail. The hero Kindzu, however, does not reach the third moment, which, in the quotation above, constitutes the only real reason for his prolonged absence. However, by the end he has fulfilled what he had in the beginning promised: 'I light the fire of a story and I douse my own self. When I have finished these jottings, I shall once again be a voiceless shadow' (Couto 2006b, 7). The notebooks remain after his demise, and they mark a powerful presence in the final lines of the novel, being clearly associated with the fecundity of the earth: 'the sheets scatter along the road. Then, one by one, the letters turn into grains of sand, and little by little, all my writings are transformed into pages of earth' (Couto 2006b, 213). Thus, if Kindzu has the potential to become a voiceless shadow, he also has the wherewithal to endow his notebooks with the power of 'ensuring the circulation of the regenerating spiritual energy that his adventure has released' (Macedo 1980, 34; our translation). His notebooks announce, through the prophecy of the enchanter in Kindzu's last dream, 'a new beginning' following the apocalyptic war, when 'the survivors will embrace life with the simple joy of young lovers' (Couto 2006b, 211). Junhito will then reassume his human form, which is to say that the nation will fully take up independence and peace.

This message of hope, dreamed in a dream of future, passes through the pair Gaspar/Muidinga as another vehicle of transmission. Kindzu's papers, transformed into pages of earth, fall from the hands of Gaspar, the illegitimate son of Romão Pinto, the fruit of the violation of black Farida or, in a final analysis, the offspring of the colonial violence wrought upon Africa. But Gaspar, re-born in the person of Muidinga, is part of the 'new beginning' announced by the enchanter.

The paths of Kindzu and Muidinga/Gaspar eventually cross, just as the spun threads cross in the multiple meanings of this complex and rich novel – a novel that is fundamentally allegorical but narrated by a pessimist in hopes of restoring our belief in the future:

> – That would be good: to teach someone to dream.
> – You don't know, son. But as long as men sleep, the land will seek ... It's that life doesn't like to suffer. The land seeks deep inside each person so as to gather all their dreams. Yes, we could say that life is the seamstress of dreams.
>
> COUTO 2006, 190

It is for this reason that the land is sleepwalking. It cannot wake before the arrival of that 'morning full of new light' (Couto 2006b, 211), when 'the tones of a song will well up, [as if they were] the gentle lull of the first mother' (Couto 2006b, 211).

3   Race Relations in *O Outro Pé da Sereia*

Turning our attention to another of Mia Couto's novels, *O Outro Pé da Sereia*,[11] it is striking that in the depiction of race relations, a central theme here, Couto also aims at a message of hope for the future. Furthermore, in both novels, the reader is asked to consider historical events in order to examine present-day Mozambique and learn the relevant lessons for the nation's improvement. Similar to events in *Terra Sonâmbula*, there are two intersecting story lines here, although in *O Outro Pé da Sereia* the chronological gap between the key narrated stories is much wider than in *Terra Sonâmbula*, extending from the sixteenth century to the beginning of the new millennium. Similar again to *Terra Sonâmbula*, characters in *O Outro Pé da Sereia* pursue their quests throughout physical and psychological space. Here, however, these quests are five hundred years apart. The reader follows the journey of Portuguese missionaries travelling from Goa to proselytize in Mozambique in the sixteenth century; but, on the other hand, the text narrates the experiences of two black Americans visiting Vila Longe, the Mozambican village where they find themselves searching for their African roots, just as Mwadia Malunga looks for her lost childhood, also in Vila Longe, and also at the beginning of the twenty-first century.

Paulo de Medeiros (2011) refers to race, violence, and representation as being 'diversely complex' and, at the same time, intertwined insofar as the first depends unconditionally on the other two. From our present perspective, Medeiros's most important contribution highlights the absence of research on race and race relations in Portugal – the centre of a one-time multi-continental empire:

> Unlike other societies where a discourse on race can be seen as constitutive of their own national identity from the start, race appears to be more of a silenced subject than an actual point of discussion in Portugal ... I think that it is also fair to say that race is practically an absent term either in academic discourse or the public sphere and yet one that is crucial to

11   The Mermaid's Other Foot.

understand some of the challenges facing Portuguese society in the present and into the future. (1)

The first question is, why discuss Portugal if the subject in hand is Mozambique, and more specifically a novel, *O Outro Pé da Sereia*. Broadly, this comes from our conviction that Couto and other writers from the Lusophone world are mainly responsible for continuing to open a space for the discussion and critique of race relations in Portugal.[12] The case of Couto's writing is interesting because he dwells between the countries, being himself Mozambican yet having a deep understanding of European/Portuguese culture, since he descends from white/Portuguese parents. Furthermore, he is one of the most widely read African writers in Portugal, his writings being not just welcomed by an academic readership but by the reading population in general. Couto's novels, which address a past shared by colonizers and colonized, have been and continue to be a vehicle through which Portugal confronts itself and its ex-colonies, by presenting us with intersections of Portugal's past pitfalls and its current relations – political, cultural and racial – with new African nations.

Another reason to believe that writers from former colonies might have an impact on the transformation of Portugal's future, by forcing it to come to terms with its colonial past, is proffered by Luís Madureira when he comments on Lusophone postcolonialism. From Madureira's perspective the former colonies have gone through a process of collective recollection of the past, in which 'incompatible appropriations of the past pave the way for a collective (and therapeutic) anamnesis, for the necessary forgetting of the brutality and of deeds of violence at the origin of every political formation' (Madureira 2008, 221). In contrast, in the former metropolis, amnesia and silence have prevailed until recently, when, in part as a result of the influence of African authors, there has been an increasing production of books dealing with the topic of race, written by Portuguese novelists, sociologists and literary critics.[13]

---

12   Writers whose names have become so familiar and cherished across a wide readership, such as Mia Couto and José Eduardo Agualusa, continually inspire discussion of themes relating to race, which tend to be absent from Portuguese academic and daily discourses. What makes this particularly interesting is that these same writers are accused by some of not corresponding exactly to the African identity they assume, but rather matching a definition of ex-colonizers taking advantage of current interest in African literature in Portuguese in the publishing world in Lisbon, while rehashing outdated lusotropicalist ideals of racial harmony and blending. Contrary to this negative view, we contend that these authors have played, and continue to play, a key role in forcing the issue of race relations on a culture inclined to ignore it or sugar coat it.

13   In the last decades, we have been witnessing a slow building up of Portugal's awareness of its colonial past, reflected on contemporary fiction. As a counterpart to a group of

In *O Outro Pé da Sereia* the concepts of memory, past, remembering, and forgetting become intertwined with race and constitute the main subject of the book. Almost all the novel's epigraphs question the representation of time and history, as can be seen in the following example: 'Here is our fate: to forget in order to have a past, to lie in order to have a future' (Couto 2006a, 75).

These epigraphs refer to and entwine two eras: 'the history of Portuguese incursions into the interior of Mozambique in the second half of the sixteenth century' (Madureira 2008, 212), and the year 2002. Such entanglements are one of the most recurrent facets of Couto's deconstruction of dichotomies. Here, he conceives of the representation of history as a blend of documented and fabricated pasts. Furthermore, the question of how Africa is perceived from the outside is a fundamental one, since it has been the object of repeated mystifications and idealizations. Besides, by representing a community that manufactures its own lies/fictions about its past, Couto shows how Africans may unknowingly or deliberately reproduce outdated, colonial ways of depicting Africa. This happens throughout the novel since the portrayed African community, arguably best epitomized in the character Casuarino, tries to convey to black American visitors an image of Mozambique that does not correspond to reality. In orders given to the community by Casuarino when he insists, 'I want everything archaic, all very rustic' (315), or in epigraphs – 'Such is our destiny: forget to have a past, lie to have a destiny' (75) – a mentality is exemplified that, like the colonial one, tries to erase reality in order to portray Africa in accordance with outsiders' pre-conceived models: in other words, as a primitive land inhabited by a backwards people, as it had been seen or imagined by mystified or mystifying colonizers.

O Outro Pé da Sereia presents a kind of laboratory of personal experiences regarding skin colour. If not all, at least many racial variations can be found in the book's almost four hundred pages. Examining the two main characters of one of the novel's two narrative and thematic lines (the one that goes back to the mid-sixteenth century), there are examples of what Boaventura de Sousa

novelists bent on imperial nostalgia (of which Manuel Arouca, the author of *Deixei o Meu Coração em África* (2005) may be a good example), Lídia Jorge, António Lobo Antunes, Helder Macedo, Teolinda Gersão, Isabel Barreno are paradigmatic canonical writers who have offered us eloquent images of the other side of a supposedly innocent colonialism. More recently, new names are appearing. Isabela Figueiredo with her *Caderno de Memórias Coloniais* (2009) was a sensation opening up controversy especially on the subject of race relations in colonial Mozambique. In 2011, two other fascinating novels were published – *O Retorno* by Dulce Maria Cardoso and *Os Pretos de Pousaflores* by Aida Gomes – also generating both acclaim and public reflection on issues of colonialism and racism, arguably its most direct corollary.

Santos defines as the Portuguese 'transit between Prospero and Caliban'. As Santos observes:

> The Portuguese, ever in transit between Prospero and Caliban (hence, frozen in such transit), were both racist – often violent and corrupt, more prone to pillage than to development – and born miscegenators, literally the forefathers of racial democracy, of what it reveals and conceals.
>
> SANTOS 2002, 24

Along these same lines, the missionary Gonçalo da Silveira is portrayed as an arrogant, violent, insensitive, corrupt, and racist missionary. For him, slaves are no more than human commodities and Africa is nothing but a poisoned continent. He shows no mercy for hungry or thirsty slaves:

> At the port of Goa, water was left out, cotton was brought in. It was left behind the water meant for the slaves, it was taken in the wealth meant for the traders. Many of the travellers in the ship's hold would not arrive at their destination, having died of thirst or having starved to death.
>
> COUTO 2006a, 188

Silveira sees slavery as 'a means of disciplining the heathens' (Couto 2006a, 188); he sees black people as savages, as lascivious, inhuman, and devoid of a soul. His mission thus presupposes a whitening of the black soul:

> In Goa he had never made friends with any African. Their dark skin did not help in seeing a soul in them. And yet it was that very opaque soul that was the ultimate goal of his journey. The whitening of these spirits – that was the purpose of his voyage.
>
> COUTO 2006a, 235

On the other hand, the trajectory of the priest Manuel Antunes moves in the opposite direction: his journey is informed by compassion for the slaves who make the '*travessia*' (the trip) in the hold of the ship, deprived of humane living conditions, pushed to the extreme of eating maps to avoid dying of hunger (Couto 2006a, 182). While crossing the Indian Ocean heading to Mozambique, Antunes questions the significance of their religious mission: 'Is there any sense in going out to evangelize an empire of which we don't know anything?' (Couto 2006a, 186), he asks himself. At the same time, Antunes is against the corruption and the debauchery witnessed in Goa, and the 'abuses and immoralities lived in the vessel of Our Lady of Ajuda' (Couto 2006a, 187). He represents a more egalitarian and humanizing view of the world:

> That wind, he thought, would sweep the whole land, it would equally strike both the weak and the powerful. And the powerful would learn that there is a power much bigger than theirs. The wind would teach them how to be small.
>
> COUTO 2006a, 189

Additionally, Antunes's journey is not only concerned with crossing the ocean but is also a personal experience of identification with the other, to the point that he himself becomes that other: 'I am moving to another race, D. Gonçalo. And the worst is the fact that I am liking better this journey than all the rest of our trip' (Couto 2006a, 190). In the figure of the priest Antunes, Couto shows the reader that race is not confined to the colour of the skin; it relates to a way of living and feeling, to morals and principles, to culture and values (Couto 2006a, 301). More poetically explained, race is the 'colour of the soul' (Couto 2006a, 236). Haunted by cruel memories, like the one of a slave who, made desperate by hunger, cut out his tongue and ate it, Manuel Antunes decides to take the name of Nimi Nsundi, who died in the ship. This name appropriation becomes the symbol of his transformation into a new, different human being. He chooses the condition of the black man, 'exiled from the past, not allowed to speak but the languages of the others, forced to opt between immediate survival and an announced death' (Couto 2006a, 302). In a final passage we see him as a *'feiticeiro'* (sorcerer), mixing pagan and Christian rituals in a harmonious manner.

Further questioning established notions of history, the novel re-examines slavery through the character of Xilundo, another black slave coming to Mozambique in the ship, who became acquainted with Manuel Antunes. Xilundo reveals that slavery was not practiced exclusively by white Europeans; he says that although he was now a slave,

> his family owned slaves. That was their means of survival: they lived off capturing and selling slaves. His father had sent him to Goa, as a servant, to punish him for serious disobedience. His father's plan was simple: he intended to prepare his son to inherit his business of selling people. In the process of being a slave he would learn how to make other people slaves.
>
> COUTO 2006a, 300

Turning now to the 2002 characters in the novel, the same type of anti-Manichaean approach is used. Tio Casuarino, the Mozambican host of two black American historians, and manager of a project to fabricate a past for the visitors, is a useful example of a corrupt African elite. His only goal is to take advantage of the foreigners' naïveté regarding Africa. As the barber Arcanjo reminds him, the land belongs to people like Casuarino (Couto 2006a, 149), who treats as inferior those who live on a different social-economic level. Casuarino reproduces European and American stereotypes about Africa, using them as means to 'sell' his country to their guests. His 'slogan was: *Everything wild, out with any trendy fads*' (Couto 2006a, 314).

Obviously, though he is a black Mozambican, Casuarino sees himself as a white foreigner; he identifies all positive and good things with the West. Using Couto's words in *Pensatempos*, we argue that Casuarino is an example of the substitution of an 'exploiting elite by another one, even though belonging to another race' (Couto 2005, 25). Also, he is native only in appearance, since he is one of those who are ready to become

> 'the black boys' of others, the foreigners. As long as these 'others' entice them with enough attractions, they'll end up selling the little of ours that is still remaining.
>
> COUTO 2005, 25

Benjamin Southman is a black American historian, who travels to Mozambique to find his ancestors' roots and to 'collect data that will confirm the hypothesis that "the stigma" of slavery and the colonial past lies at "the origin" of (or "explains") the continent's current misery' (Madureira 2008, 216). Having been raised an American, he looks at Mozambique with a certain disdain, and at pauper, begging children with condescension. Regardless of his African ancestry, he looks at Mozambique with superior eyes. Despite being black, he cannot avoid being racist himself in this context, even questioning black Africans' ability to perform certain tasks. When he is about to land in Mozambique,

> [t]he plane jolting on the old runway made it emerge, in him too, the unconfessable question: of what race might the pilot be? Might he be black, the one who was leading his fate? Without realizing it, he crossed himself.
>
> COUTO 2006a, 162

As Luís Madureira phrases it, Southman, 'like many anti-colonialist historians, endeavours to summon the agents of the empire to be judged and sentenced in absentia before the tribunal of History' (Madureira 2008, 216), but the answers to his inquiries result in slippery information, which once again complicate any fixed perspective of history.

Zeca Matambira, another interesting character in this context, sees the tight curls of his hair as 'dirt in his soul' (Couto 2006a, 249). He was raised to believe that white forms of beauty and white culture were the only patterns to be followed – a model of perfection. Matambira tried everything he could to whiten himself: 'And he remembered his cream to whiten his skin, the products to uncurl his hair, his hiding his humble origins' (Couto 2006a, 343). As a former boxer, Zeca never allowed himself to fight against a white or a mulatto:

> he could only strike a black, a man of his own race. His brain had been taught not to let him defend himself from a white man. Matambira, the promising pugilist from Tete, had been defeated by life before having stepped on the boxing ring.
>
> COUTO 2006a, 255

The final character in this context, the barber Arcanjo Mistura, seems to play the role of devil's advocate in the narrative. He refuses to participate in a strategy to deceive the foreigners, and argues that his compatriots are not respecting their 'national dignity' (Couto 2006a, 166). *Mestre* Mistura, in fact, does not believe that the colour of one's skin should interfere with any possible alliances among men. He is able to recognize the contradictions in the black American historian's pronouncements, as well as those exhibited by his own compatriots, who once fought for independence yet now use methods of governance and exploitation similar to those the colonial rulers once practiced. In a conversation with Casuarino, who tries to convince him to talk with the American visitors, the barber affirms: 'I couldn't care less that they are black. What sort of blacks are these people who are afraid of the word "black"?' (Couto 2006a, 215). When Arcanjo finally agrees to speak with Benjamin Southman, he pointedly remarks: 'You did not leave Africa when they took you in the boats as slaves. You left it when you went inside a church and kneeled before Jesus' (Couto 2006a, 218). This observation establishes Africanness not as a question of colour, of race, but as a concept that may only be defined in terms of culture, or rather, of cultures and their respective practices. Moreover, Arcanjo is against the discourse of black affirmation because he sees it as a form of racism, and as a way of allowing Africans to be complacent towards themselves. What stands out in this novel, then, is Arcanjo's message, which we see as part of Couto's humanistic project of problematizing questions of race, culture and identity: 'We have to fight in order to stop being black, in order to become persons, simply' (Couto 2006a, 219).

In *O Outro Pé da Sereia*, different points of view are intertwined in a way that allows the reader to become more sensitive to the fact that not everything is black or white: there is always a grey area that makes human encounters possible, or not. We subscribe to Niyi Afolabi's opinion that by

> providing a bridge between tradition and modernity, Portugal and Mozambique, orality and the written word, fantasy and reality, Mia Couto transforms his heritage of both cultures, the Portuguese and the Mozambican, into a hybrid cultural space which represents not only 'Mozambican identity' but problematizes such a construct.
>
> AFOLABI 2001, 160

4   Past and Future: Crossing Paths of Despair and Hope

Jorge Palma's song about Portuguese colonization, which appears as an epigraph to this chapter, claims that no one can help Portugal if it remains paralyzed in an imperialistic mind set, and keeps silent on the subject of race (as Paulo Medeiros also suggests). We believe that through the work of writers like Mia Couto, who states, '[w]e often miss the courage to look for our demons inside our own house' (Couto 2005, 95), Portugal and Mozambique can mutually help each other by building up cultural and personal bonds, and by constructing bridges across which human beings can meet and look at each other, as in a mirror. Couto appears to share this opinion whenever he expresses through his narrators and characters the sorts of views outlined throughout this chapter. After all, Couto's literary forays in Mozambican history disclose a deep belief in the redemptive power of words and of storytelling in the reinvention of its future. Furthermore, his 'pessimistic optimism' can be found in the bridges he builds, at multiple levels, between this country's past and its present, betraying his conviction that knowledge of a troubled historical process does not necessarily hinder hopes for a brighter future – as long as postcolonial Mozambican society is willing to acknowledge the ethical and political value of candid self-critical examination.

References

Afolabi, Niyi. 2001. *The Golden Cage*. Trenton, NJ: African World Press.
Arouca, Manuel. 2005. *Deixei o Meu Coração em África*. Lisbon: Oficina do Livro.
Cardoso, Dulce Maria. 2011. *O Retorno*. Lisbon: Tinta da China.

Coelho, João Paulo. 2006. *Crónica da Rua 513.2*. Lisbon: Caminho.

Couto, Mia. 2006a. *O Outro Pé da Sereia*. Lisbon: Caminho.

Couto, Mia. 2006b. *Sleepwalking Land*. Translated by David Brookshaw. London: Serpent's Tail.

Couto, Mia. 2005. *Pensatempos*. Lisbon: Caminho.

Couto, Mia. 1992. *Terra Sonâmbula*. Lisbon: Caminho.

Eliot, T.S. 1960. *Four Quartets*. San Diego, CA: Harcourt Brace & Company.

Figueiredo, Isabela. 2009. *Caderno de Memórias Coloniais*. Lisbon: Angelus Novus.

Fletcher, Angus. 1964. *Allegory: The theory of a symbolic mode*. New York: Cornell University Press.

Gomes, Aida. 2011. *Os Pretos de Pousaflores*. Lisbon: Dom Quixote.

Macedo, Helder. 1980. *Camões e a Viagem Iniciática*. Lisbon: Moraes Editores.

Madureira, Luís. 2008. Nation, Identity and Loss of Footing: Mia Couto's O Outro Pé da Sereia and the Question of Lusophone Postcolonialism. *Novel. A Forum on Fiction* 2/3: 200–228.

Medeiros, Paulo de. Race, Violence and Representation: Framing Portugal as a Post-Imperial Polity. 1–10. http://kellogg.nd.edu/projects/FLAD/pdfs/medeiros.pdf, accessed June 5, 2011.

Newitt, Malyn. 1995. *A History of Mozambique*. Bloomington: Indiana University Press.

Ornelas, José. 1996. Mia Couto no Contexto da Literatura Pós-Colonial de Moçambique. *Luso-Brazilian Review* 33 (2): 37–52.

Rosário, Lourenço do. 2008. *A Narrativa Africana de Expressão Oral*. Maputo: Texto Editores.

Santos, Boaventura de Sousa. 2002. Between Prospero and Caliban: Colonialism, postcolonialism, and Inter-Identity. *Luso-Brazilian Review* 39 (2): 9–43.

Secco, Carmen Lúcia Tindó Ribeiro. 2006. *Mia Couto e a 'Incurável Doença de Sonhar'. África & Brasil*. Letras e Laços. São Paulo: Yendis.

Venâncio, José Carlos. 1992. *Literatura e Poder na África Lusófona*. Lisbon: Instituto de Cultura e Língua Portuguesa.

Young, Tom and Margareth Hall. 1997. *Confronting Leviathan. Mozambique since independence*. Athens: Ohio University Press.

CHAPTER 9

Mozambican Capulanas: Tracing Histories and Memories

Signe Arnfred and Maria Paula Meneses

The *capulana* identifies Mozambican women in various ways. It is a piece of colourfully printed cotton material, usually 1.7 m by 1 m; it is wide enough to cover a woman comfortably. The brightly coloured cloth brings colour to the countryside's monotonous landscapes as well as to the streets of the towns. Capulanas often feature a strong central design or theme; others replicate a particular motif. Many women wear the capulana over their skirts while working in the fields in order to control the dust; others use them as a skirt/a wrapper, or sometimes as a shawl, or as a veil over heads and shoulders (in Muslim areas of northern Mozambique); some use them as a sling for carrying babies, or to wrap and carry their belongings. This versatility and usefulness explain the popularity of capulanas throughout the country.

Capulanas are fascinating, because beyond being a useful piece of clothing they are so many other things: identity markers, symbols of love, means of communication and archives of history and memories. Also, the changing history of conditions of production and marketing of capulanas is interesting, following the changes in Mozambique's own history over the last more than hundred years. Through much of this time capulanas have been an expression of the local cosmopolitanism, a particular feature of the coastal areas of Mozambique.

This chapter is about the semantics of capulanas – the manufactured pieces of cotton cloth that cross the cultural landscape of Mozambique. Looking into the meanings of the use of these textiles in the broader context of eastern Africa, we aim to discuss the memories and uses that capulanas embody, underlining their importance as markers of identity and as creative and dynamic vehicles of social interaction.

Following some notes on capulanas as markers of identity and treasured items for women young and old, we will delve into the complex history of the manufacture of capulanas, including connections of trade across the Indian Ocean, and the vicissitudes of capulana production in Independent Mozambique. The heartland of capulanas is in northern Mozambique – spreading inland from the coast, influenced by Swahili culture. Judging from historical accounts of matrilineal Makhuwa culture, capulanas played important roles in relationships between lineage heads and male dependants, as well as between in-married husbands and wives (and their matrikin). After an account of such connections – a Makhuwa history of power, gender, sex and capulanas – we go into the broader history of capulanas and kangas[1] (the Kenya/Tanzania name for this type of cloth) along the Swahili coast. The importance of capulanas in the Tufo dance culture of Ilha de Moçambique is here seen as a special case of capulana culture in Muslim/Swahili contexts. Towards the end of the paper we elaborate on capulanas as means of communication – of certain historical events in terms of their given names, and on a more personal level through their captions – a relatively recent phenomenon on Mozambican capulanas. We conclude with a note on the resilience of capulana culture, and the continued existence of capulanas as an expression of local cosmopolitanism while also condensing the complexity and diversity of social, political, and global influences.

1   Capulanas as Markers of Identity

The capulana is intimately associated with Mozambican women, acting as a core agent of communication in the continuous production of identities; it is a symbol of belonging in this south-eastern African country. Since the nineteenth century, reports about capulanas have been a constant in the socio-cultural landscapes that have come to be described as Mozambique.[2] Capulanas are part of both language and culture in this region, and have developed into a distinctive synthesis of indigenous African and foreign elements. An active agent of intercultural contacts, the capulana became over time more than a piece of cloth: in linking eastern and western shores of the Indian Ocean, it has become an important element in a complex web of intercultural contacts.

Identities are produced through social processes that create differences, including aesthetic distinctions. To dress is in itself part of a process of socio-cultural differentiation, and a form of expressing occupation, status and gender, among other elements. Far from being static, identity processes are in a state of constant change and may serve as a window through which to analyse how societies are interpreted and represented. Capulanas are greatly valued items and people feel affection for them; collected and handed down from mothers to daughters, they act as reservoirs of memory and expression

---

1   *Kanga* – from the verb ku-kanga, in Kiswahili, meaning involving or closing.
2   See, for example, Lupi (1907), Cruz (1910), and Noronha (1915).

regarding personal and collective histories of relationships and events (Beck 2000; Meneses 2003). They mark times past, yet they also mark the identities of the women who wear and use them today. Capulanas are indicators of group belonging (women with identical capulanas), and they reflect the celebration of events.

Older women, who have collected capulanas throughout their lives, keep their capulanas in wooden chests: they represent a sort of treasure, and a symbol of a woman's wealth. Some of the capulanas can be dated back to a woman's youth, and as such they trace important events that have marked her life. Some may have been handed down to her by her mother, thus representing a history which goes even further back. Others may have been offered to her by her husband, others again by her in-laws at the time of the *lovolo* (bride price), by a son returning from the mines in South Africa, or by the OMM[3] to commemorate a special political event.

Thus, when an elderly woman opens her wooden chest, she opens up a stream of memories. The capulanas tell her story and retrace the network of relationships to which she belongs. Here, capulanas act as historic documents, speaking about specific social and personal events. These old capulanas are rarely worn; they only see the light of day on special occasions, but they may be given as gifts to daughters, daughters-in-law, or other close female relatives, to mark special occasions. When the owner dies, the capulanas are passed on as a legacy to those of her descendants who are fortunate enough to be considered her heirs (Rolletta and Tocato 2004).

2   The Complex History of the Manufacture of Capulanas

The abundant literature available on transoceanic trade shows the importance of clothing in the Indian Ocean region: 'Significant Indian Ocean trade is documented since at least the early ninth century AD, with the specific commercial and cultural ties between India and East Africa over the last few hundred years well captured in the history of the emergence of kanga cloth' (Parkin 2005, 47). According to Beck (2000), for a long time kangas were also imported from Europe: Switzerland, the UK, and the Netherlands.

As in the neighbouring regions of the Swahili coast, Mozambican capulanas were initially imported mainly from manufacturing centres on the eastern shores of the Indian Ocean – from India and Indonesia among other areas, as

---

3   Organização da Mulher Moçambicana – Mozambique Woman's Organization.

well as from Portugal.[4] The capulanas from the other side of the Indian Ocean used to be printed predominantly with abstract/geometric or floral designs. These capulanas are generally sold in pairs; they follow the kanga style of having a border around all four sides (called a *pindo* in Kiswahili) and a larger motif in the middle (*mji* in Kiswahili) (Yahya-Othman 1997). The centre of the cloth might be filled with various patterns (that is, it tends not to have a large motif) and as a rule, and unlike Swahili kangas, Mozambican capulanas did not carry captions (*jina* in Kiswahili). Capulanas may have names, but that is another story, addressed below.

Portuguese-manufactured capulanas are slightly larger, made of heavier cotton material, and the patterns are woven, not printed. Portuguese capulanas can be identified by their chequered patterns, somewhat like Scottish tartans, though in cotton (not wool) and in different colours: black, dark red, off-white, sometimes with a string of blue. Portuguese capulanas occasionally have small woven patterns mixed into the overall chequered pattern, but never a central motif (see figure 9.1).

FIGURE 9.1 *Former king Ngungunyane, his wives, uncle and son, deported* (Lisbon, end of 19th century). Note the chequer-pattern in Ngungunyane wives' capulanas.

4   As various authors stress, the cloth most appreciated by the African population was that produced in Gujarati (in India). Portuguese textiles gained less acceptance.

As Isaacman notes (1996), cotton was one of the mothers of poverty in colonial Mozambique. The textile manufacturing industry in metropolitan Portugal was supplied with cotton produced in colonial territories. Indeed, the expansion of cotton production – one of the obligatory agricultural products in colonial times – saw a substantial increase under colonial reforms carried out by the Salazar regime, from the 1950s on. Benefitting from fertile soils, a favourable climate, access to ports, and to abundant labour force to be coerced into forced production, Portuguese colonial authorities chose Mozambique and Angola to become the main sources of cotton fibre for the metropolitan textile industry: 'Mozambican cotton, imported at artificially depressed prices, fuelled the Portuguese textile industry and saved Lisbon millions of dollars annually in hard currency' (Isaacman 1985, 15). Only towards the end of the Portuguese colonial administration were the first textile industries installed in Mozambique.

3   Vicissitudes of Capulana Production in Independent Mozambique

In 1975, with independence, Mozambique's capulana culture changed; the culture of capulanas persisted, but the capulanas themselves were different. At the time of independence, Mozambique had three relatively new and modern textile factories, in the north, centre, and south of the country: TexMoque in Nampula,[5] TextAfrica in Chimoio,[6] and TexLom in Maputo.[7] These factories, which before independence had mainly catered for the needs of the Portuguese community, were now re-directed for producing capulanas. In the early years of independence Mozambique had few opportunities to import goods from outside the country; thus, the logic of the government had to be geared towards self-sufficiency. Mozambique-produced capulanas were of good quality, with printed patterns and bright colours, like the ones from the Indian Ocean trade circuit, but made in a heavier (and durable) cotton quality. The majority of Mozambican capulanas from this period did not have the kanga-style border along all four edges. A typical style was to have borders along the

---

5   Texmoque, the major textile factory in northern Mozambique, was closed down for several years. Bought by Tanzanian capital, it reopened for a while as the New Texmoque, to be closed down again in 2012.

6   This textile factory, initially known as Sociedade Algodoeira de Portugal, was located in Chimoio. It was renamed TextAfrica after independence, and was in operation until its collapse in the late 1990s.

7   TexLom, one of Mozambique's largest textile factories, has resumed operations after being closed down for several years. The factory was renamed Moztex.

two long edges, and sometimes a larger motif/motifs in the middle, but otherwise they were produced in running meters, which could be cut as required, to suit the fashion tastes of women from the south and the north.[8] The capulanas with designs on all four-edges had to be cut precisely along the short edges. Throughout the 1980s however, Mozambique-produced capulanas were almost always sold (or distributed) in pieces cut to capulana size.

During this period, in the midst of the Mozambican revolution, capulanas echoed the troubled political processes that the country was undergoing. With independence, Mozambique opted to follow a UN mandate, supporting the struggle for liberation in the neighbouring countries of Zimbabwe, apartheid-era South Africa, and Namibia.[9] As a result, shortages of goods became routine. Shops were empty, food was hard to come by, and people would have starved without the ration system, which allotted a certain amount of goods – such as maize flour, sugar, cooking oil, and tea – per family per month. Those days were marked by shortages of everything, including capulanas. The factories produced capulanas, but much of this production was exported in exchange for hard currency, so badly needed at the time. With Frelimo's single-party state controlling capulana production, several commemorative capulanas were produced for local distribution to particular party friends with patterns and texts alluding to campaigns (such as alphabetization or vaccination), important political events (such as Zimbabwean independence), party celebrations, OMM conferences and the like (see figure 9.2). Party members – including those in the OMM – had privileged access to these items. On festive days the new capulana would be brought to the OMM headquarters, for all of the OMM workers to get their piece. In spite of scarcity, in this period capulanas became a national symbol to affirm identification with the construction of 'Mozambicanness', so important for the new state. And in spite of scarcity, women managed to continue collecting capulanas.

Later, after the advent of neo-liberal economic policies (from 1986 onwards), life 'normalized', in as far as there was food on shop shelves again, and for a few years it was actually possible to buy Mozambican capulanas. However with the structural adjustment policies – known as PRE[10] in Mozambique – and Mozambique's adherence to World Bank and IMF demands for open markets, local Mozambican production of capulanas soon came to an end.

---

8   While women in southern Mozambique wear the capulana fastened on their waists, in the north they wear several capulanas together, one over another, in fashionable combinations.

9   This included the closing of borders with Rhodesia (actual Zimbabwe) and tense relations with apartheid South Africa, resulting in a negative impact on the national economy.

10   Programa de Reestruturação Económica (in english, Economic Restructuring Program).

FIGURE 9.2 Women in Mayday parade 1983 wearing identical capulanas alluding to Frelimo's
IV Congress.

One after another, the country's textile factories closed down. The PRE structural adjustment policies gained ground, and while cotton was still produced
in great quantities in Mozambique, it was no longer processed in local factories; it was exported as raw material, destined for textile factories abroad. From
a consumer point of view this meant a return to pre-independence consumer
circuits, with capulanas being imported particularly from India, but also from
China and elsewhere. Thus, once again, imported capulanas from across the
Indian Ocean were for sale in shops and at markets.

During this period, every time she visited Mozambique, Signe would meet
with old acquaintances, especially a friend and colleague from their days in the
OMM, Mamã Adelina. Mamã Adelina lived in one of the Maputo townships, in
a house with just two rooms and a kitchen in the courtyard. The visits followed
a particular ritual: bags of food and a capulana would be offered to Mamã
Adelina, and every time, when Mamã Adelina received a gift of a capulana,
she would tie it around her waist, performing a dance and song of thanks –
agradecimento. Gifts of food were necessary and were gratefully received, but
only the gift of a capulana would elicit this particular song and dance. On one
occasion Mamã Adelina offered in return an old and treasured capulana of her
own; it was double-sized – two capulanas sown into one with a ribbon of lace
down the middle, a *mukume* (see figure 9.3).[11] This kind of capulana obviously

---

11   The *mukume* consists of two capulanas cut from the same piece of fabric; they are sewed
        together by a piece of white cotton lace.

had great emotional value and it felt as a very particular honour and privilege to receive this gift. Indeed, mukumes were used for covering nuptial beds; they also used to be worn by older women at special occasions, for instance, by the mother of the bride on the day of the *lovolo*[12] (Rolletta and Torcato 2004; Bagnol 2008, 257).

FIGURE 9.3
Mukume ni vemba in southern Mozambique, by mid 1920s (Santos Rufino 1929, 28).

4   A Makhuwa History of Lineage Power, Gender, Sex and Capulanas

For more than a century capulanas have been treasured from north to south of Mozambique, however with a particularly intense presence in northern Mozambique, where they have been part of intricate circuits of sex and power.

---

12   *Lovolo* generally translated as 'bride value', is part of individual and collective identity. This practice in southern Mozambique, by reinforcing kinship relationships with both the living and the dead, contributes to the re-establishment of social harmony and alliances. On these occasions, the mother of the bride wears a special capulana, a *mukume ni vemba*. The larger one, the *mukume*, is tied around the waist; the smaller capulana, the *vemba*, is worn over the shoulders like a shawl. A plain coloured blouse and a headscarf (usually in the same pattern as the *mukume*) complete the costume (Torcato 2009, 54).

Information on the history of the special role of capulanas in northern Mozambique is provided by Christian Geffray (1990), who conducted fieldwork in Erati district, Nampula province, in the early 1980s. Geffray provides a fascinating account of matrilineal circuits of power, money, and capulanas in the early part of the twentieth century.

Among the matrilineal Makhuwa (the dominant ethnic group in northern Mozambique), young men moved upon marriage to live with their spouses (this is still the case); they were expected to work for many years on their wives' matrilineal land, which was controlled by their mothers-in-law (this also still happens, but to a lesser extent). The food produced was taken to the granaries of the mothers-in-law (the grandmothers of the men's children, in other words), from where it would be distributed to the family's children and grandchildren. The young men's labour was effectively invisible in this process: the grandmothers were (and still are) perceived as the givers of food (Geffray 1990).

When the in-married men themselves get grown-up daughters, who bring in new young sons-in-law to work on their wives' matrilineal land, the men, now fathers-in-law, are absolved from their obligations to work on their wives' family land. They can start cultivating a plot of land for themselves, with sesame, groundnuts, or other products to be sold in the coastal areas. Geffray describes how these middle-aged men mobilize younger male dependents to help with the long-distance transport of the produce to the coast. The trip to the coast and back – in Erati district this would be some 100 km each way – may take two to three weeks during the lean and dry months of the year (July–August), when it is easier to walk through the bush and there is less agricultural work to be done. Once they have arrived at the coastal towns, the agricultural products will be sold to Indian or local merchants in exchange for capulanas, and possibly some other goods, but the capulanas are the most important items. The cloth, produced across the Indian Ocean region, is purchased in bales of 20–30 meters. Each helper gets a few lengths of capulana in return for his help on the journey, but the bulk of the merchandize is brought not to the homestead of the producer and owner of the sesame/groundnuts, but to the homestead of the *humu* (or *mwene*) – the head of the producer's own matrilineal lineage, the *nihimo* (which is different from the nihimo of his wife). The goods are presented to the humu by his dependent, as a mark of deference and respect. In his possession, the capulanas become tools of power and politics; they may be used to settle quarrels or conflicts between lineages; as such, the capulanas may circulate from one humu to the next. The humu uses some of the capulanas in this way as tools of inter-lineage politics; others are used as gifts to his dependents – young men of the same nihimo. These young men hand on the capulanas as gifts to their wives; what they get in return is sex and devotion.

In the Makhuwa context, a married man was (and still is) obliged once in a while to present not only his wife but also his mother-in-law with a capulana. This is essential for maintaining a good relationship with the wife as well as the in-laws. As Geffray explains:

> a man's reputation in his wife's lineage will suffer if his gifts are irregular or of poor quality. Or even worse, a repeated absence of such gifts will have as a consequence a divorce, i.e. the man will be ordered back to his own family of origin. (1990, 173)

Once in the hands of the women, the capulanas do not circulate any further: they now become symbols of female power and prestige. It is true for Mozambique as described by Laura Fair for coastal Tanzania: a woman can never get enough of capulanas (Fair 1998).

Women control the distribution of food, and they are also the experts regarding sexual relations, but for capulanas they depend on men. Until fairly recently, particularly in the coastal areas, Makhuwa women were dependent on men for any product bought with money. And even if, as sometimes nowadays, women have money themselves for buying capulanas, the proper thing is still to receive a capulana as a gift, preferably from a man. As reported by Geffray:

> if the woman had access to money, she could buy capulanas herself. This, however, is not how things ought to be; it should be the man, who buys capulanas for his wife. (1990, 175)

In the course of our own fieldwork in Cabo Delgado and Nampula provinces, similar answers were given, particularly in coastal regions. Money was seen by men and women alike to be the domain of men. In northernmost Mozambique, in the coastal areas close to Tanzania, women produce beautiful *esteiras* (coloured straw mats). Selling the mats, however, was (and still is) a task undertaken by men.

> One may say that men's exclusive appropriation of means of access to the market creates a diffuse but general dependence of women in relation to men ... Women find themselves depending on male intervention for access to certain goods, considered appropriate for the social manifestation of their status and identity (Geffray 1990, 175–176).

Thus, women's control of food (and sex) is counterbalanced by men's control of capulanas (and money). Men need capulanas in order to maintain masculine

FIGURE 9.4 Young women on their way back to the village after the rituals of initiation, in
northern Mozambique.

power, and in order to be on good terms with their womenfolk. In northern
Mozambique, giving capulanas to men in return for help with fieldwork tasks
is commonplace, whereas in southern Mozambique this would not be seen as
appropriate; in southern Mozambique capulanas are women's items.

Today, women can and do buy capulanas themselves, but they are still perceived as a special item, and in essence they should be a gift of love from a man
to a woman. A gift of love, which is also a gift in exchange for sex. Research on
female initiation rituals in Makhuwa contexts in northern Mozambique reveal
that when young women are instructed on how to conduct proper sexual relations in marriage, they are also taught to expect a gift from their husband in
exchange for 'good sex' (Arnfred 2011). This gift may take the form of money,
but it may also take the form of a capulana. On the final day of the initiation
rituals, the girls – now transformed into marriageable women, when they have
been through the ritual bath, the cutting of hair etc. – walk back to the village
clothed in new capulanas (see figure 9.4).

5   Kanga/capulana History along the Swahili Coast

The items known as capulanas in Mozambique are called *kanga* elsewhere
in East Africa. In Madagascar, where similar prints are used, they are called

lamba; in other former French colonies they are called *pagne* (a French word for a piece of cloth). In Malawi they are called *chitenge*; in South Africa a common name is *kikoi*. In the nineteenth century, printed pieces of cloth were sold along the shores of eastern Africa, brought from 'the orient'. These pieces of cloth, smaller in size, were called *lenço* in Portuguese. Women started to purchase several of them and sewed them together to obtain a larger piece of material. This explains the name – *leso* – in Mombasa and further north along the Kenyan coast (Beck 2000; Meneses 2003).

Where the name 'capulana' comes from is unknown, but it is used throughout Mozambique, and became part of the Portuguese language. There is some speculation that it might derive from Ka Polana, which is where Maputo is today and where capulanas were traded. Ka Polana supposedly refers to one of the local leaders in southern Mozambique, before the establishment of Portuguese colonial administration in the area. In any case, Mozambican women's use of capulanas indicates cultural connections along the coasts of the Indian Ocean area, including Zanzibar, Madagascar, and the Comoro Islands, as well as further along the eastern shores. Mozambican women know whether their capulanas are made in Indonesia or in the Netherlands, or come from Southern Africa and whether they have been bought at the Ilha de Moçambique or in the south. They master the details, the use of colours, dyes, and patterns, and their origins. When they make a decision to obtain one or another piece of cloth, they know why, and they know what they are using to represent their identities (Meneses 2003).

Laura Fair, who has studied historical changes in male and female clothing in Zanzibar, notes that kangas began to appear in Zanzibar at the end of the nineteenth century, with the abolition of slavery. From then on, former slaves were keen to re-identify themselves as Swahili – a freeborn, Muslim coastal community. Previously, they had seen themselves as belonging to the various ethnicities of the hinterland, such as Yao, Makhuwa, and Makonde: 'Becoming Swahili was one of many steps of ethnic re-identification pursued by former slaves' (Fair 2000, 152), and wearing a kanga became a marker of this Swahili identity.[13] Female dress for poor people, including slaves, had previously been a *kaniki*, a simple dark cotton cloth, tied beneath the armpits (see figure 9.5), whereas the purchase of kangas became indicative of growing economic power in Swahili society, as well as an expression of a local cosmopolitanism in which new political subjects could express, through their choice of clothes, a redefinition of their social importance (Meneses 2008).

---

13   These pieces of cloth were probably the result of the trade established across the Indian Ocean region. Indeed, one of the main items of trade was the *bertangil* (or *bertangim*), a piece of material in cotton, dyed in red or blue, and produced in India (Isaacman 1996).

FIGURE 9.5 Female slave construction workers wearing *kaniki*. Some of the women in the
centre are also wearing early *kanga* designs (Fair 1998, 68).

In addition to being Swahili, kanga was initially a specifically urban fashion. In
Zanzibar, in particular, urban women were fashion conscious and had access
to money: 'The reputations of Zanzibari women as highly fashion-conscious
buyers engaged in endless displays of conspicuous consumption appear to
date from this era [the early years of the 1900s]' (Fair 1998, 77). Fair reports
from contemporary statistics that prior to 1929, 'Cotton Piece Goods' (including kangas) constituted an average of 25 percent of all textiles imported to
Zanzibar, 10 percent of those imported to Tanganyika, and 8 percent of textiles
imported to Kenya and Uganda. After 1929 the percentage of printed Cotton
Piece Goods (of which, in Zanzibar, 90 percent were kangas) nearly doubled,
although for Tanganyika, Kenya, and Uganda the figures were somewhat lower:
'According to these records, even during the depression the demand for kangas
in Zanzibar remained surprisingly stable' (Fair 1998, 77).

We have no statistics on the import of cotton goods to Mozambique in the
same period (the 1920s and 1930s), but the description of Zanzibari women's
relationship to kangas make sense in a Mozambican context, especially when
one looks at photographs from that time (see figure 9.6). This seems particularly likely in northern coastal areas of the country, which are close to or
part of the Swahili region. Like in the coastal areas of Kenya and Tanzania,

FIGURE 9.6   Girls from northern Mozambique, dressed in capulanas. Image from early twentieth century (Mozambique National Archives).

Arabs – particularly from Hadramawt in Yemen – have populated the northern coast of Mozambique since the end of the first millennium. Swahili culture has emerged as a mix of this Arab influence with local African cultures.

Along the eastern shores of the Indian Ocean, the Swahilization of African Muslims affected various facets of life in this region. As Abdulaziz observes (1979, 8), this 'trend has been so forceful that most Arabs of the coast, who have settled here ... have lost their original culture and language', which has been absorbed by local cultures. On Mozambican shores, by marrying into Makhu-wa matrilineages, Arab sailors and traders ensured they were entrenched in Makhuwa kinship structures. The populations of several towns along the coast are said to be the result of such intermarriage (Bonate 2007).

In northern Mozambique, the capulana culture of the coast is defined by a distinct style. As a dress, capulanas conform to Muslim codes of modesty, al-lowing the women to cover themselves from head to foot; the motifs of many of the capulanas – both abstract and floral – come from local interpretations of Islamic prohibition of figural representation. In this context, capulanas are not just used as wrappers, but also as veils. A capulana over the head was (and remains) a sign of respectability and of adherence to Islam (see figure 9.7).

FIGURE 9.7   Women in a madrassa. Angoche, northern Mozambique, using capulanas to cover
their heads.

6   Capulanas in the Tufo Dance Culture of Ilha de Moçambique

The presence of Swahili culture in contemporary Mozambique remains evident, for instance, in the *Tufo* dance culture of Ilha de Moçambique. The Tufo dance is popular in northern Mozambique; Ilha is home to more than ten different Tufo groups, each with widely dispersed nets of daughter groups as far away as Maputo.[14]

The organization of Tufo groups resembles the organization of Islamic (Sufi) *tariqas/turuque*, some of which have their headquarters in Ilha. The history of the oldest Tufo dance group, *Estrela Vermelha* (Red Star), dates back to 1931 (Arnfred 2011). As Fair observes, in Zanzibar, the costume for *Kunguiya* dances was a kanga, with the additional aspect that all kangas worn for a particular Kunguiya dance had to be identical, 'regardless of class, status and heritage'; wearing identical kangas during the performance had the effect of 'visually marking [the dancers] as equals' (Fair 2000, 168). Tufo dancers of the

---

14   For a detailed description and analysis of Tufo dance culture, see Arnfred 2011.

same group are likewise dressed in identical capulanas. However, unlike the Kunguiya dance, Tufo is not a dance of initiation. Tufo is actually an asexual dance, with roots in Muslim respectability: it is danced in lines, partly sitting, partly standing, with movements of the arms and shoulders. Where Tufo resembles Kunguiya is in the importance of capulanas. Identical capulanas for all Tufo dancers of a particular group is a requirement, as are new capulanas for every performance, and identical blouses and headscarves (see figure 9.8). Tufo dancers have a high turnover of capulanas. A man from Ilha, Abdallah, vehemently stressed that he would never consider marrying a woman from a Tufo group, no matter how beautiful she might be; the costs of satisfying her need for capulanas – three to four a week, according to him – would be too high.

FIGURE 9.8 Seated *Tufo* dance, Ilha de Moçambique.

Also according to Abdallah, Tufo dancers do not refrain from 'negotiations with their bodies' in order to obtain the required number of capulanas (Arnfred 2011).

The Tufo dancers convey an impression of being independent and self-reliant women. The attraction and fascination associated with Tufo groups (and the reason they have dispersed to far-away non-Muslim places) is exactly this air of independence and urbanity, which is associated with modernity in a sense, even if the Tufo dance in itself is rather traditional.

Tufo keeps alive the capulana culture. Each of the groups has their own fixed combinations of colours (yellow/red, blue/white, black/white, for example). A member of each group is tasked with keeping an eye on newly arrived capulanas, placing orders on behalf of the group in the shops of the Indian traders or at the local market, whenever a nice new capulana in the appropriate colours arrives. In this context, the capulanas are consumer goods, but they are also communication devices as important as the spoken word. Furthermore, the use of capulanas may be seen as a catalyst for sociocultural grounding and as a strategy for representing the self in the diversity and movement of local populations (see figure 9.9).

FIGURE 9.9   Angoche, Mercado da Criança, 2005. Trading capulanas.

Another fashion item in northern coastal Mozambique is the *kimão*, which is a tight-fitting blouse with long sleeves and an open neck, decorated with coloured strips and zigzagging ribbons. In the early 1980s, when women assembled for meetings called by the OMM, a combination of these items formed the standard outfit: a kimão with a capulana.

During the civil war, however, from the mid-1980s to the mid-1990s, so-called *calamidades* (European second-hand clothing) in the form of development aid poured into Mozambique; kimãos disappeared, to be replaced by European t-shirts. The kimão seemed to have gone forever, yet by the end of the 2000s it had regained its place in the fashion universe of northern Mozambique, although in less elaborate form (see figure 9.10).

In their (re)appropriation of the kimão, Ilha's women lay claim to their own cultural forms. Mozambican imports are destined for the social realm of display and public communication. Imported cloth, when fashioned into kimãos, becomes a vehicle for the relocation and grounding of identity; it signifies a culturally distinct fashion statement and a social link with broader cultural contexts that are different from calamidades. The fact that objects such as capulanas, and practices such as Tufo, are continuously embraced and

FIGURE 9.10   New style *kimãos*, Ilha de Moçambique 2009.

appropriated when a new need arises makes clear their pivotal role in contemporary societies; this process reinforces the intimate connections and continuities between tradition and contemporary societies.

From the late 1990s onwards, visits to Ilha de Moçambique and Angoche
revealed close contact between consumers in Ilha (such as the Tufo dance
groups) and producers in India. The Tufo groups not only reserved particularly
nice capulanas in the right colours, they also ordered specific designs. On more
than one occasion, the adventurous group *Estrela Vermelha* ordered specially
manufactured capulanas in their own colours (yellow/red) and appropriate
designs. One of them has a large red star in the middle (*mji*), small red stars in
the corners, a red border (*pindo*), and a yellow background. It also has a *jina*
(caption) that reads *Estrela Vermelha*.

In terms of designs, Indian traders in Mozambique display good business
sense. They realized that women favour some of the old and beloved capulanas, including those produced in the Frelimo state-monopoly days. They
selected several of these motifs and sent them to factories abroad, mainly in
India, where the old designs were reproduced, sometimes in different sizes
and on materials of different quality, but it was still the same much-loved pattern. There are also a number of new patterns – and captions, previously non-
existent in Mozambique, which have started to appear, sometimes with words
in Swahili (which few in Mozambique understand), sometimes in Emakhuwa,
very rarely in Portuguese. Other capulanas display contemporary motifs, such
as cellular phones, cars, or radios. In this sense, the realm of capulanas allows
for innovation, the formulation of modernity, and for the expression of aesthetic feelings and experiences that 'speak' in women's 'own voices'.[15]

Women's taste in capulanas reveals a fine-tuning in terms of the dominant
fashion trends. In 2009, for example, chequered capulanas (produced in Portugal and quite expensive) were popular in Ilha de Moçambique. This probably
followed a fashion trend favoured by the then First Lady of Mozambique, who
had a soft spot for *mukumes* (often sewn from chequered capulana material);
another explanation may have to do with the fact that nowadays, due to liberalization of world trade, old-style Indian cotton capulanas are difficult to get
hold of. Most capulana-printed material now on sale in the shops and markets of northern Mozambique is synthetic: the colours are bright and they are
cheap to buy, but the quality is poor and they are unpleasant to wear in the
heat.

---

15   Amina C., interviewed in Angoche, 2004.

7   Capulanas Tell the History of the People

Most Mozambican capulanas do not have captions; even less so in the 1980s and 1990s. Nevertheless, many have names. The names are given and communicated as parts of local oral culture. As Rolletta and Torcato explain (2004), the process of naming a capulana is part of the marketing. When a new assortment of capulanas arrives at a store, the shopkeeper rushes to introduce the customers to the new patterns:

> The discussion that takes place, in which the trader also participates, ends with the 'baptism' of the capulana. Then other costumers come along, looking for the capulana that their neighbour showed them, and now they ask for it by name.
>
> ROLLETTA and TORCATO 2004, 28.

Indeed, this seems to have been the case with the *Nyerere* capulana, produced by TexLom at the time of the first visit of the then Tanzanian president to Mozambique.[16]

The name given often refers to a particular event at a given time, and it acts as a document or a portrait of past significant events and struggles. Such is the case of the *Nkwakwanana* capulana. In Xichangane, one of the main languages spoken in southern Mozambique, *Nkwakwanana* means 'the long march'. It refers to a practice carried out by Portuguese authorities in colonial days. If caught without a pass, African people living in the city were sent back to rural areas:[17] 'These persons were assembled, and guarded by *sipaios* [native colonial police]. They were walked out of Lourenco Marques back to their areas of origin in the countryside' (Tembe and Cardoso 1978b, 23). Another example of a well-remembered capulana is the *Mudende*. This name is also rooted in colonial days, when the Portuguese ruled that all Mozambicans should pay an annual tax. If a woman was caught without a pass and without the slip that showed her to have paid her tax, she would be sent off to forced labour – *xibalo* – for up to six months. This mudende tax hit single mothers particularly hard.

---

16   Because Tanzania was one of the main supporters of the struggle for independence of Mozambique, allowing for FRELIMO to have military bases on its territory, this visit was a celebration of friendship and liberation.

17   In order to be able to live in urban areas, Africans had to hold a pass, with the name of the employer clearly assigned. This pass (*caderneta indígena*) had information on it regarding the tax payments made by the holder.

FIGURE 9.11
TWO TRADITIONAL
HEALERS IN MAPUTO,
DRESSED IN SPECIFIC
CAPULANAS.

Another capulana that brings back memories was called *Kandya Kaia*, which means 'single mother' (Tembe and Cardoso 1978b, 24).

Capulanas also act as social manifestos. *Xivite xa va baniana* – hatred of the Banyans – was the name given in the south to the capulana used at the time when India took over Goa, Damão, and Diu, in 1961. The Portuguese, in retaliation for the Indian takeover of 'their' territories, arrested and deported all Indian citizens from Mozambique, confiscating their goods (Tembe and Cardoso 1978a, 38). In Ilha de Moçambique, capulanas also have names. For example, a capulana was named *Amala wa Azukir* (lack of sugar), remembering a particular period when no sugar was available in shops or markets.

Capulanas also speak the language of grief. Some capulanas have black and white motifs and these are used as a sign of mourning. During the funeral of a loved one, close relatives wear capulanas to cover their heads and faces, to 'hide the tears' (Rolletta and Torcato 2004). If someone important dies, women in the family buy new capulanas, to dress alike in the moment of sorrow.

Furthermore, capulanas may signify particular occupations. Traditional healers wear specific capulanas, which are restricted for ordinary people. They have only three colours – white, red and black – and display traditional patterns: a red sun, or a large snake in the centre, are quite common patterns in this context (see figure 9.11).

8 Capulanas as a Means of Communication

In recent years, even Mozambican capulanas, or kangas sold in Mozambique, have started carrying captions, or *jina*. Swahili jina are often riddles or proverbs with inherently ambiguous meanings. Saida Yahya-Othman compares them to captions on t-shirts. Sometimes they carry a message relevant to a specific situation, sometimes not. However, jina or kanga names are often used by Zanzibari women as convenient means of expression. Jina are convenient because they are not confrontational, but indirect and polite, in accordance with local norms of respectable female behaviour. No matter how direct or obscene a kanga name is, one can always claim that it was not intended to harm:

> the politeness of kanga names does not lie in the content of the message, which can be extremely blunt, aggressive and even obscene, but rather in the redressive action that the addresser takes in providing herself, and consequently her addressee as well, with an out.
>
> YAHYA-OTHMAN 1997, 140

Indeed, Yahya-Othman goes on to discuss women's use of kanga names as a form of resistance: '[Women] should always comport themselves with dignity and should not engage in open confrontation; they nevertheless can act as independent agents, in terms of the kanga names they choose, and where and for whom they wear them' (1997, 146).

Examples of captions on capulanas sold in Mozambique include: 'Provocation is not good, you should choose what to say';[18] 'Destined to be safe, I remain protected, and your evil wishes have not materialized';[19] 'A wife's beauty is in her character, not her looks';[20] 'Don't remember the evil things only, while forgetting to be thankful for good deeds'.[21]

In a certain sense capulanas may be seen as subverting the boundaries of dominant discursive practices, as part of an arrangement allowing women a

---

18 In Kiswahili 'Chokochoko si njema mchague la kusema'.
19 In Kiswahili 'Wastara nimestirika mlilolitaka halikunifika'.
20 In Kiswahili 'Uzuri wa mke ni tabia si sura'.
21 In Kiswahili 'Usikumbuke uovu ukasahau fadhila'.

degree of self-determination while remaining respectable, humble women. By communicating through capulanas, women do not speak up, but the covert writings on their capulanas act as a substitute in speaking to the public. In this context, women may be said to 'reappropriate language and the public domain' (Beck 2000, 107). As noted by Yahya-Othman, 'women use K[anga] N[ame]s as a voice which allows them to vent their feelings while avoiding direct confrontation with their addressees, and thus remain within the boundaries of propriety which are set for them by the society' (1997, 140). Women act as independent agents in terms of the captions they choose, and where and for whom they wear them. They 'have thus transformed this discursive practice to suit their own needs, and in the process have rejected the traditional view of the kanga as a 'respectable', almost sacrosanct form of dress and communication' (1997, 146).

9 Summing Up

Mozambican women have chosen capulanas as a mode of dressing since the nineteenth century; this choice has determined new forms of belonging and being, inextricably linked with global flows. Identity processes often combine the old and the new. In this sense, when analysing such processes in Mozambique, we must pay attention to cultural and temporal implications, which, as we have sought to demonstrate here, combine tradition with modern impulses. Capulanas reflect multiple belongings, negotiating women's identity between tradition and modernity. On one hand, the capulana shows the influences of the past but, on the other, it also shows how women see themselves in present-day Mozambique. Capulana culture has changed over the years, reflecting economic and political changes, globally and locally in Mozambique. Nevertheless, the capulana culture of Mozambican women has shown a remarkable resilience, making it likely that even with changing conditions of production and trade, for many years to come, capulanas will remain close to the hearts of Mozambican women. In this way capulanas are likely to remain a symbol combining multiple worlds: it provides a glimpse of a local cosmopolitanism while also condensing the complexity and diversity of social, political, and global influences.

References

Abdulaziz, Mohamed H. 1979. *Muyaka: Eighteenth-century Swahili popular poetry*. Nairobi: Kenya Literature Bureau.

Arnfred, Signe. 2011. *Sexuality and Gender Politics in Mozambique: Rethinking gender in Africa*. Oxford: James Currey.

Bagnol, Brigitte. 2008. Lovolo e espíritos no Sul de Moçambique. *Análise Social* 43 (2): 251–272.

Beck, Rose Marie. 2000. Aesthetics of Communication: texts on textiles (Leso) from the East African Coast (Swahili). *Research in African Literatures* 31 (4): 104–124.

Bonate, Liazzat J.K. 2007. Roots of Diversity in Mozambican Islam. *Lusotopie* 14 (1): 129–149.

Cruz, Padre Daniel. 1910. *Em Terras de Gaza*. Oporto: Gazeta das Aldeias.

Fair, Laura. 1998. Dressing up: clothing, class and gender in post-abolition Zanzibar. *Journal of African History* 39: 63–94.

Fair, Laura. 2000. Identity, Difference and Dance: female initiation in Zanzibar, 1890–1930. In *Mashindano! Competitive music performance in East Africa*, ed. Frank Gunderson and Gregory Barz, 143–174. Dar es Salaam: Mkuki na Nyota Publishers.

Geffray, Christian. 1990. *Ni Père, Ni Mère. Critique de la parenté: Le cas makhuwa*. Paris: Seuil.

Isaacman, Allen. 1985. Chiefs, Rural Differentiation and Peasant Protest: The Mozambican forced cotton regime, 1938–1961. *African Economic History* 14: 15–56.

Isaacman, Allen. 1996. *Cotton is the Mother of Poverty: Peasants, work, and rural struggle in colonial Mozambique*. London: James Currey.

Lupi, Eduardo. 1907. *Angoche: Breve memória sobre uma das capitanias-móres do Districto de Moçambique*. Lisbon: Typographia do Annuario Commercial.

Meneses, Maria Paula. 2003. As Capulanas em Moçambique: Descodificando mensagens, procurando sentidos nos tecidos. In *Método, Métodos e Contramétodo*, ed. Regina Leite Garcia, 111–123. São Paulo: Cortez Editora.

Meneses, Maria Paula. 2008. Mulheres Insubmissas? Mudanças e conflitos no norte de Moçambique. *Ex æquo* 17: 71–87.

Noronha, Eduardo. 1915. *Em Redor de África*. Oporto: Typographia da Empreza Litterária e Typographica.

Parkin, David. 2005. Textile as Commodity, Dress as Text: Swahili *kanga* and women's statements. In *Textiles in Indian Ocean Societies*, ed. Ruth Barnes, 47–67. London: Routledge.

Rolletta, Paula and Maria de Lourdes Torcato. 2004. *Capulanas e Lenços*. Maputo: Missanga.

Santos Rufino, José. 1929. *Álbuns Fotográficos e Descritivos da Colónia de Moçambique*. Vol. 7. Lourenço Marques, Mozambique: Broschek.

Tembe, Ofélia and Carlos Cardoso. 1978a. As Capulanas Têm Vida e História – I. *Revista Tempo*, 395: 37–41.

Tembe, Ofélia and Carlos Cardoso. 1978b. As Capulanas Têm Vida e História – II. *Revista Tempo*, 397: 22–28.

Torcato, Maria de Lurdes. 2009. Bonecas de Capulana. *Revista Índico* 44: 52–57.

Yahya-Othman, Saida. 1997. If the Cap Fits: Kanga names and women's voice in Swahili society. *Afrikanistische Arbeitspapiere: Schriftenreihe des Kölner Instituts für Afrikanistik* 51: 135–149.

CHAPTER 10

Healing the Pain of War through Art: Mozambique's Grassroots Approach to Post-conflict Resolution – Transformação de Armas em Enxadas

Amy Schwartzott

'I was warned by my commandant that if I lose my weapon it is better to kill myself.' This statement by António,[1] a former child soldier, vividly contextualizes the intrinsic materiality of weaponry and its powerful presence in Mozambique's protracted history of war. More than twenty five years have passed since nearly three decades of continuous warfare ended in 1992. António brokers the collection of arms between people who retain or have knowledge of the location of automatic weapons, bazookas, rifles, pistols, and other artefacts of war, and members of the Conselho Cristão de Moçambique (CCM) (Christian Council of Mozambique) who run a project called Transformação de Armas em Enxadas (TAE – Transforming Arms into Ploughshares). TAE collects and destroys decommissioned weapons from Mozambican wars, transforming them into art, thus revealing the potency of recycling as an artistic tool in post-conflict resolution.

Many scholars have begun to look at the importance of art as a tool for healing the pain of the past; they use memorialization and remembrance as a means by which to achieve this (Kelly 1994; Liebmann 1996; Bennett 2005; Samuels 2008). While scholars linking the arts and conflict resolution often distinguish between process and product in the role of the arts (Liebmann 1996; Epskamp 1999; Zeliger 2003), most research focuses on art as a therapeutic device, its role in the remembrance of conflict, and how it contributes to processes of community building and reconciliation.

The TAE project is innovative in that it adds another dimension by preventing conflict through its purposeful use of recycled weapons as media. By recycling weapons of war into art, healing and commemoration are achieved, but in addition, the weapons are disabled in order to prevent them being used for killing again. William Kelly, American artist and founder of The Peace Project

---

[1] Antonio, interviewed in Boane, Mozambique, October 12, 2010. António is a pseudonym. The names of the informants discussed here have been changed to protect their identity.

states, 'It has been said that a painting can never stop a bullet, but a painting can stop a bullet from being fired' (Kelly 1994, 117). Mozambique's TAE project verifies this through sculptures that maintain visceral symbolism, as art created from recycled weapons.

Recently, some scholars have begun to examine contemporary Mozambican artists using weapons as media (Faltas and Christian-Paes 2004; Spring 2005; Tester 2006; Fonseca 2012; Elmquist 2007). This chapter investigates both the impact of, and challenges facing TAE, through its program of collecting, destroying, and transforming recycled weapons from past conflicts, by foregrounding the individuals involved with the project: particularly through an examination of informants and artists involved with TAE.

Whereas internal challenges within TAE, such as strained relationships between artists and TAE administrators in its early years have been documented elsewhere (Tester 2006),[2] this chapter strives to illustrate the more recent machinations of TAE with closer regard to the individual personalities and their impact on the process and project as a whole both locally and globally. By contextualizing the ways in which past lives of recycled materials inscribe meaning as weapons are transformed into art, I demonstrate how TAE artists recycle both literally and conceptually, as they create evocative art while deconstructing Mozambican history. The visual power of TAE artworks engages viewers to remember the violence and destruction of Mozambique's extended history of war, representing the continuation of the life of a weapon through its reincarnation. TAE's purposeful destruction and transformation of recycled weapons of war enables these armaments to make visible the invisible concept of peace through the potent symbolism of powerful artworks that are composed of former killing tools. The words of a TAE informant are telling, 'these artworks are important because they transmit a feeling to us – they have a connection with our lives.'[3]

The Mozambican 'civil war' (1976/77–1992) almost directly followed the nation's battle for independence from Portuguese colonial rule (1962–1975). Due to the complexities of this conflict, including the fact that both sides received considerable external support, references to these events as 'civil war' are widely contested among scholars, and it is often referred to as Mozambique's

---

2 Tester is among the few scholars that critique TAE. He focuses largely on his viewed failings of the TAE project: including the inability of its artworks to reach a local, Mozambican audiences and problems with artists' remuneration for works created for TAE. When I began conducting research on TAE in 2008, strained relations with the artists had much improved. As will be shown below however, informants often continue to remain unrewarded for weapons presented to TAE.

3 Paulinho, interviewed in Matendene, Mozambique, December 17, 2010.

'post-independence war.'[4] It was fought between the new ruling party, *Frente de Libertação de Mocambique* (FRELIMO – Liberation Front of Mozambique), founded in Tanzania in 1962 to fight for Mozambique's independence, and *Resistência Nacional Moçambicana* (RENAMO – Mozambican National Resistance), which was founded in 1975, following independence. Renamo was an anti-Communist political organization and resistance movement.

Many scholars have debated the ways in which this post-independence conflict was precipitated by external aggressors, but the focus of the present chapter is the overall destruction caused by it, which resulted in considerable suffering throughout the country. Africanist social anthropologist Bjørn Enge Bertelsen discusses the impact of the violence of these decades on Mozambican culture, and he notes, 'relations between state and violence ... have been crucial, visible, and tangible from the liberation struggle onward' (Bertelsen 2009, 216). Mozambique's post-liberation conflict precipitated economic collapse, famine, nearly one million war-related casualties, and the internal and external displacement of several million civilians.

1 Theorizing the Recycling of Mozambique's Weapons of War

Following former UN Secretary-General Boutros Boutros-Ghali's use of the term 'peace building' in his influential 1992 report, *Agenda for Peace*, post-conflict resolution has become a fast-developing interdisciplinary field. Recent scholarship that recognizes the important role of art both in this field and in trauma studies is highlighted by Goran Hyden, who remarked to me that 'the use of art as an alternative mechanism [in post-conflict resolution] is an innovation especially appropriate in the light of rapid urbanization with its more concentrated and accessible audience'.

This research and its positing of art as integral to post-conflict resolution contributes to the limited scholarship on this topic (Liebmann 1996; Bennett 2005; Samuels 2008); in particular, it endorses TAE's use of recycling as a potent tool for peace building and peacekeeping in the Mozambican context and beyond. Seeking an interdisciplinary approach, social anthropology (Kopytoff 1986; Appadurai 1988), visual culture studies (Mirzoeff 1999), and post-conflict resolution theories are linked within this inquiry (Boutros-Ghali 1992; Sengulane 1994; UNECA 2001; as it focuses on the materiality of

---

4 Bjørn Enge Bertelsen (2009) draws attention to complexities often lost in the over-simplified terms used to describe Mozambique's conflicts, including determining when the wars actually began. See also Dinerman 2006.

TAE's assemblage arts as powerful tools for remembrance, reconciliation, and peacekeeping.

This framework for investigating TAE draws largely from Igor Kopytoff's seminal essay, 'The Cultural Biography of Things'. Kopytoff's essay focuses on an object's transformation from its initial use through its many lives, fuelling an exploration and analysis of the materiality of recycled objects that are transformed into art. Kopytoff's important question, 'How does the thing's use change with age and what happens to it when it reaches the end of its usefulness?' (Kopytoff 1986, 33) has led to the conclusion that the life of an object – such as a weapon – does not end when it is destroyed and recreated artistically: in its reincarnation as recycled material it gains more expressive power as it is transformed into art.

Kopytoff's emphasis on the object is rooted in the importance of its original identity, and the ways in which its intrinsic meaning is maintained despite its destruction and the fact that it cannot be used again. TAE physically cuts the weapons to prevent their further use, yet the recognizable shapes of gun parts remain. The iconic symbolism of the weapons as they are transformed is essential for understanding the meaning of TAE's project.

2   History of TAE

TAE initially developed within workshops and seminars as part of a strategy titled 'Preparing People for Peace', aimed at establishing peace and democracy following FRELIMO/RENAMO negotiations and the General Peace Agreement signed in Rome in 1992.[5] This peace-based initiative began in the context of *Comissão do Justiça, Paz e Reconciliação*/Department of Justice, Peace and Reconciliation (JPRC) within the Christian Council of Mozambique (CCM). Motivated by a mandate of the church to bring peace, CCM was founded in 1948. Comprised of at least twenty different religious denominations, its membership includes mainline churches brought to Mozambique by missionaries as well as indigenous local churches. Bishop Dom Dinis Sengulane was president of CCM when TAE (donor based and CCM's largest program) was initiated in 1995.[6]

Sengulane and CCM's intention was that TAE should facilitate community dialogue and civic education in dealing with reconciliation, memory, healing, and forgiveness, stating that the primary motivation following the peace

---

5   Bishop Dom Dinis Sengulane, interviewed in Maputo, Mozambique, August 21, 2009 (henceforth, name, location and date of interview: Maputo /MPM).

6   Sengulane, MPM, August 21, 2009.

agreement was for different factions to come together after the war to reunite as a nation.[7] This process included CCM/JPRC members travelling around the provinces to find out what Mozambicans feared most after the war. Sengulane explained that a woman in Nampula province asked him, 'What are we going to do with so many guns in the hands of the people?'[8] He said that he applied principles he found in the Bible: 'and they shall beat their swords into plough-shares. And their spears into pruning hooks: nation shall not lift up sword against nation neither shall they learn war anymore' (King James Version; Is 2:2–4). This well-known verse reveals not only the desire to promote peace, it also underscores a pervasive theme in Mozambique arts: recycling.

CCM's solution was that the Mozambican government and the UN should complete the disarmament program, and CCM, through the establishment of TAE, would utilize transformation as a guiding principle in its program for peacekeeping in Mozambique.[9] TAE's original plan consisted of collecting weapons, making them unusable, and of providing an instrument of production as an incentive in exchange for the weapons collected. Sengulane and other TAE religious leaders stress that they did not provide a monetary incentive because they did not wish to give the impression that they were buying guns.

Originally, incentives took the form of material objects such as bicycles, sewing machines, and ploughs. Over time, TAE has become more flexible with incentives offered, focusing on confidence building and creating an honest living for people who turn in weapons.[10] Diverse incentives such as farm implements, seeds, cement, zinc roofs, and even tickets for trips to home villages are not unusual. TAE policy stresses anonymity and the lack of involvement of the army or police when weapons are handed over; they never record any names.[11]

Weapons exchanges by demobilized soldiers, individual civilians, and, eventually, entire communities have followed similar frameworks in terms of exchanging arms for products or services. TAE representatives work to become integrated into provincial regions and to gain access to areas where heavy fighting took place during past wars; thus, while many weapons have been retrieved, considerable amounts are believed to still remain in areas such as Zambézia and Nampula provinces.

Admission into communities is achieved by focusing on traditional grass-roots ideals based on trust and the sharing of food, drink, and eventually

7   Sengulane, MPM, August 28, 2009.
8   Ibid.
9   Sengulane, MPM, August 21, 2009.
10   Sengulane, MPM, October 7, 2010.
11   Ibid.

information. After gaining a community's acceptance, TAE representatives are often led to weapons that have remained hidden since the last war.[12] In total, 129 weapons and 389 pieces of ammunition of various calibres were retrieved from three communities in Gorongosa and Buzi districts in a recent weapons collection.[13] TAE National Coordinator Boaventura Zita has commented that while the response to the project has been positive to date, 'the truth is that there are no numbers on how many weapons existed in the first place'.[14] TAE officials remain concerned about the unknown number of weapons that may remain in Mozambique and the danger this poses for maintaining the country's peace. As will become clear in the informants' stories below, in many ways, eradicating the remaining weapons is now even more important to the preservation of peace in Mozambique than it was when the war ended in 1992.[15]

3   Facilitating TAE Weapons Collection: Individual Narratives and Motives

Informants who hand over weapons to TAE have distinct histories and motivations in relation to how they acquired them and in terms of why they are now turning them over to TAE. The individual narratives conveyed here illustrate this diversity, and underscore the continuing necessity and importance of TAE's project in Mozambique, as well as revealing challenges to the project.

Several times a week, Arlindo travels from his home in Matola (an industrial suburb) to Maputo (Mozambique's capital), to facilitate a community peace project: his explanation of why he personally turned weapons over to TAE is ironic in light of this. He said,

> I try to fight like a criminal in the street. I can go into the street to show it [a gun] and that is bad. That is harmful. We know it is dangerous and I give it [to TAE] without questioning it. It is good for me.

Subsequently, when asked about the TAE project and its effectiveness, he responded,

---

12   Boaventura Zita, MPM, August 18, 2009.
13   Nicolau Ruis, MPM, November 1, 2010.
14   Zita, MPM, August 1, 2008.
15   The issue of weapons in Mozambique has been addressed by scholars in several different contexts (for example, Faltas and Christian-Paes 2004; Knight 2004; Tester 2006).

> As you know, I need something to help my life. I receive things that can help my life [incentives] and I [am] helping to save lives ... my mind gives me peace [by handing over the weapons].

Arlindo is building a cement block house using supplies he has received as incentives from TAE in exchange for weapons. When I visited Arlindo in December 2010 he had just received five bags of cement in exchange for guns he had handed in.

Paulinho is a former member of the military. He has been handing weapons over to TAE since 2001. He has revealed neither his connection to TAE to his friends and neighbours, nor the fact that his home in Matendene is a result of this connection. Paulinho said of TAE:

> This project is coming to fight against the criminals and take out weapons from the population – through incentives the population [is able] to make agriculture, construction, and other kinds of work ... it is a good project and has good impact in Mozambique.[16]

When I visited Paulinho a second time in early January 2011, he was in the process of another weapons exchange. He was offering TAE seven pistols and ammunition in the form of bullets. He told me that for the exchange of four operational and three non-operational pistols and the bullets he would receive 45 bags of cement (see figure 10. 3). Specific factors determine the type and value of incentives received by informants for weapons; more value is given to operational weapons than those that are non-operational, and weapons are generally more valuable than ammunition. Nicolau Luís, TAE Assistant Project Director, relayed the following information:

There is a table of 'rewards' for individuals to choose from when they relinquish their weapons. The most one can receive for a working AK-47 is ten metal roofing pieces (or ten bags of cement, but the roofing is more expensive). If someone does not want ten bags of cement or roofing pieces they can choose something for the equivalent monetary value (then 3750 meticais = $145 US +/-) and TAE will pay for that item.[17]

Although the informants' wishes are taken into consideration, the overarching determination of incentives is directly related to TAE's financial stability. Since TAE is donor based, incentives are contingent upon the funding/donations received. Several of the informants I spoke with shared their dissatisfaction

---

16   Paulinho, interviewed in Matendene, Mozambique, December 17, 2010.
17   Nicolau Luís, MPM, November 10, 2011.

with prolonged waiting periods for incentives promised, which they had expected to receive as soon as the weapons exchange took place. Despite this criticism, each of the informants I spoke with praised the project's mission and they continue to turn over weapons to the group. One informant's response to the question of why he continues to hand weapons over to TAE without always receiving payment is a testament to the objectives of the project:

> Well, the project is very good – fighting against bandits who get weapons, robbing cars, assaulting people on the street. For me I never stop dealing with them – even now ... most people say God exists – but who can pay me is God.[18]

Through conversations with Paulinho I learned that many of the weapons remaining in Mozambique today are held by former military combatants. Paulinho's explanation of this is revealing: 'During demobilization following the Peace Agreement the armed forces were individually responsible for turning in one weapon each. Many turned in one weapon and kept the rest they had'.[19] Paulinho's home is constructed entirely of materials he has attained from TAE incentives received for turning in weapons of war. Many TAE informants seek such supplies to build homes for themselves and their families. Because these dwellings are constructed of materials exchanged in efforts to eradicate Mozambique's remaining weapons, I refer to them as 'houses of peace' – they are visible incarnations of peacekeeping in Mozambique (see figure 10.1).

António, mentioned at the start of this chapter, is a former child soldier who began fighting for RENAMO in the civil war when he was seven or eight years old, in Inhambane and Vilankulos. Unlike many others, António was not forcibly recruited to become a child soldier. He explains,

> I started in the war service because my parents were living with the [RENAMO] soldiers. I did not know what I was doing at that time ... so [I was] not forced into it; they trained me how to deal with weapons and how to put land mines. They liked children because children have no fear to die.[20]

António now works with other ex-child soldiers, past military personnel, former combatants, and others, to recover and hand over weapons to TAE. He has

---

18   António, interviewed in Boane, Mozambique, July 7, 2011.
19   Paulinho, interviewed in Matendene, Mozambique, January 21, 2011.
20   António, interviewed in Boane, Mozambique, July 7, 2011. . For similar discussions on child soldiers in Mozambique and elsewhere see Castanheira 1999 and Honwana 2007.

FIGURE 10.1   *Casa do Paz*/House of Peace, created entirely of incentives provided by TAE exchanges with Informant, Mozambique.

been working with TAE since 2001. António's connection with the project is ongoing, as he mentioned at one of our recent meetings. Just two days earlier he had handed over 33 pistols, 3 AK47s, and 3 rockets, and he planned to collect more the next day in Moamba. Focusing on the materiality of the weapons, I asked António if he could expand upon the value given to weapons during the war. He explained that during the civil war weapons were considered more important than people; soldiers were given explicit directions to retrieve weapons immediately from their victims.[21]

António said to me that so many killings took place so frequently that there were too many weapons for child soldiers to carry. RENAMO also lacked a strong infrastructure with permanent bases, so young soldiers had to rely on hiding retrieved weapons. He further explained that in these cases he and his comrades removed ammunition and firing mechanisms, leaving piles of weapons behind for later retrieval.[22] As a result of this reality, António candidly

21   António, interviewed in Boane, Mozambique, October 11, 2011.
22   Ibid.

commented, 'If somebody wants to start a war in Mozambique [now], it is so easy because weapons are spread all over'.[23]

4   TAE Artistic Development: Past and Present

TAE's vision of transformation to peace in Mozambique also involved the question of what should be done with all the collected weapons that had been destroyed. At this point, the biblical verse, 'they shall beat their swords into ploughshares', becomes a clear source for peace and reconciliation. TAE's innovative approach to peace building uses art as an iconic visual reminder – a mnemonic device symbolizing the violence of war. By recycling weapons from Mozambique's wars and transforming them into art, TAE strives to achieve healing and commemoration. TAE's initial plan, based on a literal translation of the biblical verse, was to melt the weapons down and turn them into tools. Ultimately, this process proved too costly and was abandoned. Sengulane views the change as providential, for it would have altered the visual outcome of the weapons' transformation, permanently erasing their former identities as dangerous killing tools.

By destroying the weapons while maintaining a visual reference to what Kopytoff (1986) refers to as their 'former lives', weapons transformed into art now serve as emblematic images. The destruction of weapons of war and their transformation into art is more than symbolic. These images reflect the church mandate and focus of TAE, 'to bring peace and to forgive, not forget, and keep on touching the wound that is bleeding'.[24] Thus, in the transformation of weapons into art, the peace-building ethos of the TAE project succeeds by disarming bodies as well as minds. Simply put, the TAE project strives not only to physically remove and destroy weapons from the landscape of Mozambique, but to combine this with programs of civic education to perpetuate a culture of peace both physically and mentally. This process affects the individuals living amongst the remaining weapons, as well as the artists, viewers, and patrons; those exposed to the TAE artworks receive powerful reminders of the horror and violence of Mozambique's past.

TAE's transformation of recycled weapons of war into art began in 1997, two years after the initial project had been established. TAE was striving to glorify peace instead of war, and wished to create visual memorials of this. TAE forged a partnership with *Associação Núcleo de Arte*, a long-standing arts organization

---

23   Ibid.
24   Zita, MPM, August 1, 2008.

in Maputo. Initially, fourteen artists were involved in a workshop in which they were challenged to transform the weapons into symbols of peace. The artists' only stipulation was that they should use the weapons to create imagery associated with peace, avoiding violent themes. Otherwise, they were given the freedom to create.

More generally, but similar to CCM's grassroots TAE project, with its message of peace achieved through the purposeful collection, destruction, and recycling of weapons of war into art, the church played a key role in the mediation of the peace process in Mozambique. This process largely took place within the community of Sant Egidio in Rome.[25]

When members of TAE leadership were asked where they found their inspiration for the development of the project, they stressed that the motivation came from the Bible. When probed further about specific sources of guidance, they responded,

> not only are we collecting weapons, we are awakening ideas in grassroots organizing. We don't need fancy theories about conflict resolution ... academics want more. Bishop Tutu led programs ... peace talks come from the church.[26]

This grassroots approach to peacekeeping and reconciliation has inspired TAE artists to memorialize the destruction of Mozambique's wars through their use of transformed weapons of war. TAE artists create artworks designed to evoke the memory of Mozambique's long history of war for viewers, as well as serving as a potent process for the artists, many of whom lived through the war and are motivated to promote peace through art.

The impact and transgressive nature of TAE sculptures is largely rooted in a purposeful visual language that is created by the tension inherent in using the materiality of weapons of war in the promotion of peace. The artworks, comprised of cut and dismembered weapons of war, maintain the power of their original forms, challenging the viewer's preconceived ideals of art and beauty. These sculptures are not beautiful, nor are they easy to look at: they transform weapons from tools for killing into tools for reconciliation and peace building. TAE's narrative through the sublime imagery of weapons *transformed* presents an alternative identity for contemporary Mozambique. The artists' visual narratives move beyond Mozambique's past reliance upon socialist revolutionary

---

25   Several scholars have written on the links between the role of the church and Mozambique's peace process, including Zuppi 1995 and Anouilh 2006.

26   Interview with Reverend L. Amos/Bishop Sengulane, MPM, August 20, 2009.

imagery, which employed the iconic form of the AK47;[27] instead of glorifying war, TAE artists present contemporary Mozambican society as glorifying
peace.

TAE artists as a group display innovative explorations in their invocations
of the memory of war to move Mozambique and the world forward in peace
through remembrance. However, specific concerns have led to my selection of
the individual artists included here. In order to historicize the development of
TAE's art component, I have chosen to illustrate specific periods in the history
of the project, including artists from three distinct points: the earliest TAE artworks (1997); the middle years (2000–2005); and most recently (2010–present).
This has been done to obtain the broadest view of TAE artists' general output.
Secondly, and similar to TAE informants, each of the TAE artists has personal
motivations. The aim here has been to demonstrate a broad cross-section of
their diversity in terms of these individual motivations. A final criterion for
inclusion is to give some of the less famous artists an opportunity to have their
work more widely viewed.

Fiel dos Santos was one of the first artists to work for the TAE project when
CCM/TAE approached *Núcleo de Arte* in 1997. As with most of the TAE artists
I have interviewed, Fiel's relationship to the project is personal, He explained
that when he was 12 or 13 years old, his brother was kidnapped into service
as a child soldier for six years.[28] While one of Fiel's brothers was forcibly recruited to fight on the side of RENAMO, another brother chose to enlist on the
government side of FRELIMO to fight in the same war. Fiel's situation was not
unusual, as many Mozambican families were divided as members served on
opposing sides during the country's last war. Further elaborating on his personal connection to TAE, Fiel stated, 'I grew up during the fighting. Now it's my
time to do something for society. I want to be voluntary to work on this project.
I'm working here for my soul'.[29]

Fiel's forms evoke his curiosity about nature. He is interested in the relationship of parts to the whole, often revealing the intricacy of individual materials
in his overall constructions. Sensitive in his treatment of form and placement,
his focus on the objecthood of the weapons forces viewers to connect with the
meaning of the weapons and the intrinsic power of the violence inherent in
each one.

---

27   The current Mozambican flag, adopted in 1983, portrays the image of an AK47 assault rifle
      fitted with a bayonet, crossed with a hoe to create the shape of an X.
28   Fiel dos Santos, MPM, October 5, 2010.
29   dos Santos, MPM, August 1, 2008.

Fiel shares his lengthy tenure working for TAE with fellow artist Cristóvão Estevão Canhavato (Kester). Both artists participated in the creation of the well-known, large-scale TAE artwork, *Tree of Life*, which was formed in 2005 by four Mozambican artists: Fiel, Kester, Adelino Mate, and Hilarió Nhatugueja. British Museum Curator of African Art, Chris Spring, commissioned *Tree of Life* in conjunction with the British Museum and Africa '05, which celebrated African culture and heritage in London in 2005 (Spring 2005, 20–25). International attention has been drawn to this work, which has become both a symbol of peace and a symbol of Africa. *Tree of Life* is now housed in the permanent collection of the British Museum in London.

Kester's individual TAE artwork, *Throne of Weapons*, also in the British Museum, was one of the early works that inspired Spring to contact and ultimately commission TAE art for the British Museum (Spring, 2005, 20–25). This piece has been incorporated into the museum's *Pentonville Prison Project*– an outreach program that aims to engage in dialogue with prison populations on the subject of violence. Program Director Jane Samuels explained that the project is based on prisoner interactions with *Throne of Weapons*, which is taken around British prisons. Constructed primarily from recycled AK47s, *Throne of Weapons'* powerful visual presence is used to facilitate discussions on gun crime, violence, and peace.

Samuels refers to *Throne of Weapons* as 'an "aggressive symbol" to deal with key objectives including issues of rehabilitation and re-education (gun crime, issues of peace reconciliation, community rebuilding, and amnesty)'.[30] Both *Tree of Life* and *Throne of Weapons* highlight diverse meanings translated through the materiality of TAE artworks, as well as the continuing global impact of TAE's projects. Another example of TAE's global influence is the Peace Art Project Cambodia (PACP), initiated in 2003; it is often described as being loosely based on the TAE project, using decommissioned weapons to create art (Sasha Constable 2010).

Kester recounted that personal connections to the war inspired him to participate in TAE's project, based on several occurrences of accidents within his family resulting from the widespread use of anti-personnel mines [landmines]. Kester explained that his initial engagement with TAE was founded on the idea that 'where there are weapons there is fear'.[31] He described how he was fascinated by the possibility of creating artworks that expressed his

---

30   Jane Samuels interviewed in London, UK, October 28, 2009.
31   Kester, MPM, September 29, 2011.

creativity and emotions, while illustrating the transformation of instruments that used to kill.[32]

Kester created one of the most powerful artworks in a recent TAE exhibition held in collaboration with *Núcleo de Arte* in 2010 to commemorate Mozambique's *Dia do Paz* (Day of Peace) on October 4, 1992, which marked the end of its 'civil war'. Kester's artwork, *O Abraço da Paz* (Embrace of the Peace), represents the figures of Joaquim Chissano and Afonso Dhlakama shaking hands (Chissano was the second president of Mozambique and leader of Frelimo; Dhlakama was the second leader of Renamo). This work captures an important time for Mozambicans, symbolizing the moment peace was achieved between the warring factions. Kester's powerful artwork constructed from the recycled weapons of this same war delivers a potent TAE message, which is implicit in this large ¾ life size work (see figure 10.2).

Sengulane once explained that Dhlakama viewed TAE's project as allowing the viewer to see the end of the life of a gun.[33] As stated above, however, the present chapter argues that the TAE project does not represent the end of the life of a gun, but rather an incarnation of its many lives, in a culmination made possible by art. It allows the viewer to understand the invisible concept of peace through the viewing of recycled weapons of war.

Jorge José Munguambe (Makolwa) is an artist from Núcleo de Arte whose involvement with TAE dates back to 2000. Makolwa's personal connection to TAE is unusual in that he was sent out of the country by his family to improve his chances of surviving the war. Makolwa's motivation to create art for TAE is intrinsically linked to his personal goals in his art-making practices. He explains,

> I began making art to deal with my responses to the civil war – at this time I was creating for myself as a means of catharsis. I started to realize this was also something I could do to give back to my country – an act of creation to counter the destruction that had taken place. As I realized that my art provided something for people other than myself, I knew that I could offer a visual means to share my experiences and emotions with others.[34]

One of Makolwa's recent TAE artworks is particularly resonant of his personal connections to his country and the war. *Olhando para a frente em direção à paz, lembrando o passado* (Looking Forward Towards Peace by Remembering the

---

32   Ibid.
33   Sengulane, MPM, October 7, 2010.
34   Jorge José Munguambe (Makolwa), MPM, August 29, 2011.

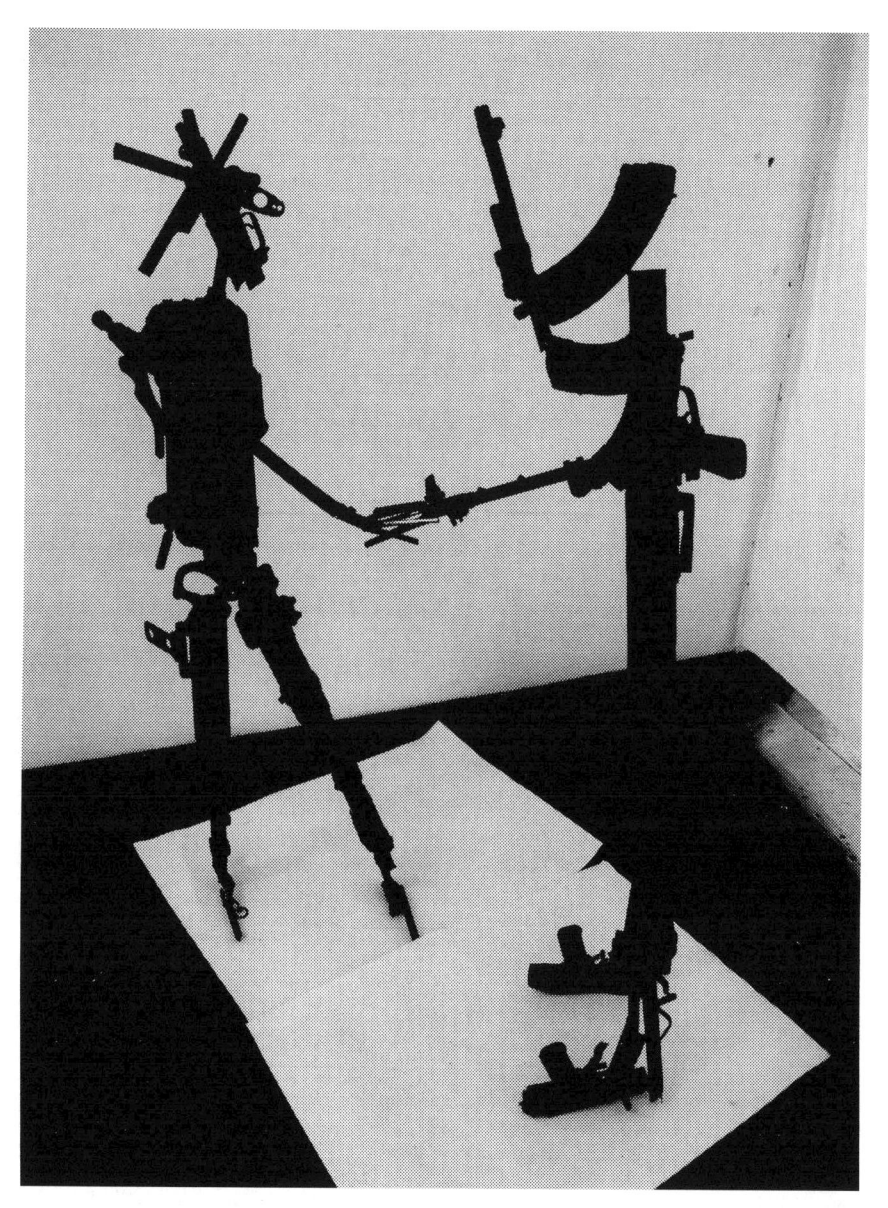

FIGURE 10.2   Cristóvão Estevão Canhavato (Kester) *O Abraço da Paz* (*Embrace of the Peace*), mixed media (recycled weapons), 2011.

Past) represents a family devastated by the war but moving ahead to survive. A mother and her young son are struggling to move forward, while the baby on the mother's back looks behind at Mozambique's past. Asked to comment on this powerful artwork and its meaning, Makolwa said (see figure 10.3),

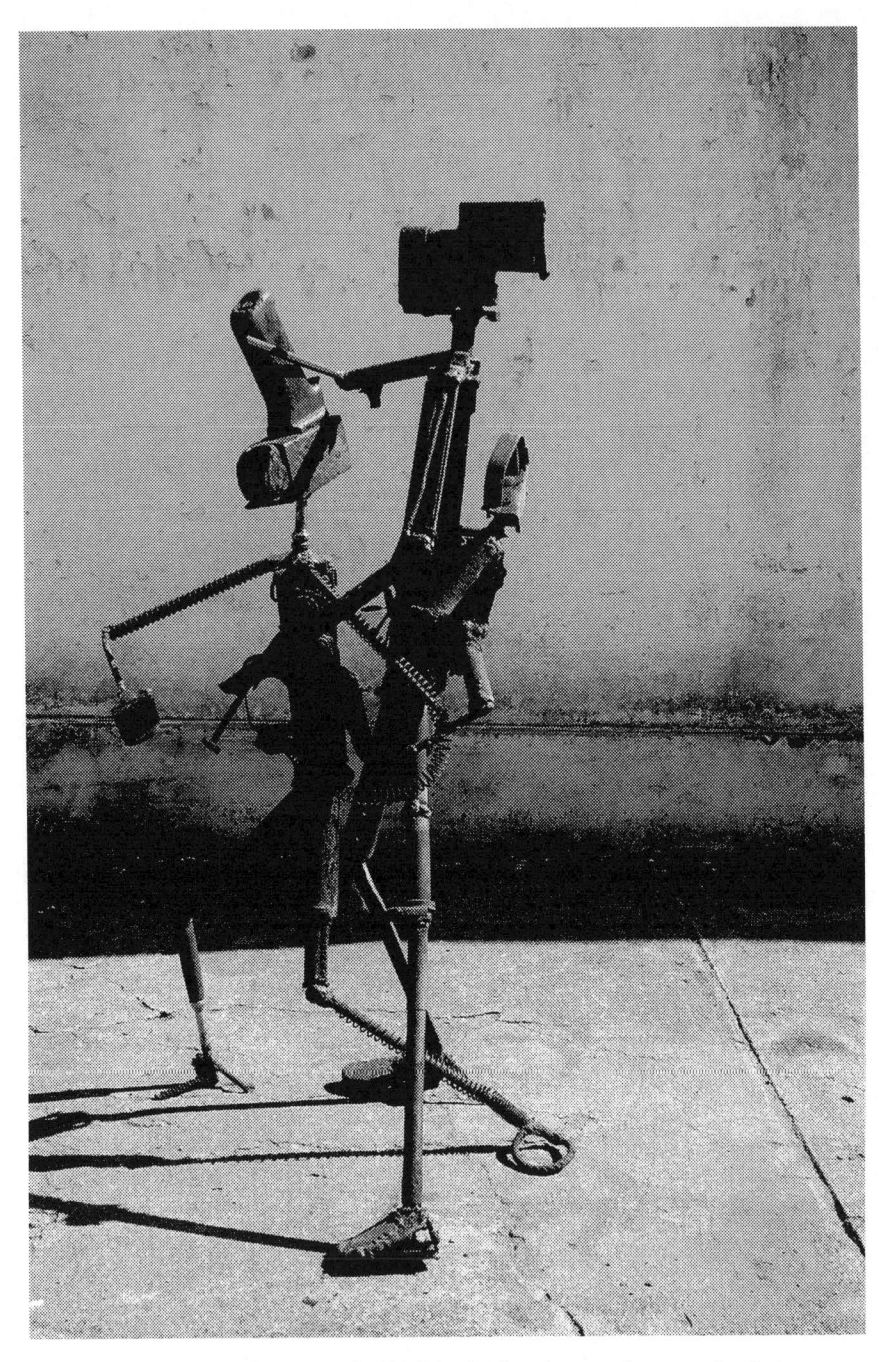

FIGURE 10.3   Jorge José Munguambe (Makolwa) *Olhando para a frente em direção à paz,*
              lembrando o passado (*Looking Forward Towards Peace by Remembering the*
              Past), mixed media (recycled weapons), 2011.

> With this work I hope to show people the guns that were used during the war to remind them of the destruction of Mozambique's struggle for independence and the civil war. By remembering the past, I hope to show Mozambicans and the world the power of peace through memories of what will never happen again.[35]

In this detailed sculpture, the gun parts are clearly shown (see figure 10.4). A closer view reveals that the young boy's head in Makolwa's piece is composed of the pistol grip of a destroyed weapon. Other recognizable weapon parts of the sculpture soon become readily identifiable, such as the trigger, trigger guard, and recoil spring from an AK47. Closely examining the many different pieces of destroyed armaments in such sculptures underscores the materiality of the weapons' original form and function. Kopytoff's notion of the lives of objects is readily inserted here as a tool for understanding the potent message revealed when the viewer contemplates the former life of the weapons depicted.

The viewer cannot help but meditate on the former life of the trigger of the weapon prominently shown here. The fact that this specific mechanism of this individual gun was quite possibly responsible for causing many deaths creates a powerful visual symbolism. The clearly recognizable gun parts resonate with their innate association with violence and death: the artists' purposeful selection of this powerful element of the weapon is here realized as the head and mid-section of the young boy.

Silverio Salvador Sitoe (Sitoe) is also from *Núcleo de Arte*; he began making art for TAE in 2010. Sitoe's creations are distinctive, as one of the pieces he created was not welded: *Dou-vos a minha Paz* (I Give you my Peace) was not only physically distinct from the other pieces but is also the work through which Sitoe has theorized on the merits of not welding weapons to create TAE artworks. When I asked Sitoe about his inspiration for this work that is not welded together, he responded, 'In my mind we don't even have money to buy bread–how are we buying supplies, machines to weld?'[36]

The theoretical framework Sitoe is developing around the concept of not welding the weapons to create artworks includes several platforms for the expansion of TAE and the sustainability of the materials. A few of the points he outlines include the ability to create quick demonstrations/performance art with strong impact at the site of the weapon's retrieval; low cost; versatility in creating the artworks (who and how); and the ability to recycle the weapons

35   Makolwa, MPM, August 1, 2011.
36   Silverio Salvador Sitoe (Sitoe), MPM, October 18, 2010.

FIGURE 10.4   Detail, Jorge José Munguambe (Makolwa) *Olhando para a frente em direção à paz, lembrando o passado* (*Looking Forward Towards Peace by Remembering the Past*), mixed media (recycled weapons), 2011.

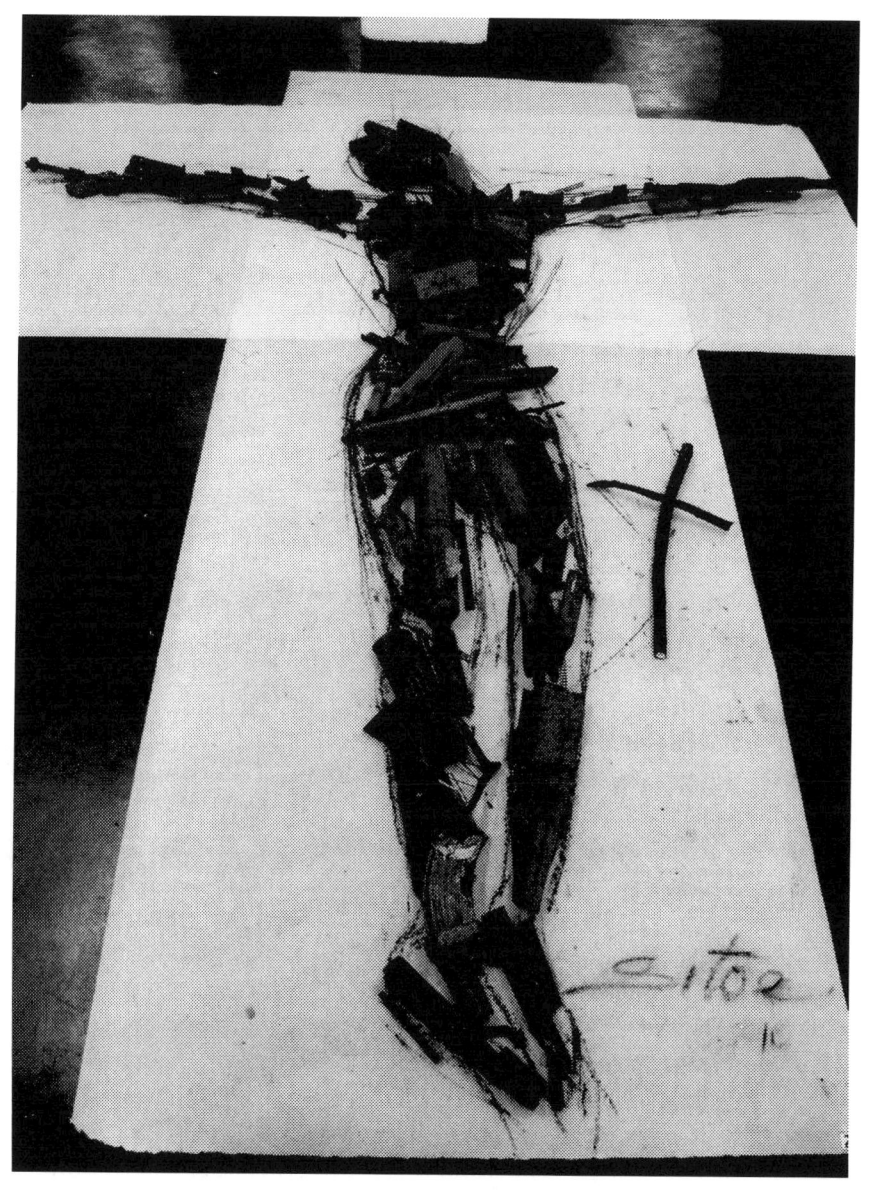

FIGURE 10.5   Silverio Salvador Sitoe (Sitoe) *Dou-vos a minha Paz* (*I Give you my Peace*),
mixed media (recycled weapons), 2011.

repeatedly.[37] Commenting further in relation to *Dou-vos a minha Paz*, Sitoe
states (see figure 10.5),

---

37   Ibid.

> Those weapons have killed people and these people are lying down now. They are bones. If you look at that picture [*Dou-vos a minha Paz*] it looks like people who have died but in a different way, with open arms – [they] embrace me although I'm dead. With these people I'm in peace.[38]

Sitoe's work draws powerful connections between the peace of the present and the conflicts of the past. His reference linking Mozambicans of the present to those who have died in past wars suggests the effectiveness of memorialization and remembrance in relation to the continuation of peace keeping in Mozambique. Sitoe's work evokes the necessity of appeasing the dead to ensure living in peace – a site that has been a growing source for scholarship on Mozambican conflicts.

5   Conclusion

The TAE project demonstrates the power of recycling and art as tools of post-conflict resolution. Inasmuch as TAE is dependent upon donors for continued success of its project, patronage of its arts is essential to insure its continuation as well.[39] As stated above, TAE artworks are complex and difficult to process visually and emotionally, as they are fraught with inherent memories of war-torn lives. As an expected result of their powerfully embedded emotional messages, individuals are often hesitant to commit to purchasing these artworks. A further factor in the difficulty of securing patrons for TAE artworks lies in the lack of widespread support of the arts in Mozambique. Although this is slowly beginning to change, it has not yet developed among the Mozambican population.[40] Finally, a fundamental critique of TAE that I have continually observed is the overall lack of visibility of the project and its art. This lack is most apparent within Mozambique.

In response to my queries surrounding its visibility, TAE National Coordinator Zita stated: 'We should have more exhibits, more debates on issues of art as an instrument of peace to show pain, expectation, and hope'.[41] As of yet, these goals have not been implemented. Ironically, as illustrated in this investigation,

---

38   Sitoe, MPM, October 18, 2010.

39   In terms of patronage, TAE artists typically receive 55% payment on sales and TAE/CCM maintains 45% of the cost of the sculptures sold unless sales are made within the context of a gallery, such as *Núcleo de Arte*, when the artists' share is diminished to accommodate a percentage for the sponsoring patron.

40   Contemporary art in Mozambique and its audiences is discussed in Schwartzott 2014.

41   Boaventura Zita, MPM, October 19, 2010.

most of the commissions for TAE arts originate outside of the country. Similarly, in terms of overall patronage, most individuals who purchase TAE arts are expats, foreigners, tourists and international museums.

TAE's future is decidedly uncertain. Development plans for TAE previously included incorporating additional recycled materials such as metal, pottery and other objects into the creation of artworks, as well as addressing ecological concerns by tackling environmental issues. Additionally, TAE Coordinators envisioned a peace institute in the town of *Liberdade*, outside the city of Maputo. This plan originally included creating an international institute where scholars would convene to teach, learn, and develop ideas surrounding peace, conflict-resolution, and the use of art as a tool in this process.[42]

TAE's plans for these developments remain unrealized. According to TAE National Coordinator Zita, 'We still have some challenges...we have problems in terms of management, for example transparency and accountability. Small grants keep the project alive (CWS, Global Ministry in USA) and since the exhibition we have electricity'.[43] Since Zita expressed these issues confronting TAE in October of 2010, the situation of TAE has worsened.

In a seemingly unending cycle, weapons continue to remain uncollected as informants remain waiting for promised incentives. Incentives cannot be provided for weapons because financial support from donors who would ordinarily provide the means for these incentives has dried up. With no support, TAE is unable to collect weapons, which does not provide materials for its artists to create artworks that would help to improve its visibility.

Despite specific challenges facing TAE, including a lack of transparency and visibility, which are currently under investigation, the artists' transformation of recycled weapons from Mozambican wars is meaningful for those engaged in, as well as viewers of, the purposeful collection, destruction, and transformation of these weapons into symbolic representations of Mozambique's continuing peace through remembrance.[44]

While Kopytoff calls for observation of the life of an object – 'How does the thing's use change with age and what happens to it when it reaches the end of its usefulness?' (Kopytoff 1986, 33) – Mozambique's TAE project represents a challenge to this appeal. Through the process of TAE's project, destroyed weapons are empowered in their transformation into art – they are strengthened

---

42   Ibid.

43   Ibid.

44   The TAE project is discussed more fully in my PhD dissertation entitled 'Weapons and Refuse as Media: The Potent Politics of Recycling in Contemporary Mozambican Urban Arts' which was successfully submitted to University of Florida in 2014, as well as several articles and book chapters (Schwartzott 2012, 2013).

symbolically as they become potent tools for peace keeping. Seemingly contradicting the original use of weapons as tools for destruction, the TAE project reveals through artistic transformation the power of recycling. TAE artists reveal and perpetuate the invisible concept of peace in their creation of iconic artworks of remembrance, reconciliation, memorialization, and peacekeeping – not only for Mozambique but globally.

Since Renamo's unilateral annulment of its 1992 Peace Accord with Frelimo's government on October 22, 2013, increasing tensions between Frelimo and Renamo indicated the return to war as a real possibility. Mutual actions resulted in lost lives on both sides of the conflict. More recently however, negotiations have been under way between Frelimo and Renamo to seek a cease-fire as deliberations continue to build a peace treaty amenable to both sides. Bishop Sengulane, long a pioneer in his quest for peace in Mozambique has been an influential figure in these proceedings, continuing his commitment in spite of his retirement as bishop in March of 2014.

I had the opportunity to speak with the Bishop as the peace talks were in progress. He relayed that with impending peace in Mozambique, 'We need to move into national reconciliation. In my retirement I dedicate myself to fullness of life'.[45] In order to facilitate this, Sengulane expressed hope that despite its current lack of resources, perhaps through government support TAE would serve a key role as facilitator in the disarmament process that would be an important part of achieving peace between Frelimo and Renamo, and the country of Mozambique as a whole.

References

Anouilh, Pierre. 2006. Des pauvres à la paix: Aspects de l'action pacificatrice de Sant'Egidio au Mozambique. *Le Fait Missionnaire* 17: 11–40.

Appadurai, Arjun. 1988. *The Social Life of Things: Commodities in cultural perspective*. Cambridge: Cambridge University Press.

Bennett, Jill. 2005. *Empathic Vision: Affect, trauma, and contemporary art*. Stanford: Stanford University Press.

Bertelsen, Bjørn Enge. 2009. Sorcery and death squads: Transformations of state, sovereignty, and violence in postcolonial Mozambique. In *Crisis of the State: War and social upheaval*, eds Bruce Kapferer and Bjørn Enge Bertelsen, 210–240. New York: Berghahn Books.

---

45   Sengulane, MPM, August 7, 2014.

Boutros-Ghali, Boutros. 1992. *An Agenda for Peace: Preventive diplomacy, peacemaking and peace-keeping. Report of the Secretary-General*. New York: United Nations Rule of Law Unit.

Castanheira, Narciso. 1999. *Ex-criança soldado: 'Não queremos voltar para o inferno'*. Maputo: ONG Reconstruindo a Esperança.

Dinerman, Alice. 2006. *Revolution, Counter-revolution and Revisionism in Post-colonial Africa: The case of Mozambique, 1975–1994*. London: Routledge.

Elmquist, Dana. 2007. Contemporary Mozambican Sculpture in a Western Marketplace: The Growing Importance of NGOs in the Art Market. MA Thesis, UCLA.

Epskamp, Kees. 1999. "Healing Divided Societies." People Building Peace: 35 Inspiring Stories from Around the World. Utrecht: European Center for Conflict Prevention.

Faltas, Sami and Wolf Christian-Paes. 2004. *Exchanging Guns for Tools: The TAE Approach to Practical Disarmament*. Bonn: Bonn International Center for Conversion.

Fonseca, Maria Emilia. 2012. *Touching Art: The Poetics and Potency of Exhibiting the Tree of Life*. Cambridge: Cambridge Scholars Publishing.

Honwana, Alcinda Manuel. 2007. *Child Soldiers in Africa*. Philadelphia: University of Pennsylvania Press.

Kelly, William. 1994. *Violence to Non-violence: Individual perspectives, communal voices*. Camberwell, VA: Harwood Academic Publishers.

Knight, Mark. 2004. Camps and cash: Disarmament, demobilization and reinsertion of former combatants in transitions from war to peace. *Journal of Peace Research* 41 (4): 499–516.

Kopytoff, Igor. 1986. The cultural biography of things: Commoditization as process. In *The Social Life of Things: Commodities in cultural perspective*, ed. Arjun Appadurai, 64–91. Cambridge: Cambridge University Press.

Liebmann, Marian, ed. 1996. *Arts Approaches to Conflict*. London: Jessica Kingsley Publishers.

Mirzoeff, Nicholas, 1999. *Introduction to Visual Culture*. London: Routledge.

Samuels, Jane. 2008. The British Museum in Pentonville Prison: Dismantling barriers through touch and handling. In *Touch in Museums*, ed. Helen Chatterjee, 253–260. Oxford: Berg.

Sasha Constable. 2010. Peace Art Project Cambodia. Art project presented at http://sashaconstable.co.uk/projects/peace-art.

Schwartzott, Amy. 2014. Weapons and Refuse as Media: The Potent Politics of Recycling in Contemporary Mozambican Urban Arts. PhD. diss., University of Florida.

Schwartzott, Amy. 2013, Transforming Arms into Ploughshares: Weapons that Destroy and Heal in Mozambican Urban Art. In *Representations of Reconciliation: Art and Trauma in Africa*, eds Lizelle Bisschoff and Stefanie Van de Peer, 110–131. London: I.B. Tauris Publishers.

Schwartzott, Amy. 2012. Recycling Weapons of War into Tools for Peace Building in Post-Conflict Mozambique. In *People Building Peace 2.0: 34–41.* Hague: Peace Portal/GPPAC.

Sengulane, Dinis Salomão. 1994. *Vitória sem Vencidos.* Maputo: Conselho Cristão de Moçambique.

Spring, Christopher. 2005. Killing the gun. *British Museum Magazine* (Spring): 20–25.

Tester, Frank. 2006. Art and disarmament: Turning arms into ploughshares in Mozambique. *Development in Practice* 16 (2): 169–179.

UNECA. 2001. Proceedings of the conference on African conflicts: Their management, resolution and post-conflict reconstruction, held at the United Nations Economic Commission for Africa, December 13–15, 2000. Addis Ababa: Development Policy Management Forum.

Zelizer, Craig. 2003. The role of artistic processes in peacebuilding in Bosnia-Herzegovina. *Peace and Conflict Studies* 10 (2): 62–73.

Zuppi, Don Matteo. 1995. A communidade de Santo Egídio no Acordo Geral de Paz. In *Moçambique: Eleições, democracia e desenvolvimento,* ed. Brazão Mazula, 114–123. Maputo: Inter-Africa Group Press com patrocínio da Embaixada do Reino dos Países Baixos.

CHAPTER 11

'Taking Ownership': The Brazilian Pentecostal Project to Change Mozambique

Linda van de Kamp

Since the early 1990s, Brazilian Pentecostal churches have occupied the urban and peri-urban centres of Mozambique; the most prominent among these has been the *Igreja Universal do Reino de Deus* (Universal Church of the Kingdom of God, known as the Universal Church) (Cruz e Silva 2003; Freston 2005; Van de Kamp 2016).[1] Pentecostal pastors run churches in various neighbourhoods, perform on radio and television, and organize 'spiritual crusades' in stadia and central city squares with the stated aim of bringing radical change to people's lives. For change to happen, the Brazilian pastors emphasize the need to break with local cultural practices that in their view are evil. They stress the existence of a war between God and Satan, between heavenly and demonic powers. This includes a concern with causes of misfortune as being located in the past: ancestors' involvements with evil spirits are believed to have negative effects on their descendants (Meyer 1998; Van Dijk 1998). The Pentecostals believe it is necessary to gain distance from such aspects of 'Mozambican culture' as kinship relations, traditional healing, and local marriage forms. They teach that it is only by becoming independent from (ancestral) kin that people's lives will change for the better.

In addition, the Pentecostals preach the 'Prosperity Gospel', emphasizing that a combative faith brings happiness, health, and prosperity in all aspects of life (Coleman 2000; Martin 2002; Gifford 2004). The Prosperity Gospel includes

---

1 In the last census of 2007, Evangelical and Pentecostal churches were counted together for the first time, as one separate category, which shows their growing importance. In Maputo city, where the Brazilian Pentecostal churches are most prominent, their share correspond to 21% of the population that assumed a religious membership; in the province of Maputo it is 16.9% (INE 2009a, 2009b). While these churches share a central emphasis on 'being born again', they encompass a variety of denominations, doctrinal lineages and practices. Within this wide array of churches, Pentecostal Brazilian churches are prominent in most of Mozambique's urban centres. The most visible Brazilian Pentecostal churches are the Universal Church, *Deus é Amor* (God is Love), and *Igreja Mundial do Poder de Deus* (World Church of the Power of God), which are characterized by a strong focus on the 'Prosperity Gospel' and the notion of 'spiritual war' (Anderson 2004, 144–165; see also Freston 1995).

a financial practice of 'sowing and reaping': the more money one offers in church, the more one may expect to earn in the future. For change to happen, converts pay tithes and additional financial offerings to ensure a more prosperous life. Towards this end, special services and courses are organized to teach people how to become successful economically. The pastors explain that one should take the initiative and demonstrate economic competence by looking for new opportunities and making profitable deals. Mozambican converts emphasize the ways in which their Pentecostal lifestyle contrasts with that of their fellow citizens; they blame them for 'holding up their hands' and 'waiting for a job and money to come'.

In studies of Pentecostal religion in Africa, a principal question is whether it is possible to speak about radical change of the kind that converts claim to experience.[2] Currently, there is a renewed interest in a historic, Weberian approach to the relationship between a 'neo-Protestant' or Pentecostal ethic and the spirit of development and change in a neo-liberal age (Meyer 2007; Comaroff 2009; Van Dijk 2010; Comaroff and Morier-Genoud 2011; Freeman 2012). According to many scholars,[3] Pentecostal Christianity might (or even should) be a leading force for change in the contemporary world in terms of bringing socio-economic and political development, and personal empowerment. The central question of this chapter is what type of change Brazilian Pentecostalism in Mozambique is bringing about, and to what extent it might be contributing to a comprehensive basis for socio-economic emancipation.

Broadly, the chapter explores the Brazilian Pentecostal contestation of the role of 'Mozambican culture' in the struggle of each Mozambican for transformation in terms of a prosperous life. In this respect I particularly want to focus on the strong emphasis placed by Pentecostals on *tomar posse* (taking ownership), which means that a born-again Christian must realize her/his destiny by taking what is hers/his, as the bishop of the Universal Church, Edir Macedo, explains (Macedo 2004a; see also Gomes 1994, 230–231). In his terms, the world belongs to God and God's belongings are to be enjoyed. Prosperity, health, and love are essential for human existence, as they are the signs of having accomplished God's creation. Furthermore, every believer must exercise his/her right to prosper. In the following I examine how this central Pentecostal attitude is incorporated by Pentecostal women in the capital Maputo, where the number of adherents is the highest in the country and nearly 75 percent of these

---

2 See, for example, Meyer 1998; Van Dijk 1998; Engelke 2004, 2010; Marshall 2009; see also Bialecki and Daswani 2015.

3 See, among others, Martin 2002; Gifford 2004; Berger 2009; Ter Haar and Wolfensohn 2011; Attanasi and Yong 2012.

are women.[4] I argue that a particular interaction between Brazilian Pentecostal pastors and gendered socio-economic and cultural dynamics in Maputo shapes life as an enterprise in which converts must take a pro-active attitude, at any cost, in order to ensure a prosperous life.

1   Upwardly Mobile Women, Family, and Work in Maputo

A significant group of Pentecostal converts in Maputo consists of upwardly mobile women – relatively well educated, and/or earning a salary – between 30 and 40 years old. Compared to other generations, younger and older, I found that converts in this generation most clearly demonstrate an ambivalent stance towards aspects of 'Mozambican culture' or 'tradition'.[5] Among the upwardly mobile members of this generation more generally, 'African culture' and 'Mozambican culture' appear to be delicate subjects. Many of them grew up in Maputo in the period after independence was declared from Portugal in 1975. The single-party Frelimo regime embarked on a revolutionary development route with a socialist orientation, which prohibited 'backward practices', such as ancestor rituals, customary marriage, and traditional healing (Mazula 1995; Honwana 2002; Lundin 2007). Speaking local languages was also strongly discouraged; at home, parents thought it better for the future of their children if they spoke the official language, Portuguese. The women could often understand the local language but it was not theirs, and they could not or did not speak it. They experienced difficulties communicating with their grandparents and other kin who were not used to speaking Portuguese. This generation internalized a distance from their cultural past (Cipriano 2011; see also Sumich 2010).

However, in the post-socialist, neo-liberal era of the 1990s, Mozambicans were called upon to valorise their past culture again, as a force with which to develop a prosperous nation (Honwana 2002; West 2005): government officials started to wear 'authentic' African clothes and 'traditional rituals' were performed during official state ceremonies; traditional healers received support; non-governmental organizations (NGOs) emphasized the importance of local cultures in their programs. Since this time, there has been a revival of

---

4   These figures are based on interviews and observations. Worldwide, Pentecostalism attracts high numbers of women with similar percentages to those found in Mozambique (Martin 2001: 56; Brusco 2010).

5   Pentecostals and non-Pentecostals often used the word 'tradition' (*tradição*) when referring to local customs, and to beliefs and rituals relating to ancestral spirits.

Mozambican identity, and discussions about what it actually is and means (see, for example, Bertelsen 2003; Santos and Trindade 2003; Meneses 2005, 2006).

Pentecostal women joined the discussions about the role and meaning of Mozambican cultures and traditions in their own forthright ways. Convert Paula[6] (aged 37) was always outspoken about her vision of *tradição*: it would disappear. Paula works at a telecommunications company and was finishing her studies at the University Eduardo Mondlane. She blames her (grand)parents for their role in traditional practices, which she felt had given her bad luck. Paula had been attending services at the Universal Church since 1994, when she had experienced depression during a time when her family was facing problems. 'In my family we have a lot of trouble with marriages', she said.[7] Only one of her five sisters had married. 'It is said that we carry the names of our ancestors and therefore our ancestral spirits. Spirits claim persons', she explained, and therefore she and her sisters would be unsuccessful in their relationships (see also Van de Kamp 2011).

Other Pentecostal women were looking for more affinity with their ancestors, but at the same time they also wanted to distance themselves from them, as in the case of Julia (civil servant, aged 40), who accuses her parents of breaking with tradition. She recalls that her father had not paid a *lovolo* (bride price),[8] and had thus brought misfortune to his children. Her father had been educated at a Catholic seminary in the colonial period and was supposed to become a priest. Julia states that her father regards local customs, such as lovolo, as barbaric; he 'had been proud of having a car and civilization'.[9] For Julia, it was his arrogance that had made him and his family poor. Her father should have paid the lovolo because without it people did not belong to any family and lacked protection from ancestral spirits. She had visited a *curandeiro* (healer) to re-balance her relationship with the family's spirits. However, when she felt that she and her relatives were only sending bad spirits to each other with the help of a *feiticeiros* (witch doctor), she went to the Universal Church to rid herself of spirits and the influence of kin. Women like Julia were experiencing problems that they believed were caused by attempts to become part of the culture of their ancestors while also wishing to leave it behind. In

---

6 All interviewee names have been anonymized; the excerpts have been translated by the author from Portuguese.

7 Interview, held on June 21, 2006.

8 *Lovolo* is a marriage payment made by the bridegroom's family to the bride's family to compensate the girl's parents for bringing her up, to establish kin relations, and to distribute and accumulate wealth and maintain the lineage (Feliciano 1998, 249–267; Junod [1912] 1996, 109–120; see also Granjo 2005; Bagnol 2006).

9 Conversation held on February 3, 2007.

this ambivalent position, Pentecostal pastors give them clear instructions: 'leave the past behind' and 'let the traditions disappear'.

There is second reason why this generation experiences this ambivalence in relation to 'tradition'. Often, their parents, family members, and sometimes their (potential) husbands expect them to be a 'traditional woman' or house-wife, but the world of education encourages them to continue studying and to pursue a professional career: it teaches them to be more critical about the traditional role of women. Their education and professional careers do not necessarily have to conflict with their roles as mothers and wives, but they often do (see also Manuel 2011).

Cases in point are Paula and Julia who are both afraid of marriage; they refuse to endure the hardships their mothers had lived through. Instead, they want to share their household responsibilities with their husbands, to aim for financial independence, and they wish to have a faithful spouse. For example, Marcia (aged 33), who has a university degree and works as a teacher at a secondary school, says: 'I want a husband who knows how to clean the house and cook'.[10] Paula, Marcia, Julia, and other women of their generation believe this to be impossible,[11] yet they still want to get married to enjoy the status inherent in marriage. While the women want to be different from their mothers, they do not know how to achieve this new life, as they lack role models and encouragement from their relatives.

A third source of ambivalence in the lives of the Pentecostal women of this generation is their struggle with limitations and restrictions in their professional careers. New institutes of higher education and study programs emerged after they had already started working. They therefore took evening classes at the public and private universities to compete in the emerging job market in the banking sector, NGOs, consultancies, tourism, and government agencies. They often complain that urban areas lack the organization required for their 'middle-class' lifestyles, such as affordable apartments in the city centre, nice shops, restaurants and other places of leisure, and access to post-graduate courses and career possibilities. Mozambique's cities do not currently have the infrastructure to provide for all these demands, and the upwardly mobile are complaining about the government's inability to organize society properly (see also Jenkins 2006, 120–124; Pitcher 2006, 98–103).

These dynamics of ambivalence – towards 'tradition', towards kin and partners, and towards the lack of socio-economic infrastructure – result in problematic access to money, distrust in (affective) relationships, and uncertainty

---

10   Interviews held on April 7 and 21, 2006.
11   Interestingly, some men accused women of not being sufficiently emancipated.

about the influence of spiritual beings. The upwardly mobile Pentecostal women feel that they cannot trust their kin and partners, that they should create their lives individually, and that they need to find strategies to live as independently as possible (see also Costa and Rodrigues 2007; Nielsen 2010). It is from within this reality that Pentecostal women participate in the marriage and business courses organized by Pentecostal pastors; they attend services for success at home, at work, and in finance and business. However, the Brazilian pastors have one clear message: they have not come to help Mozambicans, but to teach them how to help themselves. In short, they are there to teach them how to 'take ownership'.

2   Brazilian Pentecostalism and the 'Fighter Woman'

The Brazilian Pentecostal churches arrived in Mozambique at the beginning of the 1990s, when processes of democratization and liberalization were beginning (Cruz e Silva 2003). The church leaders profited from the deregulation of religious expression and the liberalization of markets and media, as in other places in Africa (Meyer 2002). During this time, Brazilian pastors began holding church services in the cinemas, bought radio and television time, and increasingly started to play a remarkable role in debates about national cultural identities, especially with regard to issues of family, marriage, and sexuality. Women who had been able to pursue professional careers as a result of a more liberal socio-economic order were particularly attracted by these messages about modern Christian life styles, ranging from fashion to sexual relationships and economics. The dilemmas and challenges experienced by these women, amongst other issues arising from changing gender roles and their relations with (ancestral) kin and partners, influenced their interest in the Brazilian Pentecostal focus on marriage, family, and spirits. The women were analysing their own situations with reference to the preaching of the Brazilian Pentecostal leaders.

With regard to the meaning of marriage, the Brazilian pastors[12] emphasize that through marriage a couple are starting a nuclear family, leaving their extended families to live their own lives. The pastors criticize local marriages

---

12   There were also Mozambican pastors and pastors from other Portuguese-speaking African countries, such as Angola. However, the Brazilians offered leadership in the Brazilian churches and most Mozambicans were only assistant pastors; they even adopted Brazilian Portuguese as their language. This seems to be changing, amongst others under the pressure of the Mozambican government who wants foreign churches to employ local pastors.

(including the practice of lovolo) for the dependence they create between the couple and the extended family, which, in their view, hampers the healthy establishment of a Christian family. The pastors express their particular disapproval of the important role of the ancestral spirits, which have to approve of the marriage during lovolo ceremonies. It is also stressed that husband and wife should spend time together, go to the cinema, or on holiday. They should try to understand each other and make each other happy.

In the past, recently married women often moved to their husband's family house but today's upwardly mobile women want to establish a nuclear household. However, they are still supposed to show their mothers-in-law affection by visiting them on a regular basis, bringing gifts, or even cleaning their houses – practices these women consider old-fashioned. Some mothers-in-law interpret their behaviour negatively, saying, 'she is forgetting her roots', 'she does not know anymore who our ancestors are', and 'she has a bad spirit'. Mothers-in-law can gain a powerful position through relations with their sons, which is challenged by upwardly mobile (Pentecostal) women. Traditionally, women's powerful positions relate to male counterparts such as (grand)fathers, husbands, brothers, and sons (Loforte 2003, 17–19). At the same time, men explain that their wives are being influenced by their own mothers, and they find it difficult to develop a life with their wives with the constant presence of her family in the household. The pastors encourage women like Marcia, Julia, and Paula to become independent of their families and local family culture.

Marcia was one of the few Pentecostal women who succeeded finding a Pentecostal partner who did want to cook and clean, and together they decided to build a Christian family. Her parents had separated when Marcia was a child and she thought that this was partly influenced by her mother's involvement with ancestral spirits. Both Marcia and her partner wanted to start their life together free from bondage to ancestral spirits. They did not want to undergo the lovolo procedures because ancestral spirits were involved and it would make them too dependent on kin ties. However, by making such a choice they created tensions with kin on both sides. At first, their parents, aunts, and uncles would not accept their choice and did not want to attend their marriage, and even though they aspired to lead their own lives, the couple also wished to maintain good relationships with their kin. After several negotiations, they decided to organize a Christian lovolo ritual without invoking the ancestors, and they invited a pastor to bless their relationship instead – a marriage ceremony that increasing numbers of Pentecostal couples were pursuing (Van de Kamp and Van Dijk 2010, 130–133). In such cases, converts were still worried that their elderly kin might have involved the family spirits, and a level of distrust and anxiety was apparent in contacts between relatives.

Paula had decided not to marry because of the violent relationship between her parents, but the pastors convinced her of the possibility of a different, happy life with a husband. She observed how the Brazilian pastors and wives went along with each other, doing everything together – they went on vacation and to the cinema, shared household tasks, and did the shopping together. She participated in 'therapy of love' sessions, in which pastors speak about themes such as 'How to find the true love' and 'Is it possible to stay happily married forever?' The central message of the therapies, courses, sermons, and booklets is to 'take ownership' of one's life. God wants his children to prosper in any way possible: they only need to act in faith.

In instructing women as to how they should take ownership, the image of the *mulher batalhadora* (fighter woman) is frequently used. One Brazilian Pentecostal female teacher states: 'A woman of God is always in control' (Cardoso 2009, 245). According to Cardoso, many women are unsuccessful in combining the tasks of going to work, taking care of the home, and investing quality time in their marriage. But God's women are fighters. They are able to take care of their home and their work, and still end the day with a perfect appearance. It is all about equilibrium, planning, and efficiency, says Cardoso (2009, 245–247). Women should organize their days and plan the hours in which they pray and read the Bible, clean the house, go to work, and spend time with their husband and their children. Women have to police themselves, and Paula and others try to follow this advice. For example, in conversation, Paula stresses that slowly her life has changed; today she can analyse difficult situations and react calmly. According to her, at her work place there are colleagues who make negative comments about her, and her relatives regularly offend her; however, she claims that she had learned to keep her mouth closed and she chooses not to respond to any such comments.

Recently, however, she has been put to the test. She started having problems with her husband 'because of the young girls who run after married men who own a car'. Paula told me how her husband had wanted to be different from his father who beat his wife and had *amantes* (lovers). But during his marriage to Paula he was becoming more like the father he so detested. According to Paula, men inherit the behaviour of their male kin. She knows, however, that this is part of the spiritual war between good and evil powers and that she is being tested. How would she deal with this situation? Would she be able to stay in control? She goes to church every day, prays in the early morning, and tries not to quarrel with her husband but to show him what true love should be like (see also Soothill 2007, 209–218; Frahm-Arp 2010, 209–244).

I followed the lives of Julia, Paula, and Marcia during my period of fieldwork that ran from August 2005 to August 2007, and I met them again in August 2008, when their situation was more or less the same. While Paula and her husband were still married, during a considerable part of the year they lived apart from each other because her husband studied abroad. Since he was not contributing much to the household finances, she was trying to find a better job now that she had graduated. She felt tired because of the daily fight for survival due to high rents, care for her children, and being uncertain of her husband's faithfulness, but she trusted that God would reward her. Nevertheless, she had become disillusioned with the Universal Church, where she felt that the pastors pressured her too much to become a successful fighter woman. She changed to the newly arrived Brazilian Pentecostal church, the World Church of the Power of God, with similar doctrines but a more relaxed atmosphere.

Julia was still unmarried, even though she dated men, and she was struggling to study for her university degree in the evenings, after work. She was tired of needing to share her income with her relatives. She had stopped attending services on a regular basis, as she was not sure if they were really helping her. Instead, she said her prayers privately and followed the church's programs on television. Marcia and her husband were doing well. They were leaders in a Brazilian church, and although their kin had predicted that they would have difficulties conceiving because they had not done the 'real' lovolo, she was pregnant.

However, when I returned to Maputo in July and August 2011, I learned that the challenges they and other Pentecostal women were experiencing in taking ownership and being in control seemed to have contributed to a new emphasis in the Pentecostal churches, which, in the Universal Church, was summarized in a new slogan: *Pôr Deus à prova* (putting God to the test) (see figure 1).

3   Putting God to the Test

As part of taking ownership and the emphasis on the figure of the 'fighter woman', converts are expected to give tithes and offerings in church. By doing so, they are deemed to have demonstrated initiative, become blessed, and have *o direito de cobrar* (the right to collect their blessings) according to Malachi 3:10, a Bible verse that was often used in services:

> Bring the full amount of your tithes to the Temple, so that there will be plenty of food there. *Put me to the test* and you will see that I will open the windows of heaven and pour out on you in abundance all kinds of good things (*Good News Bible*[13] 1994; my emphasis).

---

13   *Good News Bible* is an English language translation of the Bible by the American Bible Society. It is available on-line, at www.goodnewsbible.com.

Pastors use examples of famous people who have shown their respect for God by paying tithes, and who have been transformed into millionaires. By showing similar faith, according to the pastors, converts would be surprised. Their money supply would never dry up. On the contrary, it would continue to multiply and they would have everything they had always wanted, such as peace, happiness, health, love, and food (Macedo 2004b, 64–65). Through the money given, God is obligated to offer abundance in return.

Every Monday evening there are special services in most of the Brazilian Pentecostal churches in aid of financial success; these are mainly directed at (potential) entrepreneurs. The central message is that seemingly negative circumstances, such as lack of education and high unemployment rates, are opportunities to excel. As long as people take responsibility for their financial lives, and their lives more generally, and as long as they invest in their future, they will be successful. This was expressed in a rhetorically strong statement: 'then they *are* successful'. On the first evening of the course on doing business in the second half of 2005, the Brazilian pastor of the Universal Church had clearly stated: 'When you aren't rich, it is your own fault. It is your faith in God that will be rewarded'. At the end he said, 'You should be optimistic and not give up', and 'Don't forget that God doesn't want to look like a fool and thus will give you abundantly'. Paula, who incorporated this faith, explained to me the vital importance of changing one's life:

> In Mozambique, we are talking about the fight against poverty (*luta contra a pobreza*) but we have to fight mental poverty; it is a question of mentality. People are just sitting the whole day selling bananas and waiting for a job, but they have to do something. It is important to look forward. I have a good job and a good salary but I want to earn more money, so I'm always looking around for another job. You can't ask God and do nothing yourself.

At the time, the Mozambican government promoted particular slogans – *luta contra a pobreza* – in the fight against poverty, emphasizing that people should work hard to escape it. While this seems to resemble the Pentecostal discourse, converts are critical about their government because they feel that their leaders are not good role models and are involved with the wrong (spiritual) powers. However, the pastors know how to fight for change: by giving tithes and offerings, fasting, praying, following chains of church services, and participating in spiritual and financial campaigns, converts gain the right to collect their blessings. During services, participants offer money directed at a specific request, such as building a house. To excel, they are told, one should give banknotes, preferably in US dollars, the currency that entrepreneurs use, and which is worth far more than Mozambican currency. Competition is encouraged among the congregation for quantities of money. First, the pastors call forward those who would give US$500, then those who would give US$300, and then US$100, and so on. Converts who give coins would receive coins in return, thus, these are worthless, said the pastors. There were also special *campanhas* (campaigns) that allowed people to realize a particular dream (*meu sonho vai se realizar* – my dream will come true), such as finding a faithful husband. Jesus gave his life in sacrifice and so converts have to make (financial) sacrifices as well: they should concentrate all their energy into one request by fasting, praying, and giving money. In these campaigns, amounts of US$20,000 are no exception; such converts donate all the savings in their bank account or sell their car or their house.

I came to know many converts who went bankrupt during this process (Van de Kamp 2016), like Julia, who had eventually left the Universal Church. Her bank account was empty after offering all her money in church, but the pastor became angry with her poor results and claimed she had not dedicated herself sufficiently to the project of conversion. However, when I met her again in 2011, she had, perhaps surprisingly, returned to the church. I asked her how this could be possible after her devastating experiences. She explained that she had finally learned to take ownership and thus to take responsibility:[14]

> I have to use intelligent faith.[15] In the past I didn't use my brains; I gave what the pastor asked. Now, I give when I want to, when I feel that this is the pledge I want to participate in, otherwise it won't work.

Other converts explained to me that even pastors can be imbued with evil and can lead you down the wrong route in life, and that every convert needs to engage in self-responsibility, which is central to the Pentecostal faith. One of them, who is part of the newer generation of 15- to 25-year olds, said:[16]

> some converts are not strong enough to participate in the Universal Church. A lot of pressure is exerted on you. If you don't know what your goals and objectives are, it is possible that you will do things you probably don't want to.

14   Conversation held on August 17, 2011.
15   'Intelligent faith' – *fé inteligente*. The Universal Church's Bishop Macedo introduced this concept to stress the necessity of knowing how to use faith (Macedo 2004a, 81–83).
16   Interview held on June 23, 2006.

Apparently, Julia had not used her faith intelligently. It was her own fault that she had 'lost' all her money. At the same time, converts will only harvest what they have sown by way of offerings. By giving up and leaving the church, they cannot collect any blessings. And, like many biblical figures, they know that it might take many years to reach their destiny. They have to demonstrate that they can pass the test, and so they put God to the test with repeated tithes, offerings, sacrifices, campaigns, and prayers.

One convert told me how the pastors were calling on them to throw Bibles against the church's walls, to really put God to the test, as part of the renewed emphasis on *pôr Deus à prova*. The convert condemned this action because, like many others, she felt that their holy book should be treated with respect. Yet, this was exactly the reason that the pastors and other converts seemed to throw the Bible, to contest limitations and to force a reaction. In many ways, the Brazilian pastors and various converts intentionally performed extreme actions as a strategy to shock others and to break away from 'backward practices'. For example, they buried coffins on church premises, which outsiders understood as an offensive act that contaminated the place with the restless spirits of dead persons who could do harm (i.e., witchcraft), whereas the Pentecostals viewed this as a way to provoke these demonic beliefs; they were burying materials related to their old lives (Van de Kamp 2010). At present, they not only seem to be contesting the habits and beliefs of their fellow citizens but also God's silence. If people have offered money wholeheartedly, and prayed and fasted for years, they should provoke God, because God must give something back to them. Converts frequently understand their lack of progress as their own fault because they have not lived up to Pentecostal ideals. However, if they cannot blame themselves anymore and have indeed shown self-responsibility and dedication, then the time has come to blame God, to make a fool of him, because he is not fulfilling his promises. Such actions might finally provoke his anger and lead to his willingness to demonstrate his power, as he had done in many biblical stories in the Old Testament, which the pastors preached about.

4   Change – Helping Yourself and the Right to Prosper

Several converts explained that the financial practices of the Universal Church in Mozambique were dissimilar to those in Brazil and that Bishop Macedo was unaware of what was happening in Mozambique. Former Mozambican assistant pastors acknowledged that when Brazilian missionaries arrive in Mozambique they are shocked at the financial excesses demanded, and surprised by the ease with which 'Africans offered money in church'.[17] Converts who had been part of the church since it started in Mozambique said that financial offerings were becoming disproportionate to their income. As there seemed to be no limits to the sacrifices converts were prepared to make, amounts had increased over the years. In this sense, the interaction between Mozambican converts and Brazilian pastors has reinforced the 'sowing and reaping' aspects of the Prosperity Gospel (see Maxwell 1998).

Two interrelated developments would appear to be influencing financial practices in Brazilian Pentecostal churches in Mozambique. First, the tensions, distrust, and fear that exist in social relationships, alongside a spiritual insecurity, are shaping the desire to make some kind of a break by means of high financial sacrifices. Secondly, sacrifices are becoming part of the way in which upwardly mobile women are demonstrating their ability to pioneer and be successful in their careers and businesses, their marriage, and even in church. They have to show that they are adequately and smartly equipped, or 'sufficiently strong' to use the words of the convert cited above, to gain and set frontiers in the world until, apparently, God himself becomes the limit and needs to be confronted with Bibles thrown against church walls.

In their classic monograph about sacrifice, Hubert and Mauss (1964) focus on the destruction of the offering, the sacrificial victim, that generates spiritual benefit for the one doing the sacrificing, altering his/her state. In the sacrificial ritual the victim is destroyed, materializing a separation between the victim and the sacrificer that enables a sacred force to be made manifest. The victims of Pentecostal financial sacrifices are those who depend on the money that is offered, and who, in this context, are principally relatives and 'fictive kin' (Lundin 2007, 115–116). Knowing that money can make or break relations, converts offer large amounts of money. Tithes or normal offerings would not have sufficient impact and something bigger has to take place to show their relatives and any evil spirits that they are both serious and able to mobilize more powerful forces. Instead of their (ancestral) kin destroying them, the opposite will happen and they will triumph by becoming even wealthier. As a result, Julia and Paula no longer contribute to their parents' health costs, to the education of nieces and nephews, to the marriage costs of brothers and sisters, and are now able to invest in their own dreams.

However, converts' investments in demanding services, courses, and financial sacrifices provoke and strengthen feelings of distrust between them and their kin, their partners, and neighbours who cannot share in the wealth of their Pentecostal relative; they are afraid of losing their belongings to the church and

---

17   Conversations held in May 2007.

feel threatened by the demonization of their culture and relationships. Because converts and pastors are suspected of accumulating wealth at great cost to others, which suggests witchcraft in this context, the Pentecostal women often end up alone. Mirroring Marshall's (2009) material from Nigeria, Pentecostalism in Mozambique has an emancipatory quality, which liberates people from negative dependencies and hierarchies, yet it fails to provide a new environment for sociability and trust (see also Smith 2001; Newell 2007; van Wyk 2014).

Despite this paradox of liberation alongside uncertainty and distrust, converts stress the conviction that increasing tensions and difficulties are part of the spiritual war. The lack of trust, sociability, and support, in their view, becomes a sign of their Pentecostal commitment and is even something to nurture because it pushes them to help themselves. For example, Julia blames herself and not the pastors for having lost all her money, as she had not used her faith intelligently. Upwardly mobile converts are attracted by the fact that the churches are not places where support and sociability are central but where they are pressured to take care of themselves (van Dijk 2010). This is an attitude they aspire to, through which they can learn and demonstrate their capacities to be pioneers in the world and establish powerful positions. The appropriation of particular modes of 'taking ownership' introduces mechanisms of self-pressure to effectuate blessings that will demonstrate a convert's proven commitment and thus their entitlement to prosperity.

It is in this spirit that converts raise their children; younger converts between the ages of 15 and 25 seem to take it for granted. Compared to the older generation, younger generations are more acquainted with the current conflicts of urban society. They have grown up with the challenges and uncertainties of a neo-liberal economy and seem better equipped to deal with the demands placed on them; they demonstrate less ambiguity about both 'tradition' and their professional careers. They have clearer goals and objectives and negotiate with pastors about their sacrifices more often; they leave the church sooner if they feel their lives are not improving. The younger Pentecostals almost naturally consider the pastors as persons with whom they are doing business; consequently, they cultivate an attitude of distrust and anonymity (see also van Wyk 2011) that the older women, for example Julia, only learned by trial and error over time.

Young people's engagement with Pentecostalism demonstrates that the Prosperity Gospel is not so much a reaction to the neo-liberal capitalist economy in Maputo but it is entangled with it (Meyer 2007; Comaroff 2009), as these churches are, in many ways, operating as enterprises.[18] Furthermore, in their

---

18   For example, there is a cash machine in the new main cathedral in Maputo, at the Universal Church on Avenue 24 de Julho.

interactions, Brazilian pastors and Mozambican converts appear to expand the neo-liberal order beyond its limits by pressurizing each other to engage in opportunities and challenges with a minimum of support. Even though the Pentecostal development model that upwardly mobile women are adopting involves opening up fresh spaces and navigating new cultural and economic domains, it also means going beyond what seems feasible, in an attempt to realize heaven on earth.

Acknowledgements

My thanks go to the editors of this volume and the anonymous reviewers for their helpful comments. I am indebted to my Mozambican interlocutors who shared their lives with me. I gratefully acknowledge the Netherlands Organisation for Scientific Research (NWO), the VU University Amsterdam, and the African Studies Centre, Leiden for the (financial) support I received that enabled me to carry out this research.

References

Anderson, Allan. 2004. *An Introduction to Pentecostalism: Global Charismatic Christianity*. Cambridge: Cambridge University Press.

Attanasi, Katherine, and Amos Yong, eds. 2012. *Pentecostalism and Prosperity: The socio-economics of the Global Charismatic Movements*. New York: Palgrave Macmillan.

Bagnol, Brigitte. 2006. Gender, self, multiple identities, violence and magical interpretations in *lovolo* practices in Southern Mozambique. PhD diss., University of Cape Town, South Africa.

Berger, Peter L. 2009. Faith and Development. *Society* 46 (1): 69–75.

Bertelsen, Bjørn Enge. 2003. 'The traditional lion is dead': The ambivalent presence of tradition and the relation between politics and violence in Mozambique. In *Lusotopie 2003: Violence et contrôle de la violence au Brésil, en Afrique et à Goa*, ed. Christine Goirand, 263–281. Paris: Éditions Karthala.

Bialecki, Jon and Girish Daswani (eds.) 2015. The Anthropology of Personhood, Redux: Views from Christianity. *HAU: Journal of Ethnographic Theory* 5 (1), special section.

Brusco, Elizabeth. 2010. Gender and Power. In *Studying Global Pentecostalism: Theories and Methods,* eds Allan Anderson, Michael Bergunder, André Droogers and Cees van der Laan, 74–99. Berkeley: University of California Press.

Cardoso, Cristiane. 2009. *Melhor do que Comprar Sapatos: Várias Mensagens*. Rio de Janeiro: Unipro Editora.

Cipriano, António. 2011. *Educação, Modernidade e Crise Ética em Moçambique*. Maputo: Dondza Editora.

Coleman, Simon. 2000. *The Globalisation of Charismatic Christianity: Spreading the Gospel of Prosperity*. Cambridge: Cambridge University Press.

Comaroff, Jean. 2009. The Politics of Conviction: Faith on the Neo-liberal Frontier. *Social Analysis* 53 (1): 17–38.

Comaroff, Jean, and Eric Morier-Genoud. 2011. Twenty years after *Of revelation and revolution*: An interview with Jean Comaroff. *Social Sciences and Missions* 24 (2–3): 1–23.

Costa, Ana Bénard, and Cristina Udelsmann Rodrigues. 2007. Famílias e estratégias de sobrevivência e reprodução social em Luanda e Maputo. In *Subúrbios de Luanda e Maputo*, eds Jochen Oppenheimer and Isabel Raposo, 139–161. Lisbon: Edições Colibri and Centro de Estudos Sobre África e do Desenvolvimento.

Cruz e Silva, Teresa. 2003. Mozambique. In *Les Nouveaux Conquérants de la Foi: L'Église Universelle du Royaume de Dieu (Brésil)*, eds André Corten, Jean-Pierre Dozon, and Ari Pedro Oro, 109–117. Paris: Karthala.

Engelke, Matthew. 2004. Discontinuity and the Discourse of Conversion. *Journal of Religion in Africa* 34 (1): 82–109.

Engelke, Matthew. 2010. Past Pentecostalism: Notes on Rupture, Realignment, and Everyday Life in Pentecostal and African Independent Churches. *Africa* 80 (2): 177–199.

Feliciano, José Fialho. 1998. *Antropologia Económica dos Thonga do Sul de Moçambique*. Maputo: Arquivo Histórico de Moçambique.

Frahm-Arp, Maria. 2010. *Professional Women in South African Pentecostal Charismatic Churches*. Leiden: Brill.

Freeman, Dena (ed.). 2012. *Pentecostalism and Development: Churches, NGOs and social change in Africa*. Basingstoke: Palgrave Macmillan.

Freston, Paul. 1995. Pentecostalism in Brazil: A Brief History. *Religion* 25: 119–133.

Freston, Paul. 2005. The Universal Church of the Kingdom of God: a Brazilian church finds success in Southern Africa. *Journal of Religion in Africa* 35 (1): 33–65.

Gifford, Paul. 2004. *Ghana's New Christianity: Pentecostalism in a Globalising African Economy*. London: Hurst.

Gomes, Wilson. 1994. Nem Anjos nem Demônios. In *Nem anjos nem demônios: Interpretações sociológicas do Pentecostalismo*, ed. Alberto Antoniazzi, 225–270. Petrópolis, Rio de Janeiro: Vozes.

Granjo, Paulo. 2005. *Lobolo em Maputo: Um velho idioma para novas vivências conjugais*. Oporto: Campo das Letras.

Honwana, Alcinda M. 2002. *Espíritos Vivos, Tradições Modernas: Possessão de espíritos e reintegração social pós-guerra no Sul de Moçambique*. Maputo: Promédia.

Hubert, Henri and Marcel Mauss. 1964. *Sacrifice: Its Nature and Function*. London: Cohen & West.

Instituto Nacional de Estatística (INE). 2009a. *Sinopse dos Resultados Definitivos do 3° Recenseamento Geral da População e Habitação. Cidade de Maputo.* Maputo: Instituto Nacional de Estatística.

Instituto Nacional de Estatística (INE). 2009b. *Sinopse dos Resultados Definitivos do 3° Recenseamento Geral da População e Habitação. Província de Maputo.* Maputo: Instituto Nacional de Estatística.

Jenkins, Paul. 2006. Image of the city in Mozambique: Civilization, parasite, engine of growth or place of opportunity? In *African Urban Economies: viability, vitality or vitiation?* eds Deborah Fahy Bryceson and Deborah Potts, 107–130. New York: Palgrave Macmillan.

Junod, Henri. 1996 [1912]. *Usos e Costumes dos Bantu.* Vol. 1. Vida Social. Maputo: Arquivo Histórico de Moçambique.

Loforte, Ana Maria. 2003. *Género e Poder entre os Tsonga de Moçambique.* Lisbon: Ela por Ela.

Lundin, Iraê Baptista. 2007. Negotiating Transformation: Urban livelihoods in Maputo adapting to thirty years of political and economic changes. PhD diss., Gothenburg University, Sweden.

Macedo, Edir. 2004a. *Mensagens que Edificam.* Rio de Janeiro: Editora Gráfica Universal.

Macedo, Edir. 2004b. *Nos Passos de Jesus.* Rio de Janeiro: Editora Gráfica Universal.

Manuel, Sandra. 2011. Maputo has no Marriage Material: Sexual relationships in the politics of social affirmation and emotional stability in a cosmopolitan African city. PhD diss., School of Oriental and African Studies, University of London.

Marshall, Ruth. 2009. *Political Spiritualities: The Pentecostal Revolution in Nigeria.* Chicago, IL: University of Chicago Press.

Martin, Bernice. 2001. The Pentecostal Gender Paradox: A cautionary tale for the sociology of religion. In *The Blackwell Companion to Sociology of Religion*, ed. Richard Fenn, 52–66. Oxford: Blackwell.

Martin, David. 2002. *Pentecostalism: The World their Parish.* Oxford: Blackwell.

Maxwell, David. 1998. Delivered from the Spirit of Poverty? Pentecostalism, Prosperity and Modernity in Zimbabwe. *Journal of Religion in Africa* 28 (3): 350–373.

Mazula, Brazão. 1995. *Educação, Cultura e Ideologia em Moçambique, 1975–1985.* Lisbon: Afrontamento.

Meneses, Maria Paula. 2005. Poderes Neo-tradicionais e o Estado Moderno em Moçambique: as possibilidades da reinvenção do 'tradicional'. In *Cabral no Cruzamento de Épocas: Comunicações e discursos produzidos no II Simpósio Internacional Amílcar Cabral*, ed. Fundação Amílcar Cabral, 535–546. Praia: Alfa Comunicações.

Meneses, Maria Paula. 2006. Traditional Authorities in Mozambique: Between Legitimisation and Legitimacy. In *The Shade of New Leaves: Governance in Traditional Authority; A Southern African Perspective*, ed. Manfred Hinz and Helgard K. Patemann, 93–120. Berlin: Lit Verlag.

Meyer, Birgit. 1998. 'Make a Complete Break with the Past': Memory and postcolonial modernity in Ghanaian Pentecostal discourse. *Journal of Religion in Africa* 28 (3): 316–349.

Meyer, Birgit. 2002. Pentecostalism, Prosperity and Popular Cinema in Ghana. *Culture and Religion* 3 (1): 67–87.

Meyer, Birgit. 2007. Pentecostalism and Neoliberal Capitalism: Faith, Prosperity and Vision in African Pentecostal-Charismatic Churches. *Journal for the Study of Religion* 20 (2): 5–28.

Newell, Sasha. 2007. Pentecostal Witchcraft: Neoliberal possession and demonic discourse in Ivoirian Pentecostal churches. *Journal of Religion in Africa* 37 (4): 461–490.

Nielsen, Morten. 2010. Contrapuntal Cosmopolitanism: Distantiation as Social Relatedness among house-builders in Maputo, Mozambique. *Social Anthropology* 18 (4): 396–402.

Pitcher, Anne. 2006. Forgetting from Above and Memory from Below: Strategies of Legitimation and Struggle in Postsocialist Mozambique. *Africa* 76 (1): 88–112.

Smith, Daniel Jordan. 2001. 'The Arrow of God': Pentecostalism, Inequality and the Supernatural in South-eastern Nigeria. *Africa* 71 (4): 587–613.

Soothill, Jane E. 2007. *Gender, Social Change and Spiritual Power: Charismatic Christianity in Ghana.* Leiden: Brill.

Santos, Boaventura de Sousa, and João C. Trindade, eds. 2003. *Conflito e Transformação Social: Uma Paisagem das Justiças em Moçambique.* Vols. I and ii. Oporto: Afrontamento.

Sumich, Jason. 2010. *Nationalism, Urban Poverty and Identity in Maputo, Mozambique.* Working Paper 68, London School of Economics, London.

Ter Haar, Gerrie, and James D. Wolfensohn, eds. 2011. *Religion and Development: Ways of Transforming the World.* London: Hurst.

Van de Kamp, Linda. 2016. *Violent Conversion: Brazilian Pentecostalism and Urban Women in Mozambique.* Suffolk, UK: James Currey.

Van de Kamp, Linda. 2010. Burying life: Pentecostal religion and development in urban Mozambique. In *Development and Politics from Below: Exploring Religious Spaces in the African State,* eds Barbara Bompani and Maria Frahm-Arp, 152–168. London: Palgrave MacMillan.

Van de Kamp, Linda. 2011. Converting the Spirit Spouse: the violent transformation of the Pentecostal female body in post-war urban Mozambique. *Ethnos* 76 (4): 510–533.

Van de Kamp, Linda, and Rijk van Dijk. 2010. Pentecostals Moving South-South: Brazilian and Ghanaian transnationalism in Southern Africa. In *Religion Crossing Boundaries: Transnational dynamics in Africa and the new African diasporic religions,* eds Afe Adogame and James Spickard, 123–142. Leiden: Brill.

Van Dijk, Rijk. 1998. Pentecostalism, Cultural Memory and the State: Contested representations of time in postcolonial Malawi. In *Memory and the Postcolony: African*

Anthropology and the Critique of Power, ed. Richard P. Werbner, 155–181. London: Zed Books.

Van Dijk, Rijk. 2010. Social Catapulting and the Spirit of Entrepreneurialism: Migrants, private initiative, and the Pentecostal ethic in Botswana. In *Traveling Spirits: migrants, markets and mobilities*, eds Gertrud Hüwelmeier and Kristine Krause, 101–117. London: Routledge.

Van Wyk, Ilana. 2011. Believing Practically and Trusting Socially in Africa: the contrary case of the Universal Church of the Kingdom of God in Durban, South Africa. In *Christianity and Public Culture in Africa*, ed. Harri Englund, 189–203. Athens, Ohio: Ohio University Press, Cambridge Centre of African Studies Series.

Van Wyk, Ilana. 2014. *The Universal Church of the Kingdom of God in South Africa: A Church of Strangers*, Cambridge: Cambridge University Press, The International African Library.

West, Harry G. 2005. *Kupilikula. Governance and the Invisible Realm in Mozambique*. Chicago: Chicago University Press.

CHAPTER 12

Singing Struggles, Affirming Politics: Mozambique's Revolutionary Songs as Other Ways of Being (in) History

Maria Paula Meneses

> We will not forget the time that passed,
> Who can forget what passed?![1]

∴

Music is a fundamental mode of political expression and a political enactment. Revolutionary songs, broadcasted by the leading nationalist force against colonialism in Mozambique, FRELIMO,[2] became a significant part of developing a new sense of belonging to an alternative political project (Laban 1988; Basto 2012). FRELIMO'S national project sought to interrogate the Eurocentric political program by denouncing the colonized historiographic and biographic loci of enunciation, speaking from a new position, politically and epistemologically delinked from the colonial episteme (Mignolo 2007; Filipe 2012).

---

* This chapter is partially the result of research projects funded through by Portuguese Foundation for Science and Technology (FCT): PTDC/AFR/121404/2010 -FCOMP-01-0124 -FEDER-019531 and FEDER through the Competitiveness and Innovation Operational Program COMPETE 2020 PTDC/IVC-ANT/6100/2014 – POCI-01-0145-FEDER-016859. My thanks to all people that accepted be interviewed and to share histories with me. Also, a word of acknowledgement to the various libraries and archives consulted. Finally, to the various readers (anonymous and not) whose comments I sought to incorporate, thank you.

1 Popular song of revolutionary Mozambique. This chapter draws essentially on the analysis of the FRELIMO's revolutionary ballads and songs, produced during the liberation war and sung in the early years of independence. The majority of the lyrics used in this chapter were obtained from Radio Moçambique (records produced around mid-1970s). The revolutionary lyrics presented over the course of this chapter were sung in various languages. These are my own translations, throughout. FRELIMO was the main movement that carried out an armed struggle against Portuguese colonialism in Mozambique, becoming the party in power since independence (both in mono and multiparty contexts).

2 Through 'Voice of FRELIMO', Mozambique Liberation Front radio. From the early 1960s, FRELIMO quickly became the main symbol of struggle against Portuguese colonialism. However, other resistance movements fought – politically and with guns – against colonialism. On this topic see Cabrita (2000).

This chapter, by focusing on the instrumental use of culture in FRELIMO'S political project,[3] aims to understand the appropriation of the nation, as a political project, by the Mozambicans to become. Through unisonance, lyrics became, as I will seek to demonstrate, more than an element of shared vocabulary, they became a shared experience (Anderson 1983, 145).

Soon after the coup d'état that shook colonial Portugal on April 25, 1974 the revolutionary songs swamped national radio in Mozambique, spreading new political and geographical references for the new country that was being designed. These highly politicized lyrics embodied FRELIMO'S political vision, to be 'partaken' throughout the country. By singing, in the times of transition to independence, people showed the power to choose and support another destiny, challenging the intellectual construction of colonial epistemology.[4] In this sense, these revolutionary songs are part of the literature of combat in Mozambique (Mendonça 1988), as they helped to mould 'the national consciousness, giving it form and contours and flinging open before it new and boundless horizons', expressing the 'will to liberty expressed in terms of time and space' (Fanon 1963, 173).

This political approach towards nationalist struggles is not unique. For Philip Bohlman (2004, 120), analysing modern European contexts, nationalist music can be used in distinctive ways: to fabricate and create images of the state; to mobilize, by music, ideas that narrate an historical or political struggle, the residents of the state; and to develop, through aesthetic and musical languages, specific political missions and ideological projects.

The lyrics of FRELIMO's revolutionary repertoire[5] spoke in various languages about 'unknown' African heroes, places, and struggles, voiced another means by which to think of the political, and opened up new spaces in which to

---

3 A project that shows several similarities with the political transition in Angola. As Marissa Moorman detailed study illustrates, cultural practices are 'intimately intertwined with and productive of nationalism throughout the struggle for independence and afterwards' (Moorman 2008, 58).

4 Other forms of knowledge and experiences beyond the colonial episteme were suppressed by colonial institutions (Meneses 2011). The accumulated amnesia and the enforced silence surrounding epistemological diversity were intentional acts of forgetting, signifying a denial of any possibility of mutual recognition (Santos 2007).

5 Revolutionary songs were played everywhere, but most of them remained anonymous, particularly in the years after independence. This research interest put me in touch with several people who had been part of choirs, both during the liberation struggle and after. These interviewees were very helpful in identifying some of the composers (most of them already deceased) of the revolutionary songs, including Samuel Dabula, Simão Sipeto Tibúrcio Lindolondolo, Abílio Filipe Awendila, Jorge Zaqueu Nhassengo, Justino Chemane, Salomão Manhiça, among others.

affirm the epistemic rights of the colonially oppressed.[6] These songs anticipated radical challenges in the near future of independent Mozambique. Yet,
beyond aesthetic considerations, the lyrics' political message remained unfa-
miliar to many in Mozambique, mainly because a significant part of the urban population did not understand these native languages and were unaware
of the political projects proposed by the leading political force, FRELIMO, the
nationalist mouvement.[7] This ignorance, the result of the Portuguese colonial
educational project, reinforced the mutual ignorance that fed the controversy
surrounding interpretations of the nationalist vision for the newly country. If
we accept that the past is experienced and lived by the people, an analysis of
these songs can help decode specific social pasts in this context, opening a
window through which to explore the historical consciousness and intersub-
jectivity that still informs contemporary Mozambique.

This chapter analyses a number of revolutionary songs as a discursive site that
enabled various publics to participate in the political life of Mozambique during
the transition period towards independence. While debating the political content of these songs is nothing new in an African context,[8] a close analysis of the
political role and place of revolutionary songs as an epistemological stance is a
new area of study. This chapter argues for an interdisciplinary approach to the
liberation struggle, and for the recognition of liberation songs as key historical
documents. The country's territorial imagination was configured to supplant colonial spatial imaginaries, and this entailed new relationships that united territory, people, and historical interpretations. The lyrics are useful, then, as a means
by which to discuss political life in and about Mozambique's troubled past.

With the onset of modern colonialism in Mozambique at the turn of the
twentieth century, songs emerged as vehicles by which to reaffirm other forms
of knowledge and political positions from which to resist colonialism and ac-
celerate social change. Through satirical songs, workers could protest against
their suffering as forced labourers on large plantations, and they also used them
as a means by which to preserve their identity (Vail and White 1991). In their
songs, people sought to mediate between an idealized imagined past and the
uncertain constitution of the present, thus evaluating their destiny, and their

6   With independence, Mozambique maintained Portuguese as its official language; however,
    other languages, previously described as 'native dialects' became recognized as national lan-
    guages, and were used widely. The reference to these languages as dialects reflects the desire
    to downgrade the image of the diversity and richness of African cultures and their interac-
    tion. According to the recent national census, more than half of the population still has a
    national language as its mother language (see http://www.ine.gov.mz/iv-censo-2017).
7   Mozambique was one of the settler colonies in Africa. Over two hundred thousand settlers
    left the country following independence (Penvenne 2005, 80).
8   See, for example, Vail and White (1991), Fabian (1998); Allen (2004).

few options. In fact, these songs were revealed as useful analytical tools when extensive research on the migrant labour force in Mozambique was conducted after independence (First 1983). These brief examples connect this region with a broader African context, for songs have been interpreted as maps of experience throughout the continent (Coplan 1997; Longwe and Clark 1998). Over the last decades, songs and praise poetry[9] have been analysed both as forms of historiography (Penvenne and Sitoe 2000; Israel 2009) and as historiologies (Vail and White 1991; Fabian 1996).

Colonial narratives constructed African subjects as primitives who spoke in incomprehensible grunts and did not possess the capacity to think and decide about their own destinies. World (Eurocentric) history became the imperial road to power and domination (Wolf 1982). The colonizers drew a kind of *cordon sanitaire* between themselves and the colonized. This demarcation was activated by, and is perpetuated in, modern knowledge and Portuguese language, which are the unambiguous domains of the colonial. In Mozambique, as in neighbouring contexts, songs provided a means by which people could articulate 'the pressing issues of the day more eloquently than any political speech or historical treatise' (Pongweni 1997, 63). The revolutionary liberation songs must be understood as concrete elements that carry memories reuniting the past with the present. The message of the politics of the future was passed on through singing, since oral tradition in African languages remained the agency through which Mozambicans shaped the knowledge of another future. In short, the songs are memories of the liberation struggles that continue to carry a political message.

As Nyamnjoh and Fokwang observe (2005, 253), 'much remains to be known about the relationship between music and politics, and on how musicians, politicians and political communities all strive to appropriate each other in different ways and contexts'. The songs broadcast by FRELIMO reflected and circulated images of other social landscapes that were being built. Questioning the arrogance of knowledge promoted by colonial ideology, the nationalist liberation project openly questioned the dehumanization of Africa and of Africans by evoking other histories, other heroes, other allies, and other references. A fuller understanding of how these songs were created and appropriated by whose social forces, and when, extends our appreciation of their associations with other strong, free epistemological elements that radically challenged the colonial reality.

---

9   In Southern Africa contexts, praise poetry refers to popular indigenous oral tradition, celebrating, in a laudatory form, local heroes.

1   **The Sense of Being Part of a Broader Nationalist Struggle**

> I feel very proud of being African
> All my ancestors were -born here
> Legitimate sons of this Kingdom
> Oh my Africa, oye, oye![10]

The Indian Ocean has witnessed, for more than a thousand years, a significant transit of migrants. These movements were shaped by numerous factors that were both geographic and social in origin, and created a different sense of belonging to an interconnected African space. However, the history of this interconnectedness ruptured when the Portuguese navigator, Vasco da Gama, passed through Mozambique on his way to India in the early in sixteenth century. The subsequent Portuguese colonial projects sought to reinterpret the Indian Ocean in line with Western imaginaries.

Initially, the presence of Eastern Africa in Europe was contained in and spread through commodities, legends, and in the embellished first-hand experiences of a few hardy travellers (Santos and Meneses 2006). However, the imperial project took a new turn in Mozambique with the Berlin Conference and the Scramble for Africa in the late nineteenth century.[11] Modern colonial administration was symbolized by the imposition of political control over the territory by a foreign force – in this instance, Portuguese – that sought to incorporate and exploit it. This colonial administration drew a 'new' map of Africa, projecting a European dictum over the continent, constructed according to their knowledge and scientific horizons.

Designated Portuguese East Africa until the 1920s, Mozambique later became a geographic expression and a cultural formation defined according to imperial processes. As Europe established its distinctive identity in relation to rest of the world, this imperial process radically altered the idea of Europe, now synonymous with White Men. This also meant imposing various categories of 'non-Europeanness' and reinforced discourses of 'race (racial discrimination)' to govern and conceptualize human diversity.

According to official Portuguese rhetoric of the time, modern colonialism was not primarily about exploitation, but about exporting civilization. With the superiority of race, Catholic values, science, and capitalist economic know-how,

---

10   Popular revolutionary song of Mozambique.
11   Conveyed by Germany, this conference was attended by the foreign ministers of twelve European powers, of the Ottoman empire and the United States, carrying out lengthy discussion on how to 'scramble' the continent (1894–1895). The conference steered in a period of heightened colonial exploitation and domination by Western powers, while simultaneously eliminating most existing forms of African autonomy and self-governance.

the Portuguese insisted they had a moral obligation to redeem the 'backward heathens' of Africa by transforming them – in a distant future – into progressive citizens, ready to take their place in the modern world. According to this reasoning, the Portuguese were not pilfering land from the people who occupied the territory of Mozambique, nor exploiting local labour. Instead, they presented themselves as self-appointed trustees for supposedly vulnerable natives, who had not yet attained a stage on the evolutionary scale that would allow them to develop or make responsible decisions on their own (Meneses 2011).

The force of colonization has to be analysed in terms of what impact it had on the region by examining how the very meanings inherent in being European and being native were both objectively and subjectively constructed by the colonial experience. Within colonial juridical thought, the concept of Portuguese citizenship identified a specific, socially concrete moral standard: it applied only to white men and women born in Portugal, the 'genteel soul of colonization'.[12] The category of European defined status and determined these relationships.[13] It signified being part of a geopolitical strategy of power in a space dominated by modern eurocentric rationality, which wore the colour white.

Denying the complexity of these identity relationships has been an enduring legacy of the moral, political, economic, and scientific appropriation of the continent by the modern colonial machine. Portuguese and the African languages never met as equals, even under conditions of equality, independence, and democracy. One of first measures of the civilizing agents of Portuguese colonialism was to suppress local languages, together with the culture and the history these languages carried. Civilizing agents considered the languages of the natives to be incomprehensible, and inadequate in terms of expressing any knowledge in the arts and sciences. The inability to speak Portuguese and to produce modern knowledge became a key element that would reaffirm the inferiority of black Africans. European languages became the language of knowledge. As a result of political imposition, this knowledge would be transmitted to the natives according to what the illuminist tradition depicted as an 'assimilation process'. Even more destructive, Portuguese language and history disassociated Mozambique from Africa both politically and intellectually.

The dichotomy of black and white constituted the 'new' relationship imposed upon Mozambique with the modern colonial encounter. Africa was produced

---

12   'Amor e vinho (idílio pagão)', in an article published in the newspaper O Africano, June 11, 1913.

13   An attentive reading of the legal codes reveals an abyssal line separating nationality from citizenship. Under the Estatuto do Indigenato (Statute of Indigenous Populations), the first version from 1926, blacks were natives of Mozambique; they were deprived of citizenship rights and submitted to an extremely repressive disciplinary regime. The Regime of Indigenato was only abolished in 1961 (Meneses 2007).

as an object without a past and outside history. Hegemonic European historiography became the very embodiment of 'world history' through the artifice of exceptionalism that imposed a linear understanding of the world: a progression from ignorance (savagery) to knowledge (civilization). In Mudimbe's words, 'offering and imposing the desirability of its own memory, colonization promises a vision of progressive enrichment to the colonized' (1994, 129). To confront the colonial project would require understanding the revolutionary struggle as a cultural struggle – as a struggle for the right to write Mozambique's own history. It meant rewriting history from the subaltern's perspective, which had been made invisible by colonial power.

Radically challenging the colonial imaginary became central to FRELIMO's political project,[14] which understood the pivotal role of culture in national liberation and nation building (Mondlane 1969; Siliya 2004). This political project required another knowledge to confront the colonial loci of enunciations and to challenge the conceptual structure that guided colonial actions in political, social, and economic domains. There was a widely shared concern that the dominance of eurocentric thought would be an obstacle to the creation of a national awareness in the wake of independence. To be able to claim another history and convey it in other languages, beyond the colonial perspective, would highlight 'the possibility of moving the centre from its location in Europe towards a pluralism of centres, themselves being equally legitimate locations of the human imagination' (Thiong'o 1993, 26).

> Africa, a continent in struggle for its freedom,
> Africa is breaking the chains of the old slavery!
> Africa together fights against colonialism,
> Africa united challenges imperialism
> And we are part of the OAU![15]

Several lyrics celebrated the re-linking of Mozambique to Africa as part of the pan-African project, of which the Organization of African Unity (OAU)[16] was

---

14   It should be emphasized that FRELIMO followed a shared path with other African nationalist movements, for which the struggle against colonial rule was a struggle for culture.

15   Popular revolutionary song of Mozambique.

16   The Organization of African Unity was established on 25 May 1963, to be disbanded in 2002, and replaced by the African Union (AU). Among its main aims OAU defined the promotion of the unity and solidarity of the African states, acting as a collective voice for the African continent; the coordination and intensification of cooperation of African states to achieve a better life for the people of Africa; the defence of the sovereignty, territorial integrity and independence of African states, and the eradication of all forms of colonialism and white minority rule in the continent.

a cornerstone. The struggle for freedom was a struggle against the enslaving chains of knowledge that (re)produced a colonial idea of Africa. Reclaiming pride on its own history and culture, OAU advanced a specific nationalist project for Africa, where the eradication of colonialism in Africa was a cornerstone element. The knowledge and the messages transmitted in these revolutionary songs were not islands in themselves but part of a broader movement to be once again part of Africa, and the rest of the world, in its struggles and victories against colonialism, dependence and violence, for freedom.

2 Beyond the Anti-Colonial Paradigm

In colonial, metropolitan Portugal, the paradigm of the civilizing mission dominated for a while the political discussion on the importance of colonialism. It would also be echoed in struggles carried out by democratizing movements towards a broader and freer social participation, struggling actively against fascism and colonialism (Andrade 1998; Laban 1998). Between 1940 and the 1950s, this paradigm changed dramatically. At a time when Africa's colonies were understood as part of the Portuguese empire, the same territory was envisioned as a stronghold for revolutionary nationalism, following the path of other liberation struggles taking place on the continent.[17] Young people instigated broader discussions on the implications of colonization. They began claiming the right to speak on behalf on their own people and claiming the right to self-determination (Mondlane 1969; Andrade 1998; Craveirinha 2003). This shift can be found in several reflections written during the era, which reveal that the nationalist project was conceived, above all, as an act of culture (Cabral 1974).

The revolutionary songs recorded throughout the struggle reveal a foundational element of the peoples' nationalist movement; at the level of culture and acculturation they denounced relationships between colonialism and local elites (Siliya 2004). The main question was: from what base did African peoples look at the world? The issue was not one of mutual exclusion between Africa and Europe but concerned the source and the starting point for democratic interactions, involving all progressive forces of the world.

Languages are the collective memory, the depository of a people's history. The colonial subjects had their minds systematically (re-)educated in order to

---

17   In Mozambique, as in other contexts, one should not reduce the nationalist struggle to the armed struggle carried out by FRELIMO or COREMO (Mozambique Revolutionary Committee, a movement that was also active in the armed struggle, up to early 1970s). Political prisoners, church members, clandestine freedom fighters, etc. offered fierce opposition to colonialism.

eradicate their cosmovisions and make them forget the knowledges transmitted in their native languages. In making their culture dominant, the colonizer's aim was to suppress the capacity of the colonized to construct an identity independent of colonial references. Since 'an oppressor language inevitably carries racist and negative images of the conquered' (Thiong'o 1993, 52), the return to one's roots, in socio-cultural terms, emerged as a key political motif that was central to the empowerment of the liberation struggle (Cabral 1974).[18] Knowing oneself and one's environment is the basis of grasping the world. Instead of only one centre from which to view the world, the appeal was to allow for a radical re-centring wherein different people in the world would have their own culture and environment. Nyerere, the first president of the neighbouring country of Tanzania, remarked:

> When we were at school we were taught to sing the songs of the Europeans ... It is hard for any man to get much real excitement from dances and music which are not in one's blood (1967, 186).

The struggle itself became a moment of self-consciousness inscribed in a broader reflection on the possibility of multi-sided historical interpretations. This predication on profound political transformation was announced by the wave of political independences that crossed the continent in the 1960s, representing a revolutionary project that aimed to create new societies, free of foreign political domination and exploitation.

If the main political goal of the colonial paradigm was the inclusion of indigenous populations into the realm of Portuguese citizenship,[19] the new nationalist paradigm combined a diversity of concepts and political inspirations, which promised to unlock a diversity of possibilities of change with independence, through the amplification of the meaning of self-determination (Meneses 2007, 2015). This radical challenge translated itself into a series of messages present in the revolutionary repertoire.

> In June 1962, the Mozambican people
> Solemnly decided to open a single war front in the country,
> To struggle against our common enemy.

---

18 In several African contexts, the return, by the colonized, to their socio-cultural roots meant the return to other epistemes (re-)acquired through the nationalist struggles. This also symbolized the end of the colonial attempt to produce modern scientific knowledge as the only valid episteme.

19 That is, to transform them, in a distant future, into Portuguese citizens, having acquired the cultural skills embodied in the meaning of being Portuguese.

> Long live to FRELIMO,
> Long live to our people,
> Long live to our liberating army,
> Long live to self-determination![20]

These lyrics contrast the colonial project of Mozambique, as part of the Portuguese empire, with the idea of Mozambique struggling for the right to affirm its own future as a nation,[21] in a political message circulated by FRELIMO long before independence.

For FRELIMO, as well for the various democratic and nationalist opposition groups inside Mozambique (Souto 2007), (re)conquering the ability to tell their own history – and thus the possibility of constructing an image and an identity outside the concept of 'being Portuguese' – required a critical dialogue about the roots of contemporary representations. This critical dialogue questioned the geographies and semantics associated with concepts that insisted upon locating Africa far behind others in terms of 'progress and civilization'.

From this perspective, the liberation movement represented the most effective means by which to create unity from the various identities, thus leading a cohesive struggle against external enemies (such as colonialism, capitalism) and internal enemies (such as the local bourgeoisie, racism, and tribalism) in order to free world cultures from the restrictions of exploitation (Frelimo 1977, 134–142, 159–161, 178–179). FRELIMO sought to ground the project for a new, decolonized Mozambique in terms of the liberation of the oppressed masses' creative potential which would overcome and transform their conditions of unfreedom.

> The unity of our people,
> Forged in struggle and in torture,
> Is a safe and sound victory,
> The beginning of a new world.
> Long Live to FRELIMO, the vanguard
> Of all Mozambican people,
> Long Live to Mozambique that has given proof
> Of bravery to attain victory.

---

20 Popular revolutionary song of Mozambique.
21 Within FRELIMO, the promise of diversity (as the possibility of self-definition) within the realm of the national project, has always been a very sensitive political topic. See Cabrita (2000), Igreja (2010).

We have defeated colonialism,
We will defeat imperialism!
Our motherland will be the grave
Of capitalism and exploitation.

We are united with the world,
That is struggling against bourgeoisie,
For the power that serves the people,
Workers and Labourers.[22]

The nation-building vision pursued by FRELIMO included the political adoption of an official version of the history of Mozambique. This project was grounded in a set of collective memories of both recent and distant colonial pasts (FRELIMO 1974). In a paper published in 1986, Bragança and Depelchin highlighted the risks of a populist and acritical reading of the liberation struggle:

> One of the most fundamental problems of the existing history of FRELIMO comes ... above all, from the unquestionable manner in which this knowledge is used. The fact that the armed struggle resulted in independence in 1975 reinforced the view of the correctness of the armed struggle thereby leading to an implicit and silent consensus concerning the real causes of the victory of independence (1986, 165).

Furthermore, in alerting people to the perils of aligning this struggle with FRELIMO's history, they set the tone for scholars engaging in discussions about the role of history in the process of building a national political memory, and argued in favor of retaining complexity when analysing the history of the country's national liberation.

Oblivious to these alerts, leading politicians of FRELIMO opted for a different approach, co-opting a national historical narrative. This project aimed to invent a single past in order to create 'Mozambicans' who were united in a persistent struggle against a common enemy, without fractures and without differences (Meneses 2011).

3   Nationalist Songs and the National Project

FRELIMO carried out a complex political strategy in seeking to deal with the ambivalent and hybrid identities that constituted the intricate colonial legacy.

---

22   Popular revolutionary song of Mozambique.

As indicated above, Frelimo's politics of memory was founded upon the idea of 'not forgetting the time that has passed'. However, it concealed the different experiences and projects that were contained by the time-space unit of 'national liberation', in which they were subsumed into a single ideological standpoint: the nationalist experience of the liberation struggle.

Frelimo (1977) instated a project of radical social change – the Mozambican revolution – rather than a mere substitution of the colonial administration by local political elites.[23] The epitome of the nationalist project was the nationalist guerrilla, the inspiration for the 'New Man' and the prototype of the new Mozambican citizen. The new man was the revolutionary who identified with the people; he was a product of liberated areas, whose purity was filtered by the modern nationalism defined by FRELIMO (Meneses 2007). The liberated areas and the very struggle for liberation were understood as laboratories in which to foster counter-hegemonic spaces of resistance and affirmation of other knowledges, and a different political utopia. In this project, the diversity of memories of past nationalist struggles, or the multiplicity of on-going cultural and political struggles that would challenge the dominant references, could barely find a place (Coelho 2010).

FRELIMO will win,
FRELIMO will be the victor,
In the struggle for freedom,
FRELIMO will triumph.

Mozambique will win,
Mozambique will be the victor,
In the struggle for freedom,
Mozambique will triumph.

Africa will win,
Africa will be the victor,
In the struggle for freedom,
Africa will triumph.[24]

---

23 'Some Mozambicans conceived independence as a mere change of people in terms of the administration: expelling the Portuguese to replace them with Mozambicans, keeping intact the political and administrative colonial machine. Exploitation, oppression, and all negative effects of the colonial system would remain in place, now to be carried out by Mozambicans'. *Voz da Revolução* 5, June 1970.

24 FRELIMO anthem.

As outlined above, the nationalist paradigm required a radical vision of the new nation, and throughout the struggle, FRELIMO slowly changed its nature to accommodate this. From a movement that accumulated multiple political perspectives, it grew into a modern nationalist party by the end of the 1960s. The movement had the advantage of being an organization carrying an armed struggle under a unified leadership. The ideological project envisioned a Mozambique as a new independent nation, a fundamental part of this project. The goal was to develop a new sense of belonging based upon the colonial project that had formed the territory of Mozambique in the late nineteenth century. FRELIMO was to follow the modern (and violent in its very origins) project of building a nation-state, exercising the propensity to centralize political power through the severe exercise of economic, administrative, and historical unification. It sought to transform the presence of multiple cultural regimes into a linear sequence of historical events and policies in the name of a united front of the 'people' of Mozambique (Meneses 2007).

> We are the sons and daughters of the people,
> We are fighting led by FRELIMO.[25]

FRELIMO sought to inculcate a monolithic idea of a modern Mozambique through the lyrics of these popular revolutionary songs. The various groups that inhabited Mozambique knew little about each other, but it was important to create a sense of national unity. Thus, the imposition of a single national project over a landscape of cultural diversity restricted the potential for diversity, although the struggle for self-determination had embodied multiple cultural struggles. The construction of FRELIMO as the sole political leader of the only legitimate emancipatory struggle led other leaders and nationalist struggles to be presented as reactionary elements,[26] outside the pantheon of 'national, official memory'. These events reduced the complex history of the country's anti-colonial and nationalist struggles from the 1950s through the 1970s to a narrative of a single, unified struggle.[27]

---

25   Popular revolutionary song of Mozambique.
26   Over recent years, multiple biographies have focused on the nationalist struggle in Mozambique; they have shed new light on the intricacies of this project. See, for example, Ncomo (2003), Veloso (2007), Mboa (2009), Vieira (2010), Chissano (2011), as well as interviews published by Laban (1998).
27   FRELIMO managed to accomplish this project by channelling multiple moments and actors of the nationalist struggle into a single narrative of liberation: 'FRELIMO is the expression of people's and Mozambique's will to be free' (FRELIMO 1977, 122). The second

The tension between the modern territorial representation of Mozambique claimed in maps, legislation, and histories that were produced by the colonizers, and the successive (re-)constructions of the various identities in the geo-cultural territory identifiable as modern-day Mozambique has translated into a cohabitation of multiple senses of belonging (Santos and Meneses 2006). This cohabitation, never peaceful (even when interpreted as such by those in power), has involved little dialogue. This reality manifests itself in successive reconfigurations of conflicting identities, which have in turn generated other presuppositions and concepts. These have defined multiple geo-cultural places that came to be identified as Mozambique, but in which other peoples, and other cultural, linguistic, and religious archives were also present. The long duration of history requires some analytical breadth when focusing on the specificity and the diversity that comprises Mozambique.

4   The Making of Heroes: Founders of the Nation?[28]

One means by which to crystallize the abstract idea of nation into a solid symbol lies in the creation of heroes. Worshipping a hero can establish national self-identification, rallying a heterogeneous community (the subjugated colonial subjects) into a unified national citizenry. In this sense, heroes, together with anti-heroes, are a mechanism by which to produce political memories and a source of national history. As mentioned above, the contemporary history of Mozambique is a project of memory that is held hostage and propelled by Frelimo, the party in power. At its core lies the memory of the struggle for national liberation whose main fallen leaders became national heroes. The first heroes were guerrilla fighters, and with independence this icon was bound to that of senior politicians, projected as flawless in their credentials as freedom fighters.

The naming of heroes reflects FRELIMO's need to appeal to a common sense of belonging across Mozambique. For a while, the hero of the unitary nationalist popular movement was the collective image of the people, made flesh in the figure of FRELIMO. Praise for the leading role of the movement was decisive in reinforcing the party's authority. After all, the struggle was made up of 'sons of the people', integrated into the liberation movement, who challenged their oppressors in arms and fought for their liberation.

---

part of the project resulted in the co-optation of the nationalist struggle by Frelimo (i.e., the appropriation by a contemporary political party of the nationalist struggle).

28   This topic is also addressed in Bjørn Enge Bertelsen's chapter, in this volume.

We are the sons of the people; we are the sons of the people!
We have struggled for national liberation!
Our people has lived five centuries of slavery,
But our people never was submissive,
Today, the Mozambican people headed by FRELIMO struggles united.[29]

5   Challenging the Oppressors

As the liberation war unfolded, heroes were branded, entering the narrative of
the nationalist struggle. The construction of this national project rested upon
the politicization of past and current struggles, which was deepened through
the process of creating a collective political memory. The forming of membership to this 'imagined community' (Anderson 1983) was founded upon the
dichotomization of spaces between liberated areas controlled by FRELIMO,
and the colonial territory, populated by suspicions of collaboration. Because
a significant part of the territory of Mozambique remained mostly under
Portuguese control, it was necessary to 'purify' the country from all negative,
collaborating elements perceived as traitors to the cause of self-determination
(Meneses 2016). In the first years of independence, the icon of the 'New Man'
was created upon the figure of the revolutionary fighter: he 'produced and
struggled for the creation of the new radically distinct independent Mozambique, engaged with the struggle for world liberation from oppression.'[30]

Thus, the popular movement shifted to songs that glorified the heroes now
transformed into myth. FRELIMO sought to bridge fragmented constituencies
by valorising such heroes,[31] whose identification acted as a catalyst for the
struggle, offering a vision of a ready-to-be-born nation.

Let's go, let's go Mozambicans!
Let's sing the praises of Mondlane,
Dead for the freedom of our Mozambique.

Your blood, Father Mondlane,
Irrigates Mozambique, and the people struggling to harvest

---

29   Popular revolutionary song of Mozambique.
30   Popular revolutionary song. The 'New Man' would be created by cutting the links to the
      colonial, traditional and bourgeois past. FRELIMO's ideological project conceived the
      'new man' as the vanguard citizen – example of the success of its own proposed modern-
      izing project. On the topic of the creation of the 'new man', see Vieira (1978).
31   This goal would be continued after independence.

269

Freedom, bread and peace
Your example guides us,
Beaming our footsteps:
To serve the People.[32]

The 1969 assassination of Eduardo Mondlane, FRELIMO's first president, became a central point of reference in the revolutionary ensemble of songs. Informal choirs of freedom fighters would praise his dedication and his courage in various languages. The remembrance of past heroes was seen as being imperative in the 'freeing' of other people outside the scope of colonial historiography.

In addition to the struggle, heroes were created out of comrades in arms as a form of recognition that opposed class, ethnic, racial, or religious differentiations. The only exception was gender: the strategic recognition of heroines reinforced another perspective on the involvement and the role of women in the struggle. This is reflected in a number of songs praising Josina Machel, who came to symbolize the 'new woman' in such songs as the hymn of Mozambican women (which is still sung today).[33] Other songs embodied admiration of her character and her dedication to the nationalist cause, as evident in the following lines:

Today is the day
We remember our comrade Josina,
Our restless combatant.[34]

The selection and recognition of and heroines is an exercise in national self-identification when the idea of a nation is a little too abstract to command human allegiance readily. To create the idea of a nation FRELIMO had to personify it (Africa and Mozambique), as suffering collective bodies; national heroes and heroines provided an idea of the nation in human form. Through this process, FRELIMO became the 'voice' of the people's collective desires, assuming the right to morally determine right from wrong behaviours.

6   The Dangers of Heroism: Enemies, Anti-Heroes, and Traitors

The songs thus far reproduced show that FRELIMO, conceived ideologically as a movement powered by the people, was informed by the consciousness of

32   Popular revolutionary song of Mozambique.
33   April 7, the day Josina Machel died, was established, with Mozambique's independence, as a formal holiday, to commemorate the day of Mozambican women (instead of March 8, as in many countries of the world).
34   Popular revolutionary song of Mozambique.

a collective who felt oppressed. At the same time, the denouncing of ethnic, racial, or tribal schisms in FRELIMO, which occurred in the late 1960s (Frelimo 1977; Peixoto and Meneses 2013), was strongly criticized in the revolutionary songs. These songs were powerful rhetorical tools for transmitting the idea of a revolutionary Mozambique made up of a united people allied in their struggle with the progressive forces of the world.

Describing itself as a movement powered by the people, FRELIMO sought to direct its energies and anger towards the symbols of the Portuguese colonial state rather than another racial or ethnic group. The guerrillas and supporters of the anti-colonial struggle identified the Portuguese army and those associated with it as their enemy, as the Portuguese army was the vehicle of colonialism. Portugal's war effort on three fronts,[35] especially when Portuguese soldiers increasingly perceived the colonial war as absurd, took a toll on a regime that was being eroded anyway.[36] The songs mocked the top military and political Portuguese leaders as the nationalist struggle spread throughout Mozambique 'like a bushfire'.

> Caetano[37] careless, you are getting worse with your adventures,
> Even the chicken already knows you!
> You [Portuguese] have invaded Guinea Conakry, invaded Zambia and Tanzania
> And everywhere people speak badly about you.
> In all the bewilderment, your name pops out!
> You are no different from the hyena,
> And you are going to see the results of your acts.[38]

The vision of belonging and of nationalist aspirations corresponded with the idea of a unified people, invincible and victorious over its enemies:

> Attention, today, now!
> Enemies of Mozambique, attention!

---

35   Angola, Guinea-Bissau, and Mozambique.
36   While Portugal planned the *Nó Górdio* (Gordian Knot) military operation as the *coup de grâce* against FRELIMO, it had the opposite effect: the nationalist struggle spread throughout the country and reached central Mozambique by early 1972. Guerrilla attacks were carried out close to Beira, the second largest city in January 1974 (Couto 2011).
37   Marcelo Caetano, Head of the Council of Ministers of colonial-fascist Portugal from 1968 to 1974.
38   Popular revolutionary song of Mozambique.

> With Samora,[39]
> We are prepared to fight,
> To carry out our war,
> In Cabo Delgado, in Niassa...[40]

Assumed as a people's movement, FRELIMO sought to peel away fears of ethnic, religious, class, racial and gender divisions, proposing a broad front against colonialism, which was seen as the source of oppression.

> Forward oppressed people,
> Forward colonized people,
> Forward all; let's stand up,
> Forward, for peace – unite!

> We, the struggling people,
> Are linking the treads of a thousand struggles,
> Our decision towards Uhuru,[41]
> Freedom, independence.[42]

The songs highlight a pan-African sensibility that transcends the physical boundaries imposed by colonial geography, suggesting that the liberation struggle in Mozambique in many ways mirrored such heroism throughout Africa. The lyrics also reveal a broader dimension to this struggle. As mentioned earlier, they declare solidarity of the people's movement in Mozambique with other marginalized and oppressed peoples across the world, appealing for new geographies of proximity.

The Portuguese and several African leaders manipulated the historical construction of tribalism and racism in the context of an armed nationalist struggle against a colonial system. For many who feared the future the option was to replace the Portuguese (that is, the whites) without challenging the power structure created by colonialism. For FRELIMO,[43] the enemy was identified as

---

39   Samora Machel replaced Mondlane as leader of FRELIMO, after challenging debates over the nature of the struggle. He later became the first president of independent Mozambique. He was killed in a plane crash in 1986, the circumstances of which are still unclear today.

40   Popular revolutionary song of Mozambique.

41   Uhuru means freedom in Kiswahili.

42   Popular revolutionary song of Mozambique.

43   And other allied nationalist movements, such as the MPLA in Angola and the PAIGC, in Guinea Bissau and Cape Vert.

the colonial-capitalist system, and not a racial group. This was echoed in constant reprimands against discrimination in all its forms, and was associated with the denunciation of all political and military leaders who dared to challenge the monolithic political project of the movement: 'we were not struggling to substitute the whites by blacks' (Siliya 2004, 333–334).

> FRELIMO is endless, that is, indestructible,
> Is endless FRELIMO, is endless!
>
> Simango is reactionary,
> Reactionary Simango, he is a reactionary!
>
> Nkavandame[44] has betrayed us,
> Traitor is Nkavandame, he is a traitor!
>
> Frelimo is endless, that is, indestructible,
> Is endless FRELIMO, is endless![45]

Today, the grand narrative generated by the nationalist struggle remains the most visible form of opposition to narratives generated by the colonizers. FRELIMO nationalist project was based on the exposure of colonialism and its vices (capitalist exploitation, forced labour, discrimination, subalternization, concealing of knowledges, and oppression, gender discrimination, etc.) as the foundational material of a national project for the future. In addition to identifying national heroes, another important element in creating a national consciousness was the creation of anti-heroes as examples of those who had no place in the people's national project. From the colonial past to the modern national ideal, this narrative included anticipated futures and reconstructed pasts, with no room to accommodate other political aspirations from the people.

The idea of a Mozambique for Mozambicans emerged, in the aftermath of the armed struggle, as an organically local project that would create what came to be designated as Mozambicanness. The country's call for equality dramatically erased the differences that constituted its social fabric. At the same time, it generated profound contradictions, synonymous with continuities of past histories, practices, and political mechanisms. On the one hand, denouncing schisms in the nationalist struggle obscured the root causes of economic,

---

44 Lázaro Nkavandame, a makonde, organized a cooperative movement in northern Mozambique. Later on, he broke with FRELIMO's leadership on aspects related to the economic options in independent Mozambique, and surrendered to the Portuguese.

45 Popular revolutionary song of Mozambique.

political, and social exploitation and, on the other, it also demonstrated the complexity that constitutes the sense of national belonging that FRELIMO's national project entailed (Meneses 2007).

7   Can We Really Forget the Past?

The revolutionary repertoire touches upon a controversial question – the relationship between aesthetics and society. If the songs reflect an ambition for 'another' presence in Africa, and for Mozambique as an independent country, they also exhibit how aesthetic preferences are shaped or even determined by a certain social structure and a particular ideological perspective. As Nyairo and Ogude observe, 'music is a travelling text whose multiple meanings are contingent upon the politics of its production and consumption' (2005, 226). Musical texts are generated by and generate layered knowledges; they are entwined in the politics of production in the way audiences are incorporated, and in how audiences receive them. Since music is one of Africa's most salient forms of popular art, it forms a trenchant political site (Allen 2004, 1–3).

The intersection of music and politics demonstrates the problematic nature of FRELIMO's mode of thinking. Through the themes, concerns, and political messages of the revolutionary songs, one attends to the issues and events that constitute the movement's experiences. Sung in different languages, the revolutionary repertoire reveals words woven into the soundtrack of events, moments, and experiences. These songs' bequest is a new Mozambique, breaking away from the earlier Mozambique constructed by colonialism, riven by separate ethnic and racialized identities. The songs attest to the multiple and fluid identities that sought to define a future, postcolonial country.

A question remains: can lyrics (as a form of oral literature) be equated with historiography, adding sources to the historical record? These songs sought to produce other political references, gracing other state functions, both public and private. In this sense, the revolutionary songs reflect a specific historical discourse while at the same time they sought to reinscribe and rewrite the very historical context they were located within.

These various sources of knowledge about the revolutionary liberation in Mozambique aim to subvert the ideology that represents one officially written version of history more reliably than others. As another form of belief/ power structure, this ideological hierarchy is revealed to be merely one of several ways to ascertain historical truth in the production of history. These differences, although often silenced to a broader public, reflect distinct political interpretations of what being Mozambican means; and these silences are impossible to override.

The revolutionary songs asserted the people's right to engage in the democratic process of (re)building their identity. They were heard and played by people who would sing of their experiences, loudly repeating FRELIMO's political goals. This practice generated another version of history that reinvigorated the knowledges of the people. Such other ways of making history reflected a position of being in history as full subjects, and integrated into broader networks that project and are presupposed by the image of a collective, and the vision of the new nation.

The popular culture that FRELIMO struggled to impose (Silyia 2004) was not simply a matter of how Mozambicans aimed to see themselves, or even how FRELIMO conceived itself as the leading political force. It aimed to shape Mozambique's identity and therefore the way others read and understood their country. At the same time, these songs anticipated the potential risk of a future authoritarian leadership, which of course is what FRELIMO's single-party state was to develop into in the first decades of independent Mozambique (Meneses 2007, 2011).

Over the last two decades, a growing number of intellectuals have challenged Frelimo's efforts to monopolize the production of national history; they have done so through debating how a community[46] can heal its social wounds by facing its suppressed and almost forgotten pasts (Khosa 1990; Ncomo 2003). As Fabian convincingly agues, however, the freedom that the lyrics of the revolutionary songs generate are 'a quality of the process of human self-realization; freedom cannot be anything but contestatory and discontinuous or precarious' (1998, 21). Groups have challenged FRELIMO's attempt to claim ownership over processes of making history using the same music. The imposition of a single narrative about Mozambique's past has limited the country's ability to negotiate that past, and thus has not contributed to national reconciliation (Meneses 2011, 2015). Active steps towards reconciliation need to include a public debate and the social recognition of suffering, for the loud silences of the recent past may only be broken by including multiple voices and memories.

Overburdened by its role in carrying a sense victory for the subjugated, independence was a moment in Mozambique when various 'pasts' were silenced; it was a transition that did not necessarily entail decolonization (Bragança 1986). However, this idealized project of transition would eventually have to face the reality of multiple conflicts and antagonisms (Meneses 2012). Several writers have sought to expose questions suppressed by the 'ideality' embodied by the moment

---

46   Mozambique has endured several processes that strained the new nation, including war
      against Rhodesia (now Zimbabwe), and apartheid South Africa, and an internal civil war
      that ended in 1992 (although skirmishes, some of them rather violent, have been going on
      since them).

of independence, and have done so by representing a world marked by a series of disillusionments and violence (Khosa 1990; Laban 1998; Craveirinha 2004).

The power of popular music as political education cannot be denied. It provides an idiom and harnesses the prevalent mood for change and rebirth in the nation. Mozambique's more recent history shows how the independent state enforced a policy of amnesia and silence that eventually threatened the real decolonization process, because it suppressed memories of the processes by which the country's identity was created.[47]

Decolonization is a much wider concept than the mere winning of independence or the transfer of powers. The former focuses on a nationalist, anti-colonial struggle, whereas the latter foregrounds negotiations and planning among colonial officials and colonized elites. But decolonization also entails the exploration of dreams, the analysis of struggles, compromises, pledges, and achievements, and the rethinking of basic ideals (Sheppard 2006). Trapped in the ideality of its independence, Mozambique was subsumed by the nationalist meta-narratives of the nation's triumphal takeover. It insisted upon valorising a single narrative (including but not limited to the cult of heroes) while leaving aside the diversity of the historical processes that had affected the majority of the people.

Mozambique's real decolonization cannot be achieved by suppressing the past. In this sense, Songs are travelling texts that will invariably have multiple meanings, reaching wide audiences; they collapse simplistic ideological boundaries often used to describe difference in African politics, such as those of the rulers and the ruled. In one of his best-known records (2007), Azagaia – a well-known Mozambican rapper – intones:

I told you
That the history that you study has lies,
That your brain is washed by each grade you obtain,
That the revolution was not just made with songs and vivas,
That there were treasons, tortures and hidden histories...[48]

---

47   Political independence, at least in Africa, did not mean the end of colonialism. Postcolonial societies are based on development regimes constructed under colonial rule, which inherited the colonial inclination to excise politics from economic and administrative practice. The pre-eminent role of formal law in defining citizenship after independence draws attention to the tension resulting from the persistence of a eurocentric definition of the modern state. The contradiction between multiple political and cultural identities and realities, and the singular definition of citizenship associated with the modern state, a legacy of the colonial infrastructure of representation, continues to be a reality in contemporary Mozambique (Meneses 2012, 2015).

48   Song 'The Lies of the Truth', available at http://www.youtube.com/watch?v=b9IwDjrUNTE &feature=related accessed on July 2nd 2010.

Songs are, indeed, 'one of the fundamental mechanisms through which people indicate what they personally enjoy, approve of, identify with, recognize as true or acknowledge as ethically appropriate' (Allen 2004, 4). As such, revolutionary music both documents history and is itself history.

References

Allen, Lara. 2004. Music and Politics in Africa. *Social Dynamics* 30 (2): 1–19.

Anderson, Benedict. 1983. *Imagined Communities: Reflections on the origin and spread of nationalism*. London: Verso.

Andrade, Mário Pinto. 1998. *Origens do Nacionalismo Africano: Continuidade e rutura nos movimentos unitários emergentes da luta contra a dominação colonial Portuguesa, 1911–1961*. Lisbon: Dom Quixote.

Basto, Benedita. 2012. 'Quem é escrito?' Revolução, alteridade, experiências de reescrita e história conectada no contexto da guerra colonial e de libertação em Moçambique. *Via Atlântica*, 21: 75–92.

Bohlman, Philip B. 2004. *The Music of European Nationalism: Cultural identity and modern history*. Santa Barbara: ABC-CLIO.

Bragança, Aquino. 1986. Independência sem Descolonização: A transferência do poder em Moçambique, 1974–1975. *Estudos Moçambicanos* 5/6: 7–28.

Bragança, Aquino, and Jacques Depelchin. 1986. From the Idealization of Frelimo to the Understanding of the Recent History of Mozambique. *African Journal of Political Economy* 1 (1): 162–180.

Cabral, Amílcar. 1974. *Return to the Source*. New York: Monthly Review Press.

Cabrita, João M. 2000. *Mozambique: The tortuous road to democracy*. New York: Palgrave.

Chissano, Joaquim Alberto. 2011. *Vidas, Lugares e Tempos*. Maputo: Texto Editores.

Coelho, João Paulo Borges. 2010. Memory, History, Fiction: A note on the politics of the past in Mozambique. Paper presented at the Journées d'étude 'Il était une fois les indépendances africaines ... La fin des empires?' EHESS, Paris, October 21 to October 22.

Coplan, David. 1997. Eloquent Knowledge: Lesotho migrants' songs and the anthropology of experience. In *Readings in African Popular Culture*, ed. Karin Barber, 29–40. Oxford: James Currey.

Couto, Fernando. 2011. *Moçambique 1974: O fim do império e o nascimento da nação*. Lisbon: Caminho.

Craveirinha, José. 2003. *Poemas de Prisão*. Maputo: Ndjira.

Craveirinha, José. 2004. Saborosas Tanjarinas d'Inhambane. In *Nunca Mais é Sábado: antologia de poesia Moçambicana*, ed. Nelson Saúte, 103–106. Lisbon: Dom Quixote.

Fabian, Johannes. 1996. *Remembering the Present: Painting and popular history in Zaire*. Berkeley: University of California Press.

Fabian, Johannes. 1998. *Moments of Freedom: Anthropology and popular culture*. Charlottesville, VA: University Press of Virginia.

Fanon, Frantz. 1963. *The Wretched of the Earth*. New York: Grove.

Filipe, Eléusio. 2012. 'Where are the Mozambican Musicians?' Music, Marrabenta, and National Identity in Lourenço Marques, Mozambique, 1950s–1975. PhD thesis, University of Minnesota.

First, Ruth. 1983. *Black Gold: the Mozambican miner, proletarian and peasant*. Brighton, Harvest.

FRELIMO. 1974. *História de Moçambique*. Oporto: Afrontamento.

Frelimo. 1977. *O Processo Revolucionário da Guerra Popular de Libertação*. Maputo: Edição do Departamento do Trabalho Ideológico da Frelimo.

Igreja, Victor. 2010. Frelimo's Political Ruling Through Violence and Memory in Postcolonial Mozambique. *Journal of Southern African Studies* 36 (4): 781–799.

Israel, Paolo. 2009. Utopia Live: singing the Mozambican struggle for national liberation. *Kronos: Southern African Histories* 35: 98–141.

Khosa, Ungulani Ba Ka. 1990. *Ualalapi*. Lisbon: Caminho.

Laban, Michel, ed. 1998. *Moçambique: Encontro com escritores*. 3 vols. Oporto: Fundação Eng. António de Almeida.

Longwe, Sara, and Roy Clark. 1998. *Woman, Know your Place: the patriarchal message in Zambian popular song*. Lusaka, Zambia: ZARD.

Mboa, Matias. 2009. *Memórias da Luta Clandestina*. Maputo: Marimbique.

Mendonça, Fátima. 1988. *Mozambican Literature: from assimilation to liberation*. Stockholm: The Culture House.

Meneses, Maria Paula. 2007. Os Espaços Criados pelas Palavras: Racismos, etnicidades e o encontro colonial. In *Formação de Professores e a Questão Racial: Uma visão além das fronteiras*, ed. Nilma Gomes, 55–76. Belo Horizonte: Autêntica Editora.

Meneses, Maria Paula. 2011. Images outside the Mirror? Mozambique and Portugal in world history. *Human Architecture* 10 (1): 121–136.

Meneses, Maria Paula. 2012. Powers, rights and citizenship: the 'return' of the traditional authorities in Mozambique. In *African Perspectives on Tradition and Justice*, ed. Tom Bennett et al., 67–94. Cambridge: Intersentia.

Meneses, Maria Paula. 2015. Xiconhoca, o inimigo: Narrativas de violência sobre a construção da nação em Moçambique. *Revista Crítica de Cências Sociais* 106: 9–52.

Meneses, Maria Paula. 2016. Hidden Processes of Reconciliation in Mozambique: the entangled histories of Truth-seeking Commissions held between 1975 and 1982. *Africa Development* 41 (4): 153–180.

Mignolo, Walter D. 2007. Delinking: the rhetoric of modernity, the logic of coloniality and the grammar of de-coloniality. *Cultural Studies* 21 (2/3): 449–514.

Mondlane, Eduardo. 1969. *Struggle for Mozambique*. London: Harmondsworth.

Morman, Marissa. 2008. *Intonation: A social history of music and nation in Luanda, Angola, from 1945 to recent times*. Athens, OH: Ohio University Press.

Mudimbe, Valentin Y. 1994. *The Idea of Africa*. Bloomington, IN: Indiana University Press.

Ncomo, Barnabé Lucas. 2003. *Uria Simango: Um homem, uma causa*. Maputo: Edições Novafrica.

Nyairo, Joyce, and James Ogude. 2005. Popular Music, Popular Politics: unbwogable and the idioms of freedom in Kenyan popular music. *African Affairs* 104 (415): 225–249.

Nyamnjoh, Francis B., and Jude Fokwang. 2005. Entertaining Repression: music and politics in postcolonial Cameroon. *African Affairs* 104 (415): 251–274.

Nyerere, Julius. 1967. *Freedom and Unity/Uhuru na Umoja*. London: Oxford University Press.

Peixoto, Carolina Barros Tavares, and Maria Paula Meneses. 2013. Domingos Arouca: um percurso de militância nacionalista em Moçambique. *Revista Topoi*, 14 (26): 86–104.

Penvenne, Jeanne. 2005. Settling against the Tide: the layered contradictions of twentieth century Portuguese settlement in Mozambique. In *Settler Colonialism in the Twentieth Century*, eds Caroline Elkins, and Susan Pedersen, 79–94. New York: Routledge.

Penvenne, Jeanne, and Bento Sitoe. 2000. Power, Poets and the People: Mozambican voices interpreting history. *Social Dynamics* 26 (2): 55–86.

Pongweni, Alec J.C. 1997. The Chimurenga Songs of the Zimbabwean War of Liberation. In *Readings in African Popular Culture*, ed. Karin Barber, 63–72. Oxford: James Currey.

Santos, Boaventura de Sousa. 2007. Beyond Abyssal Thinking: from global lines to ecology of knowledges. *Review Fernand Braudel Center* 30 (1): 45–89.

Santos, Boaventura de Sousa, and Maria Paula Meneses. 2006. Identidades, colonizadores e colonizadores: Portugal e Moçambique. Project report POCTI/41280/SOC/2001. Coimbra, Portugal: CES.

Sheppard, Todd. 2006. *The Invention of Decolonization: the Algerian war and the remaking of France*. Ithaca, NY: Cornell University Press.

Siliya, Carlos. 2004. The Artistic and Cultural Production during the Liberation Struggle. In *11° Congresso sobre a Luta de Libertação Nacional*, ed. Lourenço do Rosário, 332–341. Maputo: Instituto Superior Politécnico Universitário and Ministério para os Assuntos dos Antigos Combatentes.

Souto, Amélia Neves. 2007. *Caetano e o Ocaso do Império*. Oporto: Afrontamento.

Thiong'o, Ngugi wa. 1993. *Moving the Centre: The struggle for cultural freedoms*. Nairobi: East African Educational Publishers.

Vail, Leroy, and Landeg White. 1991. *Power and the Praise Poem: Southern African voices in history*. London: James Currey.

Veloso, Jacinto. 2007. *Memórias em Voo Rasante*. Maputo: JVCI.

Vieira, Sérgio. 1978. O Homem Novo É um Processo. *Revista Tempo* 398: 27–38.

Vieira, Sérgio. 2010. *Participei, por isso Testemunho*. Maputo: Ndjira.

Wolf, Eric. 1982. *Europe and the People without History*. Berkeley: University of California Press.

CHAPTER 13

Scientific Research and Epistemological Violence

José Luis Cabaço

We are currently going through a difficult period in the field of social and human sciences, in which the mercantilism of knowledge has limited our ability to intervene innovatively. Michael Neocosmos, a renowned scholar working in South Africa, asserts that contemporary social science tends to focus on what already exists and seems unable to propose alternatives (Neocosmos 2009). This affirmation reflects the anguish of those who live at the core of the epistemological violence that characterizes the coloniality of knowledge.

However, there are encouraging signals on the horizon: mainly from the 1990s onwards, African Studies has expanded; there has been an increase in the quantity and quality of knowledge produced by African social scientists; and, above all, the in-depth problematization of epistemological questions concerning African Studies has developed to involve social scientists and scholars from different latitudes. This means, on the one hand, and regardless of diverse motivations, that concern for and sensibility towards the continent's problems is growing in various parts of the world. On the other, it is significant that African scholars seem determined to find their own path in order to know their own realities through dialogue amongst themselves and through living with the realities of the continent; they are taking part in the international debate and proposing options based on diverse accounts and experiences. Throughout the last few years, the amount of research has increased and the analyses put forward have become progressively richer – a trend also seen in the increase in works reflecting in depth on African issues. A sensibility towards the complexity and the specificities of our social realities has been growing within social science. These facts are undoubtedly encouraging.

Hence, the purpose of this chapter is to bring into this debate on Africa and Mozambique some of the concerns of a growing number of Mozambicans who work in this field of social and human sciences. Amongst these concerns, I seek to highlight the relevance of the research integrated into so-called development projects within the country, its impact on social operators and researchers, and its role in the formation of the dominant thinking in this area. Mozambique has been impoverished by a violent and brutal military conflict that evolved into a protracted civil war, which led to the complete destruction of the country's economy as well as to the deterioration of its social tissue.

These facts are at the basis of Mozambique's classification as the poorest country in the world throughout the first half of the 1990s.

In the aftermath of the signing of the Peace Agreement (Acordo Geral de Paz)[1] in 1992, the progress achieved in terms of both socio-political stability and economic recovery triggered recognition and sympathy among the international community. This international recognition turned Mozambique into a success story and a privileged partner. To the donor community, we became an example to follow in an Africa that was fragile due to the lack of qualified professionals and its infrastructural debility: Africa's current image is that of a continent dilacerated by coup d'états, poor governance, corruption, famine, pandemics and, particularly in the last decades, dominated by ethnic and religious conflicts.

The actions of the Mozambican government have been producing concrete results: macroeconomic indicators are positive; multiparty elections have taken place as regularly as defined by the constitution; absolute poverty has decreased; infrastructure has improved; the electricity distribution network is now serving new regions across the country; sanitary assistance has developed; and the school network has expanded, despite disturbing quality problems. In addition, the press has the liberty to criticize institutions. There is a remarkable effort in progress to turn Mozambique into a powerful regional energetic centre – a process that includes gas and coal beds being explored, the construction of another important hydroelectric production unit, and the initiation of oil prospecting. Whoever has travelled to Mozambique throughout the years following the civil war could not fail to notice the transformations that have occurred in an environment of socio-political pacification and normalization of the population's lives.

Nevertheless, we should not ignore the impressive differences – some still markedly colonial – that persist in economic, social, and political relations, as well as in the life conditions of Mozambicans. Within the country, distinct realities coexist, sometimes in the same physical space, and these refer, for example, to the nature of the businesses in operation, patterns of comfort and consumption, the use of technology, forms of social organization, cultural and religious practices, and processes of democratic participation.

However, material achievements have turned Mozambique into a 'success story'. Consequently, the country has benefited from the international community's privileged support through budget financing and development programs. Following the end of the civil war in 1992, the cooperation programs increased, specialized agencies and NGOs proliferated, the number of projects

---

1   See introduction to this volume.

expanded, and the number of expatriates (experts or economic operators) grew significantly.

Due to the importance that it has attained within the donor community, my country has also been the subject of many studies, and pieces of research and analysis. This work has involved such diverse fields as economic and financial activity, as well as social and political themes including poverty, gender, health, land, environment, human rights, democracy, governing, and civil society. The great majority of these works emerge from consultancies that accompany the feasibility and the particular aspects of specific projects connected with the development effort. It is common knowledge that these projects are promoted and financed mostly by foreign institutions (international bodies, governmental agencies from donating countries, NGOs, and private investors). This research has enabled data gathering and systematization, which is subsequently worked out according to the objectives that generated it. It is important to contend that they represent a useful source of information by providing studies and analyses to a range of economic and social national actors and, more generally, to all those interested in Mozambique.

In spite of these achievements, in the majority of those research-oriented projects integral to cooperation purposes, the terms of reference and the main work methodologies continue to be directed from and developed outside the country. Further, research is still being performed – or at least monitored – by foreign specialists who are hired for that purpose, or by consultancy agencies based in Mozambique. Thus, we are facing a market of services with an intensive activity in which Mozambicans participate essentially as specialized labour. The shortage of financial resources available for scientific research in various institutes, independent research centres, and centres that are incorporated in local universities – as well as the low salaries paid by national institutions to scholars and researchers – invite Mozambican organizations, research environments, and individuals to look for sources of income in this 'consultancy market'.

Importantly, this research activity has key limitations and brings about disturbing effects that relate to the selected objects of study, the investigational practices, the conceptual references, and the methodologies used: the themes correspond to the priorities and needs generated by international cooperation programs; the research usually obeys criteria that should be sanctioned by those funding the research; and, finally, the studies focus on the segmental problems of the projects and rarely provide adequate opportunities to make an in-depth critique of the causes behind the questions asked.

Furthermore, due to their quantity and to the number of researchers involved in them, these studies create a *habitus* (Bourdieu 1992), and thereby naturalize concepts and procedures. As a whole, they reaffirm and consolidate the hegemony of the thinking of the 'North' as the only source of scientific knowledge (see Hountondji 1990, 2002; Santos 2007). They naturalize concepts that should regulate research, and eliminate historical and cultural variables that condition the phenomena under study. They end up being assimilated and accepted as the only Methodology (with a capital 'M') to study, and contribute to what the international community as well as the African authorities call the process of modernization of society. This critique is valid for all areas of knowledge, but it becomes particularly relevant in the field of social and human sciences, which is more directly linked with the formation of individual and collective consciences.

In this way, in terms of the 'consultancy market', the space for creativity in research and critical reflection is limited. Focalized studies logically demand functional results for the projects that determine them; hence, the premises of their approach are only discussed on exceptional occasions. Even the public institutes and research units conform to 'market' rules, and sometimes they are complementarily conditioned by official priorities and political imperatives. From the perspective of global strategies, the economic reason puts pressure on the production of knowledge, under the guise of 'national interest'.

This happens regardless of the effort made by local scholars and researchers, who are determined to produce knowledge based on the country's problems and aim to offer elements necessary for an adequate response to real needs. In Mozambique, excellent quality research and analyses have been (and are still being) produced in prestigious institutions, such as the Center for African Studies and the Centre of Population Studies, at the University Eduardo Mondlane[2] and at the Centre of Strategic International Studies, which is linked to the Higher Institute of International Relations – to cite only the most productive cases. This academic production has been of great significance to knowledge of Mozambique's geo-politics and geo-identity. The research has questioned paths previously covered and opened new and necessary debates. However, this significant research does not have an effect (or if it does, it is only a marginal one) on the processes of decision-making and the definition of policies.

The conditions that constrain many of the commissioned works are a source of concern for a growing number of Mozambican researchers, many of them young people who work alongside some of the most renowned scholars. These researchers are confronted with crucial questions regarding the country, which they would like to have the opportunity to investigate, although these questions might not necessarily be connected with their work. In parallel, they observe the treatment of Mozambican society's problems with criteria, concepts,

---

2   The oldest public university in Mozambique.

and methods that do not address national specificities, do not consider determining variables, and do not approach essential causes (Hountondji 1995).

The studies that aim to support such projects do not, for instance, consider the variables of an international landscape and produce an analysis which uncritically borrows a reality patterned by exogenous factors. They do not stop to discuss issues such as the cultural meaning of phenomena, their representations, the interpretation and comprehension of facts, the content of symbols, the power and sense of myths, or the dimensions of space and time. In short, the majority of paradigms are 'imported' without previous questioning or adaptation to the local reality.

An effect of such uncritical importing of paradigms and research 'marketization' is that the situations under study emerge as not having a history: they are regarded as isolated facts and phenomena and are therefore treated in the same way as analogous facts and phenomena would be in any other latitude or context. Conforming in this way to a universalized model often ignores aspects that are essential to an understanding and identification of the procedures and methodologies of intervention.

I will illustrate this situation by providing an example of an urban paradigm. Several commissioned studies on the problems of Mozambican cities refer to urban spaces in which the poorest segment of the population lives in a hierarchical way. Explicitly or implicitly, the 'centre' is the *cidade de cimento* (cement city), which is urbanized and structured according to the European-colonial model. The remaining space is conceived as being subaltern and complementary, and is examined according to its deficits in relation to the 'centre'. In these studies, I do not see any trace of the stimulating contributions provided by researchers from the University Eduardo Mondlane, who are revealing sources of endogenous dynamics and specific forms of infrastructural, social, economic, and cultural organization that allow the daily survival of the peoples in those urban spaces outside the 'centre'. The few references made to these studies focus on minor details, and do not discuss the urban paradigm that is crucial for the sedimentation of universalizing thought and for the interiorization of Eurocentric concepts of modernity.

Underlying this fact is a perspective of development that emerges precisely from Eurocentric concepts of modernity. Development is presented as a univocal movement towards the model of civilization represented by the 'central' countries. As I have stated elsewhere,

> 'development' commonly connotes the extension of the Knowledge, the Technologies and the Methodologies from the hegemonic countries to the peripheral countries – an overall tendency involving the uniformization of its use and application. The question of difference is temporarily

incorporated by the cultural specificities and idiosyncrasies of each people. The 'civilizing mission' announced in the nineteenth century, thus,
dislocates its axis of religious and cultural uniformization to economic
and technological assimilation. Now, real development necessarily implies the human being's self-sustainability. It emerges from the historic
process, from the relationship between the human being and the context that surrounds him or her – nature and other communities and its
members with which he or she is acquainted. In other words, it is the
result of the dialogic relationship between the needs and the priorities
that arise in each community's life and the creative and inventive spirit
of men and women who work to integrate the communities. Ultimately,
development depends on the growing incorporation by the community
and its members of the practices and knowledge that proceed from each
new solution need.

CABAÇO 2006, 4–5

It is true that the failure of some cooperation programs, along with commitment and pressure from researchers, has been generating the revision of objects of study and methodologies. However, such an exercise invariably occurs
following the same vertical logic: new approaches must earn the scientific
and methodological approval of the 'North' before they can be applied in the
'South'.

Dissatisfaction and even indignation among some national researchers has
been leading to the creation of independent research institutions that incorporate and reinforce a new Mozambican civil society. In these institutions new
critical, social, economic, environmental, and democratic modes of thinking
are being forged, having their roots in the real society of our country. Without
intending this to be an exhaustive list, those building a reputation on such
research and social intervention include: the Institute for Social and Economic
Studies (IESE), the Civil Society Support Mechanism (MASC), the Centre for
Public Integrity (CIP), the Centre for Democracy and Development Studies
(CEDE), the Centre of Mozambican and International Studies (CEMO) and the
Centre for Civil Society Learning and Capacity-Building (CESC).

The concerns of these Mozambicans working in the field of social and human sciences are not exclusive to Mozambique. As mentioned above, they
represent a field of discussion that is becoming increasingly wide amongst
researchers and scholars throughout Africa, as well as within that growing number of people who dedicate themselves to African and postcolonial
studies. Such developments, of course, have a historical basis: since the end
of the 1960s, social sciences have increasingly and insistently questioned

authoritarian and Eurocentric ways of approaching the Other. The pioneering works of the Chicago School, and the revolution brought about by Bronislaw Malinowski (1922), had lost their impetus due to the new priorities determined by the Second World War and the restructuration of the new world order that followed it, which was conducive to the end of colonialism as a politics of territorial occupation. The bipolar world that emerged from the war forced the reorganization of strategies and, subsequently, the reformulation of principles and procedures – all of which had repercussions in social and human sciences. The contributions by Claude Lévi-Strauss (1958, 1962), who horizontalized the social practices of different cultures, and by Clifford Geertz, who declared in the 1980s that 'we are all natives now' (1983, 151), are two remarkable examples of paradigmatic revisions that stimulated academic reflection on the possible paths to be followed in any interdisciplinary approach to research problems.

The feminist movement and gender studies also had a significant impact by revealing an Other who was not geographically distant, but who had been, up to that point, conceived of as part of the Eurocentric 'Us'; suddenly, she appeared, and claimed her own identity and representation. This debate unveiled forms of oppression and discrimination within a specific social relationship – the one between men and women – that was until this point considered natural. The question of gender was in intimate dialogue with the colonial question, generating surprising analogies. Further, the questioning of paradigms so deeply rooted in Western culture opened spaces for the discussion of new approaches such as cultural studies, the polemical postcolonial studies, and science, technology, and society programs.

The production of theory and epistemological discussion amongst social scientists of the peripheral countries gave birth to supranational organizations and networks that have promoted a horizontal intellectual dialogue, as well as enlarging the scope of, and studying in depth, reflections on experiences that take place in the peripheral space. It is important to me to highlight the contributions made by the Council for the Development of Social Science Research in Africa (CODESRIA), the Latin American Council of Social Sciences (CLACSO), and the Indian Council of Social Science Research (ICSSR).

In our neighbouring South Africa (the continent's most industrialized country), we can witness an intense debate on epistemology, which is still in a constant process. I can briefly refer to the example of an ongoing project called 'Shifting Boundaries of Knowledge', which, based on the Delphi method, intends to produce a list of the problems that should interdisciplinarily be considered research priorities to question both paradigms and methodologies. Through dialogue among social scientists and intellectuals, this project represents an attempt to form a national agenda and a national research politics that are able to find solutions to knowledge demands and the specificities of African societies, and that appreciate the urgent need for an innovative approach to everyday realities in South Africa.

As far back as 1996, the Gulbenkian Commission, a research group headed by Immanuel Wallerstein, recognized the limitations and difficulties of investigation in Africa. It also acknowledged the first signs of an 'experimental process', which was an alternative to well-established approaches from the 'North'. Despite these first signs, we still have a long and difficult road ahead of us. Within the new colonial relations between central powers and peripheral countries, knowledge takes over the role that used to be performed by the occupational forces of colonial powers. The thought produced in dominant countries constitutes a referential pattern and a pattern for evaluation of the quality of scientific and technical work produced in the 'South'. Simultaneously, it is a decisive tool for the preservation of surviving concepts of civilizational superiority, which has characterized relations with the 'South' since the colonial era.

Thus, the innovative efforts of African scholars and intellectuals have yet to have a real impact on everyday lives. As a whole and in the name of pragmatism the elites across the continent have adhered to the development paradigm proposed and imposed by Bretton Woods institutions. This has maintained forms of thought that only question this paradigm on the margins of national debates and outside decision-making centres.

As mentioned above, the terms of reference integral to many of the studies that are commissioned and carried out in our countries are reflections of concepts, procedures, and methodologies transferred between very different realities. The number of studies produced, as well as the number of Mozambicans involved in them, corroborates these references, naturalizes those processes, and imposes a model. Ultimately, it renders irrelevant the nationality and origin of the consultants and researchers, providing that principles and procedures are taken into account. On important issues coupled to the organization of society, to economic and financial ordering, the concepts of development, or the concept of cooperation, there is an explicit conformity with 'what is normal' (or expected) according to hegemonic thought. The social science of the 'North' is universalized and presented as the 'real social science'. In addition, it affirms itself as opposed to other forms of knowledge, which are relegated to the category of 'interesting'.

A not insignificant number of African (and Mozambican) staff members who are educated at international universities, or at national universities that follow the same patterns and models, choose to adjust themselves uncritically to the formulas presented as state of the art. The employability and success of these staff members within the labour market depend on how rigorously they can perform such mimicry. Furthermore, universities are increasingly losing their role as centres of knowledge production, innovation, and academic debate to become formative schools for qualified labour. For the student, the know-how (*savoir faire*) becomes more rewarding and compensatory in the short term than the knowing (*savoir*). The know-how is measured according to levels of faithfulness to the parameters and objectives proposed by the majority of institutions that request those works – not according to the critical and innovative capacity of local researchers. Critical thought is socially disqualified, ostracized as abstract, and publicly denounced as an obstacle to the country's development.

In the field of knowledge, the real and divisive line between North and South is drawn in relation to epistemological approaches. According to Boaventura de Sousa Santos and Maria Paula Meneses, there are no neutral epistemologies. Reflection, they contend, should focus on the practices of knowledge and their impact on other social practices (Santos and Meneses 2010). Thus, it starts making sense if research is built on concrete questions, and if its creative and innovative potential is directly or indirectly projected into society's everyday life. The epistemological reflection that both Santos and Meneses are referring to has an implicit socio-political dimension; actually, the idea of 'understanding in order to improve' has always been subjacently present in social sciences.

The purpose of critical thought's marginalization is precisely that of interrupting or minimizing those impacts. Knowing social phenomena in depth raises the number of variables to consider, makes governing complex, increases the light shed on the stages of power, and often reveals the inconsistency of 'truths' meant to be incontestable in the name of pragmatism. To know social phenomena in depth expands society's real democracy and brings the centres of decision-making and power closer to the citizen:

It is urgent to return justice to the black continent, sharing all the knowledge over different aspects of its life, which was accumulated over the centuries, with all the people that live there. It is important to take adequate measures in order to enable Africa to proceed to the lucid and responsible appropriation of the available knowledge, as well as of the discussions and interrogations developed elsewhere. This appropriation should go side by side with the critical reappropriation of Africa's own endogenous knowledge and, above all, with a critical appropriation of the process of knowledge production and capitalization itself. (Hountdonji 2010, 129)

References

Bourdieu, Pierre. 1992 [1977]. *Outline of a Theory of Practice*. Cambridge: Cambridge University Press.

Cabaço, José Luis. 2006. Apropriação Cultural e Desenvolvimento. Text presented at the II Seminário Internacional Brasil-África. PUC-Minas: Contagem.

Geertz, Clifford. 1983. *Local Knowledge: Further essays in interpretive anthropology*. New York: Basic Books.

Hountdonji, Paulin J. 1990. Scientific Dependence in Africa today. *Research in African Literatures* 21 (3): 5–15.

Hountdonji, Paulin J. 1995. Producing Knowledge in Africa Today: the Second Bashorun M.K.O. Abiola Distingushed Lecture. *African Studies Review* 38: 1–10.

Hountdonji, Paulin J. 2002. Knowledge Appropriation in a Post-colonial Context. In *Indigenous Knowledge and the Integration of Knowledge Systems*, ed. Catherine A. Odora Hoppers, 23–38. Cape Town: New Africa Books.

Hountdonji, Paulin J. 2010. Conhecimento de África, Conhecimentos de Africanos: duas perspectivas sobre os Estudos Africanos. In *Epistemologias do Sul*, ed. Boaventura de Sousa Santos and Maria Paula Meneses, 119–131. Coimbra: Almedina.

Lévi-Strauss, Claude. 1963 [1958]. *Structural Anthropology*. New York: Basic Books.

Lévi-Strauss, Claude. 1966 [1962]. *The Savage Mind*. Chicago: University of Chicago Press.

Malinowski, Bronislaw. 1922. *Argonauts of the Western Pacific*. London: Routledge & Kegan Paul.

Neocosmos, Michael. 2009. The Political Conditions of Social Thought and the Politics of Emancipation: an introduction to the work of Sylvain Lazarus. In *Re-imagining the Social in South Africa*, eds Heather Jacklin and Peter Vale, 111–138. Pietermaritzburg, South Africa: University of Kwazulu-Natal Press.

Santos, Boaventura de Sousa. 2007. Beyond Abyssal Thinking: From global lines to ecology of knowledges. *Review Fernand Braudel Center* 30 (1): 45–89.

Santos, Boaventura de Sousa, and Maria Paula Meneses, eds. 2010. *Epistemologias do Sul*. Coimbra: Almedina.

Index